CW01335980

England's Revelry
A History of Popular Sports and Pastimes, 1660–1830

England's Revelry

A History of
Popular Sports and Pastimes
1660–1830

by
Emma Griffin

*A British Academy
Postdoctoral Fellowship Monograph*

Published for THE BRITISH ACADEMY
by OXFORD UNIVERSITY PRESS

Oxford University Press, Great Clarendon Street, Oxford OX2 6DP

Oxford New York

Auckland Bangkok Buenos Aires Cape Town Chennai
Dar es Salaam Delhi Hong Kong Istanbul Karachi Kolkata
Kuala Lumpur Madrid Melbourne Mexico City Mumbai Nairobi
São Paulo Shanghai Singapore Taipei Tokyo Toronto

Oxford is a registered trade mark of Oxford University Press
in the UK and certain other countries

Published in the United States
by Oxford University Press Inc., New York

British Library Cataloguing in Publication Data
Data available

ISBN 0–19–726321–6   978–0–19–726321–1

Typeset by J&L Composition, Filey, North Yorkshire
Printed in Great Britain
on acid-free paper by
Antony Rowe Limited,
Chippenham, Wiltshire

For David

Contents

Illustrations

Acknowledgements

This book began life as a PhD thesis at Cambridge University in 1996. I am indebted to a number of people who have advised me during the course of my research, and I should like in particular to record my thanks to the following. Gareth Stedman Jones was an inspiring supervisor, and his early criticisms unquestionably improved the dissertation on which this book is based. My examiners, Boyd Hilton and Amanda Vickery, both offered encouragement, as well as timely criticisms that helped me to take the research further. A better editor than Martin Daunton is hard to conceive. His criticisms of the first draft enabled me to improve the book's structure and argument substantially; and the good-natured efficiency with which he steered me through the completion of this book has made the experience very much easier and more enjoyable than it might otherwise have been. I should also like to express especial thanks to Vic Gatrell, who has taken a generous interest in this project, yet nevertheless been a challenging critic. Conversations with Sarah Pearsall over the years have helped me to clarify my thoughts many times, and Martin West read several chapters and gave me valuable help with the prose. John Conlin, Mark Dawson, Natasha Glaisyer, Lawrence Klein, Matthew Nudds, Robert Poole, Naomi Tadmor, Leigh Shaw-Taylor, and Chris Thornton all read drafts of chapters and contributed many helpful comments and criticisms. I would like to thank them all.

My thanks are also due to the institutions whose financial support has made possible the writing of this book. The British Academy provided the three-year studentship that permitted me to embark on the PhD; and the Institute of Historical Research a one-year fellowship that enabled me to complete it. It is thanks to a postdoctoral fellowship from the British Academy that I have been able to undertake the revisions that were needed to prepare the dissertation for publication. I must also record my sincerest thanks to the Master and Fellows of Sidney Sussex, for electing me to a fellowship, and for providing such an exceptional environment in which to live and work.

A number of travel awards allowed me to undertake the archival research this book required. The survey of town accounts that lies at the heart of the project was made possible by a series of generous research grants from Trinity College, Cambridge. Additional trips were funded by the Prince Consort and Thirlwall Fund (Cambridge University); the British Academy; and Sidney Sussex, Cambridge. My thanks are also owing to many archivists in local records' offices for help with finding and interpreting the documents in their collections. Especial thanks are due to Gill Shapland at Cambridgeshire County Record Office, for helping me so cheerfully with the county's enclosure records and maps.

Finally my sincere thanks are owing to friends and family. Most especially I owe my thanks to my parents and sisters for their constant support over many years, and their unfailing interest in 'the book' more recently. A special debt of gratitude is also owing to Matthew Nudds for years of friendship and for his unwavering encouragement to embark on the PhD. Friends—Dominique Collins, Sarah Pearsall and Peter Kail, Catherine Frances, Adam Smith, Andrew and Angela Morris, Chris Stewart, Pete and Tab Smith and Silke Arnold-de-Simine—have all encouraged me, and provided in turn the support and distraction that helped me to keep going.

Notes on the text

Throughout the text and references, whenever dates are given they are rendered as they are found in the documents. Archival records are therefore given according to the old style, that is those before 1752 are left as they were before the calendar change of that year; in published archival material, they are reproduced as found. In transcribing manuscripts, original spelling, punctuation, and capitalisation have generally been maintained, though for the sake of clarity, punctuation has occasionally been altered. Italics are in the passages quoted unless otherwise stated. Footnote entries qualified by '(loc. hist.)' refer the reader to the local history section of the bibliography; '(diar.)' to the diaries and journals section; and ('diss.') to the dissertations.

Abbreviations

AD	Archives Department
ALS	Archives and Local Studies
AO	Archive Office
Arch. Soc.	Archaeological Society
AS	Archive Service
BA	Borough Archives
BWP	*Birmingham Weekly Post*
CA	City Archives
CRO	County Record Office
LSL	Local Studies Library
RL	Reference Library
RO	Record Office
UL	University Library

I

Introduction

none that I know of
[this question is] unanswered, because not in the power of
there is nothing contained in these questions which can be answered by
me
I have nothing, Sir, to transmit to you under any of these heads[1]

The question which none of these writers, all contributors to a parochial
history of Berkshire prepared in the 1750s, could answer was the following:
what particular games, sports, customs, proverbs, or peculiar words and
phrases are used in your parts? And their inability to describe local sports
and recreations is unlikely to have been exceptional. It was shared, at least,
by all but one of the other twenty-six contributors to this Berkshire history, and its companion volumes were similarly silent on the theme of local
games, sports, and customs. It is generally admitted that the scarcity of
detailed descriptions of popular custom in early modern England has
impeded the writing of histories of popular recreation in the period.
Although the occasional literary reference, and the complaint literature
associated with clerics such as Phillip Stubbes and Richard Baxter, have
been exhaustively and imaginatively mined by historians, there is inevitably
much that such sources leave unilluminated. Given this, it is not entirely
surprising that an exceptionally wide-ranging and comprehensive account
of the festive calendar in early modern England nonetheless overlooks the
parish wakes and feasts that lay at the core of this calendar. Simple questions are left unanswered: where in the parish were the feasts held? how
long did they last? who went? and who did not? And given that very few
contemporary writers thought to record such details, providing accurate
answers to these questions will always be difficult.[2]

The focus of this study is sports and recreations over the long eighteenth century. The chapters that follow explore the history of parish wakes

---

[1] *Collections for History of Berkshire*, pp. 29, 37, 41, 85.
[2] The recent history is Hutton, *Rise and Fall*.

and feasts; civic fairs and celebrations; football, cricket, and other athletic sports; bull- and bear-baiting; and the annual celebrations of Shrove Tuesday and Guy Fawkes. Since customs and pastimes became the object of sustained scholarly research towards the end of this period, problems of evidence become ever less acute. From the outset, the framework of this research was historical; rather than describe sports as they existed in the present, scholars sought to elucidate the origins and antiquity of customs and traditions, to trace and translate accounts of sports hitherto overlooked in ancient documents, to describe customs that had disappeared. An eighteenth-century student of cockfighting, for example, sought to establish when and where the origins of the sport lay. His enquiry took him back to the Classical world, and his arguments were grounded in the careful translation of Greek and Latin texts.[3] The first book wholly devoted to popular sports was the work of Joseph Strutt, an eighteenth-century antiquary and engraver. Published in 1802, Strutt's *Sports and Pastimes of the People of England* was a work of scholarship, a synthesis of references to popular recreations contained in old and rare texts; it was not based upon the actual observance of contemporary custom. The historical orientation of early research into custom and folklore was continued in the work of local historians, who together made a major contribution to the study of popular sports in the nineteenth century. The bibliography to this book illustrates both the extent of research into sports and pastimes by such writers, and its enduring value to historians of popular recreation. And again, these authors were concerned largely, though not exclusively, with the customs and traditions of earlier generations. In fine, the impulse to describe and understand sports historically is at least two centuries old. The subject matter of this book might appear to owe its inspiration to the expansion of social history in the 1970s, but in fact the history of popular sport has demonstrably earlier antecedents, and the most appropriate starting place for this book, therefore, is perhaps not the social history of the post-war universities, but the historical interest in popular recreation that emerged at the end of the eighteenth century.

Early scholars of sports and pastimes were primarily recorders, undertaking to provide descriptive accounts of previously unnoticed local recreations for the sake of posterity. Yet, for all their descriptive leanings, their work was not without its theoretical underpinnings and, as historical interest in popular custom became more widespread, so a number of assumptions about their social significance became firmly established. By force of

[3] Pegge, 'Memoir on Cockfighting', pp. 132–50.

repetition, the assertion that the historical consequence of sports went beyond the enjoyment or otherwise they afforded their participants soon became axiomatic. Possibly sensitive to the charge that sports and diversions were an essentially trivial aspect of the past, nineteenth-century scholars posited a homology between recreation and morality. They argued that sports and pastimes merited historical interest not merely as quaint objects of curiosity, but because they provided an indication of the cultural sophistication or otherwise of those who enjoyed them. In the formulation of Joseph Strutt, 'when we follow men into their retirements, we are most likely to see them in their true state, and may judge of their natural dispositions';[4] and, according to William Howitt, '[the sports and pastimes of the people] furnish a certain indication of the real character of a people'.[5] Repeatedly, then, we are informed by folklorists and historians that a chapter on diversions has been included in their work because 'The degree of refinement in a nation may generally be known by its popular pastimes and sports';[6] or since 'The amusements of the people may be taken as a fair standard of their morality.'[7]

At the same time, the progressionist tendency of much nineteenth-century historiography—the belief in the gradual progression of society to higher forms—was also evident in local history. Different sports were presumed to belong to different stages of civilisation, and it was consequently thought possible to gauge how far up the scale of civilisation a population had moved if information about its recreations was forthcoming. Apparently in Liverpool in the late eighteenth century, 'from the customs and diversions of the people at this period, it is evident, that they had made but slow advances in civilisation'.[8] And in another time and place, '[the] amusements of this period exhibit a gradual improvement in the manners and tastes of the people'.[9]

An entirely unexceptional nineteenth-century account of popular sports may be found in John Brewster's *History of Stockton-upon-Tees,* written in the 1820s. Brewster began his account 'Of the improvement of public manners' in the late seventeenth century: we are told that, at that time, the condition of the town had been 'very low and feeble'. First among the efforts to improve Stockton was the building of a church. Then came a new

---

[4] Strutt, *Sports and Pastimes*, p. i.
[5] Howitt, *Rural Life*, ii, p. 258.
[6] Gibbs, *History of Aylesbury*, p. 551.
[7] Heaviside, *Annals of Stockton*, p. 131.
[8] Troughton, *History of Liverpool*, p. 92.
[9] Dent, *Birmingham*, iii, p. 486.

vicar, who was soon called upon to inter a 'poor person'; scandalised to learn that the funeral attendants customarily reused the same coffin for the poor, he ensured that this 'act of indecency' was henceforth swept away. Next in Brewster's narrative was the Revd Mr Skelly, who by the 'superiority of *calm reasoning*' persuaded his neighbours to leave aside the Shrove Tuesday tradition of throwing at cocks. In the present day, cockfighting was 'discouraged', and bull-baiting was 'totally suppressed'. Civilisation, it is plain, had at last reached Stockton.[10]

Yet, despite the ostensibly historical frame of reference, a curious mixing between the past and the present is discernible in Brewster's work, whereby a number of odd and apparently unrelated occurrences are ordered and made intelligible with reference to the present. Of course, by nineteenth-century standards this elision was not particularly curious: the motivation behind many studies of recreation was precisely and unashamedly to reveal the progress made in recent times, and (it was generally thought) 'we may congratulate ourselves on the improvement which has taken place'.[11] But this narrative of improvement is clearly overdetermined and, as an account of historical change, less than satisfactory. Although many nineteenth-century scholars convincingly established that popular recreations had undergone a series of noticeable changes in the recent past, their assumptions have resulted in a circular explanation of the causes of the changes described. Their understanding of recreation was based upon a number of stereotypes about which sports were civilised and which barbaric; and their narratives inspired by the faith that society ineluctably progresses from barbarism to civilisation. Their conclusions— that an earlier generation's sports indicate how uncivilised that generation had been, and that the disappearance of certain pastimes was owing to the march of civilisation—are no more than a rephrasing of these initial beliefs.

Nowhere is this form of argument more frequently encountered (and its shortcomings more conspicuous) than in the many accounts chronicling the decline of blood sports in a particular town or region. Consider, for instance, Henry Heaviside's description of the disappearance of blood sports from Newcastle: 'it is only by advancing in the scale of civilisation,' he wrote, 'that such a people are brought to have a relish for amusements of a more refined and innocent character'. But this is a rather disingenuous account of the changes Heaviside describes for, by his own admission, 'It is well the Legislature put a stop to a practice [cockfighting] so cruel and

---

[10] Brewster, *History of Stockton*, pp. 257–60.
[11] Gibbs, *History of Aylesbury*, p. 551.

revolting.'[12] A historian of Doncaster believed that 'in the gradual decline of cock fighting, bear baiting, bull baiting, and badger baiting may be traced the slow but sure progress of civilisation and refinement'; but he also added that bear-baiting at a neighbouring township eventually 'induced the magistrates to interfere with vigour and determination; and adopt measures to prevent a recurrence'.[13] One is forced to consider the possibility that the popularity and decline of certain sports depended not only upon the refinement or otherwise of those who enjoyed them, but also upon the attitudes of those who did not. In Newcastle and Doncaster, the elimination of blood sports was owing not simply to the progress of civilisation, although this was the story their historians clearly wanted to tell; the less benign influences of legislation, magistrates, and parish constables were also involved.

The same tension is apparent in other nineteenth-century discussions of popular pastimes. The many changes in the way in which the anniversary of Guy Fawkes was celebrated cannot, for example, be fully comprehended without considering the role of the lawmakers and officials who controlled, rather than took part in, the annual festival. The writer William Howitt recalled the way the Fifth of November used to be kept up; the 'state of utter riot and confusion . . . men and lads in every place, shouting, scuffling, making all the uproar, and doing all the mischief possible', and concluded 'these things have cured themselves'. Yet they did not quite 'cure themselves' in the autonomous way that he implied, for as he went on to point out, 'in towns, in general, bonfires and firing of guns are prohibited'.[14] The resident of Horsham in Sussex, who recalled that the cycle of decline and revival of the town's Guy Fawkes celebrations was related to both 'the coolness or enthusiasm of the inhabitants' and 'the opposition or indifference of the magistrates', arguably had a better grasp on the causes of cultural change than the scholars who looked exclusively to plebeian tastes and morals.[15]

It is not hard to find examples of official interference in popular recreation in the long eighteenth century. Indeed, few plebeian sports lay entirely beyond the reach of local officials. Most were endlessly promoted, regulated, and suppressed by those in positions of authority, and this involvement of the forces of law and order indicates that the significance

[12] Heaviside, *Annals of Stockton*, p. 131.
[13] Hatfield, *Notices of Doncaster*, i, pp. 72, 83.
[14] Howitt, *Boy's Country-book*, p. 80.
[15] Burstow, *Reminiscences*, p. 74.

of sports was as much political as cultural. As such, it is important that historical accounts of recreations do not attempt to collapse the customs
under discussion into straightforward indicators of the cultural tastes of the
poor, or to 'read' them in search of evidence for the level of civilisation they
had reached. Equally, their history should not be written without reference to those with the power to encourage, harass, or prohibit them.
Nineteenth-century historians were always pleased to note recent changes
in patterns of recreation, but they failed to address the way power and the
law were involved in forcing the changes described; it is to be expected that
modern histories of popular sports will not contain the same oversight.

With the passage of time, nineteenth-century scholarship on sports and
customs has been largely forgotten. These early explorations into popular
culture are now little used, and they serve as primary material for the historian of popular recreation, mined for descriptive rather than analytical
content: it is in the social history of the 1960s and 1970s, not in nineteenth-
and early-twentieth-century scholarship, that the origins of current
research into popular culture are usually located. There can be little doubt
that the histories of popular recreation that appeared at this time differed
in a number of respects from the amateur tradition that had preceded.
Social history, from the outset, was progressive and innovative, consciously
drawing upon the ideas and insights of the neighbouring disciplines of
sociology, economics, anthropology, and psychology, and through its explo-
ration of previously unstudied areas of the past, and its exploitation of new
theories and concepts, social history quickly set itself apart as a new and
pioneering sub-discipline.[16] Of course, many nineteenth-century stock
assumptions about the 'barbarity' of certain pastimes were abandoned. So
too was the belief that historical change may be explained by reference to
the inevitable progression of society towards a more perfect state of civilisation. Yet, for all its appearance of modernity, much of the social history of
this period nevertheless remained closed to the ways in which power
shaped the customs under consideration, and the history of popular recreation arguably never fully succeeded in freeing itself from its scarcely
remembered nineteenth-century antecedents.

In part, this seems to have been a consequence of the heavy reliance on
social anthropology. It is perhaps no surprise that as historians of popular
culture began to mark out and study new aspects of human existence they
turned above all to this discipline. There was a certain logic to borrowing

---

[16] See, for example, Krantz (ed.), *History from Below*; essays by Wilson and Wrightson in
Wilson (ed.), *Rethinking Social History*.

from the anthropologists, as it was they, after all, who were most deeply involved in understanding the social life of pre-industrial society.[17] Thus Keith Thomas, pioneer of social history and advocate of the value of anthropological techniques and concepts to the study of the past, cited the examples of the Dogons of the Sudan, the Trobrianders, and Maori fishermen in an article on work and leisure, in the belief that 'primitive societies' provided the 'most obvious contrast' with the working habits of the modern industrial world. He was clearly drawing upon the functional paradigm dominant in anthropology in the 1960s when he suggested that some pre-industrial recreations were the 'products of a society organized for war'; others 'explicable only in terms of the periodic release necessary in a rigidly hierarchical society'; and yet others 'reflect[ed] the web of kinship and neighbourhood'.[18] And when anthropologists shifted away from the functionalism of Malinowski, Radcliffe-Brown, and other early-twentieth-century ethnographers, social historians quickly followed suit.

Throughout the 1980s, the focus for social historians was upon the 'meaning', rather than the function, of the cultural practice they studied, and few studies of popular culture were considered complete without some discussion of how cultural practices were understood and experienced by those who participated in them. For example, a study of football in Northumberland mining communities was concerned to establish the 'meaning of the game to the miners', and the 'role it played in their lives';[19] whereas research by Douglas Reid promised to 'reconstruct the experience of the wakes and fairs of eighteenth- and nineteenth-century Birmingham'.[20] Likewise, Richard Holt's seminal text on the making of modern sports in Britain argued that the historian needs to examine the 'motives, pleasures, and values enshrined in the daily round of play. A social history of sport in modern Britain not only has to ask "What has changed and why?" but "How did people feel about the changing place of sport in their lives?"'[21]

---

[17] For a contemporary criticism, however, see Thompson, 'Folklore, anthropology and social history', pp. 247–66.

[18] Thomas, 'Work and Leisure', pp. 50–62, quotes on pp. 52–4. See also idem, 'History and anthropology', pp. 3–24.

[19] Metcalfe, 'Football in mining communities', pp. 269–91, quote on p. 269. See also idem, 'Organized sport', pp. 469–95.

[20] Reid, 'Interpreting the festival calendar', pp. 125–53, quote on p. 125.

[21] Holt, *Sport and the British*, p. 2. In addition, see David Underdown: 'Historians of popular culture inevitably have to start with the forms in which culture is expressed—the mask, the ritual, the dance . . . but the object of the exercise is to get at the values, and we can only do this by decoding the expressive forms'. Idem, 'Regional cultures?', p. 29. See also Borsay,

This emphasis on the 'meaning' of popular sports owed a clear debt to the symbolic anthropology, expounded most emphatically and eloquently, but by no means uniquely, by Clifford Geertz.[22] His innovative and extremely accessible studies of culture in the Far East offered a new interpretation of cultural practice, one which held a seductive appeal for a wide range of academics from many disciplines.[23] Geertz attempted to unravel the symbolic meaning of social activity, to decode the cultural messages contained within ritual and action, and the method of 'thick description' that he developed in order to do so was quickly incorporated into the vocabulary of historians of popular culture.

A detailed and familiar example of Geertz's 'thick description' is contained in his essay on the Balinese cockfight.[24] Long caricatured and condemned by the Balinese elite as a primitive and backward pastime, Geertz set out to understand the significance of cockfighting to those who participated, and his analysis was based upon a study of the ways in which participants betted. He demonstrated that the cockfighters systematically placed bets that were inconsistent with the goal of maximising winnings, and used this to suggest that the Balinese cockfight was more than an idle pastime motivated by the hope of petty gain. He argued that betting patterns revealed participants exploiting the fight in order to express their pride in family and village. As the stakes rose, the investment of familial pride became more pronounced, and fights in which betting were high were in Geertz's formulation a form of 'deep play', saturated with symbolism for their participants. This then formed the 'meaning' of the Balinese cockfight. The fight was not a form of mindless entertainment; it was, he concluded, 'fundamentally a dramatisation of status concerns'.[25]

But whilst offering valuable insights into the cultural resonances of cockfighting, this analysis is not without problems. It might be questioned, for example, whose meaning is being privileged, for cockfighting is hardly enjoyed by all. There are several restrictions on those permitted by Balinese

'All the town's a stage', pp. 228–58; Reid, 'Beasts and brutes', pp. 12–28; Cressy, 'Fifth of November remembered', pp. 68–90; Walsh, 'November bull-running in Stamford', pp. 233–47; Owens, 'Nationalism without words', pp. 242–69.

[22] Geertz, *Interpretation of Cultures*, pp. 3–30.

[23] For Geertz and historians, see Waters, 'Signs of the times', pp. 537–56; Biersack, 'Local knowledge, local history', pp. 72–96; Samuel, 'Reading the signs', pp. 88–109 and idem, 'Reading the signs II', pp. 220–51; Goodman, 'History and anthropology', pp. 783–804.

[24] Geertz, *Interpretation of Cultures*, pp. 412–53.

[25] Ibid., p. 437.

cultural codes to enter the cockpit, suggesting it might be prudent to qual-
ify any general conclusions concerning the role of cockfighting in Bali.
Geertz is explicit about the relevance of the cockfight for all Balinese people—'much of Bali surfaces in the cock ring . . . it is a Balinese experience,
a story they tell themselves about themselves'.[26] Yet his confidence in the
universality of his conclusions appears to rest upon an unwarranted confla-
tion of the cockfighters with 'the Balinese', for looking closely it becomes
clear that 'much of Bali' never gets anywhere near a cock ring. Children are
excluded, so are young adults, the very poor, and all women of all ages: as
Geertz noted, 'Cockfighting is . . . not for youth, women, subordinates, and
so forth'.[27] Furthermore, individuals invest status in 'deep play' rather than
in the shallow play of low-stake matches, yet deep play is hardly the
province of all. Deep play involves high-money betting, but precisely
because betting is high in this, a poor peasant society, many of the regular
petty gamblers find themselves with few opportunities for deep play. Deep
play, it turns out, is for 'the really substantial members of the community,
the solid citizenry around whom local life revolves'.[28] It may very well be
a vehicle for the expression of status concerns, but the position of high-
level betting cockfighting in Balinese culture is more marginal than Geertz
admits, and the significance of this conclusion is therefore more problem-
atical than he acknowledges. His account uncannily mimics the exclusion
of the young, the poor, and the female from an important social arena and
there is something unsettling about work that so complacently glosses these
exclusions. One is led to question what function these careful excisions of
the subordinate majority from the historical or anthropological record
might serve in our own culture. At the least, the political implications of
modern scholarship that perpetuates the marginalisation of subordinate
social groups should not be left unchallenged.

Of course, one might attempt to extend an analysis of this kind by
searching for more meanings, by seeking to recover the meaning of the
cock ring to those excluded from it, whether for reasons of age, poverty, or
gender. But, however many meanings we uncover for the Balinese cockfight, there are features of the cockfight that this approach will always fail
to capture, for the cockpit is not simply a place of play, a stage for the
ritual display of family pride; it is also a site of conflict. The urban elite and
intelligentsia do not enter the cockpit—as Geertz explained, 'It sees

---

[26] Geertz, *Interpretation of Cultures*, pp. 417, 448.
[27] Ibid., p. 440.
[28] Ibid., p. 435.

cockfighting as "primitive", "backward", "unprogressive", and generally unbecoming an ambitious nation'[29]—and they have used their powers to create criminal sanctions designed to punish anyone who does. The prohibition of cockfighting suggests a very different context for cockfighting from that stressed by Geertz—not of Balinese culture, but of Balinese politics. There are no reasons for privileging the 'meaning' of sport over the politics of sport, and there is something hopelessly incomplete about an account of popular culture which does not address the pressures—political and legal—circumscribing its very existence.

Where historians of popular recreation in England have focused upon the meaning of cultural action, very similar limitations are evident. Some of the most reflective work on recreation is contained in Ross McKibbin's studies of hobbies and gambling in early-twentieth-century Britain.[30] In keeping with the concern to understand the meaning of popular culture, his work on gambling promised to consider the 'part it played in the economic and intellectual environment of the working class', and concluded that betting was a rational activity for the working classes, offering an opportunity for mental stimulation that its members were otherwise too frequently denied.[31]

But this account nonetheless remains limited, for there are key aspects of working-class betting that it fails to investigate. A major source of evidence for McKibbin's study of gambling was police records, for cash betting was not only rational for the working classes; it was also illegal. Fines and imprisonment could, and indeed did, follow for those found guilty of placing or accepting off-course cash bets. Furthermore, the gambling laws that underpinned these prosecutions were the product of an unequal society, and embodied a very questionable sense of social discrimination: thus credit betting, inevitably the privilege of the wealthy, had not been classified as a criminal offence.[32] These partial laws bore down on society unequally, and were integral in shaping a working-class gambling culture that was fundamentally different from that of wealthier citizens. More generally, the sheer poverty of early-twentieth-century manual workers severely restricted the scale and the scope of working-class gambling, further shaping the gambling culture that McKibbin described. In sum, the

---

[29] Geertz, *Interpretation of Cultures*, p. 414.
[30] McKibbin, 'Working-class gambling' and idem, 'Work and hobbies', both reprinted in his *Ideologies of Class*, pp. 101–66.
[31] Ibid., p. 101.
[32] Clapson, *A Bit of a Flutter*, pp. 14–78.

distribution of power, authority, and wealth inflected and constrained all working-class experiences of betting. These forces lay down the possible ways in which gambling might be experienced by the working classes. They were central to defining the form that popular gambling took, and any account which fails to address them is leaving significant parts of the historical record unexplored.

When nineteenth-century researchers described the decline and disappearance of sports and customs, they neglected the ways in which power and authority had influenced these trends. It is regrettable that so much twentieth-century writing about popular custom, through its focus on meaning, similarly skirts this issue. The meanings and significance that have been variously assigned to recreations may well be valid, and they are certainly not without interest. But the privileging of meaning, and almost total exclusion of the operation of power and social inequality, has produced studies of popular culture that are at best incomplete, and at worst misleading. Though stripped of the naive teleology of nineteenth-century historiography, this methodology nevertheless appears to continue in the depoliticised tradition of writing that surfaced in the nineteenth century. It is time to develop new ways of approaching plebeian culture, to establish an alternative framework in which popular recreations may be analysed, and above all to integrate popular experiences of sports and pastimes, with the power structures that variously encouraged, permitted, and suppressed them.

It is to be doubted, however, whether recent revisionism in the history of popular culture successfully accomplishes this. During the 1990s, critics began to question many of the assumptions of the first generation of research, challenging the central supports and procedures of the first wave of research into popular custom, and rapidly establishing a new historical orthodoxy.[33] As might be predicted, at the heart of the new thinking lay a desire to introduce a greater degree of sophistication into our understanding and analyses of popular cultural practice, to 'problematise' some of the assumptions with which early researchers had worked. The idea of one common culture, a set of customs and practices shared by all the poor, was therefore challenged. It was argued that the diversity of cultural practices amongst the subordinate classes undermined the idea of one culture belonging to the poor, and suggested that historians of popular culture

---

[33] Kaplan, *Understanding Popular Culture*, esp. pp. 5–37; Harris, 'Problematising popular culture', pp. 1–27 Dentith, *Society and Cultural Forms*; Reay, *Popular Cultures*, pp. 1–3, 198–223; Mullan and Reid (eds), *Eighteenth-century Popular Culture*, pp. 1–40, esp. 1–6.

should investigate these tensions, divisions, and oppositions, rather than obliterate differences in an endeavour to provide tidy accounts of socio-cultural practices and change. We were urged to explore with greater care and precision the ways in which factors such as age, gender, religion, and locality fractured the unity of cultural practice.

Just as the notion of a culture shared by the poor has been questioned, so was the idea of a culture that is confined to the poor scrutinised and found wanting. Critics claimed that early studies of popular culture assumed the existence of two distinct social groups—the elite and the pop-ular—and believed that customs, beliefs, and values were sometimes shared by both groups, at other times the preserve of only one. It was argued that cultural practices cannot be directly mapped onto sections of society in the way this model supposes; that actions, objects, and beliefs are forever mov-ing beyond the confines of the social groups to which they are supposed to belong. The idea of 'appropriation' was introduced, not simply to express the circulation of cultural practices throughout the ranks of society, but also to emphasise the way in which these practices were simultaneously put to different uses by different social strata.[34]

It must be recognised, however, that although these ideas were defined in opposition to the first generation of research into popular culture, there is greater precedence for many of these observations than is usually admit-ted. As might be expected from an academic community in the process of carving out a new area of research, a not inconsiderable degree of effort was initially devoted to discussing and defining the subject of research.[35] And, if early researchers did not talk about the 'fracturing' or 'fissuring' of popular culture, they nevertheless captured something of these ideas in their dis-cussions about the heterogeneity of the customs and beliefs of the people they studied. Peter Burke's seminal text on popular culture, for example, devoted a chapter to exploring the 'unity and variety' of popular culture, and suggested we should replace the notion of one plebeian culture with that of numerous popular cultures, each varying according to age, gender, and location.[36] It was a constant refrain in the early literature on popular culture that the customs and practices under consideration could not be neatly located in one social group. In both discussion pieces and case stud-

[34] Many of these ideas were developed in the work of Roger Chartier. See idem, *Cultural Use of Print*, pp. 3–12.
[35] Sandiford, 'Victorians at play', pp. 271–88. See also the introductory essays in the follow-ing edited volumes: Marrus (ed.), *Emergence of Leisure*; Yeo and Yeo (eds), *Popular Culture*; Storch (ed.), *Popular Culture*; Easton et al., *Disorder and Discipline*.
[36] Burke, *Popular Culture*, pp. 23–64.

ies, it was repeatedly pointed out that an improving wing of the working classes was as hostile to certain popular traditions as the most fervent middle-class reformer; while some social elites, motivated either by a desire for social control or by traditional values, were to be found amongst the most committed and powerful defenders of plebeian culture.[37] Divisions within the culture of the common people and moments of consensus across classes were widely recognized from the outset.

It is not then in recognising the intricacies and variety of plebeian custom and culture that new writing on popular culture differs from what preceded; it is rather the handling of these contrasts that distinguishes the two traditions. If early writers had indeed noticed that the popular culture they were studying failed to correspond neatly with a particular section of society, it is nonetheless true that the ramifications of this observation were never quite fully incorporated into the final narrative. In the end, these reservations were always put to one side, carefully placed at the margins of discussion so that the main trends of social change were not obscured. There was consequently an ongoing and unresolved tension in much of this early work, an awareness on the one hand of the complexity of the relationship between the culture and the society, and a desire on the other to simplify this relationship so that some coherent story about the changing cultural life of the poor might be delineated.

The response of recent critics to this tension seems to be that we should abandon the attempt to provide general accounts of historical change altogether. Rather than cast the cultural divisions, tensions, and unexpected similarities within and between social classes to one side, this very heterogeneity is to become the focus of study; we should be concerned, in the words of Tim Harris, with 'the diversities within popular culture itself'.[38] In this new cultural history, the elucidation of difference ceases to undermine our historical narratives, it becomes the purpose of our narratives. And, in this way, the revisionist appeal for a greater awareness of the complexities of social development turns out to involve more far-reaching consequences for the study of popular culture than is apparent at first sight. The seemingly innocent call for subtlety and nuance in fact entails a fine, but powerful, redefinition of the purpose of history. The suggestion that historians should aspire to more intricate and complex accounts of the past has slipped into the historical mainstream almost unnoticed, but its simplicity

---

[37] See, in particular, Storch, 'Please to remember', pp. 71–99, esp. 76–8, 80; Vincent, 'Decline of oral tradition', pp. 20–47, esp. 40–2; Delves, 'Popular recreation', pp. 89–127.

[38] Harris, 'Problematising popular culture', p. 5.

should not be allowed to conceal that it in fact marks a departure of real significance.[39]

Furthermore, notwithstanding the new agenda that lies at the heart of recent developments in the study of popular culture, there remains something stubbornly familiar about much of the work that it has spawned. I opened this discussion by arguing that a major limitation of nineteenth-century research into popular sports was its refusal to engage with the way that structures of domination and subordination affected the history of sports in society, and suggested that more recent studies of leisure have offered similarly depoliticised accounts of recreation. The recent stress on cultural diversity and overlap brings greater sophistication to what I consider the dominant trend in late-twentieth-century research into popular culture: the attempt to uncover and understand the meaning of cultural practice. It does not, however, offer a radically new interpretation of the historical significance of these practices. It sanctions, even promotes, a scholarly approach that remains closed to the political dynamic.

It is possible to outline how these ideas about the multiplicity and diversity of cultural practices might be applied to the study of popular recreation. The idea of the 'popular' would certainly be challenged. It would be suggested, and quite justly, that supposedly 'popular' sports are not confined to a distinct social group. The eighteenth century provides several examples of sports whose appeal cut across conventional social divisions. Horse-racing, pugilism, and cricket, for example, drew support from a very wide spectrum of society, though all in very different ways.[40] Guy Fawkes celebrations, it has been repeatedly shown, rested on a complex base of support, always centred upon the poor and disenfranchised, but often extending higher up the social ladder as well.[41] Indeed it is doubtful that even the most plebeian of pursuits—bull-baiting, cock throwing, football—lay entirely beyond the reach of the middle ranks of society. In fine, our 'popular recreations' are not really 'popular' at all. Of course, the difficulty of firmly categorising the social constituency of popular sports and recreations has long been recognised, but the new cultural history suggests a novel way of handling this problem. Rather than simply acknowledge the diversity of cultural experience, the description and explication of this diversity become the focus of analysis. Thus, contrasts in the ways different

---

[39] These points are developed further in Griffin, 'Popular culture', pp. 619–65, esp. 628–35.
[40] Huggins, *Flat Racing*, pp. 38–116; Brailsford, *Bareknuckles*, pp. 23–44; Underdown, *Start of Play*, pp. 35–73.
[41] Storch, 'Please to remember', pp. 71–99; Paz, 'Bonfire night', pp. 316–28.

social groups experienced cultural practices are no longer left to sit at the margins of our accounts of popular culture, they are brought to its very centre.

My reservation with this approach is that the pursuit of such emphases risks becoming simply banal. Of course there are exceptions to any generalisations and social categorisations we make but, if social history is to avoid retreating into particularism, it is necessary to exercise judgement over where multiple meanings justify elucidation, and where their elucidation obscures alternative readings of the customs under consideration. No matter how we categorise eighteenth-century sports and their participants, there will always be exceptions to the categories we create; but it is by no means self-evident that these exceptions have greater historical importance than the gaol sentences meted out to those who refused to accept that a particular practice, in a particular time and place, had become unacceptable. Sports certainly were experienced and perceived in different ways by different social groups and, although these experiential differences are interesting, so too are their consequences. Divided perceptions had the potential to produce friction between social groups; and, in a society so advanced and unequal as industrialising England, the outcome of social conflict was always highly unpredictable.

Since the inception of research into sports and pastimes in the late eighteenth century, it has been the tendency of researchers to conceptualise popular recreations as 'folk' activities, belonging uniquely to the poor, lying beyond the reach of those in positions of authority. But few recreations ever occupied such a remote and sheltered position. Popular customs were invariably embedded in an extensive web of social relations; they were above all the site of a complex encounter between different social groups, and it is something of this encounter that I aim to capture here.[42] This is not of course to suggest that the pursuit of meaning should be abandoned, for understanding how participants perceived the activities and practices in which they engaged must lie at the heart of any piece of cultural history. It is simply that meanings and perceptions must be situated in the widest possible social and political context.

In seeking to bring the operation of power into our analysis of the meaning of popular culture, this book draws upon an older tradition in

[42] Similar ideas have been advanced by Bob Scribner: 'popular culture is . . . shaped in both conscious (and unconscious) ways from outside and from within itself, and especially "from above" by hegemonic or dominant elites wielding the kinds of political and cultural power than can set down the rules of cultural behaviour'. Scribner, 'History of popular culture', pp. 175–91, quote on p. 186. See also Storch, 'Policeman as domestic missionary', pp. 481–509.

social history, one which aimed to position recreations within a wider framework of social relations and class conflict. The pursuit of meaning has arguably been the most dominant trend in the historiography of popular culture, but it has by no means been the only one. A more radical tradition in social history turned not to anthropology, but to the modernisation theories of sociologists, and sought to tie changes in patterns of popular recreations to the industrial transformation presumed to occur in England between the late eighteenth and mid-nineteenth centuries. Though based upon a model of industrialisation that is now widely considered to be inaccurate, this style of enquiry nonetheless placed power at the centre of analysis, and suggests the basis of a new study of popular pastimes.

A particularly colourful and influential account of the impact of industrialisation was provided by Robert Malcolmson in his *Popular Recreations in English Society*. Malcolmson offered a compelling account of the pre-industrial recreational calendar, and described the changes it underwent over the eighteenth century as a result of the pressures known collectively as the industrial revolution. He accumulated scattered, but sufficiently numerous, examples of the disappearance of old pastimes in England over a period of 150 years to suggest the almost total destruction of traditional patterns of recreations by 1850, and he related this decline to contemporaneous economic change. Traditional recreations were embedded in a paternalistic, agrarian society and, as the industrial revolution broke down the traditional fabric of society, so were the vital supports of traditional recreations fatally undermined. Some regions were in advance of others, whilst some were culturally backwards; nevertheless, industrialisation and commercialisation showed little discrimination in their effects. Although Malcolmson suggested that certain regions diverged from his chronology of change, no regional peculiarities were considered to be of sufficient weight to undermine the 'basic facts of this trend'.[43]

A succession of historians filled the cultural vacuum that Malcolmson had left in the nineteenth century with a new range of commercial leisure pursuits better suited to an emergent capitalist society. In place of the annual cycle of feasts and festivals, governed by seasons and harvests, were to be found modern spectator sports and commercial music halls. By the late nineteenth century, the industrial revolution had brought the rising incomes, increased spare time, and modern transport system that spectator sports require. In response to the relentless rhythm of the factory, rules had been codified, pitch sizes standardised, and length of play fixed: sports were

---

[43] Malcolmson, *Popular Recreations*, p. 170.

now pinned down in both time and space.[44] In similar fashion, the traditional sing-along of the local beerhouse had been transformed into the commercial music hall. As befitted a capitalist society, a handful of large chains dominated the market by the century's end, and ensured the standardisation of music-hall programmes throughout the country.[45] It all amounted, in the view of one writer, to the 'urbanization, commercialisation and nationalisation of popular culture'.[46]

In these accounts, popular recreations were conceptualised as the product not simply of working-class tastes and preferences, but also of impersonal economic forces lying beyond working-class control. For these writers, the time, place, and pace of popular recreation were all shaped to some extent by contemporaneous power structures; and, although revisionists soon sought to modify this account in various ways, they continued to work with the assumption that culture and economy were inextricably linked. Hugh Cunningham's *Leisure in the Industrial Revolution* offered a comprehensive reassessment of Malcolmson's account of the impact of the industrial revolution on popular recreations. In true revisionist style, Cunningham emphasised the slow pace of change, the resilience of many traditional leisure forms, and the unexpected benefits and new opportunities presented by industrialisation and commercialisation, and his conclusions were supported by a handful of scholars working on related practices.[47] Robert Poole's research on the annual wakes in the cotton districts of Lancashire, for example, demonstrated the way in which traditional wakes entertainments continued 'with remarkable consistency', despite the rapid pace of industrialisation in the area.[48] Likewise studies of the music hall suggested that the development of this form of entertainment was only weakly influenced by the increasingly capitalist nature of the business. Peter Bailey illustrated the control that working-class audiences continued to exercise over the entertainment they were offered, and concluded that the commercial music halls of the late nineteenth century

---

[44] Vamplew, *Pay Up and Play the Game*, esp. pp. 21–43; Clarke and Critcher, *The Devil Makes Work*, esp. pp. 48–59. See also Hargreaves, *Sport, Power and Culture*, pp. 16–56; Walvin, *Leisure and Society*, pp. 2–17.

[45] Vicinus, *The Industrial Muse*; Summerfield, 'The Effingham Arms', pp. 209–40.

[46] Easton et al., *Disorder and Discipline*, p. 56. See also Alexander, *St Giles Fair*; Marrus (ed.), *Emergence of Leisure*, pp. 1–10; Henricks, *Disputed Pleasures*.

[47] Cunningham, *Leisure*, pp. 9–56, esp. 9–14. See also idem, 'Metropolitan fair', pp. 163–84.

[48] Poole, 'Oldham wakes', pp. 71–98, quote on p. 74. See also Walton and Poole, 'Lancashire wakes', pp. 100–124.

remained an autonomous expression of popular culture.[49] But none of these writers questioned the economic transformation that was presumed to lie at the heart of nineteenth-century England. In each of these studies, the drama was played out against the backcloth of the industrial revolution—universal, sweeping, and pervasive in its reach and effects. Thus, whilst the consequences of industrialisation were interpreted differently, a number of key assumptions about the nature of nineteenth-century society and economy were left unchallenged.

We have since learned to live with a very different industrial revolution—a revolution so limited, so multifarious, and so regionally confined that these attempts to generalise about the fate of popular culture during the nineteenth century appear hopelessly dated. There can be no doubting the value of this endeavour to explore the impact of economic change on cultural practice, yet economic change has thus far been conceived so narrowly that the extent to which the enterprise has even begun must be questioned. The revisionist suggestion that traditional cultural practices continued to flourish within newly industrialising districts is well founded, and it is furthermore likely that industrialisation may have encouraged the development of new popular customs and traditions. But what happened to sports and recreations outside the heartlands of the industrial revolution? The corn counties, pastoral regions, declining industrial districts in the south and south-west, ports, market towns, and historic regional centres: how did the relationship between local economic conditions and popular custom and culture work out in areas such as these? The first generation of research into popular culture made a valuable contribution to our understanding of the links between culture and economics, but with so much of the country effectively untouched by the onset of industrialisation we are forced to concede that our understanding of the ways in which economic conditions have historically influenced cultural practice still remains limited in the extreme.

It is perhaps here, then, that we need to show more sensitivity towards the heterogeneity of historical experience. When historians set out to bring a greater awareness of the complexity of popular culture, they did so by challenging the concept of the 'popular', by questioning the social following of different practices, by searching for divisions of status, age, and gender within the social categorisations that scholars had traditionally used.

---

[49] Bailey, *Leisure and Class*, pp. 154–75 See also Poole, *Popular Leisure*; Reid, 'Decline of St Monday', pp. 76–101; Stearns, 'Effort at continuity', pp. 626–55; Judd, 'Oddest combination', pp. 11–30.

But there are many other places where difference can be found, and the grounds for privileging class as the central axis around which analysis revolves have never been adequately explained or justified. Studies of the impact of the industrial revolution on popular recreations suggest an alternative place to look for variety of historical experience. They reveal that different regions and settlements had distinct patterns of recreations, and indicate that one way of resolving diversity, of making sense of the seemingly endless variations in cultural practice, might be to attend not simply to who enjoyed any given sports or pastimes, but to where they were played. Focusing upon the spaces in which games and celebrations were enjoyed promises a methodology sensitive both to regional and temporal variations in patterns of popular recreation and to the ways in which the forces of power contributed to these variations.

The specificity of regional experiences is amply confirmed by existing studies of popular recreation in the eighteenth and early nineteenth centuries. Since Malcolmson's groundbreaking national survey of popular recreations, most research has taken the form of local studies, and there is now an extensive literature exploring different sports and different regions. Wakes in Lancashire; wakes and fairs in Birmingham; fairs in London; football in Derby; camping in East Anglia; bowling in Northumbria; bear-baiting in Cheshire; festivals in Wales; cockfighting in Devon; bull-running in Stamford; and Guy Fawkes celebrations in Northamptonshire and in southern market towns—all have been described and analysed.[50] These local studies encompass a diverse set of recreations (wakes, fairs, football, Guy Fawkes celebrations, blood sports) and range across many different regions (the metropolis, provincial towns, industrial towns and hamlets, and southern rural areas). Cumulatively they have extended our knowledge of pre-industrial recreations and provide unambiguous testimony to the variety of cultural forms that existed in different locations. Yet these local studies raise almost as many questions as they answer; for, although they have repeatedly demonstrated changing patterns of sports and pastimes during the eighteenth and nineteenth centuries, their limited regional focus makes it difficult to comprehend the causes of these changes. By considering towns and regions in isolation, local histories fail to indicate whether the

---

[50] Poole, 'Oldham wakes', pp. 71–98; Reid, 'Interpreting the calendar', pp. 125–53; Cunningham, 'Metropolitan fair', pp. 163–84 and Judd, 'Oddest combination', pp. 11–30; Delves, 'Popular recreation', pp. 89–127; Dymond, 'Camping close', pp. 165–92; Metcalfe, 'Potshare bowling', pp. 29–44; Hindle, 'Custom and protest', pp. 155–78; Suggett, 'Festivals and social structure', pp. 79–112; Porter, 'Cockfighting', pp. 63–71; Walsh, 'November bull-running', pp. 233–47; Paz, 'Bonfire night', pp. 316–28; Storch, 'Please to remember', pp. 71–99.

patterns described in each case were unique to the region under consideration, or were more widely prevalent, and are unable to signal which social, economic, or intellectual factors were most important in directing the course of change.

What is required, therefore, is not the further multiplication of local studies, but a new analytical framework within which regional differences may be compared and contrasted. Using the concept of space, this book attempts to construct such a framework. Whether in urban, industrial, or rural England, all sports required space, and since the labouring poor rarely possessed any quantity of land of their own this requirement had important implications for their opportunities for recreation. The landless either awaited the patronage of landowners or appropriated public spaces for themselves—sometimes common or waste land, sometimes the village green, and sometimes public streets. Their sports were consequently dependent upon the consent of those in the local community who exercised control over these spaces, and were vulnerable to any shifts in opinion regarding the value of popular recreation that they might have. Well governed market towns, rapidly expanding industrial townships, and rural villages and hamlets provide the point of departure here. Both the pressure on open land and the policing of public space were very different in these environments, creating the possibility for distinct patterns of recreation to develop in each.

There is no template for the study of sports and space to which we may turn, as the cultural use of space has made no more than a fleeting appearance on the historiographical agenda in any field of English history. A small number of urban historians, however, have begun to consider the symbolic worth of city space, and to read cultural practices in the context of the space in which they were located. Although these studies are far from numerous, there are insights to be found here that are of value to the present work. In eighteenth-century Bristol, for example, the symbolic resonances consequent upon situating political demonstrations in the city's finest streets and squares have been analysed.[51] The use of the street for plebeian activities, both recreational and occupational, in nineteenth-century London has also formed the focus of a number of books.[52] In very different ways, these works underscore the role of topography in investing

---

[51] Harrison, 'Symbolism and location of crowds', pp. 194–213; Poole, 'Popular sovereignty and public space', pp. 40–54. See also Corfield, 'Walking city streets', pp. 132–74.
[52] Daunton, *House and Home*, pp. 11–37 esp. 15; Winter, *Teeming Streets*, passim, esp. pp. 65–79; Nead, *Victorian Babylon*, pp. 149–215. See also Croll, 'Street disorder', pp. 250–68.

popular activities with complex additional meanings, and illustrate the shifting nature of these uses and meanings over time. This book seeks to build upon the foundations laid by these urban historians, by extending their topographically sensitive studies of popular culture to different times, places, and activities. More broadly, however, it hopes to demonstrate the value of exploiting the concept of space as a tool for historical investigation outside the urban context; for, with the exception of these studies of civic space, the use of space as a category of enquiry continues to lie outside the historical mainstream.

There has been no attempt, for example, to decode the cultural value of the country's heaths, moors, and commons. An extensive historiography documenting the loss of these spaces at enclosure is dominated by economic and agricultural concerns.[53] There has been some investigation of the social conflicts surrounding the enclosure of common lands in the second half of the nineteenth century and, although these studies go beyond the agricultural ramifications of enclosure and engage more fully with plebeian responses, they too set out to situate these responses in an economic, rather than social or cultural, context.[54] And a history, whether economic or social, of the village green does simply not exist. The village green, one of the nation's best known and most loved topographical features, has attracted almost no scholarly attention, and even the simplest questions about the use, legal status, or origins of these ancient spaces remain unanswered. As this study of space moves beyond the relatively well ordered territory of the streets and squares of towns and cities, therefore, it encounters a territory that is very much less well mapped, both literally and metaphorically.

It is hoped that the advantages of using space as an analytical framework will become clear in the pages that follow, but at the outset it is important to address one possible drawback of structuring the discussion around space: the way in which this framework determines the sports and customs that lie within the scope of this work. Though ostensibly a history of 'popular recreation', this book does not engage systematically with the concept of the 'popular'. The term is employed loosely, simply to denote activities in which the poor could, and often did, participate, in contrast to those where constraints of money, time, and space conspired to

---

[53] Gonner, *Common Land*; Hoskins and Stamp, *The Common Lands*; Tate, *English Village Community*; Turner, *Parliamentary Enclosure*; Yelling, *Common Field*.
[54] MacMaster, 'Battle for Mousehold Heath', pp. 117–54; Short, 'Conservation, class and custom', pp. 127–54; Cowell, 'Commons Preservation Society', pp. 145–60.

ensure they did not; but it must be admitted that this book does not provide a comprehensive survey of all such sports and pastimes.

The list of activities that might be considered in a history of recreation is potentially long, and focusing on space places limits upon the sports and pastimes that are relevant to this book. An interest in the use of space forces attention towards activities that took place outdoors, and on public rather than private land; consequently, activities enjoyed indoors or on private premises, though they might be popular in appeal, largely fall from view. To take just a few examples, cockfighting, pugilism, and the sporting events organised around alehouses all had large plebeian followings, but all were located to some extent in private buildings or on private land. The use of private rather than public space did not of course place these pastimes beyond the jurisdiction of local officials, but it did severely restrict their scope to interfere with them, and for this reason they get little attention here. From the perspective of the annual cycle of recreation, therefore, this account contains many omissions. During the winter months, when cold weather and darkness forced revellers indoors, and in particular into the relative warmth and comfort of the alehouse, the outdoor sports and celebrations considered here diminished in importance. It is only those pastimes that help to illuminate the changing uses of particular spaces that fall within the compass of this work, and what follows is consequently far from being a complete account of the history of popular recreation during the long eighteenth century.

No less problematic than the exclusions that follow from analysing sports and recreations from the perspective of space, are the inclusions. In the eighteenth century, the range of activities that took place out of doors and on public rather than private land was wide and diverse, and this book surveys a correspondingly wide range of activities. Although many—such as football, bull-baiting, and cock throwing—had an overwhelmingly plebeian basis of support and might be loosely described as 'popular' recreations, others did not. Civic ceremonies, fairs, and cricket, for example, were all orchestrated, enjoyed, and controlled to some extent by ruling elites. Certainly the poor participated in these events, but they cannot be considered 'popular' recreations according to any customary use of the term. They get attention here because they drew large crowds of people into public areas, but clearly the term 'popular recreations' must be interpreted loosely, understood to denote plebeian involvement, rather than any more significant statement about the social constituency of those presumed to enjoy them.

This book's interests are firmly rooted in popular recreations, it being the plebeian and the playful that lie at its heart. The expression 'popular recreations' is employed here both for reasons of convenience, as well as to emphasise that it is in the recreational life of the poor that we are primarily interested; but it needs to be recognised that the fit between the 'popular' on the one hand and between 'recreations' that used public spaces on the other is imprecise. It is the use of certain types of public space that determines which activities are relevant to the discussion and which are not; and this analytic framework produces a work exploring an eclectic, and sometime curious, range of pastimes, mapping only loosely onto the 'popular'.

It is not my intention, however, to pursue these observations about the social constitution of 'popular' recreations further. The chapters that follow turn away from current concerns about the complexity of social composition, in order to investigate the more unexplored terrain of space. It is a concept as imprecise and fraught with difficulties as the 'popular', yet it nevertheless promises a new perspective on the sports and pastimes that have interested researchers for over two centuries. In the next chapter, Chapter 2, I describe these activities—the fairs, celebrations, sports, and pastimes—in detail, and introduce some of the ways in which space was critical in determining how these activities were experienced and enjoyed. The remaining seven chapters extend the discussion of these pastimes, and of the significance of their physical location, further.

The core of this book consists in three case studies, each looking at the recreations and spaces to be found in different types of settlement. We look first at the streets and squares of provincial market towns; then at the diverse vacant spaces to be found in industrialising towns and villages of the west Midlands and the West Riding of Yorkshire; and finally at the village greens of rural England. But there is no attempt here to insist that these three areas form discrete environments, each with its own and unique patterns of recreation. Woven through these case studies structured around space is a discussion of the ancient custom of bull-baiting—a practice that spans these different settlements and spaces. Popular blood sports (and their stubborn refusal to remain confined to one place) provide a salutary reminder of the difficulty of classifying sports and pastimes, and of their tendency to overspill any categories that we construct. The urban, industrial, and rural divisions that structure this research should accordingly be approached as approximate rather than absolute categories, and the continuities between different types of settlement, although they are not fully investigated here, should always be borne in mind.

The two chapters on market towns (Chapters 3 and 4) open the first of our case studies exploring the connection between sports and space. Towns were the location of a wide and varied range of sports and pastimes, and there was a correspondingly large number of different places that might be used for recreation. The space that forms the focus of these two chapters, however, is the public street, and above all the market square. Chapters 3 and 4 describe the activities that were customarily practised here between the late seventeenth century and the early nineteenth century, and chart a complex series of changes in these uses over the period. The two chapters suggest that, as well as their commercial uses, the streets and squares of early modern England had a symbolic and cultural significance, and describe a gradual but discernible redefinition of their cultural worth during the long eighteenth century. In the second case study (Chapters 6 and 7), we move to the industrial environment. Chapter 6 outlines the distinct popular cultures that existed in two contrasting industrial regions, and questions what local factors might have contributed to these regional peculiarities. Chapter 7 turns back to the theme of space, and explores the changing uses of the streets, commons, and wastes that were available for recreation in expanding industrial settlements. The third and final case study (Chapter 8) turns to the rural environment, and the focus here is upon the village green. I seek first to establish the significance of the village green, and then proceed to examine how far the enclosure movement in one rural county (Cambridgeshire) affected the survival of both village greens and of the games that had traditionally been played upon them.

The ancient custom of bull-baiting appears at a number of points throughout this book. It emerges as a butchers regulation in the first chapter on provincial towns (Chapter 3); and reappears as a plebeian pastime to which the inhabitants of Birmingham and the west Midlands were peculiarly attached in Chapter 6. Chapters 5 and 9 explore this unique, and in many ways problematic, sport further. Chapter 5 provides an intellectual history of the sport. It looks at the rapid emergence of hostile criticism about bull-baiting in the late eighteenth century, and attempts to situate this outpouring of concern within the wider context of concern about animal cruelty. In Chapter 9 an attempt is made to describe and explain the eventual disappearance of bull-baiting, and the discussion of the sport that runs throughout the book is thereby brought to a close.

As the following nine chapters progress, the true complexity of recreational life in England between the Restoration and the early nineteenth century begins to unfold. It must be admitted that the full extent of this diversity is not fully comprehended by dividing recreation into its urban, industrial, and rural components. Nonetheless, it is hoped that by focusing on space a novel and unique light can be shed upon a wide range of popular sports, games, and celebrations during the period of modernisation.

2
Popular recreations

The assault on popular recreations mounted in the late sixteenth century and first half of the seventeenth century and the spontaneous outburst of popular rejoicing at the return of Charles II in 1660 have been well documented.[1] The jubilant celebrations, the distribution of beer, bread, and meat, the loyal processions, and joyful bonfires lit to mark the King's return, were all recorded by observers glad to be witnessing such events. But while it is certain that the Restoration oversaw the immediate revival of much of the old festive calendar, the long-term changes ushered in after this flush of enthusiasm are less clear. The rapid reappearance of the old festive culture at the King's return in May 1660 was arguably of greater symbolic than practical significance. An astute observer at Oxford, Anthony Wood, noted a maypole had been set up in order 'to vex the Presbyterians and Independents', and his account of the dancers' motivation was surely not incorrect.[2] Communal feasting and drinking, dancing around maypoles and traditional sports indeed implied a rejection of the values of the Protectorate, a return to the supposed harmony and community of the pre-Civil War years. But the descriptions of Restoration revelry that were painstakingly recorded were also idealised representations of communal festivity containing a barely concealed political message. Sports, recreations, and revelling could quickly degenerate into the kind of behaviour that local communities were not inclined to tolerate, and the suspension of censure in the politically charged climate of the early 1660s provided no guarantee for their long-term security.

This book sets out to consider what did happen to popular recreation and merry-making in the period following the Restoration, and, as was outlined in the previous chapter, it does so by situating recreations in the spaces in which they were enjoyed. Let us begin, however, by looking at

---

[1] The fullest account of popular recreations in the seventeenth century is contained in Hutton, *Rise and Fall*, pp. 153–226. A wealth of relevant material from the West Country has also been analysed by Underdown, *Revel, Riot and Rebellion*, esp. pp. 44–105, 239–70.
[2] Wood, *Life of Wood*, i, p. 314.

the activities themselves in greater detail. Popular recreations are events of intrinsic historical interest: they are occasional moments of release, reversal, inversion; instances of excitement in working lives, and qualities such as these arguably become marginalised in the discussions about space that follow. This chapter sets out to bring these qualities into sharper focus. It aims to illustrate some of the ways in which space was fundamental in shaping these customs and practices, but also, more simply, to describe the long-since forgotten pastimes with which this book is concerned.

The festive calendar

The year in early modern England comprised many calendars. During preceding centuries, numerous events of Christian, pagan, legal, dynastic, and agricultural origin and significance had left their mark, creating a succession of dates scattered through the year, each celebrated with a rest from work and customary entertainments. Different seasons brought their respective celebrations and amusements, some of great antiquity, others of more recent origin, some recognised nationally, others of purely local significance.

At the heart of the recreational calendar in all corners of the country, however, lay the cycle of fairs, wakes, feasts, and revels, punctuating the year with particular force during the summer months. In the view of one commentator, 'the rustics, in general, look to wakes and fairs for their amusement'; and there is much evidence to support his view.[3] Every community enjoyed at least one annual celebration of this kind, though the exact form that fairs and feasts took varied considerably between different regions and between settlements of different sizes. In larger towns, fairs predominated. These were complex occasions, typically spanning several days, and mixing both recreational and commercial functions; fairs combined, in the words of one historian, 'the roles of market place, labour exchange [and] amusement park'.[4] In Bampton in Oxfordshire, it was noted that the August fair was both a horse market and 'a sort of carnival to all the neighbouring villages';[5] and so far as the poor were concerned, it was presumably as a carnival rather than as a horse market that the fair

---

[3] Howitt, *Rural Life*, ii, p. 273.
[4] Judd, 'Oddest combination', p. 15.
[5] Giles, *History of Bampton*, p. lxiv.

appealed. Large fairs lasted several days with at least one devoted to markets—cheese, horses, cattle, hardware, and so forth—and with plays,
booths, and races providing entertainment on subsequent days, and many
smaller fairs followed a similar pattern. The gathering of traders and large
crowds invariably attracted travelling showmen and pleasure-seekers as
well: food, drink, and merriment formed an indispensable component of
any civic fair.

The exact range of entertainments that might be enjoyed at a large
urban fair was rich and varied. An early-nineteenth-century handbill
depicting the attractions of the fair included pictures of 'Punch & his
Wife', 'Conjuring', 'Players', 'Wonderful Doings', 'a Merry Dance',
'Tyger', and 'Bear & Monkey'—suggesting an occasion comprising a
weird and wonderful mix of amusements, some familiar and others less
well known.[6] Amongst the many attractions typically to be found at a civic
fair were theatre companies showing plays to suit all tastes—melodramas,
comedies, thrillers; freak shows boasting oddities and curiosities of all
kinds, both human and animal; tumblers, rope-dancers, acrobats, and
musicians; and a wide range of novel foods and cheap consumer
goods.[7] Some of these could be seen on an occasional basis outside the
annual fair. For example, John Clifton, a carpenter living in Oundle,
Northamptonshire, saw 'Mr Longmore, the Hertfordshire Giant' and
'Peggy Morgan, the smallest woman in England', both typical fair exhibits
at the town's inn, the Swan.[8] Then there were those entertainments
unique to the fair, such as the rides and merry-go-rounds that were
becoming popular in the early nineteenth century. These had existed in
some form since at least the early eighteenth century, but they became
both more complex and more common at the century's end.[9] Together
with the plays, shows, freaks, and food they created a fairground that

---

[6] Guildhall Library, London, 'The Fair', Noble Collection, C26.5.
[7] See Muncey, *English Fairs*; Walford, *Fairs, Past and Present*. See also Hone, *Every-day Book*, i,
22 May, pp. 688–94; 5 Sept., pp. 1168–253; and the collections of the Guildhall Library, London: Osborne, 'Bartholomew Fair', Gr.3.3.1; 'Bartholomew Fair', MS. 01514; Main Print
Collection, Pr. L.26.5; Playbills Collection (fairs).
[8] Northamptonshire RO, Clifton's Day Books, 1763–1784, ZA/8732–46, 3 June 1776, 24
Aug. 1776. He also saw a small collection of wild beasts and Maria Theresa, 'the amazing
Corsican Fairy', when they came to visit his town. Ibid., 1 July 1779, 21 March 1772.
[9] See, for example, the depiction of a small horizontal swing in an untitled ballad dated
1800: Guildhall Library, London, Main Print Collection, Pr. L.26.5. A painting of the
fair at Croydon in 1833 illustrates a more elaborate ride, rotating vertically. George
Hawkins, 'Croydon Fair, 1833' (w/c & ink on paper), Croydon Art Collection, Croydon
Clocktower.

offered exhilaration and excitement. Fairs combined the old and the new; they mixed traditional entertainments with novelties; and the sheer quantity of different amusements that might be encountered there provided variety and interest and assured their enduring popularity throughout the centuries.

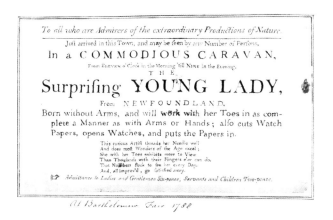

Figure 1.   Fair bills, 1788 (Guildhall Library, London, Osborne Collection, GR.3.3.1).

In smaller settlements, fairs without markets and dedication feasts, going variously by the names of 'feasts', 'wakes', 'hoppings', and 'revels', took the place of the trading fairs found in large towns. At these, many of the same shows and booths that visited urban fairs might be found (though they would be fewer in number), as might a wide range of simple plebeian games of various kinds. These 'rustic sports' included smoking matches in which contestants competed to smoke a quantity of tobacco in the shortest time; pudding-eating contests, the goal of which was to finish a bowl of hot pudding as quickly as possible; and grinning matches, in which prizes were awarded to the participant deemed to have pulled the ugliest face. Other fair-time favourites involved chasing greased pigs and rams; climbing up greasy poles for a joint of meat;[10] and races of many different kinds—wheelbarrow races, sack races, and smock races (races run by women for a prize of a smock).[11] A Shropshire folklorist was given the following account of the wakes entertainments in the small town of Ellesmere by a local inhabitant:

> I have seen men each up to his neck in a sack, with his arms tied in, and jumping a bag-race [sack race] in the market-place, [where] there was generally a wagon with eight or ten old women in it, grinning through horses' collars for a prize. Also as many old men, each supplied with a basin and spoon, and eating *hot stir*, the first who had finished to have a prize.[12]

And a Berkshire labourer recalled the annual feast held in the small village of his childhood in the following terms: 'Here [in front of the village inn] the shows were drawn up—the golden farmer in wax, the learned pig that could play cards, a fat lady, a cheap jack, and a sweetmeat and ginger-bread stall, a mouth organ and a drum. A gipsy with a fiddle sat on a platform and directed the dancing.'[13]

Rural feasts and wakes had a different origin to fairs, being rooted in the pre-Reformation festive calendar and linked to the parish's dedication saint, rather than fixed by charter. In practice, however, there was little to distinguish rural feasts from fairs, as both were held annually on a prescribed date, and both were devoted to the pursuit of pleasure. There were also strong similarities between these small rural feasts and fairs and the

[10] See the humorous description in [Darter], *Reminiscences*, p. 67.
[11] In Hertfordshire, a farmer travelled to Birch Green one spring 'being their a fair. boys running in sacks . . . Young girls for a shift deckerated with Ribons'. Hertfordshire ALS, Carrington Diary, D/EX3.31, 15 April 1805. For smock races, see Brailsford, *Taste for Diversions*, pp. 149–52.
[12] Burne, *Shropshire Folklore*, ii, pp. 445–6.
[13] Buckley, *Life-story*, pp. 28–9.

Figure 2. Isaac Robert Cruikshank, *Jumping in Sacks*, drawn by W. H. Payne, engraved by George Hunt (Bridgeman Art Library, London).

larger fairs founds in towns; although small rural feasts and wakes rarely possessed markets, a recognisable set of entertainments could nonetheless be found at feasts and fairs of all kinds and sizes, and the same mix of plays, freaks, oddities, games, and races was ubiquitous.

Although civic fairs and rural feasts used the same repertoire of entertainments, there remained a clear difference between the two, for there were certain qualities that the small rural feast or fair could never have. Visual representations of civic fairs emphasise the crowds that were drawn to these events and the carnival atmosphere consequent upon the stalls and crowds of pleasure-seekers. The small quiet fairs of rural villages could never replicate the commotion, excitement, and anonymity of the large civic fair.[14] In the hamlet of Wakering in Essex one year, for example, the fair 'consisted only of three stalls and the music and dance in the barn might be enquired for in vain'.[15] The very same stalls no doubt sometimes

[14] Samuel Colman, 'St. James's Fair, Bristol' (oil on canvas), Bristol City Museum and Art Gallery. See also the descriptions of London fairs in Judd, 'Oddest combination', pp. 11–30; and Cunningham, 'Metropolitan fairs', pp. 163–84.
[15] Asplin, 'Diary', 25 July 1826, p. 142.

visited larger civic fairs as well, but three stalls in isolation amounted to a fair which had little in common with large civic fairs, no matter what similarities existed between the stalls found at each.

The consequence of this distinction between large and small fairs is captured in the description that a doctor, Jonas Asplin, recorded in his diary of the fair held in Prittlewell, the small village in Essex where he resided in the early nineteenth century:

> Morning very fine. Arranged the stalls in front of my house. The fair is a very decent one. An exhibition on our right of a Giant, Giantess, an Albiness, a native of Baffin Bay and a Dwarf, very respectable. We had a learned Pig and Punch on our left, and in front some theatrical exhibition. All in very good order. Everything was quiet, orderly and decent.[16]

It is clear that the entertainments—plays, a few freaks, a learned pig—were identical to those that might be found at larger fairs, yet the context in which they were encountered created a very different experience. Stalls were laid out in front of the home of a local gentleman, and fair-goers were watched and supervised by substantial neighbours. It all resulted in a fair which in the view of a local notable was 'quiet, orderly and decent', and it is doubtful that large civic fairs would have attracted so much criticism throughout their long history if they had generally been quiet, orderly, and decent affairs.

The fair, then, was both universal and inclusive, attracting both genders, all ages, and individuals of all social status. Yet, despite being a universal experience, there were countless different ways in which the fair was encountered: diversity and variety lay at the heart of the fair-going experience, and there can be no easy generalisations about the place of the fair in eighteenth-century popular culture. A fundamental component of this diversity was the size of the settlement in which fairs were held. The sheer size of large civic fairs enabled them to offer things rarely encountered in labouring lives: choice, anonymity, and freedom from supervision. The entertainments to be found at a small rural feast or fair were far more limited, and there was little prospect of anonymity in a closely supervised village or hamlet; instead, fair day provided villagers with a rest from work and a day of social intercourse and good neighbourhood.

Civic fairs and their smaller rural cousins, feasts and wakes, were the most widespread and most frequent festivals in eighteenth-century England. Most large towns held numerous fairs throughout the year, the majority of which were devoted to pleasure in some small part at least; and whilst

---

[16] Ibid., 15 July 1826, p. 141.

it was unusual for villages to hold more than one feast or wake each year, the tradition of travelling to neighbouring feasts and civic fairs ensured that most rural inhabitants enjoyed a number of such events each year. The family and servants of Jeffrey Whitaker, a Wiltshire schoolmaster, travelled to no fewer than five local fairs in the course of one year, in addition to visiting the annual revel in their own village;[17] and a Yorkshire diarist likewise attended five in the summer months of 1726.[18] Few other events came round with such regularity to enliven the existence of the labouring classes.

There were, however, a handful of other dates that unfailingly brought festivity and the cessation of work. Shrove Tuesday was the oldest of these but, throughout much of the eighteenth century, the newer anniversary of Guy Fawkes was celebrated with equal vigour. Then there was a continuously changing cycle of political celebrations—the public thanksgivings held to commemorate occasions of national significance: royal birthdays, coronations, military victories, and so forth. There were of course many other dates in the calendar that were associated with celebration and festivity, but Shrove Tuesday, Guy Fawkes, and public thanksgivings brought the poor into public spaces for merry-making; and since this work is interested in the juncture between space and play, all reappear frequently within the pages of this book.

Shrove Tuesday was amongst the oldest and most widely celebrated dates in eighteenth-century England. William Fitzstephen's late twelfth-century history of St Thomas Becket included an account of cockfighting and football on Shrove Tuesday and repeated prohibition orders throughout following centuries suggest a continuous history of these customs throughout the medieval and early modern periods.[19] In the early seventeenth

---

[17] Whitaker, *Diaries:* Westbury fair (9 March 1739, p. 1); Warminster fair (11 April 1739, pp. 5–6); Edington fair (9 July 1739, p. 17); Corsley fair (30 July 1739, p. 20); Dilton Marsh fair (13 Sept. 1739, p. 25); the diarist's servants also attended Bratton revel (23–4 July 1739, pp. 19–20). See also the diary of William Cole; his servants travelled to eight fairs during the summer and autumn of 1766, though some of these trips were in search of goods rather than entertainment. Cole, *Blecheley Diary:* Brickhill fair (12 May 1766, p. 48); Leighton fair (20 May, p. 51); Buckingham fair (22 May, p. 51); Aylesbury fair (14 June, p. 58); Woburn fair (15 July, p. 70); Dunstable fair (13 Aug., p. 93); Stony Stratford fair (3 Oct., p. 132); Fenny Stratford fair (10 Oct., p. 135). In the same year servants also visited Easton feast (22 Sept., p. 125); Newton Longueville feast (19 Oct., p. 141).
[18] Hobson, 'Journal': Holmfirth feast (22 May 1726, p. 252); Dodworth feast (12 June, p. 253); Birchouse feast (17 July, p. 255); Skilston feast (1 Aug., p. 256); Woosboroug feast (14 Aug., p. 256).
[19] Hutton, *Stations of the Sun*, pp. 151–68.

century, an Oxford fellow, Thomas Crosfield, described the customs of
Shrovetide as follows: '1. Frittering. 2. throwing at cockes. 3. playing at
stooleball in ye Citty by woemen & footeball by men', and in the eighteenth century, the same handful of customs—throwing at cocks, football,
and pancakes—were universally enjoyed on this day.[20]

Cock throwing was as ubiquitous as it was simple. It consisted in teth-
ering a cock to the ground, and attempting to knock it down from a distance with wooden batons. There were no standard rules by which the
game was played, but it was conventional to charge players a few pence to
throw at the cock, and for any player who succeeded in knocking the animal off its feet to take possession of it if they were able to run and pick it
up before it righted itself. In Chichester in the late eighteenth century, the
going rate was apparently 'two pence three throws'.[21] Despite the best
efforts of eighteenth-century antiquaries, the origins of this singular
Shrovetide pastime remain unclear, though there can be no doubt that the
practice was extremely widespread.[22] It was played alongside a number of
other games involving chasing, or 'threshing', a cock or hen, and it is possible that these pastimes were of yet greater antiquity. Certainly the form of
these games was even less firmly fixed. The substantial Lancashire farmer
Nicholas Blundell provided the following description of the boys in his
village chasing a cock on Shrove Tuesday in the early eighteenth century:

> The Little Boys of this Town rann Blindfold after an other who had a Bell,
> for a Cock; when that Sport was over, they ran with their Hands ty'd on their
> backs after the Cock & took him in their Mouth; I think there were each
> time seaven; I, William Harrison, William Thelwall & several others were
> present.[23]

But there were endless local variations on these sports involving the chasing or threshing of cocks and hens. No matter how these games were
played, all were emphatically plebeian in their appeal: they were the recreations not simply of the labouring poor, but often of the children of the
poor as well.[24] They were played in some form in all areas throughout the

---

[20] Crosfield, *Diary*, 1 March 1633, p. 63. Stoolball was a form of cricket, and is described in
greater detail below.
[21] Spershott, *Memoirs*, p. 14.
[22] Ellis, *Observations on Popular Antiquities*, pp. 73–4.
[23] Blundell, *Diurnal*, iii, 22 February 1726, p. 178.
[24] Newcome, *Diary*, 4 Feb. 1661, p. 53; Newcome, *Autobiography*, i, 31 Jan. 1665, p.147. See
also Blundell, *Diurnal*, ii, 17 February 1713, p. 51. Not invariably however. His guest was one
year 'so busy shooting at the Cock he could not come, but after dinner he came and eat
some Pancakes etc', i, 3 March 1709, p. 204.

eighteenth century, and were usually followed in the afternoon by matches of football.

By the eighteenth century, Shrove Tuesday celebrations were plebeian and youthful in character. The day has been described as one of licensed misrule and, since festivities on Shrove Tuesday did occasionally get out of hand, there are some grounds for this view.[25] The day was commandeered by apprentices in early seventeenth-century London, for example, and was the occasion of rioting in Bristol and York later in the century. During the eighteenth century, the day continued to attract the attention of civic authorities, as they battled to eliminate cock throwing and the disorder with which it was frequently associated. In the nineteenth century, the day still remained a point of conflict between civic rulers and labourers; by this time, cock throwing had been largely suppressed, and it was the disorder surrounding the occasional games of street football that formed the target of local reformers.[26]

But these instances of violence and disorder were almost exclusively confined to urban areas, and in rural districts it seems less appropriate to describe the day as one of licensed misrule. The 'Little Boys' that Blundell and his neighbours watched chasing the cock posed no threat to social order—nor did the girls he saw threshing for a hen in a neighbour's field another year.[27] Elsewhere, a shopkeeper gave pennies to the girls that came 'a-singing' on Shrove Tuesday,[28] and a clergyman gave money to 'football men'.[29] Festive merry-making did not descend into disorder in these communities instead the day was one of good neighbourhood. And this contrast between urban and rural areas does not stem from any difference in the activities that were enjoyed, for communities in all areas participated in a fundamentally similar set of practices. Instead, we must look to the local environment if we are to understand why Shrove Tuesday took different forms, for the physical context within which activities such as cock throwing and football were situated was instrumental in shaping the ways in which they were both experienced by those who participated in them, and perceived by those who did not.

---

[25] See Hutton, *Stations of the Sun*, pp. 155–6; idem, *Rise and Fall*, p. 244.
[26] For the seventeenth century, see Hutton, *Stations of the Sun*. For the eighteenth and nineteenth centuries, see below, Chapter 4.
[27] Blundell, *Diurnal*, ii, 17 Feb. 1713, p. 51.
[28] Turner, *Diary*, 7 Feb. 1758, p. 135.
[29] Clay, *History of Landbeach*, p. 60.

In part this difference between urban and rural areas was simply a function of the numbers involved. The sheer number of urban apprentices and labourers that might take to the streets in a large town to throw at cocks, or (more occasionally) to play matches of football, posed problems for the maintenance of public order that did not exist at small rural gatherings. But the potential for disorder that existed in towns rested upon something more than the numbers of people involved. The location of the activities, as opposed to the extent of participation, was also significant. In towns, recreations were forced onto spaces that existed for other purposes. The market square was intended for trade, and the street designed for traffic, but on Shrove Tuesday the normal function of both of these places was eclipsed by the crowds that took over corners of the town for purposes of their own. The use of these public spaces added a further level of meaning to the activities. When the urban poor took to the streets for games and festivity, there was an implicit challenge to the normal order of things that did not exist when villagers enjoyed the same activities on their village green, or in tucked away fields, and this is why a history of recreation needs to attend to the significance of space. The cultural resonance of sports and recreations varied according to the spaces in which they were held. Different spaces had the power to invest popular recreations with new meanings, and for this reason an appreciation of space is fundamental to understanding both their appeal, and their fate.

The same observations have yet greater relevance when considering the celebration of Guy Fawkes night. Following the discovery of a Catholic plot to blow up the King and the Houses of Parliament on 5 November 1605, this day became firmly fixed as a day of celebration and thanksgiving.[30] But, as with all festivals and celebrations, its form was never firmly fixed, and the event continued to evolve in subsequent years. By the eighteenth century, it no longer occupied the central place in the cycle of observance of courtly, parliamentary, and civic elites that it once had, and its basis of support now resided in the lower ranks of society. Like Shrove Tuesday, Gunpowder Plot was celebrated universally by the labouring poor. In cities, towns of all sizes, and villages and hamlets, the day was marked with the same set of practices—the lighting of bonfires and the firing of squibs and crackers. However, just as Shrove Tuesday celebrations took a very different complexion in settlements of varying sizes, so did these Guy Fawkes activities acquire unique resonances in different places.

---

[30] For a good overview, see Cressy, 'Fifth of November', pp. 68–90.

In rural areas, bonfires were burned on vacant land, on the green, for example, or in the empty village street; but within towns they were fitted into close and crowded urban thoroughfares, where they posed both greater fire risks, and a potential problem for the maintenance of public order. Guy Fawkes was always associated with the appropriation of all and every scrap of wood for the festive bonfire; in towns, however, the streets were appropriated as well, and this added a local political dimension to the occasion. It is only in this context that the long-running and bitterly contested battles in many towns throughout the nineteenth century may be properly understood. At the heart of the ongoing conflict over Guy Fawkes celebrations lay a disagreement over the legitimate uses of civic space, and for this reason an account of the conflicts surrounding Guy Fawkes must be based upon an analysis not simply of what was being celebrated and how, but also of where.

By the eighteenth century, Guy Fawkes was a largely plebeian festival. Its origins, however, lay not in popular traditions of merry-making, but in the cycle of celebrations established in the sixteenth century by Elizabeth I. The proscription of religious festivals, holy days, and saints' days at the Reformation had severely depleted the nation's recreational calendar; in order to make good these losses, Elizabeth and her ministers had instituted a new cycle of celebrations to commemorate royal birthdays, and the anniversaries of coronations, military victories, royal marriages, and so forth.[31] The dates and events that were selected for celebration were reworked many times during the seventeenth century by a succession of Jacobean monarchs and they continued to change during the following one hundred years. In time, the anniversary of Guy Fawkes' attempt to blow up King and Parliament mutated into a plebeian festival, but a more formal cycle of political celebration promoted and controlled by civic leaders also remained in place.

These political celebrations drew upon a set of practices that had long been exploited as public demonstrations of joy. At their heart lay the ringing of bells; when the occasion was fitting, civic authorities lay on public barrels of beer, distributed roasted meat, and provided bundles of faggots so that bonfires might burn in public spaces throughout the night as well. Together, bells and gunfire, feasting and drinking, and the lighting of bonfires and candles created celebrations that drew in the whole community, and in this way, the prayers and sermons prescribed by monarchs and local elites were supplemented with entertainments that extended to all.

---

[31] Cressy, *Bonfires and Bells*, pp. 50–66.

The creation and development of this new recreational calendar has been well documented, and local politics successfully illuminated by examining the alacrity or otherwise with which the dates esteemed by monarchs were celebrated in local communities.[32] What has not been noted, however, is the extent to which the form of these celebrations differed between urban and rural areas. Expressions of loyalty could take many different forms and, although bell-ringing was observed in all places, public feasting, drinking, and the lighting of bonfires were largely the preserve of towns and cities. Indeed, the origins of these customs of bonfires, commensality, and liberality lay in medieval civic festivity and ceremony, not in rural traditions of merry-making, and they remained a distinctly urban form of celebration throughout the eighteenth century.[33]

The most magnificent celebrations were inevitably held in the capital and in large towns and provincial capitals, but the new political calendar of celebration was by no means confined to great urban centres. Indeed it is remarkable that even the smallest town mimicked the celebrations to be found in larger urban settlements, using much the same repertoire of entertainments—though their more limited resources usually ensured that such celebrations were held on a rather more modest scale. In Castle Cary, for example, a small Somerset town scarcely larger than a village, elections were marked in the traditional style, with 'Bells ringing etc, and a great procession through [Castle Cary] with Musick playing and guns firing'.[34] So was the coronation of George III: 'Bells ringing all day . . . a very large bonfire on the top of the hill and very grand fireworks in the evening with firing of many guns'.[35] Outside the urban sector, however, celebrations of this kind were rarely to be found. In rural settlements, the assembling of the local population in public places was reserved for none but the most momentous of events, and a number of years might occur between one occasion when the local populations was regaled with bonfires and ale and the next. In large and loyal towns, the anniversaries of accession days, royal birthdays, and military victories provided street entertainment for the populace on numerous occasions each year, but in villages, these occasions were usually marked, if at all, with nothing but the ringing of the church bells, and it has to be questioned what changes, if

---

[32] In addition to Cressy, *Bonfires and Bells*, pp. 50–66, 93–155 see Hutton, *Rise and Fall*, pp. 249–60.

[33] For medieval civic festivity and ceremony, see Phythian-Adams, 'Ceremony and the citizen', pp. 106–28.

[34] Woodforde, *Diary*, i, 1 March 1768, p. 71.

[35] Ibid., i, 22 Sept. 1769, pp. 89–90.

any, this brought to the recreational calendar of the inhabitants of small rural communities.

The only significant exception to this was in villages and hamlets situated close to an important county seat. Courtesy of the household of Thomas Pelham-Holles, the Duke of Newcastle and First Lord of the Treasury, the residents of the hamlet of East Hoathly in Sussex enjoyed no fewer than five rejoicings in celebration of a succession of military victories between 1758 and 1760 in the Duke's grounds.[36] But in the absence of such wealthy and politically connected neighbours, villagers enjoyed celebrations to mark national occasions only rarely. Celebrations here were infrequent, and tended to mark occasions of more local significance—the birth of an heir,[37] or an heir's coming of age or marriage.[38] National events were only occasionally celebrated, and oftentimes villages managed nothing at all. On the occasion of the King's recovery from madness in 1789, the parson at Weston Longeville in Norfolk 'heard firing of Guns from many Quarters abt Noon' but added that 'There was nothing at all done at Weston in that way'.[39] In sum, the newly created calendar of political celebrations established a form of entertainment that had a far greater impact in towns than in rural areas. It is predictable that towns were home to entertainments that were more complex, more extensive, and more varied than those to be found in villages and hamlets, that they were centres not only of trade and commerce, but also of recreation. But it should be recognised that the differences between urban and rural areas were not simply those of scale. There were also characteristically urban styles of festivity, and the street entertainments laid on to commemorate political and dynastic events are possibly the finest example of a uniquely urban form of celebration.

There were many other dates punctuating the year that brought festivity and the cessation of work. Some, such as harvest celebrations, were tied to the agricultural year; others, Christmas and Easter for example, were rooted in the Christian calendar; and all, of course, are worthy of further study. But these events were celebrated domestically, in private spaces, within homes, and on private land; and owing to the focus upon space, they get little detailed attention here. Fairs, Shrove Tuesday, Guy Fawkes, and public thanksgivings were celebrated outdoors, in public spaces. They are all considered in greater detail in the chapters that follow, but this brief

---

[36] Turner, *Diary*, 29 June 1758, pp. 155–6; 23 Aug. 1758, p. 161; 23 Oct. 1759, p. 191; 8 Dec. 1759, pp. 194–5; 7 Oct. 1760, p. 212.

[37] Gyll, 'Diary', 24 Feb. 1767, p. 219.

[38] Holland, *Diary*, 13–14 March 1818, p. 293.

[39] Woodforde, *Diary*, iii, 23 April 1789, p. 100.

introduction has already outlined the ways in which the environment in which they were held was critical in shaping their scale and significance. These dates were celebrated universally, in settlements of all sizes, and in all corners of the land, but the use of different spaces gave them unique resonances in each place.

Sports and pastimes

Alongside this ritual year was a range of sports and pastimes played throughout the year, irrespective of the seasons, and, in the second part of this chapter, we consider some of these. Our interest lies once again in those recreations that took place out of doors, on publicly owned land; though, as we shall see, whilst some such activities may be neatly classified as 'urban' or 'rural', others fit into these categories less easily, and it is therefore necessary to clarify further the topographical divisions that structure this work.

Many eighteenth-century sports have survived in some form until the present day, but the ancient sport of bull-baiting forms a venerable exception. It was abolished by Parliament in 1835, amidst extensive, self-congratulatory rhetoric, and it is worth pausing to emphasise the exceptional nature of this occurrence.[40] Local magistrates and civic corporations possessed such broad and undefined powers to regulate and suppress any activity that took place on public land that laws to prohibit specific activities were rarely required, and politicians and monarchs generally took care to avoid the controversy that might be caused by meddling in popular pastimes by resorting to existing laws regulating public nuisances and to informal mechanisms of power where possible.[41] There is something unusual, therefore, about the involvement of Parliament in the suppression of bull-baiting; and the sport and the clamour surrounding it is a subject to which we shall return repeatedly throughout this book.

Let us start, however, with an account of how bull-baiting was enjoyed. Henri Misson, a Frenchman travelling in England, was taken by his hosts to a bear-garden where he witnessed this peculiarly English pastime with a certain amused fascination. A century before the sport was targeted for special criticism, Misson provided a humorous account of the

[40] Nineteenth-century animal protection legislation is summarised in Harrison, 'Animals and the state', pp. 788–9. The law concerning bull-baiting is addressed in Turner, *Heaven in a Rage*, pp. 104–40. See also Malcolmson, *Popular Recreations*, p. 124. See also below, Chapter 9.
[41] For the case of prize-fighting, which occupied a dubious legal status, see Brailsford, *Bareknuckles*, passim, esp. pp. 10–11.

pastime, exceptional for the detail it contains, and it is worth quoting at some length:

> They tie a Rope to the Root of the Horns of the Ox or Bull, and fasten the other End of the Cord to an Iron Ring fix'd to a stake driven into the Ground; so that this Cord, being about 15 Foot long, the Bull is confin'd to a Sphere of about 30 Foot Diameter. Several Butchers, or other Gentlemen, that are desirous to exercise their Dogs, stand round about, each holding his own by the Ears; and when the Sport begins, they let loose one of the Dogs: The Dog runs at the Bull; the Bull, immoveable, looks down upon the Dog with an Eye of Scorn, and only turns a Horn to him to hinder him from coming near: The Dog is not daunted at this, he runs round him, and tries to get beneath his Belly, in order to seize him by the Muzzle, or the Dewlap, or the pendant Glands . . . The Bull then puts himself into a Posture of Defence; he beats the Ground with his Feet, which he joins together as close as possible, and his chief Aim is not to gore the Dog with the Point of his Horn, but to slide one of them under the Dog's Belly, (who creeps close to the Ground to hinder it) and to throw him so high in the Air that he may break his neck in the Fall . . . This Danger would be unavoidable, if the Dog's Friends were not ready beneath him, some with their backs to give him a soft Reception, and others with long Poles, which they offer him slant-ways, to the Intent that, sliding down them, it may break the Force of his Fall . . . But unless he is totally stunn'd with the Fall, he is sure to crawl again towards the Bull . . . Sometimes a second Frisk into the Air disables him for ever from playing his old Tricks: But sometimes too he fastens upon his Enemy, and when once he has seiz'd him with his Eye-teeth, he sticks to him like a Leech, and would sooner die than leave his Hold. Then the Bull bellows, and bounds, and kicks about to shake off the Dog . . . In the End, either the Dog tears out the Piece he has laid Hold on, and falls, or else remains fix'd to him, with an Obstinacy that would never end, if they did not pull him off.[42]

The sport was competitive, but like most pre-industrial pastimes it was not played according to a standard set of rules. Dogs were set on the bull in the way Misson described one by one, and the owner of the bull awarded prizes based upon his judgements concerning which dog had attacked the bull with the most courage and success. Spectators crowded around the event, adding to the entertainment by placing their own informal bets on the outcome.[43]

Bull-baiting was experiencing renewed popularity at the time that Misson visited the bear-garden in the late seventeenth century. Like all pastimes, baiting with animals had attracted criticism from religious reformers in the late sixteenth and seventeenth centuries agitating for a more godly

---

[42] Misson, *Memoirs*, pp. 24–7.
[43] See also Malcolmson, *Popular Recreations*, pp. 45–6, 66–7.

community. Philip Stubbes, the Puritan pamphleteer, for example, had considered it a 'woeful spectacle', and dismissed it along with most sports as a
misuse of time that could be better spent performing God's works.[44] But
civil wars and revolution had discredited attempts to reform popular culture and, although the critics of sports and recreations were never entirely
silenced, few at the time of Misson's travels in the late seventeenth century
were prepared to align themselves with the hard-line views of Puritan
reformers. At the Restoration, popular customs and rustic amusements
were generally thought to be considerably less harmful than the Puritan
zeal which had recently harassed them, and in this more tolerant climate,
the ancient pastimes of bull- and bear-baiting revived and flourished.[45]

Both of these sports date back to the Middle Ages, but whereas bear-
baiting was an entertainment patronised by royalty, nobility, and civic elites,
bull-baiting was at this time pursued for more utilitarian reasons.[46] In the
medieval period, baiting bulls with dogs was believed to improve the quality of the meat, and for this reason most medieval towns enforced local bye-
laws stipulating that bulls should be baited before slaughter. By the
eighteenth century such regulations had fallen almost entirely into disuse
but, as Misson's description makes clear, bull-baiting had an entertainment
value, and so the decline of butchers regulations ordering the baiting of
bulls before slaughter did little to threaten the position of the sport in
English society.

In order to ensure compliance by butchers with the regulations ordering the baiting of bulls, medieval towns constructed and maintained a bull-
ring, usually situated in, or close by, the market place. The small payments
required to maintain a bull-ring declined steadily through the early modern period, and during the eighteenth century they disappeared altogether;
but the bull-rings constructed by an earlier generation remained in place,
and the link between the market square and bull-baiting intact. By the
eighteenth century, the market place had been the customary location for
bull-baiting since the Middle Ages. The sport was certainly not confined to
towns, being well entrenched in London, and making frequent appearances
at country feasts and fairs as well.[47] Nevertheless, centuries of tradition

---

[44] Stubbes, *Anatomie of Abuses*, p. 179.

[45] For the revival of recreations at the Restoration, see Hutton, *Rise and Fall*, pp. 227–60;
Underdown, *Revel, Riot and Rebellion*, esp. pp. 44–105, 239–70.

[46] For bear-baiting, see Chambers, *Elizabethan Stage*, ii, pp. 449–72.

[47] In London a number of enclosed, commercial bear-pits provided entertainment for paying spectators. The largest and most important bear-garden was the Paris Garden at Bank-
side. This doubled as a playhouse, and was unsurprisingly the target of Puritan criticism

had firmly established the market square as the most fitting location for bull-baiting, and stamped the sport as a peculiarly urban pastime.

For most people, bull-baiting was a spectator sport enjoyed on a fairly infrequent basis, but there were many other sports that provided more regular entertainment through the course of the year, sports which large numbers played at some point in their lives, and which were even more widely enjoyed by spectators. Football stands out as the most important of these. It was played in all parts of the land throughout the eighteenth century, and in many different forms: sometimes by large unequal teams traversing wide stretches of common land, sometimes through the streets of towns and cities, and sometimes in a more recognisably modern form, confined to pitches of fixed size—it was a variability typical of early modern sports. No matter how football was played, however, it remained firmly rooted in the lower ranks of society. It was not unknown for social elites to participate in or promote the game, but in general they turned to sports such as hunting, coursing, and cricket for exercise, and the game of football was left largely in the hands of the common people.[48]

The absence of a significant elite following for football has ensured that little detailed evidence for the game has survived, and this makes it difficult, though not impossible, to piece together an account of the ways in which it was played. Our evidence is firmest for the great set matches, games linked to a certain date in the calendar, and played out between neighbouring settlements or parishes. As has been well documented, teams were composed of all the willing men of the two communities in these games, and they were therefore frequently of uneven size. Matches were played without identifiable positions or pitch, and local landmarks—the village cross or well for example, or the church porch—might serve as goals. The game at Seascale in Cumbria involved opposing teams attempting to force the ball into either the sea, or the golf links (common land in the east of the parish).[49] A similar annual match held at Pudsey in Yorkshire required the opposing teams to take the ball to certain points of a brook running through the village.[50]

---

throughout the seventeenth century, yet it was reopened at the Restoration, when it continued to provide entertainment for the diarists Pepys and Evelyn amongst others. See Hotson, 'Bear gardens and bear-baiting', pp. 276–88.

[48] For histories of football, see Marples, *History of Football*, esp. pp. 41–94; Walvin, *People's Game*, esp. pp. 9–30.

[49] Parker, *Gosforth Antiquities*, p. 36. See also Weeks, *Clitheroe*, p. 106.

[50] [Rayner], *History of Pudsey*, p. 197. See Chapter 6 below for further detail on football in the West Riding.

Football games of this kind were most frequently found in rural areas possessing extensive commons, but they were not unknown in towns either. A small number of games, usually held on one of the moveable feasts connected with Easter, were begun in the town centre rather than on the commons on its edge. On these occasions, the ball was kicked off in the market square at a time determined by custom, often midday, and it was pursued through the streets before the teams reached the commons at the edge of town. The game would invariably continue there for several more hours, as each team endeavoured to reach its goal, usually situated some miles distant from the market square.[51]

These annual matches always held a special place in the recreational calendar of the local communities in which they were played, providing entertainment not only for those who played in them, but also for the much larger number of spectators they drew, and booths and stalls were sometimes provided for the entertainment and refreshment of the influx of visitors. Sancton, in the East Riding of Yorkshire, for example, was only a small village, nevertheless 'many thousands from the surrounding towns and villages were wont to assemble' for the annual match.[52] In towns, the excitement surrounding these games was yet greater, as was the disruption they caused. Annual matches of football involved the complete closure of the town, with the shutting of shops and boarding up of windows. These games, in fine, were more than simple football matches: they were annual festival days, a holiday for both those who played them, and for the much larger number of pleasure-seekers who came to watch.

It is on the basis of games such as these that much of our understanding of traditional forms of football is based. It has been widely argued that popular football in the eighteenth century and earlier was invariably unruly and unstructured, and that it was not until the public schools redeveloped the game in the nineteenth century—introducing teams, pitches, and goals of fixed size—that the modern game was born.[53] Yet the traditional form of 'folk football' upon which this account is based was never widespread. Annual set matches played over wide stretches of common land have been recorded in no more than a handful of towns and villages, and these were largely confined to the northern counties of Yorkshire, Durham,

---

[51] For games of this kind, see Chapter 4 below.
[52] Smith (ed.), *Old Yorkshire*, p. 11.
[53] For the most thoroughgoing analysis of this kind, see Dunning and Sheard, *Barbarians*, pp. 2, 29–34, 65. See also Marples, *History of Football*, pp. 95–106; Walvin, *People's Game*, pp. 9–30.

Northumberland, Cumbria, and Lancashire. In the south of England, only in Cornwall (where they went by the name of hurling) and Devon have such games been noted.[54] Equally, the matches played in towns on Shrove Tuesday were far from widespread. There was a cluster of towns in Middlesex and Surrey which celebrated Shrove Tuesday with a football match, but no more than a dozen or so further towns scattered throughout the rest of the country celebrated Shrove Tuesday in this way. Games of football played by teams of unequal numbers of men through city streets, or over large, undefined pitches of common land were not widespread; and, although it is possible that other set matches of various kinds may have escaped attention, it is unlikely that there are sufficient remaining undiscovered to contradict this verdict.

This is not to argue that football was little known prior to its redevelopment in the public schools. The game was undoubtedly one of the most widely played outdoor sports, but it was usually played in a form much closer to the modern game than standard accounts allow. The great set matches played once a year in a handful of towns were festival occasions. They were exceptional, and this no doubt helps to explain why they so often attracted commentators' attention, but the absence of detailed and systematic accounts of other forms of football should not be taken as evidence of an absence of these games. Occasional references to football in a wide variety of sources indicate the existence of a game that was so well known and widespread that it hardly called for further comment.[55] Given the nature of the evidence for these games, it is difficult to establish exactly how they were played. It is certain, however, that they fail to conform to historical stereotypes about pre-industrial football.

---

[54] Paynter, *Old St Ives*, pp. 45–6; Chope, 'Football on Good Friday', pp. 113–14 (loc. hist.).

[55] For references to football, see the following: Berkshire (*Collections for History of Berkshire*, p. 55); Cambridgeshire (Denson, *Peasant's Voice*, p. 17); Northamptonshire (Clare, *Clare: Selected Poems*, p. 65); Buckinghamshire (Cole, *Blecheley Diary*, 3 March 1767, p. 191); Devon (Chapple, *Risdon's Survey of Devon*, p. 38); Essex (Malcolmson, *Popular Recreations*, p. 115); Herefordshire (*Gentleman's Magazine*, Feb. 1819, p. 110); Norfolk (Forby, *Vocabulary of East Anglia*, ii, p. 53); Suffolk (Henslow, *Enquiry into Suffolk*, pp. 24–5); Kent (Dunkin, *History of Dartford*, p. 265); Cumbria (Sedgwick, *Dent, 1868–70*, pp. 91, 192; Hutchinson, *History of Cumberland*, i, p. 224n; Whellan, *History of Cumberland*, p. 364); Lancashire (Weeks, *Clitheroe*, p. 106; Blundell, *Diurnal*, i, 23 April 1711, p. 287); Yorkshire (Cooper, *Helmsley One Hundred Years Ago*, p. 36; Gaskell, *Life of Bronte*, pp. 19–22; Dawson, *History of Skipton*, p. 188; Sharpe, *Diary*, 9 May 1829, p. 203; Walton, *Leeds Intelligencer*, 2 March 1774); Northumberland ('Football in the North', p. 55 (loc. hist.); Dixon, 'Coquetdale customs', p. 144 (loc. hist.)); Lincolnshire (*Lincoln, Rutland and Stamford Mercury*, 2 March 1810; *Stamford Mercury*, 9 January 1846).

Figure 3.   Thomas Webster, *The Football Game* (Bridgeman Art Library, London).

Football as it was played in eighteenth-century England knew no nationally agreed rules. The size of goals, pitches, and teams might all vary, so too might the length of play, but the absence of national regulations should not be confused with an absence of rules of any kind. Decisions about the nature of play were agreed before the start of the game and, where matches were played competitively, these rules were carefully enforced. The East Anglian variant of football—going by the name of 'camping'—has been better documented than most forms of football, and it clearly illustrates the extent to which the game was played by formal rules. Adverts in the local newspapers for forthcoming matches stipulated both the size of the team (usually ten men) and the length of play (usually half an hour), and indicate that an umpire of some description was present to supervise the playing of the game.[56] John Goulstone's researches on the nineteenth-century sporting newspaper, *Bell's Life in London,* support this account of pre-industrial football. He has uncovered numerous references

---

[56] *Ipswich Journal,* 21 Aug. 1741, 8 Sept. 1750, 30 Sept. 1752. Dymond, 'Camping close', pp. 165–92; See also the descriptions of camping in Moor, *Suffolk Words,* p. 63–6; Forby, *Vocabulary of East Anglia,* ii, pp. 50–3.

to football matches in all parts of England in the early nineteenth century, concluding that football was not only widespread at this time but that it was also played by locally determined, formal rules.[57]

The only athletic sport to rival football in popularity was cricket, though, in contrast to the very patchy evidence that we have for eighteenth-century football, the evidence for cricket is both extensive and detailed. The game has received the attention of countless historians, who have identified aristocrats promoting cricket in the late seventeenth century and its steady expansion and growth in popularity subsequently with the middle ranks of society.[58] Eighteenth-century newspapers advertising and reporting matches between gentlemen, and private diaries describing the participation of local gentry in cricket matches, testify to the ongoing involvement of social elites. Yet, while we have abundant evidence of cricket playing in the eighteenth century, when it comes to evaluating the position of cricket in the recreational lives of the poor, we face many of the same problems as those encountered when exploring the history of football. There can be little doubt that the game extended deep into the middle ranks of society, not least since matches of cricket so frequently appear in their diaries—emerging in those of parsons, millers, farmers, craftsmen, and shopkeepers as they, their children, and neighbours either watched or played the game.[59] Below this social level, however, the evidence is both more sparse, and more difficult to interpret.

Accounts of popular participation in cricket are rare, and our sources contain little detail on the constitution of village teams. Even the diary of the Sussex shopkeeper Thomas Turner—a source well known to historians of cricket, for its author was an enthusiastic follower of the game—contains little that clarifies exactly who was playing against whom. It is not clear, for example, who played in the matches Turner recorded between occupational groups, such as those between 'traders and farmers', though it is likely they involved very loose interpretations of these groups including their servants and labourers, simply because his

---

[57] Goulstone, 'Origins of football', pp. 134–43. See also Harvey, 'Football's missing link', pp. 92–116.

[58] Brookes, *English Cricket*, chs 3–5. See also Bowen, *Cricket*; Sandiford, *Cricket and Victorians*; Birley, *History of Cricket*; Underdown, *Start of Play*.

[59] For example, Woodforde, *Diary*, i, 29 April 1760, 14 May 1760, p. 14; Cole, *Blecheley Diary*, 30 Oct. 1766, p. 143; Crosier, 'Diary', Sept. 1786, p. 36; Page, 'Diary', 21 May 1800, p. 93, and 29 July 1800, p. 94; Burgess, *Diary and Letters*, 7 Aug. 1785, p. 6, 29 Aug. 1788, p. 60, 1 Aug. 1785, p. 7, 4 July 1788, p. 59.

small village contained so few traders and farmers.[60] Similarly, owing to
the small size of the village, it is probable that the matches Turner
described between 'the Street against the Nursery quarter' included
labourers from the two districts.[61] The match between 'eleven men of
the name John and eleven of any other name' must have had a very
broad social reach; and, if such teams could be assembled, it suggests that
men of all levels in the parish had a basic familiarity with the form and
rules of cricket.[62] Similarly a match in Panshanger, Hertfordshire,
between Lord Cowper's carpenters and joiners suggests that the labouring poor had all somehow or other managed to learn how to play the
game.[63]

It is likely that alongside the development of cricket as a gentleman's
pastime in the eighteenth century, traditional bat and ball games, going variously by the names of cricket and stoolball, continued to be played in all
parts of the country by the labouring poor. Oliver Heywood, a cleric in
Halifax, complained one Easter 'of young people and others playing at
Stool-ball, and other recreations'.[64] Nicholas Blundell once watched the
'Young Folks' playing a 'Game at Stoole Balle' in spring.[65] In the opinion
of one writer, cricket was the sport of 'the Plowman, the Labourer, and the
Artificer'.[66] 'Everyone plays it, the common people and also men of rank',
insisted a foreign observer.[67] There is even evidence of matches between
women, though, from the tones in which they were reported, these appear
to have had something of a novelty value.[68] We have little detail on the precise nature of these plebeian games, but Underdown is no doubt correct in
concluding that cricket, aristocratic patronage notwithstanding, was 'still a
people's game'.[69]

The timing of these games—Sunday afternoons and summer
evenings—confirms the participation of the labouring poor. It is clear that
football and cricket were fitted around the working week, into the spare
daylight hours when labourers were not at work. In Dent in Cumbria, a

---

[60] Turner, *Diary*, 23 Sept 1756, p. 64. Another diarist complained when his sons played cricket
with servants: see Skinner, *Journal*, 19 July 1822, p. 15.
[61] Turner, *Diary*, 17 May 1756, p. 40; 20 June 1757, p. 102.
[62] Ibid., 18 May 1760, p. 205.
[63] Hertfordshire ALS, Carrington Diary, D/EX3.31, 1804.
[64] Heywood, *Autobiography and Diaries*, ii, 15 Aug. 1681, p. 279.
[65] Blundell, *Diurnal*, ii, 14 May 1715, p. 134.
[66] *Public Advertiser*, 2 Sept. 1757. See also *Gentleman's Magazine*, Sept. 1743, pp. 485–6.
[67] de Saussure, *Letters of de Saussure*, p. 295.
[68] *Sussex Weekly Advertiser*, 17 June 1783; *Brighton Herald*, 21 Sept. 1827.
[69] Underdown, 'Regional cultures', p. 42.

vicar's son remembered how the young men of the parish would assemble at the church after the evening service and finish the day with a match of football.[70] Similar Sunday evening football games were noted in Ousby and Isell, also in Cumbria;[71] in Clitheroe, Lancashire;[72] in Helmsley, Haworth, and Burnsall, in Yorkshire;[73] and in a number of Northumberland villages.[74] In Herefordshire it was recorded that '[the peasantry] meet in large parties upon Sunday afternoons to play at foot-ball, wicket (an old-fashioned cricket), or other gymnasticks'.[75] Joseph Mayett, a Buckinghamshire farm servant, remembered how as a young man he was put to work in a garden 'after I had done my other work whilst other servants had their liberty to go to Cricket playing and other pastimes'.[76] Similarly in the village of Purton, Wiltshire, 'all the unmarried men in the village' would assemble in the evening 'after the toils of the day, to recreate themselves with a few pleasant sports'.[77]

And just as plebeian athletic sports were slotted into whichever free daylight hours were available, so were they fitted into spaces in an informal and impromptu fashion. There were no specially designated spaces for these athletic sports, and no fixed pitches, but fallow fields of the kind required for sports were abundant in the eighteenth century, and the country's heaths, moors, and commons were the customary location of the athletic sports enjoyed by the labouring poor. It was here, for example, that games of cricket were usually played. Local newspapers frequently recorded cricket matches on common land, and eighteenth-century diarists likewise reported numerous matches played on the commons. During the 1750s, Thomas Turner watched cricket in The Broyle, Broad Oak, Cliffe Hill, and Hawkhurst Common—these were all expanses of common lying within a 10–mile radius of his home in East Hoathly.[78] John Burgess, another Sussex diarist, watched cricket at Ditchling and Linfield Common.[79] These games

[70] Sedgwick, *Dent, 1868–70*, p. 91. See also p. 192.

[71] Hutchinson, *History of Cumberland*, i, p. 224n; Whellan, *History of Cumberland*, p. 364.

[72] Weeks, *Clitheroe*, p. 106.

[73] Cooper, *Helmsley One Hundred Years Ago*, p. 36; Gaskell, *Life of Bronte*, pp. 19–22; Dawson, *History of Skipton*, p. 188.

[74] 'Football in the North', p. 55 (loc. hist.); Dixon, 'Coquetdale customs', p. 144 (loc. hist.)

[75] Dunkin, *History of Dartford*, p. 265; *Gentleman's Magazine*, Feb. 1819, p. 110; Forby, *Vocabulary of East Anglia*, ii, p. 53.

[76] Mayett, *Autobiography, 1783–1839*, p. 7.

[77] Hone, *Every-day Book*, ii, col. 1207. See also Denson, *Peasant's Voice*, p. 17.

[78] Turner, *Diary*, 14 July 1755, p. 10; 17 June 1756, p. 45; 19 Aug. 1756, pp. 62–3; 17 May 1757, p. 98; 23 Sept. 1756, p. 56. See also Underdown, *Start of Play*, pp. 35–45.

[79] Burgess, *Diary and Letters*, 7 July 1785, p. 8; 1 Aug. 1785, p. 7; 29 Aug. 1788, p. 60.

were spectator events, drawing large crowds from a wide area, but it is clear that more informal games of cricket were also played by local residents on their commons. Such games have very rarely left any trace on the historical record, but Turner recorded occasional informal games of this kind on 'our common', and a note in his diary reveals local boys playing cricket on the common one spring: 'this day was played at the common belonging to this parish a match of cricket between 11 boys of this parish and 11 boys of Laughton Parish'.[80] No doubt children and others resorted to the common to play informal games of cricket whenever the opportunity presented.

Our evidence concerning the use of common land for recreation relates in most instances to games of cricket, but this should be interpreted as a reflection of the heavy involvement of social elites in the game, rather than taken to indicate the unimportance of other sports. There can indeed be little question that common land formed the location of many other, less widely reported, spectator sports. Games of football, for example, were traditionally played here. Whether it was the great set matches played annually over wide stretches of common land between settlements, or the more informal matches played on Sunday and summer evenings, the commons provided accessible open space for the game, and were regularly used for this purpose.[81] In East Anglia, camping was likewise played on the open commons. An antiquary from the Suffolk village of Rumburgh recalled that camping was the 'favourite amusement of the labouring youth of Suffolk' in the 1770s, and he cited Rumburgh Common as the place where the young people of the village played, 'two or three times a week . . . during the summer evenings'.[82]

A host of less familiar sports were also played on the commons, though since they rarely reached the attention of literate commentators our evidence for all of these is yet more scattered still. Around Lancashire, for example, the commons were the location of the popular game of prison bars—a regional running game played by men in teams. In the late seventeenth century, the Lancashire apprentice Roger Lowe travelled to Latchford Heath, where he found 'a great compeny of persons, with two drums amongst them. The young men were playing att *prison bars*, where

---

[80] Turner, *Diary*, 13 May 1762, p. 248. For further matches of cricket on common land, see Turner, *Diary*, 30 May 1758, p. 150; *Lewes Journal*, 30 July 1784; Page, 'Diary', 25 Sept 1800, p. 96, and 15 Oct. 1800, p. 96.
[81] See, for example, Parker, *Gosforth District*, p. 36; Whellan, *History of Cumberland*, pp. 235, 364.
[82] Quoted in Dymond, 'Camping close', p. 183.

I stayd awhile to see them.'[83] In the eighteenth century, servants living at a farm in Upton went to watch games of prison bars at the Meols or on the Leasowe, two different sites of meadowland a couple of miles north of the village.[84] A farmer in the village of Little Crosby, also in Lancashire, reported footraces on Crosby Marsh.[85] In the county of Durham, John Hobson watched footraces and jumping matches on 'Barnsly moor' and 'Brotherton march'.[86]

Commons were put to an extremely wide range of recreational uses, but it is important to emphasise that the use of common land for recreation was not a purely rural phenomenon. We tend to associate common land with the rural environment, but as many eighteenth-century towns were also surrounded by commons, this association is only partly correct. Neither of the two most widely played athletic sports—football and cricket—was strictly confined to the countryside. In Hornsea, for instance, football was 'much practised' on the town's commons by men from Hornsea and 'from all the country round'.[87] In the Lancashire town of Bury, it was remembered that cold weather had only added to the footballers' enjoyment: 'when it happened that the waste lands were overflowed and frozen, the satisfaction of the combatants was considerably increased'.[88] At the small Northamptonshire town of Oundle, football was played on 'the Twenty Acres'—an expanse of common belonging to the town.[89] The only requirement for football was a tract of open land. Eighteenth-century villages invariably possessed commons that served as football pitches but, owing to the small size and rural setting of many eighteenth-century towns, so did many larger settlements, thereby ensuring that football was popular as an urban sport as well.

For the same reason, cricket was not confined to villages and hamlets. The common land on the edge of towns provided land well fitted for the game, and was widely used for this purpose. In the course of the eighteenth century, many towns formed a local cricket club and, although

---

[83] Lowe, *Diary*, 18 July 1663, p. 25.

[84] [Wharton], 'Rural life and manners', pp. 140–1 (diar.).

[85] Blundell, *Diurnal*, i, 14 Jan. 1703, p. 27.

[86] Hobson, 'Journal', 14 Sept. 1730, p. 299; 26 Sept. 1730, p. 300; 28 April 1731, p. 304. See also Bee, 'Diary', 4 Nov. 1684, p. 49.

[87] Bedell, *Hornsea*, ii, p. 88.

[88] Barton, *History of Bury*, p. 41. See also Kay, *Diary*, 2 Feb. 1742, p. 47.

[89] Northamptonshire RO, Clifton's Day Books, ZA/8732–46, 30 Oct. 1771, 13 Nov. 1771, 28 Nov. 1771.

some played on specially laid out, private pitches, others resorted to the town's commons for matches. The cricketers in the Essex town of Maldon, for example, played on 'the marsh'.[90] The newly formed cricket club in Castle Cary played on the town's Port Meadow.[91] In Dorking in Surrey, the Cotmandene or Heath 'was the spot in Dorking where the old contests took place'.[92] This writer recalled 'devotees of the game from distant places, and hundreds of all classes of persons from the town and miles around' flocking to the heath to witness matches.

Such examples of urban communities using their commons for spectator sports may be multiplied many times over. At Chester, a gentleman chanced upon a footrace between a man and a boy one summer's day on the Roodee—the meadows situated to the west of the city.[93] Just outside Sheffield the unenclosed moor at Eccleshill was famous for knur and spell matches and occasional prize-fights in the early nineteenth century.[94] In Newcastle, the Town Moor was used for the spectator sports popular in the region—knur and spell, bowling, quoits, and fives.[95] In the eighteenth century, games were not fixed down in space. Each community exploited the land it had to hand as and when the opportunity presented. Commons of very different size and aspect provided space for cricket, football, and a wide range of other spectator sports, and the ubiquity of common land ensured strong continuities between the popular pastimes enjoyed in both large and small settlements.

The distinction between urban and rural areas is further confused by the tradition of travelling large distances in pursuit of entertainment. Villagers were accustomed to travelling up to 10 miles in order to enjoy the more complex entertainments to be found in cities and large towns. Consequently, even where clear contrasts between urban and rural communities did exist, the significance of this to their eighteenth-century inhabitants must not be exaggerated. More than any other occasion in the recreational calendar, fairs provided servants and farmhands with a day or more's holi-

---

[90] Crosier, 'Diary', Sept. 1786, p. 36.

[91] Woodforde, *Diary*, i, 29 April 1760, p. 14; 14 May 1760, p. 14.

[92] Rose, *Recollections of Dorking*, p. 80. See also *Cambridge Chronicle*, 8 July 1825 (Saffron Walden), 31 July 1835 (Cambridge).

[93] Prescott, *Diary*, i, 21 July 1717, p. 159.

[94] Cudworth, *Round about Bradford*, p. 346. Knur and spell is described in Chapter 6 below.

[95] Adams, *Memoirs*, ii, p. 470. See also Metcalfe, 'Organised sport', pp. 469–95, 'Potshare bowling', pp. 29–44. In coastal communities, the sands took the place of commons. The sands at Scarborough were the location of footraces, *Rockingham and Hull Weekly Advertiser*, 18 Nov. 1815.

day for travelling and recreation.[96] William Cole's servant travelled 10 miles to Buckingham fair in 1766, along with 'almost all the young People of the Parish';[97] and John Woodforde's servants regularly travelled the 8 miles from Weston Longville to Norwich in order to visit the great St Faith's Fair held in October.[98] In the early nineteenth century, the parson of a Somerset village recorded seeing 'many of my neighbours in best attire moving off' on Bridgwater Fair Day; again, this was a distance of about 8 miles.[99] Indeed, urban populations were usually insufficiently large to sustain their numerous, large fairs and this influx of visitors from surrounding rural areas was fundamental to their survival.

Fairs provided the most important annual holidays for rural labourers, but there were other occasional events to which they sometimes travelled. Grand civic celebrations, for example, were certain to draw large crowds of pleasure-seekers from the surrounding rural population. John Burgess, a Sussex craftsman, travelled nearly 10 miles from his village of Ditchling to enjoy the civic celebrations organised in Brighton on the occasion of the Duke of York's twenty-first birthday in August 1789:

> Went to Brighthelmstone to See many devertions on account of the Rial Family that is the Duke of Yorks Birth day Cricketing Stool Ball Foot Ball Dancing &c fire works &c 2 large Beast Rosted upon the Hill a large Quantity of Bread and Strong Beer Given With the Beef Some said there was 20000 people.[100]

And, if his estimate of the number of people present is accurate, so did many others from the neighbouring villages travel to town on this occasion. In Norfolk, the parson John Woodforde likewise regularly travelled to Norwich to enjoy the 'Hurly Burly' of the elections, Guild Day (the mayor's swearing-in), and celebrations to mark the King's birthday.[101]

There was also considerable travel over similar distances in order to enjoy the sporting events that might be found at neighbouring settlements. Fighting sports—wrestling, prize-fighting, cudgelling, and single stick—

---

[96] Cf. Voth's contention that there was a marked reduction in the number of holidays over the eighteenth century, as labourers worked longer hours to compensate for deteriorating real wages. See Voth, *Time and Work*.
[97] Cole, *Blecheley Diary*, 22 May 1766, p. 51.
[98] Woodforde, *Diary*, i, 17 Oct. 1781, p. 326; ii, 17 Oct. 1783, pp. 99–100; iii, 18 Oct. 1789, pp. 221–2; 17 Oct. 1792, p. 378.
[99] Holland, *Diary*, 6 March 1800, p. 27.
[100] Burgess, *Diary and Letters*, 9 Aug. 1789, p. 76.
[101] Woodforde, *Diary*, ii, 5 April 1784, p. 126 (elections), 20 June 1786, p. 250; iv, 16 June 1795, p. 205 (Guild Day); iii, 4 June 1789, pp. 195–6; iv, 4 June 1795, p. 205 (King's Birthday).

were all likely to draw large crowds from a wide distance, as were football
and cricket matches, horse-races, and puppet shows and plays. Events such
as these were infrequent and irregular, yet they completed the mosaic that
made up the recreational calendar of the labouring poor. William Cole's
servants travelled to watch a cricket match, a 'montabank', wrestling, and a
'great Cudgel-playing' in surrounding rural areas, in the course of a little
over one year;[102] and Woodforde's servants travelled to cudgelling matches,
a 'Puppett' show, and a 'Poney-Race'.[103] In Lancashire, a doctor 'Took a
Walk to Bury with great Numbers beside to see a Foot-Ball Match betwixt
Town and Country'.[104] Servants and labourers at a farm in Cheshire were
given leave to visit matches of prison bars, horse-races, a 'Mountebag', a
bull-baiting, and numerous cockfights, in addition to the annual fair at
Upton.[105] A parson's servant travelled 8 miles to Bridgwater races in 1816,
returning, according to his employer, 'very full of the Single Stick Play
which he admired very much';[106] and a Sussex farmer's sons travelled a similar distance to watch the races and prize-fighting at Lewes.[107] And so on.
Eighteenth-century diaries are filled with examples of servants and labourers travelling distances of up to 10 miles in order to enjoy recreations away
from home.

   It must be accepted, therefore, that the division of England into urban,
industrial, and rural areas that structures the chapters that follow is only
partly convincing. A number of athletic and spectator sports cannot be
neatly designated 'urban' or ' rural', since they were usually played on common land, and commons existed in settlements of every kind and size.
Moreover, the tradition of travelling undermined the importance of any
topographical distinctions that did exist. From the perspective of participants, as they crossed over these divides and enjoyed a range of entertainments both within and beyond their own locality, urban and rural
differences were arguably of no more than marginal significance.

   Yet there nevertheless remain good grounds for maintaining the topographical distinctions that are used here. If it must be admitted that there
are instances where these divisions are unhelpful, it should also be clear that
there are others where they are of especial value. Provincial towns, for

[102] Cole, *Blecheley Diary*, 30 Oct. 1766, p. 143; 26 Jan 1767, p. 179; 8 June 1767, p. 222; 9 Oct. 1767, p. 275.
[103] Woodforde, *Diary*, i, 22 June 1771, p. 110, 18 March 1777, p. 199; iii, 31 May 1792, p. 355.
[104] Kay, *Diary*, 20 Feb. 1742, p. 47.
[105] [Wharton], 'Rural life and manners', pp. 136–7, 140–3 (diar.).
[106] Holland, *Diary*, 30 July 1816, p. 276.
[107] Marchant, *Diary*, 6 May 1718, p. 183; 7 Feb. 1722, p. 191.

example, contained spaces for sports and pastimes that can justly be considered unique. As we have seen, their public streets and squares provided a
distinct location for sports and pastimes, and it is therefore appropriate to
consider these spaces in isolation. There were no squares or fine public
streets in villages and hamlets, yet these settlements also possessed distinctive spaces of their own. The village green had centuries-old links with
games and pastimes, and formed a social and cultural space that deserves
investigation in its own right. In industrial areas, recreations were enjoyed
on many of the same spaces as were found elsewhere—streets, squares,
commons, greens. As we shall see, however, industrial districts also contained rapidly growing populations, often under weak local governmental
control. These factors ensured that the control that was exercised over
these spaces was considerably weaker than that exerted in more stable
communities, and so created a new recreational environment out of
familiar components.

It is inevitable that all historical and social categories have exceptions,
but this should not discourage us from investigating the use of new categories and concepts. The purpose of this work is not to insist that a solu-
tion to all historical problems has been discovered. Space is a concept that
sometimes helps us to understand historical differences, sometimes helps us
to explain the course of historical development. Like all concepts, it has
its limitations, but it nevertheless offers new opportunities for taking the
discipline of cultural history forward.

3
Provincial towns: streets and squares, 1660–1750

In the 1860s, a historian of the small market town of Alnwick in Northumberland reflected on how different the town's market place had been when he was young. In those days, George Tate recalled, it had been the place where 'school-boy-plays' were enjoyed—and a 'cheerful merry scene' it was too. From noon until two, and again in the evening during summer, children and youths had congregated in the market place and 'heartily engaged in various amusements': games with marbles, handball, tops, skipping rope, hunt the hare, and local games, such as 'watch-webs' and 'soulum', were all played by the children 'in their respective seasons'. But how different, Tate continued, was the market place of modern times: 'the ancient privileges of children are now sadly abridged; they have been driven from the Market . . . In a quiet town, the Market Place is little used excepting on fair and market-days; our modern local improvement acts have silenced the joyful ring of youthful voices, which sounded so pleasing to a former generation.'[1] In Alnwick, things just weren't like they used to be.

The cultural critic Raymond Williams has drawn attention to the tendency of each generation of rural commentators to lament the recent passing of the old way of life, and this extract from George Tate's history of Alnwick suggests that such sentiments might not be confined to rural England: as Williams observed, nostalgia is both universal and persistent.[2] But Tate had also identified something that was little noted by contemporaries and which has largely escaped scholarly attention as well; the modern market place, reserved for traffic and commerce, had to be created, and it is not itself without a history. The recorders and describers of popular custom frequently dwelled upon the loss of playing grounds, the disappearance of old sports and traditions, the decline of occasions for friendly social interaction between rich and poor; and Williams' advice that 'senti-

---

[1] Tate, *History of Alnwick*, i, pp. 437–38.
[2] Williams, *Country and the City*, esp. pp. 9–12.

mental and intellectualised accounts of an unlocalised "Old England"' be approached with the 'sharpest scepticism' remains pertinent to any research concerned with social customs and local traditions.[3] Yet little regret was expressed over the transformation of the market square from an occasional site for recreation into a place with none but a commercial function. So much for nostalgic recollections of the days when recreation had been commonplace in town centres; the elimination of play from the market place was scarcely noticed at all, and, in this context, what seems more significant than Tate's nostalgia, is both the perception and the originality of his observation.

The change, however, was both more profound, and more protracted, than Tate suggested. In early modern England, town streets, and in particular the market place, had been an important location for popular recreation, and not only for the children's games, the 'school-boy-plays', that Tate remembered. Nor was street recreation a simple and unwelcome consequence of the municipal authorities' inability to prevent such occurrences, for the mechanisms to prohibit sports were certainly in place in early modern towns.[4] It was rather that streets, and above all the market square, were regarded as legitimate places in which recreation might be organised. The belief that popular recreation should be tucked away in little-used fields, or confined to specially designated playing grounds, has its origin in more recent times. In early modern towns, sports, celebrations, and street entertainments were routine and integral elements of urban life and, though recreation periodically attracted controversy, these were not controversies that could be resolved simply by changing the location of the pastimes concerned.

The recreational uses to which early modern streets were put have not gone entirely unnoticed in the century and a half following Tate's history of Alnwick. Pope-burning ceremonies,[5] the Lord Mayor's show in London,[6] election ceremonies,[7] and the civic ritual of eighteenth-century corporations[8] have all received some historical attention. Such events have generally been considered together under the rubric of 'street theatre': in

---

[3] Williams, *Country and the City*, p. 10.

[4] Everitt, 'Market towns', pp. 168–204, esp. 184–6.

[5] Miller, *Popery and Politics*, pp. 182–8; Harris, *London Crowds*, esp. pp. 103–13 passim, pp. 123–4.

[6] Burke, 'Popular culture in seventeenth-century London', pp. 44–6; Berlin, 'Civic ceremony in early modern London', pp. 15–27; Manley, *Literature and Culture*, pp. 212–93.

[7] O'Gorman, 'Campaign rituals and ceremonies', pp. 79–115.

[8] Borsay, 'All the town's a stage', pp. 228–58; Sweet, *Writing of Urban Histories*, pp. 256–65.

this tradition, civic ritual and ceremony are regarded as a vehicle for the expression of political and ideological messages, and a minor industry has developed which aims not only to unravel the meaning of this theatre, but also to assess how much of it was actually understood by the participants in the streets.[9] However, taking a longer chronological perspective, it is arguably the location, rather than the meaning, of these events that is most remarkable, and this—the 'street' aspect of street theatre—has received scant historical attention. Furthermore, those recreational uses of the streets which did not involve ritual or ceremony, the kind of informal play that Tate noted, and which was such a constant, yet unremarkable, feature of early modern towns, has not been considered at all. It is arguably necessary, therefore, to attempt to enlarge our discussion of civic recreations, so as to include an appreciation not simply of the politics of civic rituals, but also of the place. And it is surely also time to move beyond analysis of carefully orchestrated civic ceremony, and begin to consider the history of the informal and unofficial plebeian events that existed alongside.

This is not to suggest that the focus in the existing historiography on the symbolic meaning of sports and celebrations is misplaced, nor that the project to uncover their meaning is already complete. The point rather is that an exclusive focus on the social meaning of urban recreations in recent years has resulted in a near total neglect of a long since forgotten dimension of the early modern urban experience: the use of streets and squares for recreation as well as commerce. For all that our understanding of the timing, the politics, and the cultural meaning of civic recreations has become increasingly sophisticated, the significance of the market square in the life of early modern town dwellers has not been adequately grasped, nor have the changes in its cultural role been charted. These, then, are the themes that provide the primary focus of this chapter. We shall explore two distinct forms of street recreation in the century following the Restoration; beginning with the almost forgotten tradition of bull-baiting in the early modern market place, and moving on to consider the civic celebrations and street bonfires, made familiar through frequent descriptions by eighteenth-century urban elites and modern historians alike.

[9] In addition to the references cited in notes 5–8, see also Montano, 'Quest for consensus', pp. 31–51; Klein, 'Between the bums and the bellies of the multitude', pp. 18–26; Reay, *Popular Cultures*, pp. 143–51. See, however, the following two essays on political demonstrations and the use of public space: Harrison, 'Symbolism, "ritualism" and location', pp. 194–213; Poole, 'Popular sovereignty and public space', pp. 40–54.

FOOT BALL, Played at the Market Place, Barnet.

Figure 4.   *Football, Played at the Market Place, Barnet* (Barnet Museum, Barnet).

Butchers, bull-rings, and baitings

Many decades before the ancient British sport of bull-baiting was finally and decisively confined to history by act of parliament in 1835, its standing as a sport had been called into question and its claim to that title roundly dismissed: bull-baiting was senseless, pointless, worthless, 'sport' rather than sport.[10] But it had been considered in a very different light in the seventeenth century and before. Then not only was its status as a sport unquestioned, it was thought also to have important culinary benefits. Setting dogs on the bull immediately prior to slaughter was believed to improve the quality of the meat, in the same way as the flesh of hunted game was, and is still, supposed by some to be superior to that of animals killed swiftly. Bull-baiting, therefore, was encouraged not simply as sport, it was also promoted as a regulation for butchers. Thomas Moffett, in his *Health's Improvement,* 1655, explained as follows:

---

[10] This change of attitudes is considered in Chapter 5 below.

> Bull Beife, unless it be very young, is utterly unwholesome and hard of digestion, yea almost invincible. Of how hard and binding a nature Bull's blood is, may appear by the place where they are killed: for it glaseth the ground and maketh it of a stony hardness. To prevent which mischief . . . Bulls . . . [are] baited to death by dogs as we use them: to the intent that violent heat and motion might attenuate their blood, resolve their hardness, and make their flesh softer in digestion.[11]

And it was for this reason that regulations stipulating the baiting of bulls before slaughter had been established. Such regulations date back to at least the twelfth century, though how widespread the practice was at that time remains a matter of conjecture. During the early seventeenth century and Civil War, bull-baiting was often discouraged owing to its tendency to encourage crowds and disorder, and, though not specifically outlawed by the Protectorate, horse-races, cockfightings, bear-baitings, and stage plays all were, 'forasmuch as Treason and Rebellion, is usually hatched and contrived against the State upon such occasions, and much Evil and Wickedness committed'.[12] Bull-baiting was certainly attacked in many towns for similar reasons.

But, as a number of histories of popular festivity have suggested, the Restoration promised a return not simply to the old political order but also to ancient social and cultural traditions, and presented loyal civic leaders with the opportunity to restore customs that had become controversial during the first half of the century.[13] A few towns accordingly gave the sport of bull-baiting fresh encouragement after 1660. They ordered their flesh tasters—market searchers employed primarily to expose unwholesome meat and present butchers for combining and regrating—to search the markets for the sale of unbaited beef, and to present the offending butchers to the court with leet jurisdiction, where a small fine, somewhere generally between about two and five shillings, would be imposed. At the same time, these authorities assumed financial responsibility for maintaining the town's bull-ring. This involved occasional payments for repairing the iron ring, or for reinforcing the ring's foundations, and more frequent payments on the easily worn rope and bull collar used to attach the bull to the ring. These orders, fines, and expenses provided various opportunities

---

[11] Moffett, *Health's Improvement*, p. 61. See also Houghton, 'He is often baited almost to death; for that great exercise makes his flesh more tender', in his *Collection for Improvement of Husbandry*, pp. 286–91.

[12] *Writings and Speeches of Oliver Cromwell*, iii, pp. 484–5.

[13] See, in particular, Underdown, *Revel, Riot and Rebellion*, pp. 271–91, esp. 271–2, 280–1. See also Hutton, *Rise and Fall*, pp. 227–62, esp. 239, 246–53.

for bull-baiting to leave its mark in official records, making it possible to track the enforcement of the regulations over time.

In practice it is often difficult to establish how town authorities responded to the more permissive climate of the 1660s since, in addition to the usual hazards undermining the survival of long runs of documents, the quality of manorial record keeping deteriorated markedly following the Restoration. It is nevertheless clear that some municipal authorities did attempt to revive the custom at the Restoration by reintroducing orders directing the flesh tasters to search the markets for unbaited bulls meat.

Their efforts, however, appear to have met with rather indifferent success, for although civic leaders might embrace a return to the old ways with alacrity and enthusiasm, they encountered some difficulty re-establishing a custom which had often not been practised for several decades. In Sudbury in Suffolk, for example, the town authorities' commitment to the custom was unambiguously reaffirmed in 1665, when the new mayor ordered that the oaths of the local officials be reissued. The investigators of the flesh market were to swear to present 'all such p'sons as shall kill, or offer to sell any Bull's fflesh within this towne which hath not before been well and sufficiently bayted accordynge to the Auncient Orders, decrees, and customs of this Kingdom of England'.[14] In the two years following 1665, about half a dozen butchers found themselves presented and fined for selling 'Bulls Beefe unbaited'; but the last such presentment was made only two years later, in July 1667.[15] In Newbury in Berkshire, the newly restored custom was similarly short lived; there five butchers were presented at the court leet in 1662 for selling unbaited bulls, and the order stipulating that bulls should not be killed without baiting was reissued.[16] This order was repeated on numerous occasions at subsequent meetings of the court, but no more butchers were presented, and in 1683 the orders disappear from court records.[17] Likewise in Liverpool in 1672 two butchers were presented and fined in the Portmoot court for the 'killing of a bull unbaited',[18] but no further presentments were made, and a reissue of the bull-baiting regulations in the early eighteenth century followed 'Complaints being made that Bulls are kill'd before Baiting'.[19]

[14] Suffolk RO (Bury St Edmunds), Town Clerk's Book of Sudbury, EE501/6/170.

[15] Suffolk RO (Bury St Edmunds), Sudbury Book of Orders and Decrees, 1658–1681, EE501/2/8, 80, 95, 101, 113, 117.

[16] Berkshire RO, Newbury Court Leet Book, 1640–1723, N/AM1/1, 9 Oct. 1662, p. 95.

[17] Ibid., pp. 112, 148, 159, 179, 195, 203.

[18] Liverpool RO, Town Book, 1671–1803, 352/Min/Coul, Bk. 4, 37.

[19] Liverpool RO, Town Book, 1702–1731, 352/Min/Coul, Bk. 6, 347.

By the end of the 1670s few authorities were continuing to collect fines for unbaited beef. In Essex, the authorities in Saffron Walden collected their final fines for the sale of unbaited bulls flesh in 1673;[20] and the custom appears similarly to have fallen into disuse in Nottingham in the late seventeenth century, when the Common Council ordered that the rails about the bull-ring be taken down and used elsewhere.[21] In the north-east of England, Hedon, Bridlington, and South Shields were enforcing the regulation in the 1660s, but had all ceased to do so by the 1670s.[22] Only a handful of towns continued to enforce the regulation into the eighteenth century. At Atherstone in Warwickshire, the order concerning bull-baiting was repeated down to 1705;[23] and in Maldon (Essex), Manchester, Alnwick, and Darlington, fines for the sale of unbaited bulls flesh were regularly collected during the first quarter of the eighteenth century.[24] Ipswich and a small number of northern towns—Hull, Thirsk, and Kendal—continued to collect fines for the sale of unbaited bulls flesh until the 1750s.[25] But Skipton appears to have outdone them all, collecting its final fine for unbaited beef a decade later in 1765—a legacy no doubt of the exceptionally careful and efficient manorial government continued in Skipton throughout the eighteenth century.[26]

As these towns successively ceased to enforce the baiting of bulls before slaughter they went the way of the majority of English towns, which had

---

[20] Saffron Walden Town Council, Accounts of the Guild of Holy Trinity, ref. 314. Order in 1660; fines in several years up to 1674.

[21] *Records of Nottingham*, iv, p. 373. The bull-ring is not mentioned in subsequent accounts, though since these consist largely of vouchers rather than audited accounts it may well be that the voucher has been lost; an earlier archivist found one dated 1720, but this is no longer with the records. Ibid., vi, p. 83 and Nottinghamshire Archives, CA 1800E–G, 1801A–E, 1803E.

[22] East Riding of Yorkshire AO, Hedon Quarter Sessions Minute Book and Court Leet, 1657–1745, DDHE/5/1, Presentments 15 July 1659, 21 Jan. 1660, 3 Oct. 1662, 3 Jan. 1665, 4 Oct. 1667, 5 Oct. 1669. Purvis, *Bridlington*, pp. 247, 252, 254, 259; Hodgson, *Borough of South Shields*, p. 156.

[23] Warwickshire CRO, Miscellaneous papers concerning Atherstone, 1595–1804, MIR/9. Orders in 1686 and 1705.

[24] Essex RO, Malden Court Leet Presentments, D/B3/3/161; *Court Leet Records of Manchester*, v, p. 11; Tate, *History of Alnwick*, i, p. 432; Longstaffe, *History of Darlington*, p. 295.

[25] Suffolk RO (Ipswich), Chamberlains' Accounts, 1672–1785, C9/11/89–207. Hull CA, Chamberlains' Accounts, 1661–1800, BRF/2/517–698. Fines for the slaughter of unbaited bulls collected most years down to 1750. North Yorkshire CRO, Thirsk Manor Court Book, 1739–94, MIC 163. Presentments and orders at courts on 5 Oct. 1739, 10 Oct. 1740, 2 Oct. 1741, 5 Oct. 1744, 9 Oct. 1747, 11 Oct. 1754. Curwen, *Kirkbie Kendall*, p. 35.

[26] Yorkshire Arch. Soc., Leeds, Skipton Manor Jurors' Verdicts, 1700–1766. Fines in several years down to 1764.

long previously abandoned their attempts to force butchers to bait their bulls and made no effort to revive bull-baiting when the Restoration provided the opportunity. When the butchers' orders were reissued in 1690 in Kings Lynn, for example, no clause on the custom was included.[27] Similarly, the butchers' orders for Winchester,[28] Northampton,[29] Great Yarmouth,[30] and Warwick,[31] contained no clauses about baiting. As early as 1562, the clause referring to baiting was crossed out in the butchers regulations for Leicester.[32] At the time of the Restoration, the baiting of bulls in order to improve the quality of the meat had been neglected in most towns for many decades. The interest that some showed in restoring the custom in the 1660s appears to have been more symbolic than committed. It was primarily a statement of loyalty to the traditional customs of the past, and occasional attempts to re-establish the custom had almost all failed before the eighteenth century.

The decline of compulsory baiting of bulls for slaughter did not, however, mark the end of the custom in English towns, for it had long been appreciated that bull-baiting had an entertainment value in addition to its supposed ability to improve the quality of meat. In sixteenth-century Nottingham, the borough court had ordered the mayor to announce all forthcoming bull- or bear-baitings, so that all 'his bredren' might 'see the sport of the game after the old custom and usage'.[33] The borough of Nottingham had ended its payments to visiting bearwards by the seventeenth century; however, in a small number of towns the authorities continued to sponsor an annual festivity involving animal baiting down to the eighteenth century.[34] In Liverpool, for example, the mayor's swearing-in day was accompanied by a magnificent bear-baiting,[35] and in Beverley the new

---

[27] Kings Lynn BA, Hall Book, 1684–1731, KL/C7/12, 101.

[28] Hampshire RO, Winchester Index to Ordinance Books, W/B1/18.

[29] *Records of Northampton*, ii, pp. 280–4.

[30] Norfolk RO, Great Yarmouth Liber Ordinum, Y/C18/3.

[31] *Black Book of Warwick*, pp. 19–26.

[32] *Records of Leicester*, iii, p. 101.

[33] *Records of Nottingham*, iii, p. 449.

[34] Payments most years down to 1616. See ibid., iv, p. 353. In Winchester, the corporation passed responsibility for providing a baiting bull for celebrations from itself to local butchers in the sixteenth century. See *Transcripts from Archives of Winchester*, pp. 75–7. The city of Oxford, which had made similar payments to a bearward for much of the sixteenth century, had also ceased supporting the custom by this time. See *Selections from Records of Oxford*, pp. 285, 304, 312, 315, 324, 330, 337, 376, 383, 398, 411, 417.

[35] The custom is described in Troughton, *History of Liverpool*, pp. 93–4; and *Kaleidoscope,* 10 July 1820. The payments are recorded in the corporation's account books; Liverpool RO, Cash Books, 1730–1784, 352/Tre/1/4/1–7. Payment every year until 1764.

mayor's arrival was celebrated with bull-baitings.[36] In Chester, it was customary for the mayor to provide a bull-baiting at his departure;[37] and the
Staffordshire town of Lichfield likewise sponsored a baiting during the
annual 'Green Bower Feast'—a civic ceremony traditionally held at
Whitsun.[38]

These towns' historians have generally discussed their obsolete civic
customs with some degree of shame, holding them up as first-rate examples of the barbarity of an earlier age; but, if we attempt to move behind
the familiar shroud that two centuries of criticism have laid around these
customs, then it soon becomes apparent that they teach us more about the
past than the cultural sophistication (or otherwise) of eighteenth-century
society. In addition to the somewhat questionable evidence that bull-
baiting provides for the level of civilisation that the eighteenth century had
reached, these civic rituals suggest a different attitude towards the use of the
streets for recreations, and it is this, their location, rather than their barbarity, that is of interest here. Occasional descriptions of the baiting rituals
reveal that they were held out of doors, and indicate the possible transformation of the market square into a stage for recreation. In Liverpool, for
example, following the election of the new mayor, the bear was brought
into the New Market, and first baited at the 'white cross'; it was then 'led
in triumph to the Exchange'; to Derby Street; and finally to the Stocks
Market, being baited again at each of these places.[39] There was nothing
exceptional about the parading of the bear through the town, or of the use
of the market place as a stage for the ritual. The bull-baitings at other may-
oral ceremonies were likewise held in very central locations; at Chester, for
example, the bull-baiting took place at the High Cross;[40] and at Preston, it
was held in the market place.[41]

There is generally less evidence of civic pageantry involving bull- or
bear-baitings in the south of England, though a handful of small towns supported more informal bull-baiting customs. In Wokingham, for example,
the parish overseers annually bought two bulls to present to the populace
for baiting on St Thomas's day;[42] and in Chelmsford, Essex, the town's

---

[36] Oliver, *History of Beverley*, p. 421.
[37] Morris, *Chester in Plantagenet and Tudor Reigns*, p. 383.
[38] Shaw, *History of Staffordshire*, i, pp. 317–26.
[39] Troughton, *History of Liverpool*, pp. 93–4.
[40] Ormerod, *History of Chester*, i, p. 302.
[41] Hewitson, *History of Preston*, pp. 300–1.
[42] The custom is described in Readwin, *Account of Wokingham*, pp. 73–6. It is also noted in
the following official records: Berkshire RO, Wokingham Minutes of Common Council,

accounts books reveal the parish overseers regularly provided two bulls for a 'Bulls Baiting & Bull Feast' in the early eighteenth century.[43] Both were charitable events, serving as an occasion to distribute meat to the poor, and the location of these bull-baitings was the centre of the town. Following the annual bull-baiting at Wokingham, one correspondent to the local newspaper described the 'triumphal introduction' of the bulls to the stake; he reported the bulls 'being driven in the true bull-baiting stile to the most conspicuous parts of the town'.[44] In another year, it was noted the bull-baiting took place 'in the centre of the Market place'.[45]

But bull-baitings, paid for and organised by civic leaders, were rare in the eighteenth century. In the view of the civic elite, animal baitings tended to be undignified events. They encouraged local men, women, and children to crowd the streets with their fighting dogs and, no matter how magnificent the bull or bear the corporation had procured, the participation of so many working men unfailingly conferred a plebeian touch to the proceedings. Most corporate towns chose to celebrate their new mayor's inauguration in a far more dignified fashion: church services, bell-ringing, stately processions, and splendid feasts formed the core of their inaugural ceremonies, events at which the local population were welcomed, if at all, as mere spectators. As Peter Borsay has observed, civic ceremonies were supposed to inspire the awe and respect of the governed; and since bull-baitings failed to do this it is not surprising to find they were rarely included in official pageantry.[46]

Yet though the funding of bull-baiting by the civic elite was unusual, the maintenance of a bull-ring at which the populace organised their own entertainment was not. The financial accounts of many towns reveal the chamberlains renovating their bull-ring at the Restoration. In some instances this was accompanied by the reissue of regulations ordering the baiting of bulls by butchers before slaughter, but in most towns such regulations were not revived, and the bull-ring existed simply for the purpose of entertainment. As with many customs, the old sport was given new life

---

1749–1833, Wo/AC1/1/2, 8 Nov. 1786. See also the Overseers' Accounts, 1766–73, D/P154/12/3. Payments towards a bull in 1767, 1772, and 1773. Two deaths at the annual bull-baiting were recorded in the town in 1794 and 1808. See the Parish Register, 1761–1812, D/P154/1/2.

[43] Essex RO, Chelmsford Poor and Rate Book, 1713–1739, D/P94/12/5. Payments in 1713, 1716, 1720, 1723, 1724, 1728.

[44] *Reading Mercury*, 22 Dec. 1787.

[45] Ibid., 27 Nov. 1786. See also ibid., 25 Dec. 1786.

[46] Borsay, 'All the town's a stage', pp. 239–43.

by the return of Charles II, and once again it is possible to establish how long after the Restoration civic authorities continued to support the custom by tracing the payments for the bull-ring recorded in their annual accounts.

In some towns this patronage was short lived; the Cambridge treasurers, for example, made their final contribution towards the city bull-ring in 1661, paying 9s 6d 'for setting down ye Bull ring on the pease hill';[47] and Louth (Lincolnshire), Plymouth, Totnes, and Weymouth all made their final payments before 1680.[48] In contrast, however, to the short-lived attempts to collect fines for the slaughter of unbaited bulls, it was not unusual for town authorities to defray the costs of maintaining the bull-ring for several decades following the Restoration. The small town of Lymington, Hampshire, disbursed sums on bull rope and on repairs to the bull collar several times after 1660, making its final payment in 1699.[49] In Doncaster, Bristol, and Worcester the final payment towards the bull-ring appears similarly to have been made in the 1690s;[50] while Boston (Lincolnshire),[51] Kings Lynn,[52] Wolverhampton,[53] Southampton,[54] Salisbury,[55] and Great Yarmouth[56] all continued to maintain a bull-ring until the eighteenth century. The corporation at Winchester, though no longer providing a bull for baiting, was still maintaining its bull-ring in the eighteenth

---

[47] Downing College, Cambridge, Cambridge Treasurers' Accounts, 1662–1741, Bowtell Bequest/E3. Payment in 1661.

[48] Lincolnshire Archives, Louth Wardens' Account Book, 1551–1686, LGS/B/3/1. Payments in 1660, 1661, and 1672; Bracket, *History of Plymouth*, p. 112; Stainthorpe, 'Bull ring at Totnes', p. 107 (loc. hist); *Descriptive Catalogue of Documents of Weymouth and Melcombe Regis*, p. 45.

[49] Hampshire RO, Lymington Town Book, 1613–1729, 27M74/DBC2. Payments in 1675, 1682, 1687, 1699.

[50] Doncaster AD, Chamberlains' Accounts, 1661–1707, AB/6/1/2/22–47; Latimer, *Annals of Bristol*, iii, pp. 485–6; Noake, *Worcester in Olden Times*, p. 109.

[51] Lincolnshire Archives, Boston Chamberlain and Treasurer Accounts, 1695–1787, 4/B/4–80. Payment in 1700.

[52] Kings Lynn BA, Chamberlains' Accounts, 1669–1708, KL/C39/105, payments in 1674, 1679; KL/C39/107, payments in 1680, 1682; KL/C39/108, payment in 1703.

[53] Wolverhampton ALS, Wolverhampton Town Constables' Accounts, 1688–1737 and 1746–50, DX/79/1. Payment in 1705.

[54] Southampton AS, Chamberlains' Accounts, 1660–1723, SC/3/23–41. Accounts survive for less than a third of this period. Payments in 1704 and 1707.

[55] Wiltshire and Swindon RO, Salisbury Chamberlain and Treasurer Account Rolls, 1683–1712, G23/1/47. Payments in 1705 and 1710.

[56] Norfolk RO, Great Yarmouth Audit Books, 1707–1757, Y/C27/4–8. Payments in 1708–9, 1711, 1715–17, 1726.

century; it made its final payment in 1741.[57] In Bury St Edmunds, the chamberlains continued occasionally to defray the costs of bull-baiting until 1739,[58] and in Worksop the last payment for the bull-ring was made in 1753.[59] Those towns which reintroduced baiting regulations for butchers tended to maintain the bull-ring several decades beyond the collection of the final fines for unbaited meat. Saffron Walden paid for bull rope until 1712;[60] Maldon hired someone for 'keeping the bull-rope' until 1754;[61] and in 1750 an Alnwick labourer was paid 10d for going to the neighbouring town of Alnmouth 'for a rope to bait a Bull'.[62] In addition there was the handful of towns—Ipswich, Skipton, Hull, Thirsk, and Kendal—that were continuing to collect fines for unbaited bulls until the 1750s. Each of these towns was also maintaining a bull-ring. Bull-rings, it is clear, were unexceptional for much of the century following the Restoration, and so, we may surmise, was bull-baiting an ongoing practice in eighteenth-century towns.

Although establishing the existence of municipal bull-rings is time consuming, it is considerably more straightforward than investigating their use. Answering simple questions, such as who used them? and when did they use them? is difficult since accounts of the uses to which they were put—in literature, in the press, in private diaries—are extremely rare. There are certainly accounts of bull-baiting in other places and at other times, but the bull-baitings organised by private initiative at the civic bull-ring were rarely reported, and this makes it difficult to produce a reliable reconstruction of such occasions.[63]

It is possible, however, to comment on the location of these events. Civic bull-rings were invariably constructed in very central locations and, although the exact form of the entertainment enjoyed at them is not easily recovered, the significance of the space in which they were enjoyed is

[57] Hampshire RO, Winchester City Accounts, 1726–1822, W/E1/148–202. Payments in 1738 and 1741.
[58] Suffolk RO (Bury St Edmunds), Bury St Edmunds Book of Accounts, 1695–1778, D6/5/2. Payments in 1719, 1724, 1739.
[59] Nottinghamshire Archives, Worksop Constables' Accounts, 1720–1811, PR 22,770. Payments in 1724 and 1753.
[60] Saffron Walden Town Council, Accounts of Guild of Holy Trinity. Last payment in 1712.
[61] Essex RO, Chelmsford, Maldon Chamberlains' Accounts, 1660–1690, D/B3/3/86–107; 1737–1760, D/B3/3P524–39. Payments every year down to 1754.
[62] Tate, History of Alnwick, i, p. 432.
[63] For bull-baiting in other contexts, see Malcolmson, Popular Recreations, pp. 45–6, 66–8; Reid, 'Beasts and brutes', pp. 12–17. Bull-baiting and bear-baiting in industrial areas are explored further in Chapter 6 below.

not beyond investigation. In Cambridge, for example, the bull-rings were located at Peas Hill, a narrow street leading from the market square; and Bridge Street, a major road leading out of the town.[64] Nor was there anything unusual about the location of the bull-rings in Cambridge. Similar central locations for bull-rings have been noted in other large towns— Bristol, Canterbury, Preston, and Totnes, for example, all housed a bull-ring in their market squares[65]—as well as in a much larger number of small provincial towns.[66]

Figure 5.   Thomas Barritt, *Bear Beating with Wheelbarrow*, 1749 (Chetham's Library, Manchester, Manchester Scrapbook).

[64] Downing College Library, Cambridge, John Bowtell, 'Unpublished History of Cambridge', Bowtell Bequest/63, vii, p. 2756.
[65] Latimer, *Annals of Bristol*, iii, p. 486; Hasted, *History of Kent*, xii, p. 647; Hewitson, *History of Preston*, p. 118; Stainthorpe, 'Bull ring at Totnes', p. 106 (loc. hist.).
[66] For bull-rings in provincial England, see Turner, 'Petworth', p. 137 (loc. hist.); Le Blanc Smith, 'Snitterton bull ring', p. 146 (loc. hist.). For Yorkshire, see Barker, *History of Wensleydale*, p. 163; Balderston and Balderston, *Ingleton, Bygone and Present*, p. 20; Bedell, *An Account of Hornsea, in Holderness*, p. 88; Cowling, *History of Easingwold*, p. 73; Fairfax-Blakeborough, *Life in a Yorkshire Village*, p. 15; Fisher, *History of Masham*, p. 58; Hartley and Ingilby, *Yorkshire Village*, p. 100; Jones, *History of Harewood*, p. 168.

These bull-rings not only testify to the existence of bull-baiting, they also tell us something about the use of public space in the early modern town. The location of the rings suggests that the civic centre was not privileged for traffic and trading, but was a space shared by traders and residents for business and pleasure alike. The market place was a large open space situated in the centre of town. It was well fitted for bull-baiting, providing sufficient space for both the tethered bull and dogs, and for the crowds that the event would invariably attract, and the recreational value of this land was clearly not lost on contemporaries. In addition to being a place in which the market was held, the evidence from the bull-rings suggests that the early modern market square might be used for plebeian recreation—it was a sometime playground for those with nowhere else to play. The early modern town was consequently considerably more noisy and disordered than its modern counterpart, and its centre the site not only of markets and trade but of a chaotic and boisterous spectator sport as well.

It is also likely that plebeian town dwellers exercised a degree of control over the streets they lived and worked in, since the evidence suggests that it was they, not civic elites, who determined the timing and frequency of the entertainment held at the bull-rings. The absence of commentary on the use of bull-rings has already been noted, yet bull-baitings held in the centre of town can hardly have been beyond the notice of eighteenth-century town dwellers, and the failure of urban elites to comment on this aspect of urban life would therefore imply that they had little to do with the bull-rings they maintained. Their silence suggests that bull-baiting in the eighteenth-century town was overwhelming plebeian in its appeal, and points to the existence of a level of street entertainment in eighteenth-century towns beneath the concern of genteel commentators. The bull-rings indicate that the recreational uses of the streets went beyond the civic ceremonies which were funded and controlled by the urban elite, and carefully and frequently described by both eighteenth-century town dwellers and modern historians. They reveal that town streets in early modern England were also the site of a long-forgotten informal and entirely plebeian recreation.

These comments are confirmed by the account of an annual bull-running custom held in the small market town of Oundle, contained in the diary of a local resident, John Clifton. Bull-running consisted in letting a bull loose to run through the streets, and the information that Clifton's diary contains concerning the annual bull-running sheds valuable light on the use of the streets in a small eighteenth-century town for recreation.

John Clifton, a carpenter (initially a journeyman and later a master) living in Oundle, kept a daily journal for the two decades between 1763 and 1784, many of which have survived and are now stored in the record office at Northampton.[67] Initially, his day books were a business diary, almost entirely devoted to recording the work he was engaged in, but gradually, during the 1770s and 1780s, the day books were used to record an ever increasing number of social events. Even in the early years, however, the routine work books were enlivened by what seems in Clifton's eyes, to have been the event of the year—the bull-running. Indeed, during the 1760s, this event was the only social occasion to be noted from one year to the next. Clifton's diary forms a unique record of the Oundle bull-running, and it is worth noting that it is only owing to the chance survival of his day books that we know anything of this plebeian festival at all.

From Clifton's diaries, we learn that it was customary in Oundle to turn an angry bull out in the streets one afternoon between Christmas day and early January. The event entirely lacked the structure of the very stylised bull-running held each November at nearby Stamford; indeed every aspect of the sport was liable to be altered according to each year's circumstance. The date varied from year to year; it was usually in the first week of January, but could be as early as 26 December,[68] and was one year delayed until 29 January.[69] Though most years there was just one bull-running, in some years the sport was repeated a second time—though the results might be disappointing; in 1781, for example, 'the Bull that was runn last week, was runn again to Day in the Market Street, & a Heifer also but they made very little sport'.[70] More rarely, Clifton did not record any bull-running over the Christmas period, which, given his palpable interest in the sport, probably implies no bull-running was arranged.[71]

In principle, either one or two bulls were turned out to be run, but in practice, each year's sport was made from the animals at hand: one year two bulls provided spectators with an impromptu 'battle with them';[72] another time the sport was made with two heifers;[73] and another with a 'Bull & a

---

[67] Northamptonshire RO, Clifton's Day Books, 1763–1784, ZA/8732–46.

[68] Ibid., 26 Dec. 1768, 26 Dec. 1776.

[69] Ibid., 29 Jan. 1770.

[70] Northamptonshire RO, Clifton's Day Books, 1763–1784, ZA/8732–46, 1 Jan. 1781, 31 Dec. 1763, 9 Jan. 1764, 28 Dec. 1767, 2 Jan. 1768.

[71] No bull-runnings were recorded in 1772–3. On 3 March 1781, Clifton noted that he was 'once more up town, which is the first time since ye Bullrunning [1 Jan.]'.

[72] Ibid., 31 Dec. 1770.

[73] Ibid., 7 Jan. 1782.

Sag'.[74] In February 1784 two hogs were run in the streets, and one broke Clifton's shop window 'in such a manner as I never [saw] one broke before'.[75] Flexibility was the essence of the bull-running; it was held on any date that was locally convenient, and with any animals available. It was sport fitted around working life, as and when the opportunity presented.

An angry bull-running through town streets obviously presented some risks; when a 'Sulky Bull' was run one year, a man 'narrowly escaped being much hurt by him'.[76] But the bull-running involved a degree of violence and danger that was in no way exceptional in the eighteenth century, and it seems to have been precisely the danger that provided the sport's main attraction, as the following remarks by Clifton on a good and a bad year's sport make clear:

> A Steer runn'd, at Elton to Day & it was the best and wildest & made the most pushes of any that has been runn'd for a great many Years past.[77]

> To Day we had two Bulls runn'd in the market street, & they might as well have runn'd me, for the poor beasts were no more mad than I am, & I can hardly walk five yards.[78]

Excitement, danger, and unpredictability seem to have been the essential qualities of the occasion; a quiet, tame animal offered no sport. An element of local pride may also have helped to add interest to the proceedings: 'A Bullrunning to Day at Elton & it was a remarkably good one again—it had no horns. Elton has brought the honour of Oundle quite into the Dust for Bullrunning. Ahh poor Oundle.'[79]

In old age, when Clifton was too ill to attend the bull-running, he continued to remark the absence of workmen on the day of the bull-running, and sometimes recorded their thoughts about the entertainment. It clearly remained, as ever, the high point in Clifton's social calendar, a moment of excitement and adventure that enlivened daily life. How far his enthusiasm was shared by his neighbours is a matter of conjecture, but we can be certain that there was little escaping the bull-running, whatever one's opinion of it. For one or two afternoons of the year, the whole town was given over to the people's sport.

---

[74] Northamptonshire RO, Clifton's Day Books, 1763–1784, ZA/8732–46, 26 Dec. 1776.
[75] Ibid., 5 Feb. 1784.
[76] Ibid., 1 Jan. 1776.
[77] Ibid., 18 Jan. 1776.
[78] Ibid., 31 Dec. 1778.
[79] Ibid., 30 Dec. 1778.

Similar bull-running customs have been recorded in a number of towns close to Oundle during the late eighteenth century, and it is likely the inspiration for many of these came from nearby Stamford, where a particularly elaborate bull-running ritual, reportedly dating from the twelfth century, was held every year on 13 November.[80] In Bridge Casterton, for example, it was customary for the new rector to provide a calf to be run for by women on his arrival,[81] and in Wisbech, Cambridgeshire, bull-running was a Shrove Tuesday tradition.[82] Clifton referred to a bull-running at the neighbouring village of Elton. An annual bull-running was also held at Scrivelsby in Lincolnshire;[83] and in Peterborough a bull-running was organised to celebrate Lord Nelson's victory in 1799.[84] There is little evidence, however, to indicate that the practice of bull-running extended far beyond this region.

There are clearly a number of differences between these bull-runnings and the more widespread practice of bull-baiting. Bull-running was not fixed in space in the way that bull-baiting was: the chasing of a bull or heifer through the streets involved considerably more disruption in the town than the baiting of a bull fixed to a bull-ring in the market square, and this no doubt helps to explain why bull-running was an occasional pastime, an annual festival, whilst bull-baiting was enjoyed on a more regular basis throughout the year. Both sports, however, illustrate the phenomenon that forms the central focus of this chapter: the use of public streets and squares for popular recreation in eighteenth-century towns. The streets formed the course for the bull and his pursuers, and the market square provided the location for the bull, dogs, and crowds of men and women that formed a bull-bait. It matters little how frequent these pastimes were. They are of historical significance not for their frequency but rather for what they reveal of the potential uses of city streets. Bull-baitings and bull-runnings indicate the possible uses to which these spaces might be put, and make clear how wide the limits of their use were, even if these limits were reached only occasionally. Moreover, the transformation of public spaces that accompanied these pastimes was not entirely within the control of civic elites. The use of public spaces by civic elites for the pomp and splen-

---

[80] A good account of the Stamford bull-running may be found in Malcolmson, *Popular Recreations*, pp. 47, 126–35. See also Walsh, 'Bull-running in Stamford', pp. 233–47.
[81] *Northampton Mercury,* 10 Dec. 1785.
[82] Gardiner, *History of Wisbech*, p. 25.
[83] de la Pryme, *Diary*, 12 Aug. 1696, p. 109.
[84] *Lincoln, Rutland and Stamford Mercury*, 18 Jan. 1799.

dour of their rituals has been widely appreciated. The history of bull-rings, however, indicates that those much lower in society also regarded the streets as a place that they might use for recreation. The streets and the market square of every town existed primarily for commercial purposes, yet they might occasionally be appropriated by all for recreational activities as well.

We have seen, then, both the widespread practice of maintaining a bull-ring at the Restoration and the end of these payments in the century following, and it is time to consider the possible significance of this research. The temptation is to construct a story about the enthusiasm of civic elites for bull-baiting at the Restoration, and their gradual withdrawal from the ancient tradition in the century following, though this, I believe, ought to be resisted. The civic accounts reveal simply that urban officials maintained the amenity, not that they ever used it, and the failure of local elites to describe the use of their bull-rings at any time throughout the period points against their participation in bull-baiting. It is arguably more constructive to use this evidence to probe the cultural history of the market place in the early modern town. There is no evidence that bull-baiting appealed to all sections of society, yet the official payments for the municipal bull-ring suggest that the propriety of recreation in the market square had a broad social purchase. It is possibly here, then, that the real significance of the evidence presented in this chapter lies; the contributions to the bull-ring are of interest not for the light they shed on the sporting preferences of civic elites, but rather for the evidence they provide for an official sanction of popular recreation in the town centre. They suggest that it was uncontroversial that the centre of town should double as a playground when the markets were quiet or closed.

It is surely in this context that the decline of payments for the civic bull-ring in the century following the Restoration should be located. We are accustomed to linking the decline of bull-baiting with the emergence of new concerns about animal suffering, and it is not inconceivable that the withdrawal of funds reflects the emergence of hostility to the violence inherent in the sport of bull-baiting.[85] It is an argument we shall consider further in due course; for the present, however, let us pursue further these ideas about the location of bull-baiting. Given that the bull-rings were located in the market place, the end of payments might reflect not hostility towards bull-baiting, but hostility to the use of the public streets for this traditional

---

[85] See, for example, Thomas, *Man and Natural World*, p. 159; Turner, *Reckoning*, pp. 15–37; Kean, *Animal Rights*, pp. 31–2. However, see also Malcolmson, *Popular Recreations*, pp. 118–26.

pastime, a questioning of the propriety of popular recreation in the town centre, the beginning of a cultural redefinition of the legitimate uses of the market place. The evidence presented so far is insufficient to decide between these two alternatives, so let us turn away from the plebeian pastime of bull-baiting and consider how other recreational uses, broadly defined, of markets squares and streets fared in the century following the Restoration.

Bonfires and ale

By the eighteenth century, bull-baitings and bull-runnings resided largely in plebeian hands, but alongside these almost forgotten plebeian affairs lay a much more familiar cycle of public celebrations and civic rituals controlled and orchestrated by local elites. These civic celebrations have formed the focus of a number of studies, and it is not my intention to revisit this ground.[86] Instead, my purpose in what remains of this chapter is to analyse one element of public celebration: the lighting of bonfires in the public streets and market square. Of course, these bear no more than a passing resemblance to the bull-baiting that we have just considered. In contrast to the informal and overwhelmingly plebeian tradition of bull-baiting in the market place, the bonfires customarily lit there were usually orchestrated by civic elites, and for this reason it might be objected that the differences between bull-baitings and bonfires are more compelling than any similarities. Furthermore, these bonfires invariably formed one component of large and complex celebrations, and it is in some degree artificial to consider civic bonfires in isolation from the bell-ringing, sermons, and dinners that accompanied them. As an account of civic celebrations, it must be admitted that what follows is partial and incomplete. The focus of my enquiry, however, lies not in eighteenth-century civic ritual and ceremony, but rather in the recreational uses, broadly defined, of public streets in early modern England. In contrast to the bell-ringing, sermons, and dinners, bonfires always took place out of doors and on public land, and they always attracted large crowds of merry-makers from all walks of life. Bonfires were the most simple, most frequent, and most widely enjoyed form of street entertainment in early modern towns, and for this reason they merit further consideration here.

---

[86] An excellent general history of civic celebration may be found in Cressy, *Bonfires and Bells*, pp. 50–189. See also Hutton, *Rise and Fall*, pp. 227–62.

Although civic celebrations for events of local or national significance—royal birthdays, military victories, political anniversaries, and so
forth—were familiar in all parts of the country, the routine provision of
bonfires and ale appears to have been most heavily concentrated in the
south-east of England. In Kent, for instance, several boroughs paid for bonfires to entertain the populace at festive occasions. In Dover, the chamberlains funded between five and eight bonfires every year until the 1730s.[87]
In Maidstone and Queenborough, there were fewer bonfires, though in
both towns beer was occasionally provided 'for the populace', the two corporations similarly making their final payments in the 1730s.[88] Sandwich
also regularly paid for bonfires in the seventeenth century[89] and, in
Gravesend, the corporation continued to provide them during the first half
of the eighteenth century.[90] Faversham was the only borough in Kent with
the appropriate surviving records which made no contribution towards
public bonfires. Similarly many of the boroughs in Berkshire paid for
bonfires: they were particularly frequent in Abingdon, where the chamberlains paid for up to eight bonfires every year until 1788, and gave details of
each one in a section of their accounts entitled 'Ringing & Bonfires'.[91] In
Maidenhead, between one and two bonfires were provided each year at
various dates, and barrels of beer were occasionally given away.[92] In
Reading, bonfires organised for the populace appear to have been rarer, but
the barrels of beer distributed with them no doubt ensured their success.[93]

Few counties contained so many small towns regularly lighting bonfires
at the corporation's expense as Kent and Berkshire. Instead, the public funding of popular celebrations tended to be the preserve of cities, regional capitals, and county towns, as small towns generally lacked the resources to make
ongoing contributions to popular entertainments. Many of the small and
decaying boroughs of Wiltshire and Suffolk, for instance, spent little or no

[87] Centre for Kentish Studies, Dover Chamberlains' Accounts, 1660–1783, Do/FCa/6–7.
[88] Centre for Kentish Studies, Maidstone Chamberlains' Accounts, 1693–1750,
Md/FCa/1694–1750, payments for beer in 1704 and 1736. Queenborough Chamberlains'
Account, 1611–1785, Qb/FAg/1–3, payments for beer in 1701, 1713, 1731, 1762.
[89] Centre for Kentish Studies, Sandwich Treasurers' Accounts, 1664–1779, Sa/FAt/40–1.
[90] Centre for Kentish Studies, Gravesend Chamberlains' Accounts, 1653–1784, Gr/FAc/2–3.
[91] Berkshire RO, Abingdon Chamberlains' Accounts, 1702–1787, A/FAc/5–10.
[92] Berkshire RO, Maidenhead Bridgewarden Accounts, 1662–1738, M/FBa/2. Payments in
1690, 1692, 1701, 1712, 1718, 1727.
[93] Berkshire RO, Reading Chamberlains' Accounts, 1690–1771, R/FA3/52–94. Payments in
1690, 1694, 1695, 1707, 1708, 1712, 1726.

money on entertainments;[94] though the corporations at Bath, Salisbury, Ipswich, and Bury St Edmunds all funded bonfires in the early eighteenth century.[95] In Staffordshire, Stafford and Wolverhampton both regularly provided bonfires in the first half of the eighteenth century, but Walsall managed just one bonfire in the century following 1660.[96] In the north of England, the provision of festive bonfires by civic authorities appears to have been less consistent—in Yorkshire, for example, there is no evidence that any of the corporate towns regularly defrayed the cost of street celebrations[97]—but there was nevertheless a scattering of small and large towns funding public rejoicings across the north.[98]

It should not be concluded that bonfires in the streets did not exist outside the incorporated towns that routinely used civic funds for this purpose. The practice of street celebrations certainly extended beyond large towns as local notables, often involved in local government but acting in an unofficial capacity, took responsibility for the organisation and funding of such events in smaller towns without the public funds to provide for entertainments of this kind. For example, at Castle Cary in Somerset, celebrations for the coronation of George III were 'All at Mr Creed's, Mr Hindley and Mr Potts and Mr Duck's expense'.[99] The provincial newspapers affirm that the provision of firewood and beer by the local elite in small towns, though more irregular than the officially funded entertainments common in cities and large towns, was not unusual.

---

[94] Wiltshire and Swindon RO, Wilton Burgess and Chamber Accounts, 1640–1811, G25/1/92–3; Calne General Book and Accounts, 1561–1814, G18/1/1; Marlborough General Account Books, 1572–1771, G22/1/205/2–3. Suffolk RO (Ipswich), Orford Chamberlains' Accounts, 1714–1767, EE5/5/1.

[95] Bath and North East Somerset RO, Bath Chamberlains' Accounts, 1657–1724, 650/1/2. Wiltshire and Swindon RO, Salisbury Chamberlain and Treasurer Accounts, 1683–1814, G23/1/47–50. For Ipswich, see footnote 25. For Bury St Edmunds, see footnote 58.

[96] Staffordshire RO, Stafford Chamberlains' Accounts, 1699–1704, 1729–1744 D(W)O/8/2; Wolverhampton ALS, Wolverhampton Town Constables' Accounts, 1688–1750, DX/79/1; Walsall AS, Walsall Mayors' Accounts, 1633–1714, 277/13/56–102.

[97] No payments for bonfires in Beverley (East Riding of Yorkshire AO, Beverley Account Rolls, 1660–1728, BC/II/6/70–126; Account Book, 1735–91, BC/IV/1/2); Doncaster (references in footnote 50); Hull (references in footnote 25); Richmond, Ripon, and Scarborough (North Yorkshire CRO, Richmond Chamberlain Accounts, 1663–1692, 1776–1832, MIC 3386; Ripon Mayors' Accounts, 1656–1819, MIC 2140; Scarborough Chamberlains' Accounts, 1660–1683, MIC 1345; 1729–1826, MIC 2415, 2423); Sheffield (Sheffield Archives, Sheffield Burgery Accounts, 1566–1811, TT13–14).

[98] *Constables' Accounts of Manchester*, iii, pp. 1–120, passim; Furness, *History of Penrith*, pp. 182–3; Dawson, *History of Skipton*, p. 377.

[99] Woodforde, *Diary*, i, 22 Sept., 1769, pp. 89–90.

There is a clear difference between these donations of wood and ale and the bull-rings we considered in the first part of this chapter. Though bull-baiting might fairly be described as a plebeian pastime, the distribution of bonfires and ale cannot. These bonfires were lit in places and at times that were decided by local elites, and although enjoyed by all they were ultimately in the control of civic elites. These celebrations were political occasions, their moment and scale determined by the public statements of loyalty that local officials wished to make; they belong, as their recent historians have shown, to the political as much as the social history of towns.[100] But the emphasis on the politics implicit in public celebrations in much recent historical enquiry has obscured an equally significant facet of these events: the occasional transformation of streets and squares into a site of recreation. In all towns, north and south, large and small, the location of festive bonfires was the same: the streets and above all the market place formed the stage for the celebrations, the theatre for the audience. For example, at the celebrations in Worcester for the coronation of George II, 'All the Streets were illuminated with . . . Bonfires'; and at Northampton there was 'particularly a vast large [bonfire] on the Market-hill'.[101] At Alnwick, tar barrels were fired at the market place in celebration of the King's birthday in 1733; and following the election of Sir Edward Stanley at Preston in 1736, 'Bonfires blaz'd in every Street'.[102] During celebrations in York in 1745 to commemorate George II's birthday, 'four Bonfires were made in the principle Streets of the City'; and at Bristol, during celebrations following the failure of the Excise Bill, there were 'large Bonefires lighted throughout the City and Suburbs . . . in Broad Street . . . and at Queen's Square'.[103] Such examples may be multiplied many times over. Bonfires were a common feature of eighteenth-century civic celebrations, and their location was always the public street.

The strong beer and ale, sometimes recorded in civic accounts but more often donated by local notables than by corporate authorities, were also traditionally distributed at the market cross. In Louth, the town accounts noted that ale was distributed at the Market Hill;[104] at Durham, wine and 'Plenty of Strong Beer' were distributed to the 'Populace at the Fountain in the

---

[100] See, in particular, Cressy, *Bonfires and Bells*, pp. 50–66, 93–189; Hutton, *Rise and Fall*, pp.246–60. For interpretations of popular participation in celebrations, see Wilson, *Sense of the People*, pp.117–36. esp. 125–7; Rogers, *Crowds, Culture, and Politics*, passim.

[101] *Newcastle Courant*, 4 Nov. 1727; *Northampton Mercury*, 16 Oct. 1727.

[102] *Newcastle Courant*, 17 Nov. 1733, 1 May 1736.

[103] *York Courant*, 5 Nov. 1745; *Northampton Mercury*, 23 April 1733.

[104] Lincolnshire Archives, Louth Wardens' Account Book, 1735–1777, LGS/B/3/2.

Market place' in celebration of the King's birthday in 1727.[105] In Manchester, on the occasion to mark George III's coronation in 1761, 'three Stages were erected, one in St Ann's Square, one at the Cross, and one at Withy Grove, from which a Number of Barrels of Beer and Wine were distributed amongst the Populace'.[106] On the more infrequent occasions that meat was roasted and distributed amongst the poor, this too took place in the market square: in Bath, for instance, 'an Ox was roasted whole in the Market Place' for George II's coronation; and at Alton, Hampshire, 'an Ox was roasted whole in the middle of the Town' one Guy Fawkes night.[107]

Above all, the streets were filled with people on these occasions, as descriptions of public celebrations by diarists occasionally indicate. On 'Guild Day', the annual day of the mayor's swearing-in at Norwich, the parson John Woodforde noted: 'I walked thro' St Giles's Street . . . the Street was full of People . . . The Market Place was also full of People and quite down to St Andrew's Hall.'[108] And during celebrations for the taking of the 'Carribee Islands' from the Dutch the same diarist noted, 'The market place was full of People this evening and very noisy.'[109] In Manchester, during festivities for the success of Wellington's army in France in 1814, a diarist, Absalom Watkin, noted that 'the crowd was great and the press extreme' in the Market Street.[110] These patriotic celebrations engulfed the town, bonfires and people filling every square and street: the market place and market cross provided the central focus of the entertainment, but the celebrations spilled beyond into the surrounding streets, leaving no part of the town untouched by the public rejoicing. And this was no accident; this was how it was supposed to be. These celebrations, as their historians have demonstrated, were political in intent and, in order to make a convincing public statement of loyalty, thanksgivings and celebrations needed to embrace the wider population. The use of public space was integral to this. Bonfires lit in strategic corners of the town; food and drink distributed from its symbolic heart—the market cross; and crowds of people filling the streets gave these occasions a physical presence and underscored the messages of communal solidarity they were intended to convey. Clearly the location of civic

[105] *Northampton Mercury*, 6 Nov. 1727.
[106] *Manchester Mercury,* 2 Nov. 1791.
[107] *Newcastle Courant*, 21 Oct. 1727, 17 Nov. 1733. See also *Northampton Mercury*, 28 Sept. 1761.
[108] Woodforde, *Diary*, i, 20 June 1780, pp. 286–7.
[109] Ibid., i, 15 March 1781, p. 304.
[110] Watkin, *Diaries of Watkin*, 18 April 1814, p. 12.

celebrations—this use of streets and squares—is no less significant than their timing and politics.

Celebrations in cities and large market towns during the eighteenth century were eclectic affairs, embracing a wide variety of forms in addition to the bonfires and ale that I have emphasised here, and it should not be believed that street bonfires formed a growing, or particularly significant, element of civic ceremony in the eighteenth century. It is not my intention to provide a comprehensive account of civic ceremony, but rather to explore the history of the use of public streets for popular entertainments, and in this light the role of civic officials in providing wood for bonfires lit in the streets is clearly significant. The bonfires and ale tell of a society which agreed it was fitting that celebrations should take place in the public streets, in spite of the obvious inconveniences consequent upon lighting bonfires in generally narrow thoroughfares, and distributing free ale to crowds assembled in the public streets. In early modern England, the squares and streets were intended primarily for traffic and trading, but this was not their only function. The streets provided a valuable open, public space that might be given over to the poor at certain times for recreational purposes. Furthermore, the civic elite not only consented to the occasional eclipse of business and commerce by popular festivity for most of the century following the Restoration, they actively encouraged it.

But, as we have seen, the eighteenth century witnessed a steady decline in the funds that larger and richer towns were making available for public bonfires. By the middle of the eighteenth century the majority of towns had ceased making financial contributions to either bull-rings or bonfires, and in the following two decades almost all towns made their final payments. It is a development much easier to describe than explain. The corporate accounts that have been used here testify to a steady decrease in the willingness of civic officials to fund bull-rings and bonfires, but rarely indicate why the decision to withdraw funding had been made. In the 1780s the authorities of both Beverley and Wokingham announced that bull-baiting was henceforth prohibited on town land, but neither gave any account of their orders.[111] In Abingdon, it was simply noted, perhaps sulkily, in the 'Ringing and Bonfires' section of the accounts that bonfires were 'not allowed'.[112] In Preston, when the corporation directed in 1726 that it

---

[111] Berkshire RO, Wokingham Minutes of Common Council, 1749–1833, Wo/AC1/1/2. Order against bull-baiting on 10 March 1784. Order against bull-baiting in Beverley on 5 Dec. 1786. *Beverley Corporation Minute Book*, p. 69.
[112] Abingdon Chamberlains' Accounts, 1702–1787, A/FAc/5–10.

would no longer defray any bull-baiting costs, it explained that 'the power and authority of the magistrates or other civil superiors hath not been sufficient upon these occasions to restrain the turbulent and unruly passions of the common people',[113] though whether other towns were having problems with the people's 'turbulent and unruly passions' is simply unknown. In most places, the bull-ropes and bonfires silently disappear from the records, and it is consequently difficult to reconstruct reliably the forces underpinning this development.

There has nevertheless developed a consensus that the end of these civic customs should be understood in the context of increasing social divisions. It was first suggested by some of the more romantically inclined late-eighteenth-century chroniclers of local tradition that the emergence of a novel gulf between the rulers and the ruled underpinned the recent passing of many local customs;[114] and similar arguments, stressing the urban elite's increasing awareness of social difference, continue to find favour amongst historians today.[115] The withdrawal of civic notables from time-honoured civic customs is related to the emergence of a self-consciously 'polite society' during the eighteenth century, with its concomitant polarisation of elite and popular culture. It is argued that the social elite increasingly disdained the close contact with their social inferiors that traditional civic celebrations involved, and consequently adopted more socially exclusive entertainments—assembly rooms, races, concerts, and so forth—abandoning boisterous traditional festivals to the enjoyment of the populace.

But these arguments presume a period of classless sociability in the early eighteenth century that is difficult to recognise in the material surveyed here. There is certainly no evidence that the civic bull-ring was a site of promiscuous social mixing: with the exception of a handful of ritual bull-baitings held in no more than half a dozen towns, the urban elite appears never to have participated in the sport organised at the bull-ring. In early-eighteenth-century Chichester, for example, it was the 'lower sort' who were 'much given to mean diversions such as bull-baiting'.[116] Even the bonfires, though certainly belonging to celebrations that were not purely

---

[113] Lancashire RO, Preston White Book, PMC/1/2, 11 Nov. 1726.

[114] See, for example, Throsby's discussion of the Easter Monday cat hunt in Leicester; or Shaw's account of Lichfield's Whitsun bower. Throsby, *History of Leicester*, p. 166; Shaw, *History of Staffordshire*, i, p. 318.

[115] Malcolmson, *Popular Recreations*, pp. 50–71, 158–71. See also Borsay, 'All the town's a stage', esp. pp. 246–52; following in particular Burke, *Popular Culture in Europe*, pp. 270–81. For a qualified endorsement of Borsay's views, see Sweet, *Writing of Urban Histories*, pp. 256–64.

[116] Spershott, *Memoirs of Spershott*, p. 14.

plebeian in their appeal, provide slim support for the golden age of social harmony that is supposed to have existed in the early eighteenth century and before. As I have stressed, eighteenth-century civic celebrations were complex occasions, and involved far more than the bonfires and ale to which I have drawn attention here. Urban celebrations also comprised sermons and services, processions and dinners, and consequently involved all sections of the urban community. Yet, in spite of the involvement of all local citizens, social distinctions were carefully observed at all times. In practice, the street bonfires were the most emphatically plebeian element of civic celebrations: bonfires and ale were intended primarily for the entertainment of the populace, whilst more select events were held indoors for the enjoyment of the civic elite.

Newspaper descriptions repeatedly demonstrate this distinction: rather than the 'mingling of elites and plebeians round the bonfire' identified by Robert Storch, we encounter instead the populace celebrating in the streets, and the corporate body consuming sumptuous private banquets behind closed doors.[117] At celebrations in Southwark to commemorate Admiral Vernon's victory in 1745, for example, 'a large Bonefire rais'd near two Stories . . . afforded great Diversion to the Populace, among whom were generously bestow'd several Hogsheads of Strong Beer . . . the Gentlemen in the Hall in the mean time regaling themselves in an harmonious Manner with drinking Healths . . .'[118] At Bristol, the 'Mob' burnt effigies in the street during celebrations following the failure of the Excise Bill in 1733; 'In the mean time the Merchants and Principal Traders were assembled in a great Body at the Council-house, by Invitation.'[119] At Morpeth, celebrations for the King's birthday involved a large bonfire in the market place, where the health of His Majesty and all the royal family were drunk, 'after which the Magistrates, Burgesses, Gentlemen Volunteers &c retir'd to an Entertainment'.[120] In fact these social divisions cut far deeper than this. In between the fine banquets of the corporate body and the bonfires and ale of the populace in the streets, might be found any number of private dinners at local inns for different social groups—societies of tradesmen, political societies, friendly societies, and so forth. No doubt many of these individuals repeatedly crossed spatial boundaries throughout the celebrations, sometimes celebrating in the streets, sometimes enjoying private celebrations indoors. Yet, despite the broad social appeal of civic celebrations, the point concerning the

---

[117] Storch, 'Please to remember', p. 71.
[118] *Leeds Mercury*, 11 Nov. 1740.
[119] *Northampton Mercury*, 23 April 1733.
[120] *Newcastle Courant*, 12 Oct. 1745.

observance of deeply entrenched social distinctions holds: those celebrating around the bonfires lit in the streets were predominantly the urban poor and, though they might at times be in the company of their more affluent neighbours, the significance of this social contact should not be overestimated. So far as bull-rings and bonfires had ever encouraged interaction between the different ranks of society, it was a meeting that had been structured by a very acute sense of social hierarchy, and the end of official payments for bonfires and bull-rings does not suggest a fundamental alteration in the nature of social relationships.

I would argue that the decline of municipally funded recreation should not be located in a novel breakdown in inter-class harmony, but rather in the history of urban improvements. The market place and surrounding streets were the location of the bonfires lit to mark royal anniversaries, birthdays, and military victories, and it was also here that bull-rings were constructed and bull-baitings held. In addition to its primary, and most familiar function—the holding of markets—the eighteenth-century market place was a recognised site of recreation. In the words of the cultural historian, for most of the century following the Restoration, in addition to providing a physical space, the market square provided a cultural space; an arena for the pomp and splendour of carefully orchestrated civic ritual, election ceremonies, and so forth, and for the plebeian pastime of bull-baiting, largely beyond the interest and control of the ruling elite. The decline of official payments for bull-rings and bonfires needs to be understood in this context. This was not the consequence of new ideas concerning the impropriety of rulers and ruled participating in traditional activities, but rather it was symptomatic of a progressive narrowing of the cultural space provided by streets and squares in the eighteenth-century town, a breakdown of consensus concerning the right of the poor to appropriate the streets for activities of their choice at the time of their choosing.

The evidence presented here suggests that a significant modification of our understanding of the history of the eighteenth-century town is required. The narrative of eighteenth-century civic improvements is well known, described most forcefully and most coherently by Peter Borsay, but extended, refined, and largely endorsed by a far larger number of scholars.[121] The physical transformation of the eighteenth-century town—the

---

[121] Borsay, *Urban Renaissance*, pp. 60–79. Some recent contributions to the history of the eighteenth-century town include, Corfield, *Impact of English Towns*, pp. 172–8; Mitchell, 'Development of urban retailing', pp. 259–83, esp. 266; McInnes, 'Emergence of Shrewsbury', pp. 53–87; Girouard, *English Town*, pp. 9–30, 75–188; Stobart, 'Shopping streets', pp. 3–21; Reed, 'Transformation of urban space', pp. 615–40.

paving schemes, the street-widening projects, the clearing of shambles and stalls, the construction of new shops and malls, of walks and promenades, the development of street cleaning and street lighting—have all been recorded. However, missing from this story of urban improvement has been an account of the cultural transformation these physical changes involved for those who had traditionally worked and played there. Civic improvement was accompanied by new ideas concerning who might use the streets and when. As the physical layout of towns was altered, so the social value accorded to streets and squares subtly changed. The eighteenth-century town witnessed not simply innovations in building and planning; it also, as we have seen here, took its first steps towards redefining the permissible uses of streets and squares, initiating the closing down of central open spaces to plebeian sport and public celebration, and the setting apart of the civic centre for traffic, commerce, and trading.

This process was both protracted and complex. Though eighteenth-century records contain evidence of new thoughts about the use of urban space, these ideas were not quickly translated into reality, for civic traditions of several centuries' standing were not to be easily erased. There was no clear, linear decline of street recreations in the eighteenth century, but a complex renegotiation of the legitimate uses of urban space, and it is the purpose of the following chapter to consider this development further.

4
Provincial towns: streets and squares, 1750–1830

The previous chapter considered the customs of baiting bulls and burning bonfires in the market square in the century following the Restoration, and drew attention to the subtle changes in the ways that civic authorities regarded these pastimes during the period. But bull-baiting and bonfires were by no means the only form of recreation to be found in the streets and squares of eighteenth-century towns. These pastimes are in some ways easier to capture than others, since the regular payments that civic authorities made for bull-rings and bonfires have ensured they left a clear mark on the historical record. There were many other events, however, which, though they failed to leave a mark on the civic records, filled the streets in an essentially similar way. Some, such as fairs and coronation celebrations, had the backing and support of civic elites; while others, the festivities enjoyed at Shrovetide and Guy Fawkes, for example, were purely plebeian affairs, lying largely beyond the concern of local leaders. Street recreations, therefore, were considerably more extensive and diverse than those considered in the previous chapter, and it is time to expand that discussion to include practices such as these. This chapter sets out to extend the analysis of street recreations begun previously in two ways. On the one hand, it continues the history of street recreations chronologically, looking at the fortunes of events once funded by civic elites in the years following the end of these payments. On the other, it turns to consider forms of civic recreations that were not routinely funded by the public purse, looking first at the cycle of pleasure fairs and occasional public celebrations, and then exploring more ephemeral events, the uncharted terrain of plebeian street recreation.

Fairs and celebrations

The most regular and enduring recreational events throughout the eighteenth century were the trade, hiring, and pleasure fairs punctuating the calendar of towns across the country. Many of these fairs were of considerable antiquity. There is evidence of fairs of Roman and Anglo-Saxon origins, and chartered fairs increased rapidly in number in the three centuries following the Norman conquest. By the fifteenth century an extensive network of fairs covered the land, and further foundations in the early eighteenth century extended this network yet further. Although edicts in the Middle Ages had attempted to restrict fairs to larger settlements, the ongoing grants of new charters to small towns and villages had encouraged the development of this network over the subsequent centuries and served to ensure their ubiquity in settlements of all sizes by the eighteenth century.[1]

Just as fairs had spread to every kind of settlement, so their number and timing fitted no strict patterns. No town was without at least one annual fair, and in many places considerably more were held throughout the year. Northampton, for example, was home to no fewer than eight annual fairs for most of the eighteenth century; by the middle of the nineteenth century, this number had risen to thirteen.[2] In the small Yorkshire town of Skipton, ten fairs for the sale of livestock and cloth were held annually in the middle of the eighteenth century, and fairs everywhere were held at all times of the year.[3] Many older fairs had been originally linked to the Church, and were consequently held upon Sundays and on feast days. Edicts of Edward III and Henry IV had largely succeeded in removing fairs from Sundays, but this nevertheless left scope for wide variation in their timing.[4] They were held throughout the year for periods varying between one day and two weeks. The very long timeframe of their history had resulted in a diverse set of practices in every aspect of the nation's network of fairs by the eighteenth century.

The passage of time had similarly ensured that the location of fairs was subject to a number of variations. Just as the timing and duration of each fair was fixed by either charter or custom, so the site of every fair was fixed. Many of the earliest foundations had stipulated church land—often the churchyard itself—as the ground for the fair. Statutes from the thirteenth century had prohibited the holding of fairs in churchyards, and, although

---

[1] For general histories of fairs, see Walford, *Fairs, Past and Present*, pp. 12–53; Muncey, *Old English Fairs*, pp. 1–19; Addison, *English Fairs*. Much of the most valuable work on fairs has taken the form of local studies. See, for example, Hulbert, 'Survey of Somerset fairs', pp. 83–159; Walker, *Essex Markets and Fairs*, esp. pp. 36–43; McCutcheon, *Yorkshire Fairs*.

[2] Muncey, *Old English Fairs*, pp. 145–6.

[3] Owen, *Account of Fairs*, p. 87.

[4] Walford, *Fairs, Past and Present*, p. 34; Muncey, *Old English Fairs*, pp. 9–10.

their frequent repetition suggests that these orders were often ignored, by the fifteenth century the elimination of fairs from churchyards had been largely completed.[5] By this time they had migrated beyond churchyards and were to be found scattered upon spaces of every kind—urban streets and squares, commons, greens, and, in some instances, private land. Within towns, the market square and surrounding streets had emerged as the most common site for the holding of fairs. It was customary for large markets to overspill the market square and fill surrounding streets, and fairs tended to occupy civic spaces in a similar way.

Most civic fairs were important trading marts, devoted largely or wholly to the sale of horses, cattle, sheep, cheese, textiles, iron goods, china-ware, and other commodities. They were, therefore, an extension of the usual trading functions of the town, and so the use of central trading spaces was entirely fitting. A local resident recalled how the livestock for sale at the monthly stock market in Dorking had lined the town's streets: 'The horned cattle occupied the south side of High Street, from Chequer Yard to the Red Lion Hotel. The sheep pens, on the same side of the road stretched from the hotel named to the White Horse Inn, while a similar space was covered on the opposite side of the street by additional pens for sheep and pigs.'[6] The goods for sale at fairs filled the streets in the same way. At Wellington, cattle were penned in the town's three main streets—Mantle Street, High Street, and South Street—and 'stalls were erected on every available spot';[7] and at Winchcombe, 'The whole of North Street was full of horses tied up as close as they could stand, while the side lanes . . . were practically blocked'.[8] At hiring fairs, servants for hire lined themselves down streets in identical fashion. At the hiring fair at Leeds, for example, 'they [the servants] range themselves on either side down the principal street (Briggate), and there are inspected and questioned by those who are in quest of servants';[9] and in Swindon, servants seeking situations rendered 'the foot-ways in the High Street . . . literally impassable' at the time of the hiring fairs in the middle of the nineteenth century.[10] Visual evidence reinforces this point. Paintings from the eighteenth and nineteenth centuries depict horses and cattle lined down the streets, and market squares transformed into grids of pens for pigs and sheep.

[5] McCutcheon, *Yorkshire Fairs*, pp. 20–7.
[6] Rose, *Recollections*, p. 69.
[7] Humphries, *History of Wellington*, p. 232.
[8] Oakey, *Reminiscences*, p. 16.
[9] Robinson, *Dialect of Leeds*, pp. 420–1 (loc. hist.).
[10] Morris, *Swindon Fifty Years Ago*, p. 310.

In general, however, fairs were much more than markets. There is evidence from the Middle Ages of fairs offering many and varied entertainments, and in the following centuries the importance of fairs in the provision of recreation did not diminish.[11] Establishing the extent of recreation at fairs is difficult though, since it has traditionally been their commercial, rather than recreational, aspects that have attracted notice. Lists of fairs published in the eighteenth century noted no more than a handful as 'for pleasure', though since these were drawn up for the information of farmers and traders they are likely to under-represent the extent of recreation.[12] Certainly many of those listed in directories as trade fairs were noted elsewhere for their entertainments. For example, the Leeds fair held annually in July was described simply as a horse and hardware fair in Owen's *Account of Fairs*, yet the local newspaper one year contained an account of four dogs pulling a cart as one of 'many other Varieties to entertain the Populace at our Fair', and this coupling of trade and pleasure was not unusual.[13] As at Leeds, most fairs combined both commercial and recreational functions, with traders typically departing before the close of the fair, and the final days being given over to the pursuit of pleasure. The arrival of fairs consequently involved not merely an extension of trade into civic streets, but also a change in their normal use. All civic fairs brought showmen and pleasure-seekers to town, as well as dealers and traders, and, over the course of the eighteenth century, the provision of entertainment at fairs became increasingly pronounced.

Already in the early eighteenth century, a small number of fairs had been stripped of much of their trading function and were devoted largely to the pursuit of pleasure. The great fair at Bury St Edmunds was described by Defoe in the 1720s as 'a fair for diversion, more than for trade', a fair 'for toys and trinkets',[14] and a few of the large London fairs were likewise famed for the number and quality of their theatrical shows rather than as markets.[15] This trend accelerated over the following century, as improved transport and communications, industrial development, and urban growth

[11] See, for example, Morley, *Memoirs of Bartholomew Fair*, pp. 57–62, 71–2, 120–1; Walford, *Fairs, Past and Present*, pp. 166–9.

[12] The most comprehensive lists are provided in Owen, *Account of Fairs*; and Ogilby and Morgan, *Traveller's Pocket Book*, both of which were first published in the 1750s, and went through numerous revised editions.

[13] Owen, *Account of Fairs* p. 85; and *Leeds Mercury*, 4 July 1727. See also the conclusions reached in Malcolmson, *Popular Recreations*, pp. 20–4.

[14] Defoe, *Tour Through Great Britain*, i, p. 51.

[15] See Morley, *Memoirs of Bartholomew Fair*, pp. 333–421; Rosenfeld, *Theatre of London Fairs*. See also Judd, 'Oddest combination', pp. 10–30.

helped to establish alternative forms of trade, and to diminish the importance of fairs as trading marts. By the early nineteenth century, the scale of
trade at many of the country's great civic fairs had significantly declined,
and in some towns the historic trading fairs had given way to newly created pleasure fairs. In Oxford, for example, the older chartered fairs had
largely decayed by the nineteenth century, and had been eclipsed in significance by the St Giles Fair, a newly established unchartered pleasure fair,
held annually early in September.[16] Similarly Manchester's historic trading
fairs had all declined by the nineteenth century, and the Knot Mill Fair had
emerged as the city's largest—an unchartered fair which had been established in the late eighteenth century, and which, from its origin, had been
wholly devoted to pleasure.[17]

Yet, notwithstanding the changing nature of many fairs, the location
invariably remained the same. Those held in town streets continued in their
traditional place, in spite of the disruption the influx of traders and
pleasure-seekers caused to the normal business of the town. Fairs brought
stalls, shows, and milling crowds into the trading centre of towns. At

Figure 6.   William Weekes, *Street Acrobats*, 1874 (Sotheby's Picture Library, London).

---

[16] See Alexander, *St Giles Fair*, pp. 1–8.
[17] Page, *Manchester Fairs*, pp. 10, 16–17.

Kingston upon Thames, a writer described the 'forest of booths erected in the Market Place' offering an 'ample supply' of entertainment to the country people who flocked to the fair.[18] In Bury St Edmunds, the Bury Fair brought entertainments as varied as an 'Amazing Corsican Fairy' measuring only thirty-four inches high, a menagerie of 'wild productions', 'rope dancing, tumbling, postures, and dancing', and 'An Extraordinary Spotted Boy from the Caribee Islands' to the Angel Hill, a wide open street on the eastern edge of the town, adjacent to the Abbey.[19] At such times the usual trade and traffic in the town were necessarily suspended. Henry Thirlway, a Ripon stationer, provided an unusually detailed account for the way in which the fair filled the centre of a market town in the middle of the nineteenth century. He wrote:

> I never saw more shows. Thornes and Rickartims, two theatrical companies, filled the square, except a small space occupied by a wild beast show; near the church was a company of rope-dancers to be seen for a penny, and at a little distance a menagerie contained in four or five caravans besides an elephant which walked about the show . . . Besides these [shows] were several minor ones. About 1/2 past seven the elephant walked through the fair preceded by their band of music. Walked home.[20]

And this use of central streets and squares for entertainments and booths at fairs continued through the century. A description by a local historian of the transformation of the centre of Enfield by the arrival of the fair each year in the late nineteenth century indicates how little had changed: 'for three days the town, from the corner of Silver Street to the Market Place, was crowded with the stalls of the vendors of oysters, cockles, mussels, sausages and gingerbread, skittle alleys, nut shooting and wheels of fortune, the Market Place itself being occupied by roundabouts, swings and a huge monster booth'.[21] Again, nineteenth-century visual evidence reinforces these points. Nineteenth-century art reveals markets squares filled with pleasure rides, stalls and crowds of people. Fairs required a complete cessation of the normal business of the town: both central and side streets were rendered impassable by stalls, tents, booths, and pleasure-seekers.

There had been a vein of criticism about fairs running throughout their long history. The crowds, gambling, dancing, theatre, and mixing of the

[18] Biden, *History of Kingston*, p. 70.
[19] Glyde, *Folklore of Suffolk*, pp. 274–6; *Ipswich Journal*, 24 Sept. 1743; Oakes, *Diary*, ii, pp. 148–9.
[20] North Yorkshire CRO, Thirlway's Journal, 1835–1859, MIC 2563, 22 June 1843. See also his comments on the entertainments in Ripon. Ibid., 21 Aug. 1843, 18 Aug. 1844.
[21] Whitaker, *Account of Enfield*, p. 86.

sexes to be found at any fair provided ample ground for complaint, and concerns about the vicious consequences of public gatherings had punctuated the history of fairs down the centuries. The Restoration muted much of the hostility towards popular recreations that had surfaced in the sixteenth and seventeenth centuries, yet complaints about the pernicious consequences of fairs never completely disappeared in the following century and, from the 1760s, magistrates in a small number of counties took steps to limit unchartered fairs on the grounds they were injurious to the inhabitants' morals.[22] In 1761, magistrates in Essex ordered the suppression of fairs at Pebmarsh, Boxted, Ardleigh, Asheldham, Little Wakering, Barling, Alphamstone, and Belchamp Otten on the grounds that they were 'pretended fairs', an excuse for the gathering of 'loose, idle and disorderly persons' and for 'many unlawful games [and] plays besides drinking [and] other debaucheries'.[23] They issued further orders against unchartered fairs the following year and again in the 1780s; in the following decade, magistrates in Surrey followed suit.[24] From the 1780s, reforming local magistrates were offered further support by the newly refashioned reformation of manners movements. These societies, modelled on the reformation societies of the late seventeenth century, predictably included fairs amongst their many targets for reform.[25] The Society for the Suppression of Vice objected to illegal fairs as a nuisance 'of the very worst description'. Its members argued that such amusements 'tended to impair their [the lower classes'] health, to injure their circumstances, to distress their families, and to involve them in vice and misery'.[26]

But there was nothing new about these fears that fairs were injurious to public morals. Such views had been voiced periodically throughout their history, and their reappearance at this time marked no break with earlier criticisms. Given our interests in the use of space it is significant that no concern about the location of fairs may be found in these objections. The ancient custom of holding fairs in central streets and thoroughfares had not yet become controversial, and it was only several decades later that system-

---

[22] For eighteenth-century criticism, see Sheldrake, *Description of Turton Fair*. Such criticism increased in volume in the following century. See, for example, Dillon, *A Sermon on the Evils of Fairs; Devil at Greenwich Fair*; Chester, *Statute Fairs: Their Evils*.

[23] Golding, 'Fairs in Essex', p. 62.

[24] Malcolmson, *Popular Recreations*, pp. 149–52. The Surrey order is reprinted in Radzinowicz, *History of English Law*, iii, pp. 491–3.

[25] See Innes, 'Politics and morals', pp. 57–118; Radzinowicz, *History of English Law*, iii, pp. 141–65, 191–3.

[26] *Address to the Public*, p. 63.

atic steps to clear them out of central streets were initiated in provincial England. In the earlier part of the century, the idea that the location of civic fairs caused an intolerable inconvenience to residents had yet to be formed, and grievances continued to be articulated in the older language of morals and manners.

Fairs, then, were deeply integrated into the fabric of urban life. Although the eighteenth century witnessed many attempts to improve the fabric of civic centres, fairs were left largely untouched by these developments. Nor was it simply the trading element of fairs that ensured their survival in the nineteenth century, since the decline or disappearance of trade from fairs provided no serious check to their continuation. Many fairs were purely recreational events, yet they continued to be held in market squares and the surrounding streets. The central location of civic fairs was a custom of many centuries' standing, and it was not easily eroded.

In a similar way, central streets and squares continued to be used to celebrate events such as coronations, royal marriages and birthdays, anniversaries, and significant military victories; and, although the form and style of these celebrations underwent a number of changes in the second half of the eighteenth century, the use of central urban spaces remained an important element of civic festivities well into the nineteenth century. Like fairs, civic celebrations had a long history, though they had evolved through the course of the centuries to a far greater extent. As early as the fourteenth century, an elaborate civic ritual year had developed in towns, involving processions and pageants carefully orchestrated by guilds, religious houses, and urban elites.[27] The Reformation brought a relatively swift end to those forms of ritual that were religious in character, though, rather than undermine civic ceremonial, this simply initiated changes in their form for, in subsequent years, new rituals rapidly developed and filled their place.[28] In the late sixteenth century alternative, secular forms of ceremony and ritual centred upon the mercantile and governing elite were established. New celebrations commemorating royal birthdays and accession days, and military victories were instituted, and this calendar continued to flourish through the following century.[29]

It is widely appreciated that this new Protestant calendar of celebration had supplanted the older cycle of saints' days and religious observances by the seventeenth century. What has been less widely recognised, however, is

---

[27] Phythian-Adams, 'Ceremony and the citizen', pp. 106–28; Hutton, *Rise and Fall*, pp. 39–44.
[28] Berlin, 'Civic ceremony in London', pp. 15–27; Montano, 'Quest for consensus', pp. 31–51.
[29] Cressy, *Bonfires and Bells*, pp. 50–66, 93–189; Borsay, 'All the town's a stage', pp. 228–58.

the continuously changing form that civic celebrations took. The Protestant calendar created in the late sixteenth century drew upon the traditional repertoire of celebratory styles—bells and bonfires, prayers and processions, feasting and drinking—and, although the dates that were celebrated continued to change through most of the seventeenth and eighteenth centuries, these forms of celebration remained largely intact. From the late eighteenth century, however, the style of civic ceremonial began to differ in a number of far-reaching ways; by the nineteenth century, civic celebrations were beginning to look quite different from those of earlier times.

At the heart of this development lay a committed and largely successful attempt on the part of civic authorities to bring a greater degree of order and control to public demonstrations of loyalty. The earliest and most straightforward indicator of this was the ending of bonfires in public streets and squares. We noted in the previous chapter that many municipal authorities had provided wood for the lighting of bonfires on numerous occasions throughout the year for many decades into the eighteenth century. The end of official payments did not result in an immediate disappearance of bonfires in the streets, but it did in time result in a substantial decrease in their use to mark commemorative events, and this in turn led to a curtailment of the opportunities for plebeian festivities in the public streets. It is difficult to provide an accurate reconstruction of exactly who had ever enjoyed these bonfires, though the laconic and rather formulaic accounts to be found in local newspapers suggest that they were left burning through the evening for the amusement of the populace. The poor spent the evening celebrating outdoors around bonfires, whilst civic elites retreated indoors to enjoy drinking and private dinners at considerable expense and in their own company.[30] Local newspapers reveal that provincial notables continued to mark anniversaries and royal birthdays in the second half of the eighteenth century with bell-ringing and private dinners, with possibly an illumination—the lighting of candles in windows—in the evening, but that the bonfires for the populace which had previously concluded the community's celebrations were quietly dropped. The end of regular payments for festive bonfires consequently brought about a reduction in boisterous outdoor festivities, whilst leaving the more orderly bell-ringing, sermons, and dinners in place. For much of the second half of the eighteenth century, the only events to be routinely celebrated with bonfires were military victories. Long-running wars with France and America ensured the appearance of traditional-style public celebrations in a number

---

[30] See Chapter 3 above.

of years in the late eighteenth century, though these in time petered out as well.[31] Thus street bonfires and the distribution of ale at the market cross, whilst not instantly disappearing, did become increasingly infrequent during the second half of the eighteenth century; by the century's end, the era of routine lighting of several bonfires each year had drawn to an unmistakable close.

By the nineteenth century, the appearance of the local community celebrating in the streets was considerably more unusual than it had been the century before, and festivities which drew in the urban population at large were confined to events of particular national significance. Thus it was historic moments such as the signing of peace with France in 1802, the fiftieth anniversary of George III's coronation in 1809, the General Peace of 1814, victory at Waterloo in 1815, the coronations of George IV in 1821 and Queen Victoria in 1838, and the passage of the Reform Bill in 1832 which assembled the local community in the streets in the traditional way, rather than the regular cycle of royal birthdays and anniversaries. However, as these festive events became more infrequent, so they also became ever more elaborate and extensive. A number of years might pass between civic celebrations of this kind but, when they occurred, they were planned and executed with a far greater degree of care than previously, and on a scale that the eighteenth century had rarely seen.

Something of the contrast may be captured by comparing the fiftieth anniversary celebrations of the coronation of George III in the early nineteenth century, with those of the original event in 1761. The coronation was celebrated in all towns in the traditional way: with processions, bell-ringing, and gunfire in the morning; and in the evening, bonfires, meat, and ale in the streets for the populace, and private dinners at town halls and inns for local elites. In Derby, for instance, 'in several of [the streets] a Sheep was roasted whole . . . Bonfires blaz'd in every Street of the Town, Fireworks of various Kinds were played off in several Places'; and at Ashbourne 'many fat Sheep [were] roasted whole in several Parts of the Town, as it contains many Streets'.[32] In Sheffield, there was 'in every Street a large Bonfire, at several of which Sheep were roasted whole, and the People din'd in Publick'.[33]

Celebrations at the time of the fiftieth anniversary of George III's coronation, though in some places bearing many similarities to the original event, were generally more sedate affairs. A number of towns celebrated the

[31] See, for example, *Leeds Intelligencer*, 7 Jan. 1777, 20 March 1781, 5 Aug. 1793.
[32] *Derby Mercury*, 2 Oct. 1761.
[33] Ibid.

occasion in time-honoured fashion, with sheep or oxen roasted whole at bonfires in the streets, and distributed to the populace with ale.[34] Yet many others dispensed with the roasting of meat in the streets, preferring to distribute charity in the morning before church services—typically a gift of either beef or mutton, bread, and sometimes, though not invariably, a quantity of ale.[35] An editorial in the *Rockingham and Hull Weekly Advertiser* considered that the example set by Leeds—no public dinner and no beer for the populace—was a laudable one. Although enthusiastic about the forthcoming anniversary, this provincial paper believed that the occasion called for 'no "boisterous" expression of joy'.[36] In some towns, dinners were moved indoors: at Dunstable, for example, dinners were provided for the populace in the local inns.[37] Other towns upheld the tradition of dining outdoors, though in a manner that had little in common with the roast oxen and beef that had been enjoyed at the coronation celebrations of fifty years before. The nineteenth century witnessed the innovation of laying tables in the streets at which the local population sat down and dined in public, and a number of towns celebrated George III's anniversary in this new way. At Northampton, where dinner was served at tables laid in the streets, the local paper proudly reported that 'the greatest order, decorum and good humour prevailed'.[38]

Subsequent celebrations were increasingly likely to involve this kind of careful organisation. For example, in Reading, at celebrations for the General Peace in 1814, '80 principal tables, each 40 feet long, 480 stewards appointed with carvers, and at a given signal 6000 persons sat down to a splendid old English hot dinner'.[39] At Horsham, an elderly inhabitant recalled how at the coronation of Queen Victoria each child was provided with a knife, fork, and mug, and a ticket on which was printed 'Victoria, Crowned 28TH June, 1838'.[40] Civic leaders were exercising more careful control over every aspect of public festivity, and these celebrations were

---

[34] Buckingham and Bedford, *Northampton Mercury*, 4 Nov. 1809; Wellingborough, ibid., 28 Oct. 1809; Otley, *Leeds Mercury*, 28 Oct. 1809.

[35] Higham Ferrars, Harborough, *Northampton Mercury*, 28 Oct.1809; Oundle, Stony Stratford, Huntingdon, ibid., 4 Nov. 1809; Peterborough, *Cambridge Chronicle*, 4 Nov. 1809; Alford, *Lincoln Mercury*, 10 Nov. 1809.

[36] *Rockingham and Hull Weekly Advertiser*, 30 Sept. 1809.

[37] Dunstable, *Northampton Mercury*, 4 Nov. 1809.

[38] Northampton, *Northampton Mercury*, 28 Oct. 1809; Towcester, ibid., 4 Nov. 1809.

[39] [Darter], *Reminiscences*, p. 55. See also *Reading Mercury*, 18 July 1814, 30 June 1838.

[40] Burstow, *Reminiscences*, p. 43. See also Henry Thirlway's account of Queen Victoria's coronation in Ripon: North Yorkshire CRO, Thirlway's Journal, 1835–1859, MIC 2563, 28 June 1838.

consequently becoming considerably more orderly events. In reality, it sometimes proved difficult to control public behaviour, and the distribution of ale often had predictable results. In Manchester, for example, one inhabitant noted that at the celebrations for George IV's coronation, 'men, women and children lay dead drunk in the streets and many of those who could still use their limbs were fighting in the most brutal manner'.[41] At Stowey in Somerset, during an illumination for Nelson's victory in December 1805, a parson found the town 'very lively', and he and his friends 'did not stay long as there were Squibs thrown about'.[42] But the intentions of civic leaders are clear: throughout the country they were seeking to bring a greater degree of order and decorum to civic celebrations, and to redefine the way in which public spaces were used during these events.

Yet no less significant than the ever-evolving form of civic ceremony and celebrations was the ongoing use of the streets and squares for, despite these changes in the structure of civic ritual, public streets continued to form the location of all such events. Nor should this observation about the location of civic festivities be regarded as self-evident. The use of central urban spaces to commemorate events of religious, local, and national significance had always been integral to civic celebration. It ensured the involvement of the whole local population, and served to underscore the messages of loyalty and community contained within many public celebrations. These were points noticed many years ago by the historian of medieval Coventry, Charles Phythian-Adams. He observed:

> Hocktide games took place 'in' the city and not on adjacent waste ground; maypoles stood over the street; bonfires burnt on them; 'pageants' trundled through them ... Such practices are not only a reminder that medieval streets were as important for recreation and marketing as for communication; rites and processions, like the carriage through the streets of the Corpus Christi host or the Midsummer fire, periodically added a mystical dimension to this utilitarian valuation of the immediate topographical context. While doing so, they underlined further the physical inescapability of communal involvement.[43]

---

[41] Watkin, *Diary*, 19 July 1821, p. 51. Similar observations were made by Thomson, *Autobiography*, p. 46; Burstow, *Reminiscences*, p. 44.

[42] Holland, *Diary*, 5 Dec. 1805, p. 123. See also the parson's experiences at a 'great rejoicing' on account of the General Peace at Bridgewater: 'We got a position in a room on the Cornhill where we could see the Bonfire and Squibs and Rockets thrown. In a narrow passage we had a Squib thrown amongst us and Margaret's gown was burnt and when we got upstairs a Squib with a stone was thrown through the window and the broken glass flew to Mr Symes face.' Ibid., 12 April 1814, p. 262.

[43] Phythian-Adams, 'Ceremony and the citizen', pp. 121–2.

Figure 7.   James Pettrey Hunter, *The Market Place, Wisbech, on the Day of the Coronation of Queen Victoria, 28 June 1838* (Wisbech and Fenland Museum, Wisbech).

The dates, style, and meaning of civic festivity had undergone countless changes in the four centuries following the medieval patterns of ritual that Phythian-Adams was describing, yet his observations are not without relevance to the historian of nineteenth-century civic ceremony, for the use of public streets for celebrations continued to lie at the heart of these events, just as it ever had. The position of public celebrations helped to ensure they involved the entire community, and served to invest them with particular local significance.

It is, of course, difficult to establish exactly how individuals understood the celebrations in which they participated, or to recapture their appreciation of the use of central civic spaces. Furthermore, it is certainly possible to overestimate popular understanding of the use of these spaces. Historians of Restoration processions have demonstrated that the messages contained within civic pageantry were frequently lost on much of the crowd, that many turned out simply for the fun of the occasion.[44] The same was no doubt true of nineteenth-century civic ceremonies. Yet,

[44] Miller, *Popery and Politics*, pp. 183–4; Harris, *London Crowds*, pp. 123–4; Klein, 'Between the bums and the bellies of the multitude', pp. 18–26; Reay, *Popular Cultures*, pp. 143–51.

although popular experiences of ritual and ceremony are difficult to recover, it is possible to comment upon the way in which the use of central civic spaces contributed to these experiences. The position of these events gave them a physical presence that ensured their relevance to the entire local community. The frequency with which nineteenth-century autobiographers recalled grand civic celebrations from their childhood testifies to the impact of these occasions in provincial communities. A public rejoicing frequently stood out as the only event from childhood that writers recalled. An elderly shoemaker from Horsham could 'recall particulars of the event [Reform Dinner, 1 August 1832] as if they took place but last week'.[45] Another wrote, 'the coronation of Queen Victoria lives in my memory from the illuminations which marked the rejoicing in our town . . . All are as fresh as ever.'[46] An inhabitant of Thame in Oxfordshire recalled, 'a great stir was made in our little town' at the time of Queen Victoria's coronation,[47] and the appropriation of public streets was a significant factor in this, since celebrations which filled central spaces could hardly fail to draw in the community at large. Although the form of civic celebrations continued to change over the long eighteenth century, their location remained the same and this ensured significant continuities with earlier periods.

We are thus drawn once again to the conclusion that the market square had strong historic links with recreation which were not easily eroded. The moments at which the community filled civic streets for communal celebration were certainly more infrequent by the nineteenth century, yet they had not disappeared and street festivities continued to play some role in urban life. Although it would be possible to understand the changes outlined here in terms of decline, this is arguably not the most fitting way to conceive the history of civic ritual since the market square and central streets did in fact continue to serve as a space for recreation and celebrations. Successive generations reworked the form and style of civic celebrations, but the use of public streets and squares continued to invest such events with particular local significance and communal value.

---

[45] Burstow, *Reminiscences*, p. 26.
[46] Adams, *Memoirs*, ii, p. 130. See also Carter, *Memoirs*, p. 43; Thomson, *Autobiography*, p. 46.
[47] Hobley, 'Autobiography of Hobley', p. 331.

Street play: cock throwing, football, and Guy Fawkes

Some forms of recreation managed to adapt and survive into the nineteenth century but there were others that fared less well. Fairs and public celebrations, for all that they drew in the community at large, were ultimately controlled by civic leaders. The time of their holding, their duration, extent, and position, were all in the gift of civic leaders, and this sharply differentiated them from those recreations that lay outside their control. A range of more informal recreational practices had always existed alongside the large-scale, formal events orchestrated by civic leaders. We considered one such example at length in the previous chapter: bull-baiting, although practised at a bull-ring maintained by civic officials, was essentially independent of elite control. As we noted there, it is difficult to reconstruct how the sport was enjoyed, since its distance from civic elites ensured that descriptive accounts of the pastime are rare, yet payments for bull-rings provide unequivocal evidence that the market place was occasionally transformed into the site of a popular recreation, all aspects of which were largely determined by members of the community far removed from official positions of power. Nor was bull-baiting the only such recreation to fill civic streets. Although other plebeian street games have generally left little mark in official records, it is possible to piece together some account of informal recreations played in the market square and surrounding streets. And it soon becomes apparent that in the eighteenth century activities that lay beyond elite sanction and involvement fared very much less well than those that lay within.

The Shrovetide sport of throwing at cocks is one such plebeian pastime. It had very rarely received official encouragement. Ronald Hutton has found churchwardens in Pinner providing cocks for the populace to throw at and returning the profits to parish funds in the seventeenth century, but throwing at cocks was so simple and so cheap to organise that it was a national pastime in England despite an almost total lack of elite patronage.[48] It was a plebeian sport. Cock throwing was rarely referred to by the writers of diaries and, when it was, they were not recording their own participation, but what they had observed. Thus Samuel Pepys one year 'looked out at window; saw the flinging at cocks';[49] and Nicholas Blundell wrote in his diary one Shrove Tuesday, 'My Wife and I saw them throw at the Cock in the Townfield.'[50] It was, furthermore, a young person's sport.

---

[48] Hutton, *Rise and Fall*, p. 229.
[49] Pepys, *Diary*, ii, 26 Feb. 1661, p. 352.
[50] Blundell, *Diurnal*, i, 17 Feb. 1708, p. 163.

Henry Newcome, a seventeenth-century clergyman, reported his children's participation in throwing at cocks each year. He repeatedly expressed concern that his children might get hurt, and his fears were one year confirmed when 'Daniel's hat on his head was shot through with an arrow'.[51]

In rural areas, the village green or a fallow field was usually used for throwing at cocks but, in towns, churchyards and streets formed the location of the sport. In York in 1672, apprentices 'plaid in the minster-yeard, throwing at a cock'; and in early-eighteenth-century Chichester 'scarcely a churchyard was to be found' without its cock throwers on Shrove Tuesday.[52] An account of London at Shrovetide by a Dutch visitor describes the way in which apprentices took over the street on this day:

> Their entertainment [on Shrove Tuesday] is to throw at the cock. In London one sees in every street, wherever one goes, many apprentice boys running with, under their arms, a cock with a string on its foot, on which is a spike, which they push firmly into the ground between the stones. They always look for an open space, and, for a penny, let people throw their cudgels from a good distance at the cock, and he, who kills the cock, gets it.[53]

There was no official sanction of throwing at cocks, and this pastime was consequently very different from the fairs and ceremonies considered in the first half of this chapter. Shrove Tuesday was a moment when the young and plebeian took possession of the streets: as a visitor to London in the early eighteenth century noted, 'it is even dangerous to go near any of those places where this diversion is being held; so many clubs are thrown about that you run a risk of receiving one on your head'.[54] It is not surprising, therefore, to discover that as civic elites sought to improve urban centres and to impose more order on civic celebrations during the eighteenth century, the annual custom of throwing at cocks found itself the focus of criticism. Being the pastime of plebeian children, it was an easy and early target of reform.

Norwich appears to have been the first town to attack the seasonal sport since the Restoration, beginning its campaign in 1719. In that year, the town's court of mayoralty recorded the following:

> Whereas complaint has been made to this court of a great disorder committed by Apprentices and Others in the Castle Dykes and other places in this Citty under pretence of camping and throwing at cocks I am hereby to order

[51] Newcome, *Autobiography*, i, 31 Jan. 1665, p. 147.
[52] Heywood, *Diary*, i, 11 Feb. 1672, p. 345.
[53] Shellinks, *Journal of Shellinks*, p. 73.
[54] de Saussure, *Letters of de Saussure*, p. 294.

that if any further disorders be committed by the meeting of 3 or more upon
the like pretence, in the Castle Dykes or in any other parts of this Citty, they
will be prosecuted for a Ryott.[55]

In subsequent years, the city's mayors elaborated the case against throwing
at cocks in greater detail: in 1722 it was prohibited because of the 'great disorders committed by diverse idle persons';[56] in 1723 the court expressed
concern about 'the damages that have happened and are like to happen
again by the said lamentable practice';[57] and in 1731 the people involved
were 'ill-disposed' and 'disorderly'.[58] The court continued to repeat its
orders against cock throwing in much the same language every year until
the 1730s, when it began simply to note that it had been agreed to pay for
advertisements in the newspapers prohibiting throwing at cocks 'as usual'.
These notices appeared most years until 1756, when the record gives out.[59]
The next mayor's court book begins in 1767, by which time the court was
no longer advertising the illegality of throwing at cocks. Nevertheless, the
corporation had made consistent efforts to suppress the sport for a period
of over thirty years.

    Few attempts to abolish throwing at cocks were initiated so early as
those in Norwich. In Portsmouth, the corporation ordered the prohibition
of the pastime in 1720,[60] but otherwise campaigns against cock throwing
were rare in the first half of the eighteenth century. From the 1750s, however, towns everywhere were beginning to take steps to end the custom.
The authorities at Newbury, Sheffield, Wakefield, Doncaster, Reading,
Northampton, Bristol, and London all prohibited throwing at cocks during
the 1750s.[61] In 1762, constables were paid to walk the streets to prevent the
sport in Nottingham.[62] The magistrates at Colchester issued an order
against throwing at cocks in 1664;[63] and Guildford issued notices prohibiting the throwing at cocks 'either in High Streets, Backsides or Church Yards

[55] Norfolk RO, Court of Mayoralty Book, 1719–1729, Case 16a/28, p. 16.

[56] Ibid., p. 139.

[57] Ibid., p. 182.

[58] Norfolk RO, Court of Mayoralty Book, 1729–1736, Case 16a/29, p. 129.

[59] Norfolk RO, Court of Mayoralty Books, 1719–1758, Case 16a/29–31. Exceptions 1720,
1725–7, 1739, 1744–7, 1750, 1752, 1754.

[60] *Extracts from Records in Portsmouth*, p. 515.

[61] Berkshire RO, Newbury Borough Sessions Minute Book, 1739–1785, N/JQ/1/2, 29 Jan.
1750; Sheffield Archives, Sheffield Burgery Accounts, 1566–1707, TT13, payments in 1752
and 1756; Banks, *Walks in Yorkshire*, pp. 84–5; Hatfield, *Notices of Doncaster*, i, p. 75; *Gentleman's
Magazine*, Feb. 1752, p. 89.

[62] *Records of Nottingham*, vii, p. 26.

[63] *Ipswich Journal*, 25 Feb. 1764.

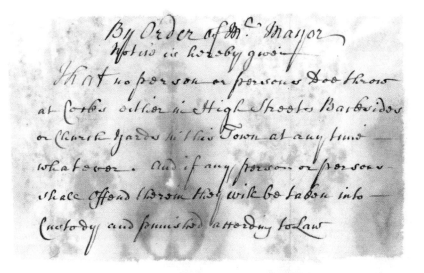

Figure 8. Guildford Mayors' Order against throwing at cocks on Shrove Tuesday (Surrey Record Office, Guildford Muniments Room, Guildford Mayors' Proclamations, BR/OC/2/7).

in this Town' in February 1766.[64] In Gravesend the chamberlains made payments for the crying down of cock throwing 1784.[65] Very similarly worded condemnations of throwing at cocks appeared in all the Liverpool papers in 1787, possibly at the instigation of the ruling body.[66] There is also evidence from Worcester, Ely, Abingdon, Dover, and Wisbech that civic rulers were endeavouring to prevent the practice in the late eighteenth century.[67]

Local people were often slow to comply with these new orders. In 1759 the justices for the Isle of Ely, Cambridgeshire, expressed exasperation that their repeated orders had yet to be obeyed,[68] and the corporation of Abingdon paid for 'Drawing a Cry and fair copy of the Bellman

[64] Surrey RO (Guildford), Guildford Mayors' Proclamations, BR/OC/2/7(1).
[65] Kent RO, Gravesend Chamberlains' Accounts, 1784–1852, Gr/FAc/4.
[66] *Liverpool General Advertiser*, 15 Feb. 1787; *Williamson Liverpool Advertiser*, 19 Feb. 1787.
[67] For Worcester, see Noake, *Worcester in Olden Times*, p. 109. The references for Ely, Abingdon, Dover, and Wisbech are given in footnotes 68–71 below. Robert Malcolmson provides examples from Castor (Northamptonshire), High Wycombe, and Manchester. See idem, *Popular Recreations*, p. 120. The suppression of throwing at cocks is also discussed in Hutton, *Stations of the Sun*, pp. 158–9.
[68] *Ipswich Journal*, 17 Feb. 1759. The quarter sessions minute book has not survived, so it is not possible to establish how often the order had been repeated.

agt. throwing at cocks' most years between 1776 and 1787.[69] Dover first paid its crier for 'forbidding throwing at cocks' in 1781, and continued to pay the crier every Shrove Tuesday for nearly quarter of a century.[70] Towns from all parts of the south of England were taking steps to prevent the custom; though the repeated orders suggest that the decline was sometimes protracted, the intention of town rulers was unambiguous.

So far as this development has attracted historical comment, it has generally been related to humanitarianism; but, although a handful of pamphlets and articles with what might be loosely termed humanitarian concerns may be identified, the language of compassion is conspicuously absent in local archives. In local records, it is disorder rather than cruelty that emerges as the authorities' central concern. The magistrates at Wisbech, for example, expressed concern that throwing at cocks was 'an encouragement to Idleness and Vice, and is always attended with Riots and Disorders'.[71] At Portsmouth, the mayor and justices were moved to act owing to the 'riotts, quarrells, and other mischeifs' often occasioned.[72] In Norwich, as we noted, throwing at cocks was suppressed in order to 'prevent such disorders as usually arise therefrom'.[73] In Newbury, the justices simply presented 'as a Nuisance the throwing at cocks in the public streets'.[74] Repeatedly, civic authorities were challenging the continuation of a sport that was at best a nuisance to those not participating, and at worst encouraged disorder. One finds little that suggests a rise in humanitarian sentiment. Though the prohibition orders did occasionally condemn cock throwing as cruel, the emphasis was placed squarely on the inconvenience of the sport in public streets, and on the disorder and mischief it potentially encouraged. Of course, humanitarian concerns may have been of slightly greater relevance than official documents suggest since these sources, by their nature, would stress the more prosaic benefits of reform, but it seems that a quite different process was also at work. The invasion of children and working people on the streets, with their cocks and missiles, had always constituted a minor public nuisance. It occurred, however, only once a year, and the annual day of misbehaviour had previously been tolerated. The

---

[69] Berkshire RO, Abingdon Chamberlains' Accounts, 1775–1788, A/FAc/10.
[70] Centre for Kentish Studies, Dover Chamberlains' Accounts, 1700–1829, Do/FCa/7–8. Malcolmson gives a similar example from Northampton in his *Popular Recreations*, p. 121.
[71] *Ipswich Journal*, 17 Feb. 1759, 14 Feb. 1760.
[72] *Extracts from the Records in Portsmouth*, p. 515.
[73] Norfolk RO, Court of Mayoralty Book, 1747–1758, Case 16a/31, 160; *Norwich Mercury*, 10 March 1753.
[74] Berkshire RO, Newbury Borough Sessions Minute Book, 1739–1785, N/JQ/1/2.

change that was taking place in the second half of the eighteenth century was not a rise in humanitarian sentiment, but an erosion of this tolerance, and it was driven by a novel disinclination to endure the inconvenience of plebeian recreation in the public streets.

The campaign initiated against throwing at cocks in the middle of the eighteenth century was consequently narrower than has generally been assumed. The moral outbursts contained in newspapers and periodicals rarely commented upon the location of the sport, but in practice official action to suppress throwing at cocks was almost entirely confined to urban areas. The only rural magistrates to have taken steps to prohibit throwing at cocks in the eighteenth century were those of Essex where, in 1758, the justices at the quarter sessions in Chelmsford issued orders to all the con-stables in the county to suppress the sport on the forthcoming Shrove Tuesday.[75] The court was clearly motivated by the same concerns as their urban counterparts; its orders indicated that 'the many Riots and Mischiefs, and other Disorders committed by Persons following the cruel Practice' had determined them to 'prevent all such unlawful and disorderly Meetings and Practices'. This, however, appears to have been the only example of rural magistrates attempting to suppress the custom. Furthermore, the county of Essex had a very long tradition of moral regulation, and it is arguably more appropriate to view these orders against cock throwing in this context, rather than as a reflection of growing concerns about the treatment of animals.[76]

It is also probable that the Essex magistrates' orders met with very much less success. It was not possible for rural magistrates to effect proper super-vision of their constables in isolated areas, and this made their chances of success far slimmer. In neighbouring Cambridgeshire, city officials strug-gled to make their constables enforce orders prohibiting cock throwing: John Paris and George Brooks, both constables of Cambridge, were con-victed at quarter sessions in 1759 for failing to assist in apprehending all persons guilty of throwing at cocks on Shrove Tuesday,[77] and the difficulty of supervising constables in rural Essex would have been considerably greater. Certainly the constables failed to bring any offenders to quarter sessions following the magistrates' orders, and it is likely that in Essex, as elsewhere, the decline of the custom occurred considerably later.[78] In

---

[75] *Ipswich Journal*, 21 Jan. 1758.
[76] Wrightson and Levine, *Poverty and Piety*, pp. 110–41.
[77] *Annals of Cambridge*, iv, p. 302.
[78] Essex RO, Process Book of Indictments, 1742–1762, Q/SPb/14.

Warwickshire, for example, the justices were taking steps against the custom in the 1810s and 1820s; and in Buckinghamshire and Sussex, local historians working in the late nineteenth century gathered oral evidence for
its continuance in the rural villages a few decades beyond this.[79] The relative complacency of rural inhabitants to the sport reinforces the suggestion
that it was its location, rather than its morality, that underpinned the campaign against the sport in the eighteenth century. The orders against cock
throwing were almost entirely restricted to the public streets and squares;
they were inspired, that is, by concern about activities in certain places, and
not by more abstract concerns about qualities intrinsic to the sport itself.

Given the increasing hostility with which civic leaders viewed cock
throwing in urban centres, it is unsurprising to discover that a range of
other popular street games became the target of criticism in the second half
of the eighteenth century. The custom of playing football through the
streets—most common on Shrove Tuesday, but played in some towns at
other Easter festivals or on Christmas day—was viewed with increasing
hostility over the course of the century. Football at Shrovetide may once
have been as ubiquitous as throwing at cocks, but it had long attracted
criticism from the authorities on the grounds that it encouraged disorder
and distracted from archery practice, and had been subject to frequent
prohibition orders from the fourteenth century. By the eighteenth century,
although the game was still widely played on open land, a slow process of
attrition had eliminated football from the streets of most towns. By this
time, annual set matches of street football were played in no more than a
dozen or so places in the Midlands, Middlesex, Surrey, and in the outlying
counties of the north; and, although some of these games may indeed have
been several centuries old, it is likely that others, particularly some of those
in Middlesex and Surrey, were of more recent origin.[80] However, despite
the doubtful origins of many of these matches, football played through the
streets on Shrove Tuesday was regarded as an ancient local tradition in the
small number of communities in which it was played, and was invariably
prized accordingly.

Like cock throwing, football had only rarely enjoyed official support
but, whereas throwing at cocks was largely a children's pastime, set matches

---

[79] For Warwickshire and Buckinghamshire, see Malcolmson, *Popular Recreations*, p. 121; for
Sussex, see Bell-Irving, *Mayfield*, p. 16 (loc. hist.).
[80] Malcolmson, *Popular Recreations*, pp. 36–7; Hutton, *Stations of the Sun*, pp. 159–63; Marples,
History of Football, pp. 24–94; Walvin, *People's Game*, pp. 13–14, 17. See also two valuable local
studies: Alexander, 'Shrove Tuesday football', pp. 197–205; Delves, 'Popular recreation', pp.
89–127.

of football were very much the preserve of adult males. And, although these games did not attract official support, they certainly drew in individuals from the higher ranks of society. Reports of street football from the early nineteenth century frequently indicated the participation of respectable citizens; local notables occasionally even enjoyed the honour of opening the game. In Kingston-upon-Thames, for example, it was the mayor's privilege to kick the first ball,[81] and at Dorking, it was recalled, 'one of the principal tradesmen usually gave the first kick'.[82] Yet, this participation of local notables notwithstanding, these matches were widely agreed to be disruptive occasions. At the very least, street football caused disruption to the normal business of the town, requiring as it did the shutting of shops and the barricading of windows. At Hampton-on-Thames, for instance, where a match of football was played in the town each Shrove Tuesday, a local historian recalled how for much of the day 'trade was at a standstill, shops were closed, whilst the windows of most of the houses in the street . . . required the protection of hurdles &c'.[83]

Never exceeding more than one day a year, these matches arguably caused considerably less disruption to the normal business of the town than pleasure fairs, often spanning several days, and returning a number of times each year. Yet games of street football involved the invasion of the populace into the streets, giving these recreational events a very different quality from the civic fairs, sanctioned by the royal charters stored in the chests of the civic corporation. Football had no such official sanction, and it occupied a very different position in urban affairs from events managed and controlled by the ruling elite. Everywhere, street football was associated with chaos and disorder. At Ewell in Surrey, 'there were no sides, but free kicking by men and boys who rushed after the ball'.[84] A number of writers commented upon how the game was played with 'much spirit' or 'great spirit'.[85] In Dorking, football was played 'with a roughness extremely dangerous to the limbs of competitors'.[86] Furthermore, these games were essentially beyond the control of civic rulers. The great annual football match in Derby, a local historian remembered, was an occasion on which 'the unrestrained people took possession of the streets'.[87] Football matches permitted an uncontrolled, and

[81] Alexander, 'Shrove Tuesday football', p. 199.
[82] Rose, *Recollections*, p. 84.
[83] Ripley, *History of Hampton-on-Thames*, p. 108.
[84] Willis, *Short History of Ewell*, p. 107.
[85] Biden, *History of Kingston upon Thames*, 59; Fishwick, *History of Kirkham*, p. 206.
[86] *Notes and Queries*, 3rd ser., 2 March 1862, p. 224.
[87] Keys, *Reminiscences*, p. 36.

largely unsanctioned, descent of local men into the trading heart of the town, and this appropriation of the streets by the urban poor distinguished street football sharply from civic fairs and celebrations.

Attacks on street football at Shrovetide were always more infrequent than those against cock throwing, reflecting the much more limited extent of the practice, yet there are key similarities between the fortunes of the two pastimes over the eighteenth century. For example, moves to suppress street football followed a similar chronology to those against throwing at cocks, being initiated around 1750 and gathering pace towards the close of the century. In the eighteenth century, the authorities at Derby and Kingston both made repeated, though unsuccessful, attempts to prohibit the annual Shrove Tuesday football match in their towns; and in the nineteenth century the local authorities of most of the towns where the game persisted began taking similar steps to remove the game from their streets.[88]

Furthermore, it is possible to identify an essentially similar motivation for this interference. Just as the suppression of cock throwing was overwhelmingly an urban phenomenon, so these concerns about football were focused upon the game when played in civic streets and squares. At Kingston, for example, the magistrates gave notice of their intention to suppress the practice in 1799, giving as their reason simply 'the great nuisance' it caused to 'the Inhabitants and . . . persons travelling through the Town'.[89] Accordingly the resolution to many of these conflicts over football was to move the offending game out of the streets and onto fields on the outskirts of town. A contributor to the local paper during renewed conflict over the Derby match in the 1840s insisted that he had no wish to 'deprive the lovers of this sport of their enjoyment', but nevertheless felt it necessary 'to condemn the fitness of the place of its competition . . . instead of emanating from the centre of the town, let them assemble in the Siddals, or some such place, so as not to interfere with the avocation of the industrious part of the community'.[90] The Shrovetide match at Alnwick moved to a meadow provided by the Duke of Northumberland; and that at Twickenham to a field belonging to a certain Mr Cole. Similarly the matches at Kingston and Ashbourne both moved to fields on the periphery of town in the second half of the nineteenth century.[91]

---

[88] See Malcolmson, *Popular Recreations*, pp. 138–45. Also Delves, 'Popular recreation', pp. 89–91.

[89] Cited in Malcolmson, *Popular Recreations*, p. 139.

[90] Quoted in ibid., p. 143.

[91] References all quoted in ibid., pp. 142–3.

Not only these set matches, but also more informal football in the streets at other times of the year were countenanced with increasing intolerance as the century progressed. The streets had long formed the location of informal games of football between young men, most of which have left no mark of any kind on the historical record. James Spershott's memoirs of Chichester in the early eighteenth century recalled 'footballing in the streets day after day in frosty weather to the advantage of the glazier',[92] and, although Spershott's comment provides an isolated description of eighteenth-century street football, similar games were no doubt as common as frozen streets. All were viewed more doubtfully as the century wore on. In the 1740s it was decided at Worcester that 'football kicking' was unacceptable.[93] The game was also attacked in Louth in the 1750s.[94] The motivation behind these actions appears once more to have been to prevent the use of the streets for the purpose of recreation. When the Hull magistrates fined a man 40 shillings for playing football in the Sculcoates, the local newspaper justified this action by explaining that the police had been ordered to prevent any persons 'playing at games in the streets troublesome to the inhabitants'. Recent matches of football, the paper added, had been 'to the great annoyance and personal danger of the public'.[95]

It is clear that there was nothing about the playing of football that offended civic leaders. It was the location of the sport that was contentious. Football was just one of a range of plebeian street games that found themselves targets of repression in the eighteenth century, and the impulse behind these attacks on traditional games stemmed invariably from concerns about the location of the activity, rather than from any deeper anxieties about the activity itself. In the 1780s, the corporation at Gravesend paid its crier to prevent 'Air Baloons';[96] and the vestry at Wakefield paid its bellman to cry down 'flying kites in the streets'.[97] In Manchester, the Shrove Tuesday custom of lifting was cried down several times in the 1750s and 1760s; and in Worcester, in 1772, the corporation spent 2s 6d, 'for proclaiming not to throw snowballs'.[98] It was also around this time that the

---

[92] Spershott, *Memoirs*, p. 14.

[93] Noake, *Worcester in Olden Times*, p. 197.

[94] Lincolnshire Archives, Louth Wardens' Account Book, 1735–1777, LGS/B/3/2. Payment in 1754.

[95] *Hull Advertiser and Exchange Gazette*, 25 April 1818.

[96] Centre for Kentish Studies, Gravesend Chamberlains' Accounts, 1706–1784, Gr/FAc/3. Payment in 1783.

[97] Banks, *Walks in Yorkshire*, p. 86.

[98] Noake, *Worcester in Olden Times*, p. 197; *Constables' Accounts of Manchester*, iii, pp. 68, 81, 108–9, 119, 126, 163–4, 346.

authorities of Stamford began to take steps to prevent the annual bull-running in the streets of their town.[99] The authorities in Hull took action against the craze for 'velocipedes', an early form of bicycle which emerged in the 1820s. An editorial in the local newspaper complained one week about velocipedes on the foot pavements 'to the great annoyances of the passengers and inhabitants', and reported a 5 pound conviction for the same the next week.[100] In 1810, the practice of boys skating on the streets during cold weather had distressed inhabitants of the same town: the local paper reported that it had seen 'several ladies exceedingly annoyed by impertinent lads'. It continued: 'we beg with due respect to our magistrates, once more to suggest the propriety of some precautionary measure for the prevention of that most dangerous practice, skating in the streets during a frost'.[101]

The final decades of the eighteenth century saw determined resolution on the part of civic leaders to clear plebeian games of all kinds out of public streets. Their actions were motivated not simply by concern over the use of streets and squares for recreation, since their ongoing patronage of fairs and civic celebrations indicates that some measure of recreation in civic centres was broadly tolerated. At stake were concerns about order and control. It was plebeian recreations that were targeted for reform, games that were played without official sanction or involvement, and which threatened peace and order within the town. Yet it should not be assumed that civic rulers were entirely successful in their attempts to limit street recreation. Although they did restrict both cock throwing and football on Shrove Tuesday, their attempts to curtail the disorder associated with that other annual plebeian festival, Guy Fawkes, met far greater resistance, and were only partially successful. The fortunes of the annual celebrations on Fifth of November during the late eighteenth and early nineteenth centuries indicate not only that different sections of the urban community held different views about the legitimate uses of the public streets, but also that the urban poor, whilst without legal sanction for their views, were not without resources to enforce definitions of their own.

Guy Fawkes had traditionally been one of the most widely celebrated anniversaries. As monarchs and civic leaders refashioned the recreational calendar in the late sixteenth and seventeenth centuries, there emerged many variations in the occasions that local communities chose to com-

---

[99] Walsh, 'November bull-running', pp. 234–7.
[100] *Hull Advertiser and Exchange Gazette*, 3 July 1819, 10 July 1819.
[101] *Rockingham and Hull Weekly Advertiser*, 15 Dec. 1810. See also ibid., 5 Jan. 1811.

memorate, but the commemoration of Guy Fawkes' attempt to blow up the Houses of Parliament was almost universally recognised as an occasion fit for public celebration. As early as the 1620s, it had emerged as the most popular state commemoration in the calendar, 'far surpassing', in the opinion of Ronald Hutton, 'the royal birthday, accession day, or coronation day'.[102] And the occasion succeeded in maintaining this popularity for much of this and the following century. It is clear, even at this early date, that the celebrations extended far beyond the bell-ringing and gifts of wood provided by civic officials; and by the time of the Restoration, Guy Fawkes night had acquired all the characteristics that distinguished it from other occasions. In the 1660s Samuel Pepys noted boys flinging 'crackers' in the streets and bonfires so thick that coaches could not pass.[103] A Dutch visitor in 1662 likewise reported bonfires and 'a great lot of fireworks . . . let off and thrown amongst the people'.[104] Though state sponsored, most aspects of the annual celebration were firmly in the hands of the local population.

So when civic authorities ended their gifts of wood for the populace the impact was barely discernible. The custom largely disappears from official records, though there can be little doubt that it continued in the traditional way. Provincial newspapers periodically commented upon the 'usual demonstrations of joy',[105] the 'usual rejoicings',[106] or the 'usual solemnity'[107] on the anniversary of the Gunpowder Plot, and it is clear from the criticism about the custom that emerged in the late eighteenth century that Guy Fawkes celebrations had in no way diminished in the intervening years. In Cambridge in the 1780s, for example, it was celebrated 'in the *usual* manner, with squibs, crackers, rioting and mischief'.[108] By the nineteenth century, Guy Fawkes celebrations had in many places reached a large scale. A historian passing through Coventry in 1814 saw 'not less, I think, than twenty very large Fires in the narrow streets of that city, around which the thoughtless rabble were at the same time throwing firebrands, discharging pistols, guns &c'.[109] In Lincoln, in 1822, the local newspaper noted that 'the

---

[102] Hutton, *Stations of the Sun*, p. 395. See also ibid, *Rise and Fall*, pp. 183–5; Cressy, *Bonfires and Bells*, pp. 141–55.
[103] Pepys, *Diary*, 5 Nov. 1661, 5 Nov. 1664.
[104] Shellinks, *Journal of Shellinks*, p. 172.
[105] *Leeds Mercury*, 11 Nov. 1777.
[106] Ibid., 6 Nov. 1781.
[107] Ibid., 10 Nov. 1772.
[108] *Cambridge Chronicle*, 11 Nov. 1786.
[109] Farey, *General View of Derbyshire*, iii, pp. 629–30.

only thoroughfare through Lincoln was occupied from one extremity to the other by large bonfires, and fireworks of every description'.[110]

Inevitably, as throwing at cocks and playing football in town streets became unacceptable, so did the lighting of bonfires and fireworks on Guy Fawkes night become controversial. The boroughs of Kent, many of which had enthusiastically promoted bonfires in the early eighteenth century, were amongst the earliest towns to attack bonfires and fireworks in the streets at Guy Fawkes. Faversham, for example, first announced its intention to prevent Guy Fawkes celebrations in 1770, when it offered a reward of 10 shillings to be paid upon the conviction of every person selling or firing rockets or squibs in the town.[111] Dover and Gravesend issued similar orders the following decade.[112] Further attempts to abolish bonfires and fireworks in the streets may be found across all parts of England. In Guildford, an undated notice from the late eighteenth century forbidding all bonfires and squibs in the town survives;[113] the authorities of Louth,[114] Southampton,[115] Ipswich,[116] Worcester,[117] and Bath[118] all announced orders against bonfires and fireworks in the streets before 1800. By the nineteenth century, these actions had become extremely widespread, and may be found in many of the towns studied here: Sandwich, Leeds, Wakefield, Sheffield, Hull, Ripon, Lincoln, Northampton, Bristol, Cambridge, Stafford, Walsall, Birmingham, and Hitchen all attempted to suppress Guy Fawkes celebrations in the first quarter of the nineteenth century.[119] The researches of Robert Storch, Bob Bushaway, D. G. Paz, David Cressy, and

---

[110] *Stamford Mercury*, 8 Nov. 1822.

[111] Centre for Kentish Studies, Faversham Wardmote Book, 1741–1820, Fa/ACS, Year 1770.

[112] Centre for Kentish Studies, Dover Chamberlains' Accounts, 1700–1783, Do/FCa/7, 5 Nov. 1781; Gravesend Chamberlains' Accounts, 1706–1784, Gr/FAc/3, 29 Nov. 1784, and every November between 1789 and 1802.

[113] Surrey RO (Guildford), Guildford Mayors' Proclamations, BR/OC/2/7(3).

[114] Lincolnshire Archives, Louth Wardens' Account Book, 1735–1777, LGS/B/3/2, payments for crying against fireworks in 1765, 1774, 1776.

[115] *Hampshire Chronicle*, 10 Nov. 1788, 16 Nov. 1789.

[116] *Ipswich Journal*, 5 and 12 Nov. 1791.

[117] Noake, *Worcester in Olden Times*, p. 62.

[118] *Bath Journal*, 28 Sept. 1761.

[119] Sandwich (Centre for Kentish Studies, Sandwich Notices and Orders, Sa/Z6); Leeds (*Leeds Mercury*, 27 Sept. and 1 Nov. 1791, 2 Nov. 1816, 8 Nov. 1817); Wakefield (*Wakefield and Halifax Journal*, 23 Oct. 1822); Sheffield (*Sheffield Iris*, 4 Nov. 1823); Hull (*Rockingham and Hull Weekly Advertiser*, 13 Oct. and 10 Nov. 1810); Ripon (North Yorkshire CRO, Thirlway's Journal, 1835–1859, MIC 2563, 5 Nov. 1849); Lincoln (*Stamford Mercury*, 11 Nov. 1808, 10 Nov. 1809, 10 Nov. 1815, 10 Nov. 1818, 8 Nov. 1822, 11 Nov. 1825, 10 Nov. 1826, 9 Nov. 1827); Northampton (*Northampton Mercury*, 5 Nov. 1801); Bristol (ibid., 2 Nov. 1811);

Ronald Hutton have uncovered many more in other regions.[120] Attempts to suppress popular Guy Fawkes celebrations were made in towns in every part of England, and the provincial newspapers that reported these actions were unanimous in their support.

Yet, in contrast to orders prohibiting cock throwing on Shrove Tuesday, which generally produced the desired effect within a number of years, these attempts to restrict bonfires and fireworks in public streets were rarely respected. Orders against bonfires and fireworks were disobeyed from the outset. In Faversham, a loose document from 1785 containing notes of a meeting of the town's 'principal inhabitants' discussing new measures to prevent bonfires and fireworks in the streets, suggests that their attempts during the previous fifteen years had not been successful;[121] and in Gravesend, the town crier was paid to cry down fireworks in early November for almost twenty years following the first such payment in 1784.[122] And such experiences were entirely typical. In Lincoln, the local newspaper noted magistrates' orders against lighting bonfires and throwing fireworks had simply created a 're-action', which had in turn produced a mob 'determined not to be so deprived of their long-established yearly sport'.[123] Few towns had managed to diminish the scale of popular Guy Fawkes celebrations to any significant extent by the end of the eighteenth century. Instead, prohibition orders triggered a set of battles that were to run in many towns through much of the first half of the nineteenth century.

These battles can only be understood if the significance of the location of Guy Fawkes celebrations is properly grasped. Universally, bonfires were burned in the centre of town—'in the middle of the market place',[124] 'on the Market Hill',[125] 'at the Market Cross'.[126] At the same time, squibs,

---

Cambridge (*Cambridge Chronicle*, 2 Nov. 1810); Stafford (*Staffordshire Advertiser*, 8 Nov. 1828); Walsall (ibid., 11 Nov. 1837); Birmingham (*Aris's Birmingham Gazette*, 11 Nov. 1822); Hitchen (Hertfordshire ALS, Minute Book of Special Sessions for the Half Hundred of Hitchen, 1808–1825, PS12/2/3, order against fireworks and bonfires in the town every year 1815–23, except 1816).

[120] Storch, 'Please to remember', pp. 71–99, esp. 74–7, 86–93; Bushaway, *By Rite*, pp. 67–71; Paz, 'Bonfire night', pp. 316–28; Cressy, 'Fifth of November', pp. 68–90, esp. 84–5; Hutton, *Stations of the Sun*, pp. 393–407.

[121] Centre for Kentish Studies, Faversham Draft Orders, Fa/AZ/79.

[122] Centre for Kentish Studies, Gravesend Chamberlains' Accounts, 1784–1852, Gr/FAc/4. Payments in 1784, 1789–1802.

[123] *Lincoln Mercury*, 11 Nov. 1808.

[124] Hird, *Annals of Bedale*, p. 86; Swanton, *Bygone Haslemere*, p. 287.

[125] Hobley, 'Autobiography', p. 332.

[126] North Yorkshire CRO, Thirlway's Journal, 1835–1859, MIC 2563, 5 Nov. 1838.

crackers, and rockets were fired there and in the streets around. To build fires in any other location was unthinkable. Consequently, occasional attempts to lure the people away from the streets to a municipally funded bonfire on fields at the edge of town were destined to fail. At Southampton, for instance, the mayor made a present of one hundred faggots to the populace on the condition that the bonfire should be made on the Marsh rather than at the Market Square; but as soon as the fire burnt out the populace assembled in the town and built another in its centre.[127] At Exeter, the mayor 'purchased a variety of fireworks to be let off in the field near the Alexandra Nurseries' in an attempt to prevent the annual bonfire in the Cathedral Yard. But here as well the people returned to the town once the display was over and set about constructing bonfires in the traditional place.[128]

Such attempts to provide bonfires and fireworks in an alternative place were doomed to failure, since it was not the bonfires in and of themselves that were valued. Guy Fawkes celebrations were about more than bonfires and fireworks to those who participated in them. They were an integral part of the urban experience, the moment each year when the usual order of things was inverted, when those who generally stood outside the formal mechanisms of power temporarily took control over their local environment. Following Guy Fawkes celebrations in Colchester in the 1840s, it was noted: 'On occasion of public rejoicing, there are collected a number of idle and loose characters, fully ripe for any mischief. So it was this evening; about forty such paraded the High Street, armed with great cudgels and walking six abreast to the annoyance of the peaceable spectators.'[129] At Burford, Oxfordshire, 'The town was entirely given over to the rough element.'[130] At Dorking, 'the streets of the town were the scene of unrestrainable lawlessness'.[131] It was the one night of the year when the urban poor became masters of the streets, the last remnant of a centuries-old tradition of plebeian recreation in public thoroughfares. And given this, the tenacity with which they held onto the custom may be more readily understood.

We have traced in this and the previous chapter the history of popular recreation in civic streets and squares from the Restoration until the early nineteenth century. It is clear there was much diversity in the way that different recreational traditions fared, and it is difficult to resolve the various

[127] Bushaway, *By Rite*, p. 68.
[128] Cossins, *Reminiscences*, p. 68.
[129] Wire, 'Diary', 5 Nov. 1846, p. 179.
[130] Quoted in Bushaway, *By Rite*, p. 73.
[131] Rose, *Recollections*, p. 88.

trends that have been identified here into a neat, linear narrative. Indeed, the value of general conclusions must be questioned, since the history of the cultural and recreational uses of urban streets overspills any timeframe we might attempt to impose. The Restoration was deployed here as the starting point for discussion, but this is clearly not the origin of street games, simply a date of convenience. Determining a point of conclusion is even more problematic, as there is no time at which street recreations drew to a close. This account ends in the early nineteenth century, but fairs, civic celebrations, and Guy Fawkes night all continued to evolve through the century, adapting to the changing conditions imposed by urbanisation and population growth. Street recreations should arguably be conceived in a framework of ongoing change that could be continued until the present day.

Nevertheless, a handful of general conclusions hold out. Fairs were unquestionably the most resilient of the street recreations surveyed here; and civic celebrations and public thanksgivings, though much changed in form, likewise managed to survive in their traditional location. But, alongside these customs that managed to adapt to the harsher climate of the later eighteenth century were others that made the passage less successfully. The eighteenth century undeniably witnessed a gradual erosion of those that were more plebeian in character: football and cock throwing were largely eliminated, and Guy Fawkes celebrations were put under pressures that eventually resulted in significant changes in their form.

The transition that had occurred is captured in an account of anniversary celebrations in the small Northamptonshire town of Towcester in 1809. Here, as elsewhere, a large-scale public demonstration of joy was anticipated in order to celebrate the fiftieth anniversary of George III's coronation. The 'opulent inhabitants' of the town agreed that 'the Market hill appeared to be the best adapted for the festal scene', and they set about organising a public dinner fit for the event to include all local inhabitants, both humble and mighty. They ascertained the probable expense of entertaining upwards of 1,000 inhabitants with roast beef, plumb pudding, and ale, purchased provisions, and then instructed the town crier that 'the presence of the poor inhabitants, men, women, and children, was requested for the occasion'.[132] Though well intentioned, it was an invitation that would have made no sense at the time of the Restoration. It is a measure of how much had been accomplished over the eighteenth century that the urban poor were now tolerated in the civic centre by invitation only.

---

[132] *Northampton Mercury*, 4 Nov. 1809.

5

Bull-baiting: intellectual history

The reasons for the disappearance of blood sports in England have perhaps been considered too obvious to merit deep reflection. No one questions the cruelty or barbarity of bear-baiting or cockfighting. It is considered natural that as society became more civilised and refined, so more people would 'see' the cruelty inherent in blood sports, and be inclined to reject them. Thus historians have tended to anchor campaigns to abolish animal combat sports in increasing compassion for animals. Keith Thomas has argued that effective campaigns against these recreations stemmed from 'a combination of religious piety and bourgeois sensibility'; Ronald Hutton has related them to 'a growth in humanitarian sentiment'; and Richard Ryder to 'genuine humane feeling'.[1] Such trends—an increase in compassion for animals, the decline of blood sports—have been treated as normal, rather than problematic. Even Robert Malcolmson, who was by no means dewy-eyed about the march of progress, was forced to concede that greater concern for animal suffering had helped to number the days of certain animal sports.[2]

I think these connections between a rise in sensitivity for animal suffering and the suppression of time-honoured recreations have been too quickly made. Furthermore, these assumptions have inhibited historical enquiry into these sports, and more specifically into their disappearance from England. If blood sports are 'barbaric', we can explain the eventual disappearance of sports such as bull-baiting by appealing to the apparently timeless tendency of societies to move towards a state of civilisation. If certain sports are cruel, then their elimination becomes simply a question of timing; their inherent cruelty ensures the inevitability (and propriety) of their eventual disappearance, and all that needs to be explained is why it was at *this* time that large numbers of people began, at last, to realise that

[1] Thomas, *Man and Natural World*, p. 159; Hutton, *Stations of the Sun*, p. 357; Ryder, *Animal Revolution*, p. 89. See also E. S. Turner, *Heaven in a Rage*, pp. 65–75, 119–20; Harrison, 'Animals and the state', p. 786; J. Turner, *Reckoning*, pp. 15–37; Kean, *Animal Rights*, pp. 31–2.
[2] Malcolmson, *Popular Recreations*, pp. 124–5.

these sports were unacceptably cruel. In the nineteenth century, the timing of most historical change was explained with reference to the march of civilisation; modern historians of blood sports rightly eschew this version of history and, in a period of rapid economic, demographic and social change, they have had no difficulty in suggesting alternative contenders. Humanitarianism, evangelicalism, modernisation, urbanisation—all have been invoked to explain why educated society at last became sensitive to the cruelty of certain popular blood sports.

But the most cursory glance at blood sports in other contexts—for example, foxhunting in England, cockfighting in France, bull-fighting in Spain—suggests that modern societies do not invariably turn to parliament to prohibit sports that involve animal blood. There was, of course, nothing natural or inevitable about the decline of plebeian blood sports in the early nineteenth century, and we are closing down enquiry into a corner of English social history with no good reason if we continue to accept that popular blood sports were simply a casualty of the passage of time. Discussions about blood sports were complex, and took a far from predictable form: the complaints that emerged in the late eighteenth century were not the spontaneous flowering of humane sentiment, the inevitable product of an industrialising, modernising, civilising society. Not only were they constructed and disseminated in a historically specific way, but the relationship between these complaints and the actual elimination of blood sports from England was likewise historically specific. The emergence of new concerns about popular blood sports and their eventual disappearance were complex historical events and the relationship between the two is not something that can be simply assumed. But let us begin at the beginning. Arguments which tie the elimination of blood sports to a rise in humanitarianism are built upon an assumption that concern for animal suffering was becoming increasingly widespread. Let us therefore attempt to establish the extent of concern for animal suffering in eighteenth-century England.

Compassion for animals?

There was undoubtedly some quickening of interest in animal welfare in the late eighteenth century. Following a near total silence on the problem of animal cruelty through most of the century, the final decade saw a small flurry of publications addressing the treatment of animals. Yet, although this period witnessed an interest in animal welfare that was greater than anything known previously, the tracts, sermons, and pamphlets concerned with

animal welfare remained few in number, and discussion on the treatment
of animals was far from widespread. According to the *Eighteenth-century
Short Title Book Catalogue,* there were no more than fifteen pamphlets,
books, and sermons wholly or in large part focused upon the treatment of
animals published before 1800. Roughly half of these were printed in the
1790s, the others had appeared sporadically from about 1760; none was
reprinted.[3] It is not difficult to find contemporaneous issues which gener-
ated a very much larger number of texts. Richard Green's catalogue of
eighteenth-century anti-Methodist publications lists 606 items in its bibliography, though considerably less mainstream topics also managed to
arouse a greater level of interest than animal welfare.[4] Leland Warren, for
example, has shown that more than fifty works were produced before 1800
largely concerned with the topic of conversation, and that many of these
passed through numerous editions.[5] From the 1790s, a pattern of about five
works published each decade largely devoted to the treatment of animals
was established, and a few of the more popular works were reprinted; but
it was not for a further forty years, until the 1830s, that the annual output
increased noticeably from this. Thus the record from the publication of
works concerned with the treatment of animals would suggest that the
topic was of very marginal interest in the eighteenth century. According to
this, albeit rather crude, measure, the promotion of more careful use of the
art of conversation was more interesting to the middle classes than the
problem of animal cruelty.

The case for eighteenth-century interest in the treatment of animals
looks slightly stronger if the periodicals are included in our survey. Steele's
and Addison's early-eighteenth-century papers, the *Tatler* (1709–11) and
Guardian (1713), both included an essay on the treatment of animals, and
they appear to have set a tradition that many of their successors continued.[6]
The *Gentleman's Magazine,* established in 1731, included two articles in its
first decade; the *London Magazine,* founded a year later, included an essay
entitled 'Cruelty to animals' in its first number.[7] Other major eighteenth-
century review journals, such as the *Monthly Review* and the *Critical Review,*
and literary magazines, such as the *European Review* and the *Universal*

---

[3] There are, in addition, a very small number of texts cited in eighteenth-century review
magazines, such as the *Monthly Review,* of which no copies appear to be extant, and which
are therefore not included in the *Eighteenth-century Short Title Book Catalogue.*

[4] Green, *Anti-Methodist Publications.*

[5] Warren, 'Turning reality round', p. 66.

[6] *Tatler,* 16 Feb. 1710; *Guardian,* 24 May 1713.

[7] *Gentleman's Magazine,* Jan. 1736, p. 10, Jan. 1737, pp. 6–8; *London Magazine,* May 1732, p. 65.

Magazine, all included essays on the treatment of animals, as did many of the less long-running ones.

But the form and quality of these contributions varied widely, and it is not possible to place them all squarely in the animal protection tradition. Some took the form of fiction and poetry, and may perhaps be more appropriately placed in a literary tradition;[8] others, such as controversial pieces about cruelty to insects, and the cruelty of hunting, elicited responses rejecting the arguments;[9] yet others were no more than ten or fifteen lines long.[10] Furthermore, owing to the eighteenth-century convention of reprinting pieces from rival publications, the same essays tended to reappear more than once, thereby slightly reducing the number of original contributions. Even if we count all these contributions in the most inclusive way possible, we are forced to conclude that animal cruelty was not widely discussed in the eighteenth century: a few of the more ephemeral papers never addressed animal cruelty; and though the more substantial papers generally did, contributions tended to be sporadic.[11] The *European Magazine* and *London Magazine* both produced only one or two essays on animal cruelty a decade throughout the century.[12] In the *Gentleman's Magazine* there were initially rather more than this, though interest seemed to wane in the second half of the century; but in the *Universal Magazine*, there were far fewer.[13] In the two major eighteenth-century review magazines we find one, the *Monthly Review,* with rather more than two contributions each decade; and the other, the *Critical Review,* with fewer.

[8] See, for example, *Gentleman's Magazine*, June 1747, p. 292; *Adventurer*, 18 Nov. 1752, pp. 22–30, 13 March 1753, pp. 217–22; *World*, 19 Aug. 1756, pp. 145–52; *Literary Magazine*, May–June 1756, pp. 102–3.

[9] For insects, see *Gentleman's Magazine*, Sept. 1771, pp. 401–2; Nov. 1771, pp. 486–7. For hunting, see *Monthly Review*, Sept. 1781, pp. 220–1; this review elicited a pamphlet 'Hunting vindicated from cruelty, in a letter to the Monthly Reviewers', reviewed in the *Monthly Review*, July 1782, pp. 21–4. See also ibid., July 1782, pp. 17–21.

[10] See, for example, *Gentleman's Magazine*, Jan. 1753, p. 5.

[11] For papers that never considered the issue, see *Rambler*, 1750–2; *Gray's Inn Journal*, 1752–4; *Bristol and Bath Magazine*, 1782–3. *Analytical Review*, 1788–99, is one major periodical that never gave the subject serious attention.

[12] The actual dates are *European Magazine*, Nov. 1786, pp. 321–3; Jan. 1796, pp. 51–3. *London Magazine,* May 1732, pp. 65–6; Dec. 1747, p. 606; July 1748, pp. 291–2; June 1753, pp. 132–4, 279–80; Feb. 1763, pp. 70–1; July 1768, p. 343; Jan. 1774, p. 20.

[13] The dates are *Gentleman's Magazine*, Jan. 1736, p. 10; Jan. 1737, pp. 6–8; June 1747, p. 292; April 1749, pp. 447–8; Jan. 1750, pp. 18–19; Nov. 1752, pp. 522–5; June 1754, p. 255; Feb. 1756, p. 56; May 1761, pp. 201–2; Jan. 1762, pp. 6–7; Feb. 1781, p. 72; Jan. 1789, pp. 15–17; Sept. 1800, p. 848. *Universal Magazine*, Feb. 1759, pp. 58–9; April 1782, pp. 176–8; March 1786, pp. 146–7; Dec. 1788, pp. 287–9; Jan. 1800, pp. 5–10.

In general, as with books, pamphlets, and sermons, the periodicals' concern with animal cruelty was more sustained from the 1790s, remaining nevertheless at a fairly low level. We also find, however, that interest divides quite clearly along political lines: certain periodicals, for example the *British Review,* founded in 1811, and the *Quarterly Review,* started in 1809, printed no articles on the treatment of animals in the first quarter of the nineteenth century; yet others, for example the *British Critic,* founded 1793, and *Blackwood's Magazine,* founded 1817, printed articles that either opposed or ridiculed the animal protection message.[14] By contrast, those that regularly participated in discussions of the treatment of animals had distinctive political–religious profiles. It was in periodicals which were nonconformist in religion and liberal in politics, such as the *Eclectic Review* and *London Magazine,* that most of the articles about cruelty to animals were published.[15] Other periodicals committed to animal protection include the *Methodist Magazine, Wesleyan Methodist Magazine,* and *Primitive Methodist Magazine.*[16] All periodicals, however, were outdone in concern for the treatment of animals by the *Monthly Magazine,* in which editorials discussed the progress of animal protection societies and legislation, important parliamentary speeches were reprinted, and regular and occasional correspondents sent in examples of cruelty to animals they had witnessed. During some years (for example, 1808 and 1809) the *Monthly Magazine* addressed the problem of animal cruelty in almost every issue; it was not until the 1820s and 1830s that any other paper gave animal cruelty such a high profile.[17] However, the *Monthly* was not only a liberal, nonconformist paper; its editor was also a vegetarian, and cruelty to animals was no doubt a subject close to his heart—such characteristics make it far from representative of early-nineteenth-century society. This survey of the monthly periodicals in the eighteenth and early nineteenth centuries does not then alter the picture of very limited concern for animal welfare before 1800, increasing only gradually after that date. It also suggests, however, that the higher levels of interest were, at least initially, not the consequence of a general raising of

---

[14] *British Critic,* Sept. 1800, p. 334; *Blackwood's Magazine,* Nov. 1827, pp. 587–93. See also articles in the *Edinburgh Review,* April 1803, pp. 128–36; Jan. 1809, pp. 333–43.
[15] See *Eclectic Review,* May 1809, p. 485; Feb. 1810, pp. 184–6; Aug. 1810, pp. 756–7; Nov. 1810, pp. 975–97; June 1813, pp. 634–45. *London Magazine,* Nov. 1822, pp. 388–402; Dec. 1822, pp. 531–6.
[16] *Methodist Magazine,* Nov. 1807, pp. 490–9; Dec. 1807, pp. 540–52; Sept. 1813, pp. 704–6; Oct. 1814, pp. 790–2. *Wesleyan Methodist Magazine,* Sept. 1822, p. 582; May 1826, pp. 310–15. *Primitive Methodist Magazine,* 1819, pp. 7–8, 56–7, 218, 132–3; 1821, pp. 12–14; 1823, p. 255.
[17] For example, the *Mirror of Literature, Amusement, and Instruction,* 1822–49.

awareness of the problem of animal cruelty, but rather of the emergence of a distinct socio-religious grouping committed to improving the lot of animals: we find, that is, a small but vociferous pressure group in the midst of a wider public largely indifferent to cruelty to animals.

Finally, the local newspapers lend considerable support to this view. With estimates of weekly circulation figures of up to 10,000 copies, local newspapers were more widely read than both books (editions typically ran to about 1,000 copies) and periodicals (monthly circulation figures of the more popular periodicals surveyed above were generally between 3,000 and 5,000); and they are therefore a useful gauge of public opinion.[18] They contain few expressions of compassion for animals before the nineteenth century, and almost nothing to indicate that new concerns about cruelty towards animals were spreading through society.[19] Animals appeared frequently in the columns of the provincial newspapers, but papers almost never addressed the issue of animal cruelty: animals appear as 'stolen or strayed' horses and dogs; as prize pigs and cattle;[20] as freaks (deformed animals were usually newsworthy);[21] as so many vermin killed by sportsmen;[22] as exhibits in a menagerie well worth a visit;[23] as horses or dogs or livestock killed by lightning (or meeting some other untoward premature death);[24] as infant-killing pigs;[25] as cocks about to fight;[26] as bulls to be baited,[27] but not as suffering creatures to be pitied and protected.

[18] Figures cited in *English Literary Periodicals*, ii, p. xvii.

[19] These comments are based upon the *Norfolk Chronicle*, *Norwich Mercury*, *Sussex Weekly Advertiser*, *Northampton Mercury*, and *Newcastle Courant* during the years 1760–1800.

[20] For John Smith's 'thumping large Hog', see *Sussex Weekly Advertiser*, 22 March 1779—on this occasion the public were invited along to watch the slaughter. For a fat sheep, see *Northampton Mercury*, 20 Jan. 1787. For a fat ox, *Newcastle Courant*, Feb. 1807.

[21] *Norfolk Chronicle*, 12 April 1783; *Northampton Mercury*, 9 Jan. 1802.

[22] *Norwich Mercury*, 22 Oct. 1768; *Norfolk Chronicle*, 31 March 1781.

[23] *Northampton Mercury*, 2 Dec. 1776, 13 Dec. 1794; *Norwich Mercury*, 18 Jan. 1783.

[24] Six cows fall down a pit, *Norwich Mercury*, 16 Jan. 1768; a horse killed by bees, ibid., 2 July 1768; animals killed by lightning, *Newcastle Courant*, 21 July 1783, 16 July 1792; a sheep dug out alive after lying under snow six weeks, ibid., 15 Jan. 1785; four horses in a pit explosion 'torn to pieces, and [thrown] to an astonishing height in the air', ibid., 6 Dec. 1773.

[25] *Northampton Mercury*, 5 June 1790, 19 Nov. 1791. On one occasion a pig killed a man; see *Newcastle Courant*, 28 Jan. 1786.

[26] Notices of forthcoming cockfights were extremely common down to 1800. See, for example, *Newcastle Courant*, 7 June 1760; *Norwich Mercury*, 14 March 1767; *Sussex Weekly Advertiser*, 19 March 1787; *Northampton Mercury*, 1 Jan. 1791.

[27] Reports in *Northampton Mercury*, 7 Jan. 1781, 10 Dec. 1785; *Norfolk Chronicle*, 31 March 1781. Adverts in *Sussex Weekly Advertiser*, 26 Nov. 1787, 17 and 24 Dec. 1787, 17 March 1788, 15 Dec. 1788.

A rare exception to this indifference to animal cruelty may be found in the *Norfolk Chronicle* in 1783, when a reader wrote to remonstrate against the cruel treatment endured by horses at the hands of drovers. But the letter was a response to a report of a farmer's servant beating a ewe to death in the previous week's paper, and there had been no remark or comment on the servant's actions either there, or in the *Norwich Mercury* which had also reported the case.[28] Thus if the most forward-thinking metropolitan presses were generally unenthusiastic about animal protection, the less progressive local papers, and their readers, were almost entirely indifferent. The animal protection message appears to have made little impact on provincial England before the nineteenth century. Although books, pamphlets, and periodicals all provide some evidence for concern about animal suffering in the eighteenth and early nineteenth centuries, the local press indicate the restricted extent of these concerns. Their indifference towards concerns about animal suffering undermines the contention that a widespread change in attitudes towards the treatment of animals occurred before the 1820s.

Evidence from eighteenth-century private diaries and journals further reinforces the suggestion that novel concerns about cruelty to animals had not penetrated deep into provincial England. Journals and diaries indicate that animals were generally regarded as property rather than pets; thus it was the purchase, fattening, disease, sale, slaughter, and death of animals that were routinely recorded, not their well-being, foibles, and temperament. Ill health or suffering in animals were viewed uncompromisingly through the prism of economics, not compassion, as the musings of William Holland, a Somerset parson, upon the subject of his lame horse demonstrate. He rode his horse out one day, although,

> [it] seemed very lame and [had] a stiffness in the left front leg and he is uncommonly thin and poor . . . The horse continued indifferent and weak but in coming homewards towards the Blacksmith's down he went to the ground and there we lay sprawling. I soon got up and the horse afterwards. This will not do, I cant think what is the matter with him . . . I only consider him taken on a trial . . . the horse is not well, he has worms I think. I have not paid for him yet neither am I inclined to.[29]

The very prosaic terms in which the killing of animals was recorded powerfully reinforces the impression that animals were viewed primarily in economic terms in the eighteenth century:

[28] *Norfolk Chronicle*, 12 July 1783; *Norwich Mercury*, 19 July 1783.
[29] Holland, *Diary*, 11–12 Feb. 1812, p. 231.

My old dog Quon was killed and baked for his grease of which he yielded 11lb.[30]

The Grey Colt could not rise, so we knocked it on the head this morning. Sold the skin for 2s.[31]

I had a mad dog in my kennel, and was obliged to kill all my hounds. Six of them were all hanging at the same time.[32]

[Ordered] Phin. Penn. to take out the cart Team the old horse named Duke being worn out with age & useless & not able to earn his meals in order to be killed for Mr Shelleys dogs.[33]

Dogs killed the tame rabbits. Hanged the dog Sanco this afternoon.[34]

Had the Horse over to Mr Marchants Street that horse I Bot the 19 Instant killed him for the Dogs.[35]

The quotations illustrate that animals were regarded as a form of property in the eighteenth century; when they had ceased being useful, they were killed. Owners were not sentimental about this, and they rarely expressed sorrow or sadness over the loss of an animal, though the financial implications of an animal's death were likely to be commented upon. Indeed, the diaries suggest that economic historians who have attempted to evaluate the financial significance of the animal population in pre-industrial England have been more faithful to contemporary perceptions about the place of animals in society than the intellectual historians who have detected increasing concern about animal welfare during this period.[36]

This leaves the argument that the decline of blood sports was a consequence of a new appreciation of animal suffering standing on weak foundations. It is not that intellectual historians who have identified a shift in opinion regarding the proper treatment of animals have been incorrect, but the extent of this shift must be challenged. Examples of concern for animal suffering may be found, yet they are simply too few to sustain the view that attitudes towards animals were sharply redefined during this period, and it

---

[30] Richards, 'Extracts from diary', 16 Sept. 1698, p. 412.

[31] Marchant, *Diary*, 24 Jan. 1718, p. 182.

[32] [Stapley], 'Domestic habits', 5 Oct. 1739, p. 51 (diar.).

[33] Tompkins, 'Diary', 28 Jan. 1769, p. 21.

[34] Hardy, *Diary*, 31 July 1780, p. 37.

[35] Burgess, *Diary and Letters*, 27 Dec. 1788, p 96.

[36] Thompson, 'Horse sense', pp. 60–81. Compare with Harwood, *Love for Animals*; E. S. Turner, *Heaven in a Rage*; J. Turner, *Reckoning*; Thomas, *Man and Natural World*; Ryder, *Animal Revolution*; Kean, *Animal Rights*.

is unconvincing to anchor the disappearance of certain blood sports in the rise of new concerns about animal cruelty when no such shift can be located.

How then are we to explain the decline of blood sports? Certainly it is not possible to appreciate the fortunes of blood sports in the nineteenth century without investigating further the concepts of cruelty and compassion, but we need to understand these terms differently. A language of cruelty was deployed but, rather than assume this language maps onto a newly awakened sensibility towards animal welfare in a neat and straightforward way, it is necessary to think more carefully about the role that language played in forging these sensibilities. In essence this requires turning around the central assumption of the existing historiography—situating discussions of blood sports not as reflections of a shift in attitudes towards animals, but as the source of new ideas. Within the space of a few decades, the long neglected sport of bull-baiting became one of the most widely debated cultural issues of the day, and, rather than appeal to a barely discernible compassion for animal suffering, it is to this discourse that we must turn if we are to understand both the place of popular blood sports in English society, and their eventual disappearance.

A new discourse

It is not hard to find discussions of popular blood sports in the late eighteenth century. We noted in the first chapter how difficult it was to reconstruct bull-baiting in market towns, owing to the near total absence of commentary upon the pastime that was enjoyed at municipal bull-rings. Yet, within decades, discussions of bull-baiting could be found almost everywhere. A plebeian pastime that had long been situated on the periphery of public consciousness moved rapidly and decisively to the centre, and the manner in which it did so raises a number of questions to be explored.

The awakening of interest in popular blood sports is nowhere seen more clearly than in the periodical and newspapers presses. Discussions about animal cruelty in the books and pamphlets dedicated to animal welfare ranged over issues as varied and specialist as riding post-chaise,[37] epicurism,[38] horse-racing and trotting races,[39] the dissection of live animals in

---

[37] *Familiar Essays*, p. 164; Richmond, *Sermon on Sin*, pp. 11–12.
[38] See Granger, *Apology for Brute*, p. 14; Macaulay, *Essay on Cruelty*, p. 37.
[39] Drummond, *Rights of Animals*, pp. 98–100.

universities,[40] and the gentlemen's sports of hunting, shooting, and fishing.[41] We have already noted that these themes made little impact in papers and periodicals, but such indifference towards animal protection did not extend to popular blood sports. These publications generally were interested in the problem of blood sports, and they tended to pay greater attention to a small number of popular pastimes than to any of the other issues associated with the animal protection debate.

Consider, for instance, the eighteenth century's foremost monthly magazine, the *Gentleman's*. The paper began criticising the Shrove Tuesday sport of throwing at cocks in its first decade and regularly inserted critical notices and letters about the custom until the 1760s. Other forms of animal cruelty were occasionally featured in the magazine—hunting was once condemned, as were insect anatomists, 'barbaric drovers', and trotting matches—nevertheless, until the 1760s condemnations of throwing at cocks formed the staple of their discussions about the treatment of animals.[42] From that date, however, the periodical inexplicably lost interest in the ancient Shrovetide sport. After 1762, just one further article on cock throwing appeared and, with the end of the paper's interest in cock throwing, discussions of animal cruelty petered out virtually altogether for the next fifty years. For a few decades, throwing at cocks had captured public interest, but the problem of animal cruelty more generally apparently failed to sustain interest.

The *Gentleman's* major rival, the *London Magazine*, also gave uneven coverage to different instances of animal cruelty. During its first two decades, it printed a number of general essays concerned with the treatment of animals, but from the 1750s the paper's concern for animals waned and its focus narrowed. From 1754 until the paper's demise in 1785 a further three articles on animal cruelty were printed; in contrast, however, to the earlier essays, which had each considered several examples of the mistreatment of animals, all of these were wholly devoted to condemning either throwing at cocks or cockfighting.[43] And the same pattern is identifiable in many other periodicals. The short-lived nineteenth-century *London Magazine*, 1820–9, carried two articles on animal cruelty during its lifetime, the longest and most significant of which was a piece of fiction

---

[40] Youatt, *Humanity to Brutes*, pp. 194–206.
[41] Young, *Essay on Humanity*, pp. 73–85.
[42] *Gentleman's Magazine*, Jan. 1737, pp. 6–8; June 1747, p. 292; April 1749, pp. 147–8; Jan. 1750, pp. 18–19; May 1761, pp. 201–2; Jan. 1762, pp. 6–7; Feb. 1781, p. 72.
[43] References in footnote 13 above.

critical of cockfighting.[44] The *British Critic,* a nineteenth-century review magazine, only twice considered animal cruelty before 1810, and on both occasions addressed the problem of bull-baiting.[45] The *Mirror* was another nineteenth-century periodical that failed to investigate animal cruelty beyond blood sports—even going so far as to rename Richard Martin's Cruelty to Animal's Bill the 'Bear-Baiting Bill'.[46] It is by no means accurate to suggest that all eighteenth- and early-nineteenth-century periodicals were interested in cruelty to animals only in so far as it involved cock-fighting and bull-baiting: some of the major periodicals, such as the *European Magazine* and *Monthly Review,* showed no significant bias towards popular blood sports in their analyses of animal cruelty; nor did the *Universal Magazine,* once it began addressing the subject at all in the 1780s. But in general the magazines tended to be selective in their concern for animal suffering, and the trend was to focus on a small number of animal sports.

This tendency was most marked, however, in local newspapers. In contrast to their near total silence on the subject of animal protection, vitriolic condemnations of bull-baiting, and more rarely cockfighting, had become commonplace in these publications by the nineteenth century. In fact, until the 1790s, local papers had carried occasional reports and advertisements for 'rustic' sports such as bear- and bull-baitings and bull-runnings. A procession of bulls, badgers, and bears recently (or soon to be) baited appeared in the columns of local papers through much of the eighteenth century. A bear-baiting on ice at Bridgwater, a bull-running for women at Bridge Casterton,[47] a bull provided by the gentlemen of Newcastle for the amusement of the poor,[48] a bull-bait on the race course at Ipswich,[49] and numerous bull- and badger-baits at inns and public houses around Sussex, Essex, and Berkshire were amongst the entertainments offered to the readers of local newspapers.[50]

---

[44] *London Magazine,* Nov. 1822, pp. 389–402.

[45] *British Critic,* Sept. 1800, p. 334; May 1802, p. 542.

[46] *Mirror,* 28 July 1825, 4 June 1825.

[47] *Northampton Mercury,* 7 Jan. 1781, 10 Dec. 1785.

[48] *Newcastle Courant,* 21 Jan. 1768.

[49] *Ipswich Journal,* 30 Oct. 1784.

[50] In *Sussex Weekly Advertiser,* report of a badger-bait 13 May 1770, adverts for bull-baiting 24 Dec. 1787, 15 Jan. 1788. In *Chelmsford Chronicle,* adverts for bull-baiting 31 Dec. 1784, 23 June 1786. In *Reading Mercury,* adverts for bull-baiting 15 Feb. 1779, 1 May 1780, 6 Nov. 1786. See also *Leeds Intelligencer,* an accident at a bull-bait at Beeston, 3 Sept. 1782; *Nottingham Journal,* a bull-bait in Newark market place, 6 Jan. 1781; *Aris's Birmingham Gazette,* accident at bull-baiting, 6 Sept. 1790; *Stamford Mercury,* city chamberlains provide two bulls for baiting 9 Nov. 1721; *Northampton Mercury,* bull-baiting at a wedding Sept. 1722, a bull race 26 May 1724.

The final decade of the eighteenth century marked a watershed in the reporting of the plebeian sport of bull-baiting by local newspapers. After 1790, advertisements for bull-baiting no longer appeared, and the occasional reports of local bull-baits were replaced by hostile accounts of the sport, not only in their locality, but countrywide.[51] By the end of the century this transition was complete; and any evidence of bull-baiting that came to the newspapers' notice was universally condemned.

The switch is clearly demonstrated in the response of the local Berkshire newspapers to the annual custom of bull-baiting on St Thomas's day in Wokingham. Throughout the eighteenth century, the parish overseers organised an annual bull-baiting in the town, according to the terms of an unusual charitable bequest made by a local butcher, George Staverton. In 1661, Staverton had bequeathed six pounds annually from the rent of his house in Staines to buy a bull to be baited, slaughtered, and distributed amongst the poor on St Thomas's day, 21 December.[52] In time, the value of Staverton's property increased, enabling the parish overseers to purchase two bulls, both of which the overseers subsequently presented to the populace for baiting on St Thomas's day.[53] The custom attracted no comment throughout most of the eighteenth century, indeed advertisements for the event were occasionally printed.[54] In the 1780s, however, the attitude of the leading local paper—the *Reading Mercury*—sharply altered. The *Mercury* printed a number of hostile reports of the custom, condemning it for its 'unparalleled brutality' and 'inhumanity',[55] though the outrage expressed at this time proved to be ephemeral. There was no further discussion of the Wokingham bull-bait for a further two decades, although the custom continued until the 1820s.[56] Like many provincial papers, the editors in Reading alternated between moral outrage and total indifference. In this

---

[51] See, for example, *York Courant*, 21 Oct. 1790; *Leeds Intelligencer*, 27 Aug. 1792; *Bury and Norwich Post*, 7 Nov. 1792, 4 Nov. 1801; *Aris's Birmingham Gazette*, 8 Oct. 1792, 12 Nov. 1792, 4 Feb. 1811, 2 Sept. 1811; *Northampton Mercury*, 24 Nov. 1792, 18 Dec. 1824; *Hull Advertiser*, 19 Dec. 1801.

[52] Readwin, *Account of Wokingham*, pp. 73–6.

[53] Berkshire RO, Wokingham Minutes of Common Council, 1749–1833, Wo/AC1/1/2. The lease was renewed for 12 pounds a year, 8 Nov. 1786. See also the Overseers, Accounts, 1766–73, D/P154/12/3. Payments towards a bull in 1767 (3s 6d), 1772 (41 10s) and 1773 (31 2s 6.5d).

[54] *Berkshire Chronicle*, 16 Dec. 1774; *Reading Mercury*, 18 Dec. 1786, 22 Dec. 1788, 20 Dec. 1790.

[55] *Reading Mercury*, 27 Nov. 1786. See also ibid., 18 and 25 Dec. 1886, 23 June 1787, 24 Dec. 1787.

[56] Ibid., 26 Dec. 1808.

respect they were typical of the provincial presses, yet the rapid switch in their response to the annual custom, and the inconstancy with which they expressed these new ideas, should cause us to question what really under-pinned the language of cruelty that was now deployed.

Perhaps part of the reason for the newspapers' tendency to focus on animal combat sports is explained in an editorial comment in the *Mirror* in July 1826. It apologised to correspondents whose letters had not yet been printed in the following way: 'it frequently happens, that articles on tem-porary subjects, or subjects that excite interest at the time, have a prece-dence over those of a general nature . . . Attention to the topics of the day is necessary.'[57] And this is clearly exactly what animal combat sports had become—a lively topic for discussion. There was little general interest in the subject of animal cruelty; blood sports, however, had become (to rephrase the *Mirror*) a subject that 'excited interest'.

And it was not simply the periodicals and newspapers that began to take an interest in popular blood sports; a similar interest may be found across a broad range of writing. In what follows, a number of different types of work—sporting dictionaries, natural history, folklore, and local history—have been subjected to scrutiny. Almost identical accounts of bull-baiting can be found in this diverse range of publications, and it is possible to trace with some accuracy the entry of this newly fashioned account of bull-baiting into the records. These writers displayed no interest in the animal protection debate, yet in a similar way to the contributors to papers and periodicals they picked up and propagated a number of ideas about the cruelty of popular blood sports. It is clear that a wide range of publications was involved in disseminating new ideas about blood sports.

Let us begin by considering sporting dictionaries. These reference books, written by and for the gentleman sportsman, were originally con-cerned solely with traditional country sports. Nicholas Cox's *Gentleman's Recreation,* 1677, which formed the prototype of the genre, consisted in four books—devoted to hunting, hawking, fowling, and fishing. Richard Blome added cockfighting to this list of sports in the title page of his *Gentleman's Recreation,* published nine years later. Until the second half of the eight-eenth century, sporting treatises, as titles such as *The Sportsman's Dictionary; Or the Country Gentleman Companion in all Rural Recreations* suggest, were wholly devoted to the gentleman's sport.[58] Something of the priorities of

---

[57] *Mirror,* 1 July 1826.
[58] See also Markham, *Country Contentments*; Seymour, *Compleat Gamester.* There were also books devoted to individual sports; see, for example, R. H., *Royal Pastime of Cockfighting.*

these books is captured in Blome's proudly stated reason for including a chapter on cockfighting: 'since many of the *Nobility* and *Gentry* delight in this noble Diversion, I shall conclude with a compendious *Treatise* thereof'.[59]

The sporting dictionary remained popular throughout the eighteenth century, with the publication of new books and re-editions of the most successful ones, but from the 1790s the strict focus on gentlemanly recreations began to be relaxed, with the most significant addition for our purposes being entries under 'bull' and 'bull-dog'. It was not that the books ceased to be written by gentlemen for gentlemen, but rather that these gentlemanly sportsmen suddenly developed a novel taste for writing and reading about the sport of bull-baiting. The new entries on popular sports were often short and usually took very similar form. Whatever the date the book was actually written, bull-baiting was described in essentially the same way: as a barbarous sport, once popular but now on the decline; 'in various districts of England, this breed [the bull-dog] is still preserved in its native purity, by that class of people who delight in bull-baiting and fighting of dogs, both of which amusements, alike inhuman, are now happily on the decline'.[60] It was supposed to be symbolic of the enlightened times that few now countenanced such barbarity: while that 'barbarous amusement [bull-baiting] continued in vogue, various instances of savage fortitude have occurred in the feats of this breed, which would rarely be credited in countries where the diversions are more rational and elegant'.[61]

The newly founded *Sporting Magazine* was very similar to the sporting reference books in both content and outlook, though it initially took no consistent line against baiting. In the early years, a few articles critical of bull-baiting were printed, but others were included in which no criticism was made.[62] For example, the magazine reproduced and explained an engraving of a combat between a renowned bull-dog, Bottom, and a man, expressing no reservations about the propriety of such antics.[63] In December 1801, however, it reproduced three letters printed in Stamford newspapers about the annual bull-running in that town. The numerous hostile contributions that the paper published in the following months

[59] Blome, *Gentleman's Recreation*, p. 277.
[60] [Maxwell], *Field Book*, pp. 74–5.
[61] Osbaldiston, *British Sportsman*, p. 81.
[62] Critical pieces in *Sporting Magazine*, April 1795, pp. 54–5; Aug. 1795, pp. 260–2; May 1800, p. 80. Uncritical pieces in ibid., Oct. 1793, p. 77; Jan. 1794, pp. 188–9.
[63] Ibid., frontispiece to vol. 18 (1801), article at Nov. 1801, p. 8. See also the engraving of a bull-baiting, July 1796, p. 123.

resolved any previous uncertainties concerning the magazine's attitude towards the popular pastime, and it rapidly established itself as the foremost critic of bull-baiting, frequently and gleefully pouring scorn and derision on this 'sport'.[64]

The sporting dictionaries and papers were not alone in their newfound interest in bull-baiting. In books about popular customs and folklore, and in local histories which included a chapter on popular pastimes, the same development may be observed. Comparisons are difficult, since writing on popular traditions was not extensive prior to the late eighteenth century, but in the few works printed before that date animal sports had not been singled out for particular criticism. John Aubrey, for example, had nothing to say about cockfighting on Shrove Tuesday, except that the Athenians had passed a law instituting cockfighting on a certain day of the year after a military victory.[65] Similarly, at mid-century, the historian Charles Deering referred to the now disused obligation of Nottingham butchers to bait bulls before slaughter, without further comment.[66] By the late eighteenth century, however, scholars discussing popular sports and pastimes never failed to heap especial opprobrium on bull-baiting, throwing at cocks, and sometimes cockfighting, and it had become almost impossible to refer to these pastimes without repeating a number of well-worn conclusions. Throwing at cocks, for example, was typically cast as a 'barbarous custom':[67] but fortunately, these 'vulgar dissipations'[68] were disappearing; 'so much have they declined in late years that . . . in a short time it is probable they will be discontinued and forgotten'.[69] This was 'much to the credit of the present generation . . . [it is] to be attributed to the increased morality of the inhabitants'.[70] In Beverley in Yorkshire, the local historian declared that cockfighting had 'declined in proportion with the moral improvement of the people'.[71]

Bull-baiting was discussed in very similar terms. The sport was described as a barbarous diversion, but one which had much declined of late, owing to the recent moral improvement of the people. The historians

---

[64] The letters on the Stamford bull-running are in *Sporting Magazine*, Dec. 1801, pp. 132–4. See also Jan. 1802, pp. 197–8; Feb. 1802, pp. 266–9; March 1802, pp. 340–2; April 1802, pp. 36–8; May 1802, pp. 101–02.

[65] Aubrey, *Remaines of Gentilisme*, p. 35.

[66] Deering, *History of Nottingham*, p. 125.

[67] Cole, *History of Higham Ferrars*, p. 213.

[68] Hutchinson, *View of Northumberland*, p. 8.

[69] Dunkin, *History of Bicester*, p. 276.

[70] Clarkson, *History of Richmond*, p. 294.

[71] Oliver, *History of Beverley*, pp. 422–3.

of Stamford, Beverley, Axbridge, Birmingham, Liverpool, Ludlow, Hornsea, Stockton-upon-Tees, and Chester repeated this account of popular animal sports.[72] Three historians of Derbyshire weighed in against blood sports,[73] as did all the most significant early-nineteenth-century scholars of popular pastimes.[74] The writers of letters and accounts of travels in England also shared this view, there being no substantial difference between Robert Southey's letters from the fictional Espriella, and E. M. Woodward's travel guide, *Eccentric Excursions*.[75] These writers' remarks were all so similar to those already described that no further comment on them is necessary.

In some instances, the transition that had occurred by the late eighteenth century may be observed with particular clarity. The ancient bull-running at Tutbury, for example, was studied by two scholars in the late seventeenth century. Though both seemed a little doubtful about the crowds that gathered to watch each year, they were nevertheless impressed and interested by the antiquity of the custom.[76] Samuel Pegge, working in the 1760s, was also more interested in the origin of the custom, than the disgrace of it.[77] Stebbing Shaw, a local historian returning to the subject at the very end of the eighteenth century, saw the custom quite differently; after quoting large extracts from Robert Plot's earlier account, Shaw added that the bull-running 'of late years has become so inhuman a practice by the promiscuous multitude, as to be a disgrace to themselves and their country ... this ancient meeting was got to so great a pitch of madness, and cruelty, that, not content with torturing the poor animal alone, [the mob] fell in the most sanguine manner upon each other'.[78] Other early-nineteenth-century scholars who described the ancient customary bull-runnings used similar, and increasingly familiar, terms to condemn it.[79]

---

[72] Drakard, *History of Stamford*, pp. 401–3; Oliver, *History of Beverley*, pp. 421–2; *Gentleman's Magazine*, March 1805, pp. 203–4; Drake, *Picture of Birmingham*, p. 83; Troughton, *History of Liverpool*, pp. 92–4; *Description of Ludlow*, p. 28; Bedell, *Account of Hornsea*, ii, p. 88; Brewster, *History of Stockton*, p. 260; Hemmingway, *History of Chester*, p. 230.

[73] Pilkington, *View of Derbyshire*, ii, p. 55; Farey, *View of Derbyshire*, iii, p. 628; Glover, *History of Derby*, p. 309.

[74] Strutt, *Glig-Gamena*, pp. liii–liv, 256–9, 281–5; Hone, *Every-day Book*, pp. 252–5, 978–1006; Aspin, *Picture of Manners*, p. 281. See also *Popular Pastimes*, pp. 19–23.

[75] [Southey], *Letters from England*, pp. 413–14; Woodward, *Eccentric Excursions*, pp. 92–3.

[76] Blount, *Fragmenta Antiquitatis*, pp. 168–75; Plot, *History of Staffordshire*, pp. 435–40.

[77] Pegge, 'Bull-running at Tutbury', pp. 86–91.

[78] Shaw, *History of Staffordshire*, i, pp. 52–5.

[79] See, in particular, Strutt, *Glig-Gamena*, pp. 277–80; Howitt, *Rural Life*, ii, pp. 273–4. See also Farey, *View of Derbyshire*, iii, p. 230.

The same pattern of rewriting accounts of popular traditions is evident in the history of one of the earliest accounts of popular pastimes, Henry Bourne's *Antiquitates Vulgares,* 1725. Bourne, researching in the 1720s, had written a chapter on Shrovetide customs, but had not discussed throwing at cocks. When John Brand, the antiquarian, reissued this work in the 1770s with copious commentary of his own, the Shrovetide section now included a section on 'the barbarous Custom . . . of *throwing at cocks* . . . It is an Amusement fit only for the bloodiest Savages, and not for humanised Men, much less of Christians!'[80] Brand continued to work on popular pastimes through the rest of his life. His research was published posthumously by Henry Ellis in 1813; and by the time of his death, lengthy and hostile sections on bull-baiting, bull-running and cockfighting had all also been prepared.[81]

One final collection of texts—popular natural history books—may be used to demonstrate the way that attitudes towards blood sports were rapidly changing at the end of the eighteenth century. Since there was very little that was distinctive in their approach to animal cruelty and animal sports, these texts may be quickly summarised.[82] Revd W. Bingley's compendium of British quadrupeds, for example, used sections on the 'ox' and the 'bull-dog' to offer rather unoriginal condemnations of bull-baiting—a 'detestable practice' which, 'thanks to the increasing humanity and civilisation of the people, is, however, now on the decline'.[83] Bingley could not discuss the domestic cock 'without a few observations on the savage diversion of cockfighting; which (to the disgrace of a Christian country) [was] encouraged'.[84] Thomas Pennant's *British Zoology* did not originally include a section on cockfighting, an oversight which he corrected in 1781 with a chapter entitled 'Of cockfighting'. By this date he had come to believe that 'some account of the barbarous custom of cockfighting . . . will be no improper appendage of the history of our domestic birds'.[85]

In common with all the other authors we have considered, the natural historians were selective in their concern for animal suffering. Thomas Bewick thought that setting dogs on a bear was an 'inhuman diversion, chiefly confined to the idle and the vicious', but had nothing but praise for that 'favourite

---

[80] Brand (ed.), *Observations on Antiquities*, p. 230.
[81] Ellis (ed.), *Observations on Antiquities*, i, pp. 56–68, 476–90; ii, pp. 283–6.
[82] For an account of popular natural history during the eighteenth century, see Ritvo, *Animal Estate*, pp. 6–42.
[83] Bingley, *Memoirs of Quadrupeds*, pp. 395, 118.
[84] Idem, *Animal Biography*, ii, p. 412.
[85] Pennant, *British Zoology*.

diversion' of the English, foxhunting.[86] Meanwhile Bingley seemed to for-
get about his concern for animal welfare altogether at various points, revil-
ing bull- and bear-baiting one moment, but marvelling at the bull-dog's
strength and courage when considering lion-baiting and badger-baiting the
next.[87] Finally, many of the entries were simply out of place. In John Bigland's
Letters on Natural History, for example, the reader encounters a discussion
about which of Spanish bull-fighting and English bull-baiting was most
manly, and which was most cruel—an unusual topic to find in a natural
history book, even by the eclectic standards of the eighteenth century.[88]

If these writers said little that was original about popular blood sports,
the fact they said anything is nonetheless of real historical interest. By the
early nineteenth century the change of opinion concerning popular animal
sports was total. A handful of sports that had previously been condoned and
quietly ignored, moved to centre stage and, within the short period of a few
decades, a new discourse, a new set of beliefs, was first created, and then
consolidated through endless repetition. Throwing at cocks and bull-baiting
had been utterly discredited, and cockfighting was rapidly joining these
sports as a disgraceful and intolerable diversion. It is not simply the extent
of the criticism about these sports that is remarkable, there is also something
curious about their content. Different writers, at different times, and
speaking of different sports all repeated an essentially identical account:
popular blood sports were savage and barbarous, but happily now on the
decline. Criticism of these ancient pastimes was not only ubiquitous, it was
also suspiciously formulaic.

Constructing cruelty

It should by now be evident that the criticism of popular blood sports that
emerged in the late eighteenth century is very much less straightforward
than has usually been assumed, yet the puzzles posed by this new discourse
go beyond those already outlined. The rapid diffusion of this prescribed
account of bull-baiting and other plebeian blood sports is clearly problematic, but it must also be questioned why it was these particular pastimes
that formed the focus of so much discussion. Our own feelings are that
bull-baiting was a savage and barbarous activity, and we therefore readily

[86] Bewick, *History of Quadrupeds,* pp. 281–3, 305.
[87] Bingley, *Animal Biography,* pp. 225, 265, 244, 388–9.
[88] Bigland, *Letters on Natural History,* p. 186.

understand why this pastime was so roundly criticised. Indeed, condemnations of blood sports as inhuman and cruel scarcely register, so well do such views chime with our own. But we need to pause for thought, for though bull-baiting may indeed have been savage and barbarous, the same was true of many of the other sports that were widely tolerated, encouraged even, in many of these publications. Why, then, were bull-baiting, cock throwing, and to a lesser extent cockfighting singled out for attention? We need to consider why it was that these sports were labelled cruel, whilst similar activities largely managed to escape criticism of any kind.

The problem is illustrated most clearly in the sporting dictionaries, and in the way in which they handled sports that were in most respects identical. Bull-baiting, badger-baiting, and badger-hunting are not greatly different. Bull-baiting, as we have seen, was a contest between dogs in which each dog attacked individually a captive bull in order to demonstrate his strength and courage; the principle of badger-baiting was essentially the same—it involved placing a live badger in a hole dug in the ground, and setting dogs loose one by one in an attempt to dislodge the animal. In badger-hunting, several dogs are set loose upon a wild badger either to capture it ('having taken a live and lusty badger, if you would make sport, carry him home in a sack, and turn him out in your courtyard, or some other inclosed place, and there let him be hunted and worried to death by your hounds'[89]) or to kill it outright. In fact all hunting with dogs involves this principle: trained dogs are set on wild animals which use their 'cunning' to defend themselves—that is, they flee for their lives. Animal baiting, in contrast, uses captive animals whose defence is their strength. The language used to describe these sports, however, can make it very difficult to recognise any similarity between them, as becomes apparent when descriptions of the different sports are compared. Hunting a badger, for example, was usually described in a factual tone, with details omitted. The sport was described in the following terms by Osbaldiston:

> stop all the burrows, except one or two, and therein place some sacks, fastened with drawing strings, which may shut him in as soon as he strains the bag . . . the sack slips off the hoop and follows him into the earth where he lies entangled till he is taken . . . to dig the badger out of his hole . . . you should have a pail of water to refresh the terriers when they come out of the earth to take a breath and cool themselves.[90]

---

[89] *Sportsman's Dictionary.*

[90] Osbaldiston, *British Sportsman*, p. 40. See also the descriptions in Blome, *Gentleman's Recreation*, p. 90; *Sportsman's Dictionary*, 'badger'; [Maxwell], *Field Book*, p. 29; Harewood, *Dictionary of Sports*, pp. 29–30.

Very different were the accounts of bull-baiting. Neutral language was replaced by colourful and imaginative descriptions that leave the reader in absolutely no doubt about the right moral conclusions to be drawn:

> A poor innocent bull was dragged into the town, amidst the shouts of an applauding multitude: it was taken to the Castle-hill, tied to an iron ring with ropes, and then torn and worried by dogs . . . Here the unhappy victim, a horrid spectacle, was baited, lacerated and harassed until four o'clock.[91]

> The poor animal had been privately baited in the morning, and goaded with sharp instruments, in order to render him furious enough for public exhibition, which he afterwards experienced, tied down with ropes, baited by dogs, and gored by brutes in the shape of men.[92]

It is highly debatable whether it is more cruel to set dogs on a bull tied to a stake or on a badger in its den, but these accounts hardly encourage such reflection. Their use of language almost guarantees revulsion of the one, and deflects attention from the other; language has been used to invest certain activities with cruelty. In Henry Alken's badger-hunting chapter, the badger was 'vermin'; but when describing badger-baiting, the animal was recast as a 'most quiet and harmless creature'. Badger-baiting was an 'amusement for the dissipated and vulgar of all descriptions . . . Whilst we decry, and denounce at the bar of humanity, these infamous and torturing propensities, we have not one word to urge against fairly hunting the Badger in the field.'[93] But, from the badger's point of view at least, this distinction was quite artificial; it was Alken's descriptions that made the contrast between the hunting and baiting of badgers convincing, not any qualities inherent to the sports themselves. In John Lawrence's work, a similar discrimination is evident. Lawrence was a vet who also wrote extensively about sports; he reviled bull-baiting, which involved finding pleasure in 'witnessing the lingering tortures and excruciated sensibility' of an animal.[94] Foxhunting, however, was quite different: 'no true and lawful, that is to say, rational, useful, and delightful sports, would be interrupted by this regulation . . . I shall be found . . . a willing, although perhaps a weak advocate, for all those sports, which inspire mirth and hilarity, and promote health'.[95] It took only

---

[91] *Stamford Mercury*, 10 Nov. 1802.

[92] *Sporting Magazine*, Dec. 1801, p. 133. See also Taplin, *Sporting Dictionary*, pp. 92–101; Alken, *National Sports*, 'badger-baiting', 'bear-baiting'; Harewood, *Dictionary of Sports*, pp. 64–8.

[93] Alken, *National Sports*, 'Running a badger to bay', 'Badger-baiting'.

[94] Lawrence, *Treatise on Horses*, i, p. 125.

[95] Ibid., pp. 125, 127.

a little artistic licence to make these distinctions convincing; it is doubtful, however, how well they would bear closer scrutiny.

These extracts from Alken and Lawrence also reveal that an effective way of discrediting bull-baiting involved denying that the sport was really a sport at all. In the hostile literature, writers were unanimous that bull-baiting was an utterly senseless pastime; the element of combat between the animals was neglected, and the purpose of the sport, it was claimed, was simply to subdue the bull—to injure it in the greatest possible degree. Thus, according to the self-styled 'Benevolus', writing in the *Sporting Magazine*, a forthcoming bull-bait advertised prizes in order to encourage owners from a great distance to bring their dog, so that 'the destined victim may not die *too easy a death*'.[96] In Lincoln, a bull was attached to the stake so that it might undergo 'all the torture that savage dogs and unfeeling spectators could inflict',[97] and at Beverley, the bull was simply 'intended to be tortured'.[98] To add insult to injury, the baited bull, these writers insisted, was usually of the gentlest temper: we have already encountered in the previous pages a 'poor animal', a 'poor innocent bull', and an 'unhappy victim'. Capel Lofft wrote: 'I hear that this noble but wretched animal was

Figure 9.   'Bull-Baiting' (Henry Alken, *The National Sports of Great Britain*, London 1903)

[96] *Sporting Magazine*, April 1802, p. 38.
[97] *Lincoln, Rutland and Stamford Mercury*, 8 Nov. 1811.
[98] *Rockingham and Hull Weekly Advertiser*, 28 April 1810.

perfectly gentle and inoffensive when turned out.'[99] Another journalist complained that 'so broken was [the bull's] spirit, or so inoffensive was it in its nature . . . that it was led along without any resistance, like a lamb'.[100] The pages of hostile depictions of bull-baiting, particularly those in newspapers and magazines, are filled with a grim procession of normally sweet tempered bulls, mangled, bloody, and torn beyond recognition.

Having dismissed the possibility that sport was the motivation behind bull-baiting, it was possible to provide an alternative account: inhumanity, barbarity, pure viciousness lay at the root of the sport; clearly, this could not be allowed to continue. According to William Taplin, bull-baiting was popular with 'the butchers and lower orders . . . abandoned miscreants', and 'the most unfeeling, and least humane, part of the very lowest, and most abandoned orders of the people . . . *brutes*; the very scum and refuse of society from every part of the surrounding country'.[101] Elsewhere, participants were condemned as 'the most stupid, ignorant and uncivilised part of our countrymen', or yet more simply, as society's 'dregs' and 'scum'.[102]

In fact, many accounts of popular sports were essentially pieces of fiction, and bore little or no reality to the actual sports. Consider, for instance, how William Taplin described bull-baiting:

> those gentlemen best calculated to appear in the character of *desperados* begin the attack, by the most dreadful noises of different kinds, *bellowings, hooings,* and *hissings,* consisting of a complication horrid beyond description, whilst the abandoned crew of *ragamuffins* are in this way, with their shouts and *huzzaings,* endeavouring to irritate him . . . the first dog is suddenly let loose . . . The scene now advances to a state of confusion exceeding all *humane* conception; the howling of the dogs . . . the roaring and dreadful bellowings of the bull . . . the dangerous pressings, and incessant hollowing and huzzaings of the *crowd* . . . all contribute to a scene from which the thinking mind retreats with horror.[103]

Newspaper writers were no less creative. One article, for example, began thus:

---

[99] *Sporting Magazine,* Dec. 1802, p. 132

[100] *Aris's Birmingham Gazette,* 7 Oct. 1792.

[101] Taplin, *Sporting Dictionary,* pp. 44, 93–6. Likewise, when Pierce Egan's fictional hero Tom went to the Westminster pit to watch a monkey-baiting he found 'a motley group . . . all in rude contact, jostling and pushing against each other'. Egan, *Life in London,* p. 259.

[102] Granger, *Apology for Brute Creation,* p. 12; *Clemency to Brutes,* p. 28; Styles, *Animal Creation,* p. 58.

[103] Taplin, *Sporting Dictionary,* pp. 98–9.

> A few days ago [a correspondent] beheld a scene upon the public road
> in a neighbouring parish, that deeply affected his feelings. One of these
> cruel diversions was just over, and the relentless mob were leading the
> mangled object of their outrage from the place where it had been
> baited . . .[104]

It is clear that much of the reporting of animal sports consisted in elaborate embellishment of a number of actual events—the setting of dogs on a
bull—but establishing exactly how far they are from the truth is difficult,
given that hostile accounts such as these form the bulk of all the descriptions of bull-baiting that we have. There is, however, an alternative picture
of animal baitings that may be constructed from sources that did not
directly oppose themselves to the sport. Until the second half of the eighteenth century, the travel journals of foreign visitors and private English
diaries occasionally described bull-baiting. Oftentimes these records contain little or no descriptive detail of the events. A few, however, contain
detailed accounts of the sport their author had witnessed, and these
descriptions diverge in a number of significant ways from those to be found
in sporting dictionaries, natural history books, works of folklore, and local
newspapers.

   In about half of the travel journals and travel diaries it is possible to
establish whether the bull or the dog suffered most. In all but one instance
the bull (or occasionally the bear) gained the advantage over the dogs. This,
for instance, is what Thomas Platter saw:

> a large white powerful bull was brought in, and likewise bound in the cen-
> tre of the theatre, and one dog only was set on him at a time, which he
> speared in such a masterly fashion, that they could not get the better of him,
> and as the dogs fell to the floor again, several men held the sticks under them
> to break their fall, so that they would not be killed. Afterwards more dogs
> were set on him, but they could not down him.[105]

Many other witnesses provided similar accounts. In 1710, Von Uffenbach
found: 'about thirty dogs, two or three at a time, were let loose on [the
bull], but he made short work of them, goring them and tossing them high
in the air above the height of the first storey'.[106] The Duke of Wirtemberg
noted: 'four dogs at once were set on the bull; they, however, could not gain
any advantage over him, for he so artfully contrived to ward off their attacks
that they could not well get at him; on the contrary, the bull served them

---

[104] *Aris's Birmingham Gazette*, 8 Oct. 1792.
[105] Platter, *Platter's Travels*, p. 169.
[106] Uffenbach, *Travels of Uffenbach*, p. 59.

very scurvily by striking and butting at them'.[107] Finally the agriculturalist John Houghton, wrote: 'I believe I have seen a dog tossed by a bull thirty, if not forty foot high; and when they are tossed either higher or lower, the men about strive to catch them . . . Notwithstanding this care, a great many dogs are killed, more have their limbs broke . . .'[108]

Private diaries generally provide fewer details about the spectacle. They nevertheless unambiguously confirm that the bulls proved to be a formidable opponent for the dogs. In August 1666 Samuel Pepys went to the bear-garden and 'saw some good sport of the bull's tossing of the dogs— one into the very boxes'.[109] Four years later John Evelyn visited the bear-garden, where he too saw 'one of the Bulls toss'd a Dog full into a Ladys lap, as she sate in one of the boxes at a Considerable height from the *Arena*'.[110] An Essex aristocrat, Sir Humphrey Mildmay, frequently provided a bull for baiting, and occasionally noted that a dog had been killed, but he never reported that the bull had been injured.[111] Nicholas Blundell, a Lancashire farmer, also laid on an occasional bull-bait for his workers' entertainment, such as this one in July 1712: 'I Baited a Large Bull . . . he was never baited before as I know off, yet played to admiration . . . I think there was not above two Doggs but what were very ill hurt, some Sticked into the Side or Lamed or very ill Brused, I gave a Coller to be played for but no Dogg could get it fairly.'[112] Sylas Neville, a Norwich doctor, once went to a bear-baiting at Islington; although he did not like the sport, he nevertheless conceded that 'the poor animal . . . was not much hurt'.[113] Finally, a Cambridge fellow, Thomas Crosfield, concluded: 'in the throwing or tossing of the dogs often they are kill'd or maimed, but yt to save them men run & catch them in the fall . . . otherwise they should be quite quasht, maimed or slaine by the Bull'.[114]

The travel journals and diaries indicate that bull-baiting derived its interest from a spirited defence on the part of the bull. Thus, one regular

---

[107] Rathgeb, 'Narrative of excursion', p. 46 (diar.).

[108] Houghton, *Collection for Husbandry*, p. 290. See also Hentzner, *Journey into England*, p. 42 (bull-baiting was 'not without great risque to the dogs'); Misson, *Memoirs*, pp. 24–7.

[109] Pepys, *Diary*, vii, 14 Aug. 1666, pp. 245–6.

[110] Evelyn, *Diary*, ii, 9 June 1670, pp. 105, 112.

[111] Mildmay, *Humphrey Mildmay*, pp. 105–12.

[112] Blundell, *Diurnal*, ii, 15 July 1712, p. 26. See also 8 Sept. 1712: 'My Black-Bull was Baited at Mrs Ann Rothwells, there played but three right Doggs & two of them were ill hurt', p. 33. The third time Blundell recorded a bull-bait, he did not give any details of the event. See ibid., iii, 28 Nov. 1723, p. 121.

[113] Neville, *Diary*, i, 28 Oct. 1782, p. 299.

[114] Crosfield, *Diary*, 1 Feb. 1636, p. 85.

participant of the sport complained when the two bulls in his town's annual bull-running had been of a mild temper: 'they might as well have runned me,' he noted, 'for the poor beasts were no more mad than I am, and I can hardly walk 5 yards'.[115] The sport was therefore not so sense-less as was generally argued. It was not an eruption of uncontrolled bar-barity. Its purpose was not to injure, overwhelm, or subdue the bull, simply in order to gratify the vicious passions of the lower orders, but to establish a hierarchy of strength and courage between the dogs and bull. Of course, we may have little sympathy with this as a sporting prin-ciple, but we should recognise that it formed a staple and entirely uncontroversial element of most rural sports two centuries ago. In this context, the criticism of popular blood sports, which at first sight seems so self-evident, is very much less easy to understand than common sense would suggest.

Clearly, the eyewitness accounts of bull-baiting found in travel journals and diaries form a sharp contrast to the endless stream of poor, innocent, inoffensive, harmless bulls found in the books and papers surveyed above, and it suggests that the account presented there is misleading in a number of key respects. This observation is not intended to vindicate bull-baiting from cruelty; well trained dogs could seriously injure the bull, and sensa-tional reports about cruelty committed by the human spectators probably had some basis in fact.[116] Furthermore, a case could certainly be made for cruelty to dogs. Given that the dog would attack whatever its owner told it, setting it on an animal twenty times its size might well be construed as cruel. The point simply is to highlight the discrepancies that exist between descriptions of bull-baiting to be found in a wide range of sources hostile to the sport, and the eyewitness accounts.

Discussion about bull-baiting was extremely widespread by the early nineteenth century, but at the heart of this discourse lay a number of fac-tual errors and misrepresentations of popular blood sports that cannot be ignored. They suggest that these hostile critics had little or no personal experience of the sports they were discussing. These writers had not per-sonally witnessed the disgusting and appalling scenes of cruelty that they feared continued. Their judgements were not based upon an informed appreciation of what the sports involved; they were no more than unre-flecting repetitions of a commonplace. In fact, the account of popular blood

[115] Northampton RO, Clifton's Day Books, ZA/8732–46, 13 Dec. 1778.
[116] See, for instance, the case of the crowd at Bury St Edmunds cutting off a bull's hoofs in order to enrage him, reported in *Monthly Magazine,* Dec. 1801, p. 464.

sports that rose to such dominance was essentially unrelated to the sport itself. The rapid and extensive diffusion of a handful of ideas about bull-baiting is noteworthy, but it is no less remarkable that these ideas were based upon a stereotyped account of bull-baiting that bore little reality to any sports that the lower orders had ever enjoyed.

It is clear that the emergence of new ideas about popular blood sports in the late eighteenth century poses many problems. It is possible to demonstrate that blood sports were set apart and targeted for especial criticism; yet, however carefully we look at contemporaneous discussion of bull-baiting, it seems to raise as many questions as it settles. Why did criticism emerge at this time? Why was it these sports that were singled out? And why did commentary of popular blood sports always take the same form: that is, that they were barbarous and inhumane, but much on the decline?

There are speculative answers to these questions that we can give. We can point out, for example, that the late eighteenth century was a period of rapid economic and demographic change, and suggest that social upheaval produced a hardening of attitudes towards plebeian blood sports. We might equally draw attention to the French Revolution, and suggest that the alarming upending of traditional social certainties in 1789, and in particular the sanguinary chaos into which the Revolution subsequently descended, encouraged new anxieties at home about pastimes that were bloody in nature. But whilst such trends might have encouraged new concerns about popular gatherings of all kinds, none seem quite equal to answering the questions posed. Blood sports, after all, were not the only occasions at which the masses gathered; bull-baiting and cock throwing were occasional and non-political activities—hardly the stuff of revolutions. Social and political change at home and abroad might have increased concern about social disorder and plebeian violence on a general level, but it is precisely the specificity of this discourse that poses the greatest problems, and it cannot be adequately explained by appealing to broader social forces.

To search for the social origin of this shift in opinion is surely to ask the wrong question, for it is clear that this discussion relates only loosely to any sports that had ever existed. We have been dealing in this chapter not with a sport, but with an idea, a concept that was both powerful and enduring. This idea was certainly founded upon a set of popular practices but, once established, it quickly took on a life of its own, spreading through society and snapping the connection it had once had to any sports that had ever been played. It took no longer than a generation to fashion a new opinion of bull-baiting, and to disseminate this to a public which in most instances had never even witnessed a bull-bait. A powerful idea was thus created, an idea that was to shape both future policy, and subsequent generations' perceptions of cruelty, compassion and their location in class, for many years to come.

6

Industrial towns and townships, 1750–1840

In Chapters 3 and 4 we looked at the history of popular sports and celebrations in English towns. The focus was on historic market towns: many were incorporated, and many were consequently large, wealthy, and comparatively well governed. Owing to their size and wealth, these were towns in the van of the eighteenth-century civic improvement movement, and were precisely the kind of town upon which Peter Borsay's well known theory of an eighteenth-century urban renaissance was based.[1] But what about those towns that Angus McInnes has identified, towns that 'displayed few of the symptoms' of Borsay's urban renaissance?[2] It seems that any history of popular recreation should include some detail on the fortune of sports and games in towns like these. The eighteenth century witnessed the growth of many towns with no pretensions to gentility. Towns could grow yet remain poor. Throughout the industrialising regions of northern and central England, eighteenth-century demographic change consisted in large additions to urban labouring populations, rather than the emergence of a culturally confident middle class, with an expanding retail sector and army of skilled craftworkers to service its needs. In Bolton, for example, fully half of the town's population in the 1830s were said to be employed in work connected with the textile trade.[3] Such towns had very different social and economic profiles from those of the market towns and provincial capitals considered in Chapters 3 and 4, and the availability and control of public space for popular recreation were likewise very different. It is by no means evident that these industrial towns were on the same cultural trajectory as provincial market towns, and it cannot be taken for granted that it was simply a question of time until they began to identify with, and set out to imitate, towns such as Reading, Cambridge, Lincoln, or Sandwich.

It is precisely in the cultural differences that existed between regions that the interests of this book lie, and in this and the following chapter we

---

[1] Borsay, *Urban Renaissance*.
[2] McInnes, 'Emergence of Shrewsbury', p. 83.
[3] Figures quoted in Hammond and Hammond, *Age of Chartists*, p. 80.

look in detail at the towns and villages of south Yorkshire, south Lancashire, the north-east, and the Midlands in an attempt to establish more firmly the extent to which these industrial communities constituted a distinct environment in terms of sports, recreations, and popular culture. These districts contained their share of medium and large towns—Manchester, Birmingham, Leeds, Nottingham, Newcastle, Wolverhampton, Bradford, Bolton, Halifax, Sheffield, to name a few—all undergoing improvements in varying degrees. Grimly overshadowing any 'improvements' introduced in these towns, however, were the rapid urbanisation and industrial growth that were transforming the regions at the same time.[4] As new employment possibilities attracted large numbers of rural migrants, populations settled both within the historic towns, and outside the traditional areas of settlement, in industrial villages, hamlets, and townships. The industrial townships in the Black Country, the pit towns of the north-east coalfield, and the mill towns and villages of south Yorkshire and south Lancashire loom large in histories of the industrial revolution, but have never found their way into histories of civic improvement, and it is important that our survey of popular recreation in eighteenth-century towns extends to cities, towns, and suburbs such as these.

This and the following chapter attempt to do so. Both consider the history of popular recreation in the industrialising regions of England, but each has a distinct objective. In this chapter we explore the concept of an 'industrial popular culture'. This chapter describes the sports and pastimes that were enjoyed in two contrasting communities in the early nineteenth century: the West Riding of Yorkshire and the west Midlands. It demonstrates the very different patterns of popular recreations that prevailed in each and sets out to consider how such marked divergences between the cultural practice of the two regions had been formed. Chapter 7 turns back to the theme of space, and aims to position the sports and pastimes described here more firmly in their topographical context. It might be said, therefore, that this chapter explores popular recreation from the viewpoint of the region, whilst the following sets out to pursue the same activities from the finer perspective of space.

---

[4] Trinder, 'Industrialising towns', pp. 805–29; Rowlands, *West Midlands*, pp. 171–5, 236–51.

Local contrasts: popular recreations in the west Midlands and south Yorkshire

At the heart of the recreational calendar throughout these industrial districts lay the dedication feasts of parish churches and chapels, popularly known in the west Midlands and the north-west as 'wakes', and across Yorkshire as 'feasts'. In contrast to market towns, where fairs, Shrovetide, and increasingly Guy Fawkes formed key events in the annual festive calendar, these wakes and feasts stand out as the most significant moment in the festive year in major industrial towns and in the hamlets and villages around them. Celebrations to commemorate the foundation of the parish church date back to at least the early sixteenth century and, like much popular festivity, they had come under attack in the half-century before the Civil War, but resurfaced with the restoration of Charles II.[5] When they reappeared they were no longer linked to parish finance, and the absence of institutional support makes it difficult to establish the geographical extent of dedication feasts over the eighteenth century. However, recent commentators have concluded that wakes were widespread across the Midland and northern counties, as well as in the Thames Valley, only becoming rare in East Anglia and the south-east, where their place was taken by small fairs without markets.[6]

Nowhere, however, did they continue more vigorously than in the industrial regions of the north.[7] As in other parts of the country, the evidence for these events is patchy, but a range of different sources suggests that all settlements in the region, no matter how small, enjoyed at least one annual celebration of this kind. In south Yorkshire, local newspapers rarely reported feasts: they tended to be reported only when accompanied by some mishap—such as the affray between labourers on the 'new navigation' and those from Knottingley, in October 1822; no more than half a dozen have been recorded in papers.[8] Local histories, mostly dating from the second half of the nineteenth century, provide a more comprehensive

---

[5] Hutton, *Rise and Fall*, pp. 118–20, 218–20, 229, 243.

[6] General surveys of wakes in Hutton, *Stations of the Sun*, pp. 348–59; Malcolmson, *Popular Recreations*, pp. 16–19.

[7] For Lancashire, see Poole, 'Wakes, holidays', pp. 32–43 (diss.); ibid., 'Oldham wakes', pp. 71–98.

[8] Darrington (*Wakefield and Halifax Journal*, 25 Oct. 1822). Also Beeston (*Leeds Mercury*, 10 Sept. 1825); Bingley (ibid., 4 Oct. 1823); Darnall (*Sheffield Independent*, 15 July 1820); Darton (*Sheffield Mercury*, 12 Aug. 1820); Huddersfield (*Leeds Mercury*, 15 Sept. 1810); Lindley (ibid., 13 July 1811).

overview of parish feasts—over thirty in all, spread throughout the West Riding, have been recorded in such sources.[9] But the writing of local histories was of course rather unsystematic, and parish feasts were no doubt also popular in the many villages and hamlets without historians. A mill-owner from Bramley, near Leeds, noted feasts in no fewer than five of the industrial hamlets around Leeds, none of which was recorded in the *Leeds Mercury*, and only two of which have been recorded in other printed sources.[10] It seems reasonable to conclude that these plebeian and privately organised festivals were to be found throughout the manufacturing districts of the West Riding—in large towns, villages and even the smallest industrial hamlet.

Similarly in the west Midlands, wakes, though imperfectly documented, were undoubtedly widespread in the early decades of the nineteenth century. In the largest regional centre, Birmingham, a number of different wakes were held throughout the summer months: there were at least three in the heart of the town, and many more scattered throughout the city's suburbs.[11] The major Staffordshire towns—Lichfield, Newcastle, Stoke, and Leek—each held an annual wake.[12] Wakes were held in many of the townships of the Black Country—over a dozen have been recorded[13]—

[9] Almondbury ([Easther], *Glossary of Almondbury*, pp. xv–xiv); Attercliffe, Bradwell, Crookes, Derwent, and Little Sheffield (Leader, *Old Sheffield*, pp. 201, 211–12); Alverthorpe (Clarkson, *Memories of Wakefield*, p. 60); Baildon, Shipley, Wilsden (Cudworth, *Round about Bradford*, pp. 337, 306, 222); Balby, Bentley, Conisbrough, Hexthorpe, Mexbrough, and Norton (Hatfield, *Notices of Doncaster*, i, pp. 80, 82–3); Birstal (Cradock, *Parish of Birstall*, pp. 27–8, 158); Cawthorne (Pratt, *History of Cawthorne*); Ecclesfield (Gatty, *Life at One Living*, p. 39); Honley (Jagger, *History of Honley*, pp. 146–7); Mirfield, (Pobjoy, *History of Mirfield*, p. 207); Morley (Smith, *History and Antiquities of Morley*, pp. 121–5); Oakworth, Keighley, and Exleyhead (Holmes, *Keighley Past and Present*, pp. 145, 150); Otley (Grainge, *History of Trimble*, p. 205); Pudsey ([Rayner], *History of Pudsey*, p. 194); Rothwell (Batty, *History of Rothwell*, p. 217); Sheffield—feasts at Broad Lane and the Wicker (Leader, *Old Sheffield*, pp. 200–1); Skelmanthorpe ([Marsden], *Reminiscences*, p. 7).
[10] Rogerson, 'Diary of Rogerson', Bramley, 25 July 1808, p. 86; Pudsey, 30 Aug. 1808, p. 87; Armley, 4 Sept. 1808, p. 87; Farsley, 3 Sept. 1809, p. 101; Horsforth, 24 Aug. 1812, p. 142.
[11] Deritend, Chapel, and Bell wakes (Hutton, *History of Birmingham*, pp. 133–5). Others mentioned in Edgebaston (*Birmingham Journal*, 13 Sept. 1828); Beech Lanes (*Aris's Birmingham Gazette*, 1 Nov. 1824); Ninevah (ibid., 10 Jan. 1825); Little Hockley Pool and Handsworth (ibid., 13 Oct. 1828).
[12] Lichfield (*Staffordshire Advertiser*, 25 Oct. 1828); Newcastle (ibid., 21 Sept. 1822); Stoke (ibid., 9 Aug. 1823); Leek (ibid., 2 Nov. 1822). No record of wakes at Stafford has been found.
[13] Bilston (*Staffordshire Advertiser*, 8 Sept. 1823); Bloxwich (*Aris's Birmingham Gazette*, 24 July 1769); Hales Owen (*Birmingham Weekly Post* (hereafter *BWP*) Notes and Queries, no. 2037); Handsworth (*Aris's Birmingham Gazette*, 13 Oct. 1828); Oldbury (*Birmingham Journal*, 12

and were also widespread in villages and hamlets in other parts of Staffordshire.[14]

Though many of these wakes and feasts were of fairly recent origin, they drew upon much older traditions of community and hospitality.[15] It was customary to clean homes in preparation of the wake and the annual celebration provided the occasion for much family visiting. Around Sheffield, it was thought that 'the best thing about that festival [Broad Lane feast] . . . was that it partook very much of the spirit and character of a social gathering of relatives and friends'.[16] Likewise, an inhabitant of Morley looked back at the village feast of the early nineteenth century, and concluded that the real enjoyment 'was in the fact that from far and wide would the stray members of a family converge towards their birthplace, to join the family circle at this festive season'.[17]

This tradition of travelling also ensured that most of the inhabitants of these regions would enjoy more than one annual wakes holiday. All annual celebrations of this kind attracted large numbers of visitors, both friends and others, from surrounding districts, and because neighbouring settlements celebrated wakes at different dates, there were numerous opportunities for reciprocal visiting throughout the period from early July to early December in densely populated industrial areas. An elderly buckle-maker from Birmingham remembered that the various parish and neighbouring wakes provided the opportunity for working men to enjoy a wake 'nearly every month'.[18] Even in the more isolated industrial towns in northern

---

Sept. 1829); Rowley Regis (*Aris's Birmingham Gazette*, 26 Oct. 1835); Rushall, Walsall (*Staffordshire Advertiser*, 25 Nov. 1826); Smethwick (ibid., 21 Oct. 1826); Tettenhall, Wolverhampton (*Wolverhampton Chronicle*, 29 Nov. 1815); Tipton (*Aris's Birmingham Gazette*, 9 Aug. 1824); Wednesbury (ibid., 4 Oct. 1824); West Bromwich (ibid., 17 Nov. 1823); Willenhall (*Staffordshire Advertiser*, 27 Sept. 1834).

[14] Wakes in Betley (23 Oct. 1819); Burslem (6 July 1822); Cheadle (3 Oct. 1835); Gnosal (25 Aug. 1827); Great Haywood (9 Oct. 1830); Hanley (12 Aug. 1820); Lane End (6 Dec. 1828); Penkridge (18 Oct. 1823); Uttoxeter (28 Sept. 1822). All dates from *Staffordshire Advertiser*.

[15] For the creation of new wakes and feasts in industrial districts, see in particular Poole, 'Wakes, holidays', pp. 32–43 (diss.); Reid, 'Interpreting the festival calendar', pp. 125–53.

[16] Leader, *Old Sheffield*, p. 200.

[17] Smith, *History and Antiquities of Morley*, p. 122.

[18] *Morning Chronicle*, 27 Jan. 1851. Cf. the millowner from Leeds for whom the repeated absence of millworkers during the feast season formed an ongoing source of irritation : 'I wish the devil had him who first instituted feasts . . . Only Scribblers and Stocks Running to-day. Our Slubbers have not given over feasting yet; they have done nothing those three days past; they are a set of clever fellows.' Rogerson, 'Diary of Rogerson', 30 Aug. 1809, p. 100. See also 30 Aug. 1808, p. 87; 22 July 1811, p. 123; 26 Aug. 1811, p. 124; 27 Aug. 1811, p. 124; 22 Aug 1812, p. 141.

Staffordshire most communities could expect to enjoy more than one wakes holiday.[19]

In most respects these occasions differed little from the feasts and wakes that had existed in the region in earlier, more pastoral times. They were occasions of purely local significance, and were celebrated with much the same range of entertainments that might be found at any country feast or fair. In Pudsey, for example, a local historian remembered 'pitching the bar, wrestling, hunting the pig, sack, smock, and wheelbarrow races' at the local feast.[20] Similar entertainments prevailed in the west Midlands: the local newspaper reported donkey and sack races at Betley wakes in 1819, and shows and races at Burslem in 1822.[21] Later in the century, inhabitants of Birmingham remembered 'dancing, drinking, singing, fighting, skittle play-ing, racing, jumping in sacks, dipping in tubs of water for money', and 'grinning through collars . . . leaping in sacks . . . bobbing at treacle rolls [and] climbing up poles for legs of mutton' at the town's annual wakes.[22]

Yet, although wakes and feasts in all industrial areas drew upon a shared set of customs and entertainments, it must also be noted that there was one region that diverged significantly from this generally consistent pattern. This was the west Midlands, and the wakes here were distinctive on account of the bull-baitings, which formed an indispensable part of the week's entertainments. In contrast to other regions, whether rural or indus-trial, every wake in Birmingham and the Black Country was opened with a celebratory bull-baiting, and wake-goers could expect to enjoy many more during the course of the week. No west Midlands wake was consid-ered complete without its bull-baiting: they were integral to popular cele-brations in this part of the country, sufficiently deeply rooted to lead one local historian to refer to 'the fetishism of the bull-baiting cult' in the region.[23]

The excitement began the day before, when local people could come and inspect the bull that had been provided for their sport. At Handsworth, for example, 'the bull was always got in readiness on the Saturday before the wake, and kept at the Jolly Bacchus stables, to be inspected by the company

---

[19] Similarly, the inhabitant of one village in Derbyshire remembered how 'three of four other villages expected to their share of the "fun"' at the time of the wake. *BWP* Notes and Queries, no. 2086.

[20] [Rayner], *History of Pudsey*, p. 194.

[21] *Staffordshire Advertiser*, 23 Oct. 1819; 6 July 1822.

[22] *BWP* Notes and Queries, no. 1639. Birmingham RL, [Jaffray], 'Hints for a history of Birmingham', 174534, ch. 16.

[23] Hackwood, *Old Sports*, p. 319.

visiting the house all day on Sunday'.[24] The entertainment began early the following morning, when the organisers of the sport endeavoured to walk the bull to the stake: at the appointed place, large crowds would have already assembled. In 1828 a constable directed to suppress a bull-baiting found 'upwards of a thousand persons assembled' between seven and eight on the Monday morning, and the bull already fixed to the stake.[25] A Handsworth man remembered finding it 'astonishing the number of people who came from Birmingham to see the first "out" of the bull by six o'clock on the Monday morning'.[26]

A wake always signified a bull-baiting, and the opening bull-baiting was a critical moment in the wake. It brought the crowd together at the beginning of the week's festivities, and ushered in the holidays that were to enliven the following three or four days. A good opening baiting was a matter of local pride in the Black Country townships, and stories about the theft of bulls the night before the wake were consequently long remembered.[27] The opening bull-bait lay at the core of the week's holiday, and was a central and distinctive feature of popular sports in this region.

This centrality of the bull-baiting to the annual wake is exemplified in many ways. One resident remembered a wake where there were no fewer than seven bulls lined up for baiting, but it was not unusual for three or four to be provided in the course of one wake.[28] Local ballads celebrated the tradition of bull-baiting at the wakes, and in the memories of the contributors to the Notes and Queries columns of the *Birmingham Weekly Post* the two events, wakes and bull-baitings, were similarly run together. Bull-baiting was not confined to the wakes: in Birmingham, one inhabitant remembered, the bulls were sometimes brought into the town after being baited at wakes nearby; 'these were chance baitings, however,' he added. 'The regular matches were got up during the holidays or wakes.'[29]

The popularity of animal baitings was not confined to the west Midlands, but was a characteristic shared by a number of industrial areas. The historian of the Lancashire wakes, Robert Poole, has observed that they were 'were notorious for blood sports and violence'; and bull- and

---

[24] *BWP* Notes and Queries, no. 34. In Broseley, Shropshire, 'to prevent the bull being tampered with' a man was usually employed to watch over it the previous night. Randall, *Broseley*, p. 181.

[25] *Aris's Birmingham Gazette*, 13 Oct. 1828.

[26] *BWP* Notes and Queries, no. 34.

[27] *BWP* Notes and Queries, no. 3287. See also Hackwood, *Old Sports*, pp. 316–17.

[28] *Morning Chronicle*, 3 March 1851. See also *BWP* Notes and Queries, no. 2037.

[29] *Morning Chronicle*, 3 March 1851.

Figure 10.   Photograph of the Old King and Queen Inn (Keele University Library,
Warrillow Collection).

bear-baiting were both common at Cheshire wakes.[30] Bull-baits were also
popular at wakes in the mining districts of Shropshire and in parts of
Derbyshire,[31] and they were certainly not absent in the West Riding either.
Yet, although bull- and bear-baiting continued as popular wake-time entertainment in these industrial regions many decades after they had begun to

---

[30] Poole, 'Wakes, holidays', p. 127 (diss.).
[31] Burne, *Shropshire Folklore*, ii, pp. 446–9; Smith, 'Memoir', pp. 181–2; *BWP* Notes and
Queries, no. 2086.

disappear from rural feasts and fairs, in none did their popularity match, or even come close to matching, the esteem with which they were held in Birmingham and the Black Country.

Consider, for example, the feasts of the West Riding of Yorkshire. Local newspapers provided occasional accounts of bull-baitings at local feasts during the first quarter of the nineteenth century;[32] and local historians writing in the second half of the century had no difficulty gathering recollections of baitings at feasts from their neighbours which they presented in addition to their own. Thus Henry Clarkson had 'lately had some conversation with an old inhabitant of Flanshaw, who tells me he has a perfect recollection of seeing a Bull Baiting take place'. Clarkson continued: 'though I do not remember Bull Baitings, I can well recollect, on several occasions, seeing Bear Baitings; which used to take place annually at Alverthorpe, a suburb of Wakefield, on the occasion of the "feast", in a field'. This sorry bear apparently spent his life 'in being baited at the village feasts'.[33] Alfred Easther, another Yorkshire folklorist, thought that bull-baiting continued at the dedication feast in Almondbury, outside Huddersfield, until 1824. Easther recalled that the bull had been brought from Flockton, an industrial village sitting in the middle of a triangle formed by the towns of Huddersfield, Wakefield, and Barnsley, and, like Clarkson's bear, it was kept 'for the express purpose of being baited at wakes, feasts &c'.[34] This Flockton bull was also remembered by inhabitants of Honley, another suburb of Huddersfield; other keepers of baiting animals were remembered in Ardsley, Ecclesfield, and Hemsworth, and a further three from Sheffield have been recorded.[35] In addition, bull-baiting was remembered in connection with the feasts in Pudsey, Exleyhood, Bingley, Skelmanthorpe, and at several feasts around Doncaster and Sheffield.[36]

Yet whilst bull- and bear-baiting were common in the West Riding, there is little to suggest that they formed a particularly significant element of the entertainments. There is scant evidence of any ritual surrounding these events; the Flockton bull, for example, was decorated with ribbons,

---

[32] See the references in footnote 8 above.

[33] Clarkson, *Memories of Wakefield*, pp. 59–60.

[34] [Easther], *Glossary of Almondbury*, p. xv.

[35] Jagger, *History of Honley*, pp. 147–9; Roberts, *History of Lofthouse*, ii, p. 46; Gatty, *Life at One Living*, p. 25; Hatfield, *Notices of Doncaster*, i, p. 80; Leader, *Old Sheffield*, pp. 209–11; *York Courant*, 21 Oct. 1790.

[36] [Rayner], *History of Pudsey*, pp. 195–6; Holmes, *Keighley Past and Present*, p. 149–50; Speight, *Chronicles of Bingley*, p. 274; [Marsden], *Reminiscences*, p. 7. For Doncaster and Sheffield, see the references in footnote 35 above.

and heralded by a band of music, but otherwise local inhabitants recalled few instances of ritual surrounding animal baitings. There are no accounts of animals being stabled in the town for the scrutiny of feast-goers the day before the feast begun, and no recollections of large crowds assembling in expectation of the animal's arrival. Joseph Rogerson, the millowner from Bramley, noted several feasts in the surrounding villages, but only one bull-baiting.[37] The arrival of a bearward was left to chance, a welcome but by no means indispensable component of the annual feast. And this suggests that bull-baiting occupied a very different position in the recreational calendar of this region. The relative indifference of feast-goers in the West Riding of Yorkshire to bull- and bear-baitings throws into relief the unique attachment of the inhabitants of the Black Country to this ancient pastime. Its high profile during the wakes in Birmingham and the west Midlands was not shared by all industrial areas; and consequently the especial significance of bull-baiting to this community cannot be explained simply with reference to the onset of industrialisation.

Nor indeed was it simply during the annual wakes that the contrasts between the popular cultures of these two regions were apparent. Shrove-tide, for example, was a significant date in the festive calendar in settlements situated in every corner of the country. The inhabitants of industrial cities, provincial towns, villages, and hamlets all drew upon a shared set of practices on this day—cockfighting, cock throwing, and football. But, despite this shared heritage, the form that the celebration took was nonetheless subject to marked regional contrasts. In the west Midlands, it was the blood sports, the cockfighting and throwing at cocks, which dominated the day. One inhabitant recalled the preparation of cocks continuing for several weeks in anticipation of the 'coming battle' on Shrove Tuesday;[38] and another looked back at the crowds of colliers and others that had 'flocked into Wednesbury' on Shrove Tuesday, in order to enjoy the cockfighting— 'the grand [event] of the year'.[39] The ancient custom of throwing at cocks was likewise particularly vigorous, and appears to have been slower to decline here than elsewhere.[40] In Birmingham, throwing at cocks developed into a spectator sport in the early nineteenth century: the sport consisted in shooting at the cock with a gun, rather than knocking him down with wooden batons; apparently, however, 'the birds breast acted as a shield,

[37] Rogerson, 'Diary of Rogerson', 28 Aug. 1809, p. 100.
[38] *BWP* Notes and Queries, no. 1921.
[39] Birmingham RL, 'Newspaper cuttings', 302127, p. 183.
[40] Reminiscences of throwing at cocks in the early nineteenth century: Scarratt, *Times in Potteries*, p. 121; *BWP* Notes and Queries, no. 1921.

and to kill the cock at one shot was not so easy a matter'.[41] In this form, the sport reportedly continued until the 1860s. It is also notable that the other activity to be widely practised in many areas on this day—football— was never mentioned with respect to either Birmingham or the Black Country.[42] The failure of the region's inhabitants to recall matches of football on Shrove Tuesday does not of course unequivocally establish that the game was not played, but it does suggest that the football, if played at all, occupied a position of relatively minor importance besides the real business of the day—the cockfighting and throwing at cocks.

Cockfighting was by no means confined to Shrove Tuesday: it was popular all over the west Midlands at other times of the year as well. One writer referred to the 'cockfighting mania' that had prevailed in the early nineteenth century, and its prominence during the Shrovetide holidays was doubtless built upon the fact that it was so deeply entrenched in Black Country society.[43] It was remembered that in the early part of the nineteenth century cockfighting contests in the Black Country were 'extremely frequent',[44] and that 'very few public-houses in the Black Country towns [were] considered perfect without their cock-pits'.[45] At the Blue Ball Tavern at Wednesbury, Monday was 'the great day' for cockfighting, though 'it was carried on at other times of the week' as well.[46] Likewise in Birmingham, Monday was the established day for cockfighting, particularly during winter.[47] In that town, one writer listed half a dozen public houses that were remembered half a century after the suppression of the sport as 'notable cocking-fighting houses', and added that there had been 'several others, now forgotten'.[48] The sport was no less popular in other parts of Staffordshire, which remained a stronghold of the sport until the twentieth century, long after being outlawed in the 1840s.[49]

The other major popular sport in the west Midlands was pugilism, and it was practised throughout the year. 'Prize-fighting held sway in a large

---

[41] *Birmingham Gazette and Express*, 9 Oct. 1908. Birmingham RL, 'Newspaper cuttings', 302127, p. 183.

[42] *BWP* Notes and Queries, no. 1921.

[43] Walsall AS, 'News cuttings', vi, p. 86. See also Birmingham RL, 'Newspaper cuttings', 302127, p. 183.

[44] *BWP* Notes and Queries, no. 3332.

[45] Ibid., no. 3319.

[46] Sandwell Community History and Archive Service, 'Wednesbury Notes and Queries', 'A cockpit at Wednesbury'.

[47] *Morning Chronicle*, 3 March 1851.

[48] Birmingham RL, 'Newspaper cuttings', 302135, p. 119.

[49] For cockfighting continuing at Lichfield, see *Birmingham Daily Mail*, 17 April 1874.

Wednesbury Cocking.

At Wednesbury there was a cocking,
  A match between Newton & Scroggins.
The Colliers and Nailors left work.
  And all to old Spittle's were jogging
To see this noble sport
  Many noted men resorted,
And though they had but little money,
  Yet that they freely sported.
There was Jeffery & Colburn from Hampton
  And Dusty from Bilston was there,
Plummery he came from Darlaston,
  And he was as rude as a bear
There was Old Will from Walsall,
  And Smacker from Westbromwich come
Blind Robin he came from Rowley,
  And staggering he went home.
Ralph Moody came hobbling along,
  As though he some cripple was mocking
To join in the blackguard throng,
  That met at Wednesbury Cocking;
He borrow'd a trifle off Doll,
  To back Old Taverner's grey.
He laid four pence halfpenny to four pence,
  Then lost and when broken away.
But soon he return'd to the pit,
  For he'd borrow'd a trifle more money,
And ventur'd another large bet
  Along with blobber mouth'd Coney;
When Coney demanded his money,
  As is common on all such occasions,
He cry'd b—st thee if thee don't hold thy
    peace,
  I'll pay thee as Paul paid the Ephesians.
Scroggin's breeches were made of Nankeen
  And wore very thin in the groin,
In stooping to handle his cock,
  His b——ks burst out behind!
Besides his shirt tail was bes—t,
  Which caused amoug them much laughter
Scroggins turn'd himself round in a pet,
  And cry'd b—g—rye, what is the matter?
The merning's sport being over,
  Old Spittle's a dinner proclaim'd,
Each man should dine for a groat,
  If he grumbled he ought to be d—d ;
For there was plenty of beef,
  But Spittle he swore by his troth,
That never a man should dine,
  Till he'd eaten his noggin of broth.
The beef it was Old and tough,
  Of a bull that was baited to death,
Barney Hyde got a lump in his throat,
  That had like to have stopped his breath
The company all fell into confusion,

At seeing poor Barney Hyde choaked,
  They took him into the kitchen,
  And held his head over the smoke.
They held him so close to the fire
  He frizzled just like a beef steak,
Then they threw him down on the floor.
  Which had like to have broken his neck ;
One gave him a kick on the stomach,
  Another a thump on the brow,
His wife said throw him into the stable,
  And he will be better just now.
Then they all returned to the pit
  And the fighting went forward again,
Six battles were won on each side,
  And the next was to decide the main,
For they were two famous cocks,
  As ever this country bred,
Scroggins's a duck-winged black,
  And Newton's a shift-winged red,
The conflict was hard on both sides
  Till brassy wing'd Blacky was choak'd,
The colliers were nationly vext
  And the nailors were sorely provok'd;
Peter Stevens he swore a great oath
  That Scroggins had played his cock
    foul,
Scroggins gave him a kick on the head,
  And cried, Yea, God d— thy soul.
The company then fell in discord,
  A bold fight did ensue,
kick b—and bite was the word,
  Till the Walsall men all were subdu'd ;
Ralph Moody bit off a man's nose,
  And wish'd that he could have him slain
So they trampled both cocks to death,
  And then made a draw of a main.
The cock-pit was near to the church,
  An ornament unto the town,
On one side au old coal pit,
  The other well gors'd round;
Peter Hadley peep'd through the gorse,
  In order to see them fight,
Spittle jobb'd his eye out with a fork,
  And said b—t thee it served thee right,
Some people may think this is strange,
  Who Wednesbury never knew,
But those who have ever been there
  Won't have the least doubt but it's true;
For they are all savage by nature,
  And guilty of deeds the most shocking
Jack Baker whack'd his own father,
  And so ended Wednesbury Cocking.

25

Figure 11. *Wednesbury Cocking* (William Salt Library, Stafford).

part of the Black Country', and informal set-tos were extremely common: 'hardly a week passed without matches being arranged either between local youths or men of note' a working man recalled in the late nineteenth century.[50] In the Potteries, boxing was 'in great favour' in the early nineteenth century.[51] The south Staffordshire collieries had their own championship and, at one colliery, every Monday was largely given over to prize-fighting.[52] Fields to the north-west of the city provided the location for many of these prize-fights,[53] and the wakes provided the occasion for many more—for 'plenty of unprofessional boxing'.[54]

As with the other sports of the region, pugilism was by no means confined to this district. Pugilism was a spectator sport with national appeal, and the tendency of men to fall to blows was familiar everywhere. However, the evidence suggests that fighting sports had a particularly high profile in the west Midlands, and that rates of participation were also high. One resident recalled that Birmingham during the 1830s had been 'quite a nest of young pugilists', and that there might be so many as half a dozen battles held on the fields and waste that surrounded Birmingham on a single evening.[55] The Staffordshire newspapers contained numerous reports of fights that had ended in death—some had been organised challenges, and others had begun as personal, often drunken, quarrels.[56] One can assume that these cases represent a very small minority of the fights contested, and that fist-fighting was an extremely common occurrence.

Besides bull-baiting, cockfighting, and boxing, the sports that inhabitants of Birmingham and its suburbs most frequently recalled were badger-baiting and dog-fighting. The requirements of both of these sports were few and simple; for this reason, both were practised on a very regular basis across the seasons. In the opinion of one inhabitant, badger-baiting had been 'almost as common as cock-fighting'.[57] Dog-fighting was likewise

---

[50] Walsall AS, 'News cuttings', vi, p. 86; Birmingham RL, 'Newspaper cuttings', 302127, p. 183.

[51] [Shaw], *When I was a Child*, p. 190.

[52] Sandwell Community History and Archive Service, 'Wednesbury Notes and Queries', no. 379; *BWP* Notes and Queries, no. 3368; *Staffordshire Advertiser*, 20 Jan. 1827.

[53] *BWP* Notes and Queries, no. 384.

[54] *Morning Chronicle*, 3 March 1851. See also *BWP* Notes and Queries, no. 3287.

[55] *BWP* Notes and Queries, no. 384.

[56] *Staffordshire Advertiser*, 19 July 1819, 13 July 1822, 5 April 1823, 7 Jan. 1826, 27 May 1826 (two separate incidences), 15 July 1826, 25 Nov. 1826, 13 Jan. 1827, 31 March 1827, 22 Sept. 1827. See also *Birmingham Journal*, 8 Aug. 1829.

[57] *Morning Chronicle*, 3 March 1851. He considered that both had been more frequent than bull-baiting which was 'a more costly, and consequently a rarer source of amusement', largely confined to the wakes.

simple to organise and extremely common. It was thought by one resident to have been 'in vogue' in the early nineteenth century.[58] Oldbury was remembered for its dog-fights in the street and rat-killing contests;[59] and a resident of Birmingham recalled that dog-fights were 'got up' every Monday.[60] The simplicity with which these sports were fixed also ensured that both proved difficult to eradicate. The workman of Birmingham who recalled the dogfights on Mondays suggested that dog-fighting continued until at least the 1850s: 'there are a few still in the summer time, when the men do not think much of walking a few miles out of this overgrown town to some quiet part of the country'.[61]

And no less significant than the popularity of these activities is the indifference with which certain other sports were regarded. Team sports, athletic sports, and games of skill were all little known in this region. Some form of football has been recorded in every corner of the land, but in the west Midlands it appears to have been largely confined to the young: 'Our sports used to be cock-fighting, bull-baiting, skittle-playing, quoits, foot-ball, leapfrog, &c.' recalled one inhabitant of Birmingham in the 1850s. He claimed that bull-baiting, cockfighting, and ratting had held little attraction to him, but added 'I know these sports were very common among the workmen, and were more talked about and thought of than such games as foot-ball, "foot and horse shoe" (leap-frog), or prison bars, which were more popular among boys and young lads'.[62] Another resident recalled a playing space that had been used by workmen and young men of the town for playing 'foot-ball, leap-frog, and other games of the sort', though he too added that such games had been less popular than blood sports.[63] None of the dozens of locals who contributed to the discussions of sports and pastimes in the Notes and Queries columns of the *Birmingham Weekly Post* in the 1860s referred to the playing of cricket or football in the early nineteenth century. Their extensive recollections were focused exclusively upon the wakes, blood sports, and pugilism, and, though it would be mistaken to conclude from this bias that athletic sports such as football were not played, it certainly suggests they occupied a position of lesser importance.

[58] Walsall AS, 'News cuttings', vi, p. 86.
[59] Hackwood, *Oldbury Round and About*, p. 310.
[60] *Morning Chronicle*, 3 March 1851.
[61] Ibid.
[62] *Morning Chronicle*, 27 Jan. 1855.
[63] In his opinion, 'cock-fighting and more brutal amusements were more popular than healthy games'. *Morning Chronicle*, 3 March 1851.

The contrast with the sports and recreations of the West Riding of Yorkshire is immediately clear. There was much overlap in the recreations that were practised in these two contrasting industrial communities, yet in each region certain sports occupied a position of particular importance, while others were of more marginal significance. Thus bull- and bear-baiting, as we have already seen, were well-established pastimes throughout the towns and villages of south Yorkshire, though they had none of the symbolic meaning that they so clearly had at the wakes of Birmingham and the Black Country. Likewise, prize-fighting was practised here as else-where, though there is little to suggest that it stood out as a particularly sig-nificant form of recreation in the way it did in the Black Country. There were certainly fewer deaths from fighting noted in the local papers;[64] and fighting and wrestling were mentioned in connection with the feasts by only a small number of writers. In the words of one historian, prize-fights on the moor at Eccleshill were 'occasional'.[65] It seems to have occupied a similar position to bull-baiting—a pastime with which all were certainly familiar, but one that was not inordinately prized.

Football, by contrast, clearly occupied a more significant position in the recreational calendar of the towns and villages of south Yorkshire. No doubt much of this football would have consisted in the informal kicking around of a ball perennially popular amongst young men, but what most writers thought worthy of record were the great set matches played between parish teams at specific moments of the calendar. Around Huddersfield, for exam-ple, it was the 'great games of football' played at 'festal seasons' that that dis-trict's historian noted; and in Pudsey, the 'great excitement' caused by the 'great set matches' was described.[66] At Lofthouse and Rothwell a match was played annually on Shrove Tuesday; and at Morley and Slaithwaite football was 'only indulged in during the Christmas festivities'.[67] Around Keighley, matches were played 'township . . . against township, and village against vil-lage' and annually 'the great set matches between the town and parish of Keighley' caused particular excitement.[68]

[64] See, however, *Sheffield Independent*, 15 July 1820, 22 Aug. 1835; *Sheffield Mercury*, 14 Oct. 1820.

[65] Cudworth, *Round about Bradford*, p. 346.

[66] [Easther], *Glossary of Almondbury*, p. xix; [Rayner], *History of Pudsey*, p. 197.

[67] Roberts, *History of Lofthouse*, ii, p. 30; Batty, *History of Rothwell*, p. 216; Smith, *History and Antiquities of Morley*, p. 128; Sugden, *Slaithwaite*, p. 64. Quote from Smith.

[68] Holmes, *Keighley Past and Present*, p. 61. See also Jagger, *History of Honley*, p. 145. See also the battle for possession of Lawe Hill between 'Thornes and Wakefield's lads'. Clarkson, *Merry Wakefield*, p. 64.

This is not to suggest that a non-violent team sport took the place of prize-fighting in the West Riding, since in its traditional form football was often regarded as a combat sport rather than as a team game. For example, in the opinion of Richard Holmes, the historian of Keighley, football was 'sometimes carried to a riotous and dangerous extent'.[69] Alfred Easther, master of the grammar school at Huddersfield and historian of the district, thought that the games would 'astonish the athletes of our days [1880s]'. During the course of a match between Almondbury and Farnley on Christmas day, 1819, he remembered, 'many ferocious kicks were given and received . . . even when the ball was scores of yards away men stood kicking each other violently'; furthermore, 'the kicks were by no means child's play, as they were all administered in clogs'.[70] Almost all of the Yorkshire historians who remembered early-nineteenth-century inter-village football matches commented on the violence of the play, and noted how peaceable the modern game of football was in comparison with the old. As the historian of Pudsey opined, it would be voted 'tame and insipid, and . . . only fit for children'.[71] It was, however, a relatively structured and organised form of violence, quite unlike the slugging out between individuals carried out on the wastelands that encircled Birmingham. Certainly, in both regions, violence was an established and entirely unexceptional element of recreation; but violence was channelled in different ways, and there can be no easy generalisations about the coarse brutality of the early industrial worker.

Football matches provided exercise and exhilaration for the men who played in them, but they also had a significance to the broader community, providing an opportunity for the expression of village identity and pride. Unlike the modern game developed in the second half of the nineteenth century, in which team support became very much a male preserve, the spectatorship of these games was not confined to the male population, and they could be expected to attract large crowds of all ages and both sexes. Just as the crowds that waited hours in the Black Country to witness the wake's opening bull-bait were filled with women as well as men, so annual football matches were not gender specific in their appeal, and the outcome of matches was the focus of local pride for every member of the community.

[69] Holmes, *Keighley Past and Present*, p. 61.
[70] [Easther], *Glossary of Almondbury*, p. xix.
[71] [Rayner], *History of Pudsey*, p. 196.

There are no examples of the inhabitants of one Black Country township competing against those of another in such a formal and structured way, but feelings of parish loyalty were not unknown in Black Country townships and, in the absence of competitive team sports, they necessarily found expression in other forms. There was, for example, much pride in every township concerning their annual wake; evidence of township solidarity is contained in accounts of the regular attempts by the young men of one township to prevent those from a neighbouring township attending their wake. As one resident recalled:

> At Wake times it was a frequent occurrence for a certain section of the dwellers of Willenhall to forbid the natives of Darlaston, Wednesbury, Bloxwich and Bilston to visit their Wake. These warnings were seldom heeded . . . and many a broken crown and severe battles were the result of encounters on many occasions.[72]

Of course, the opening bull-baiting, in which so much significance was invested was a particular focal point for parish pride, and was for this reason also uniquely vulnerable to sabotage. According to one contributor to the Notes and Queries columns of the local newspaper, it was 'common practice to steal each other's bulls and bears'.[73] Such attempts, though rarely successful, were part and parcel of the mayhem and mischief associated with the annual wakes, and an effective way of one township attempting to establish supremacy over another.

Likewise all other sports popular in the west Midlands were occasionally enjoyed competitively between townships, and thereby became the focus of parish pride. For example, dog-fighting, though essentially a sport between individuals, could easily be, and often was, organised into matches between neighbouring townships. As one resident recalled: 'Dogs from one district were pitted against those from another, just as rival teams from one town encounter another in a game of football.' Some of the 'fiercest fights' apparently resulted from meetings of dogs belonging to Oldbury and Rowley owners.[74] Cockfighting matches could likewise be organised competitively between different settlements. One resident of Wednesbury recalled: 'There were times when two towns would club together for providing and training a number of cocks in order to give some neighbouring town a sound thrashing. On more than one occasion Willenhall and

[72] *BWP* Notes and Queries, no. 3287.
[73] Ibid., See also Hackwood, *Old Sports*, pp. 316–17.
[74] Walsall AS, 'News cuttings', vi, p. 86.

Wednesfield have thus become allies.'[75] Pride in locality was characteristic of all these industrial communities, and the sports they prized the most were invariably the vehicle through which that pride might be expressed. Thus, just as violence was focused in distinct ways, so the different industrial cultures provided unique outlets for their sense of community. In the case of the West Riding, parish pride was based upon team cooperation between inhabitants of the village. Team cooperation of this kind was largely unknown in the west Midlands, but their sports and pastimes were nonetheless a valuable mechanism through which members of the different townships might express their pride in community and locality.

Finally, and again in contrast to the Black Country, a game of skill—knur and spell—was popular in south Yorkshire. The game was played with a type of wooden bat (the spell), and a ball (the knur), and the object was to hit the ball through wide, but very distant goals. It was played by boys in teams, but adult matches were usually played between individuals, and could attract large numbers of spectators. The moor at Eccleshill was famous for knur and spell matches prior to enclosure in the 1840s.[76] In the opinion of one writer the sport had been 'much more popular' than football in the early part of the century;[77] and at Rothwell it remained popular into the late nineteenth century, although 'it does not meet with much esteem from the highest society'.[78] The sport was clearly dependent upon the large heaths and moors around Yorkshire, but there were also certain qualities inherent in the game that deserve emphasis. It was a game of skill, requiring careful practice. As one local historian explained, knur and spell required 'steady nerve and pluck, and it was absolutely necessary for the players in the midst of all the excitement to keep perfectly cool'.[79] Such qualities were not called for by the blood sports so beloved by the inhabitants of Birmingham and the west Midlands, though skill and expertise were perhaps directed into the breeding and training of animals to some degree instead.

It is clear, therefore, that there were many differences between the popular sports enjoyed in the two regions. The most striking was the enduring popularity of blood sports and combat sports in the west Midlands. Bull-baiting, cockfighting, badger-baiting, dog-fighting, and fist-

---

[75] *BWP* Notes and Queries, no. 3319.
[76] Cudworth, *Round about Bradford*, p. 348; see also p. 90.
[77] Smith, *History and Antiquities of Morley*, p. 130.
[78] Batty, *History of Rothwell*, p. 215.
[79] Smith, *History and Antiquities of Morley*, p. 132.

fighting—it was widely agreed that these pastimes had dominated the recreational hours of working men in the early part of the nineteenth century. Each of these sports was enjoyed in some form in other parts of the country as well, yet contemporary songs and ballads celebrating blood sports and pugilism, and the detailed recollections of these pastimes that inhabitants of the district provided later in the century, are testimony to the scale and significance of these pastimes in the west Midlands; it is this, the intensity of working people's attachment to these pastimes, that is exceptional. All these pastimes were familiar in the West Riding as well, but none stood out in this way; football and knur and spell were the sports that dominated here. The working people of these two districts did not inhabit different cultural universes; both possessed a recognisably similar popular culture, and the differences between the two regions were those of emphasis rather than of form. The same dates and occasions—Guy Fawkes, Shrove Tuesday, and feast days—were celebrated, and much the same sports and games were played, but each region made something very different of these shared practices. Over the years, different communities had fashioned distinct and unique local cultures from a common set of resources.

Understanding cultural difference

In order to understand the distinct cultural patterns outlined here, we need to be clear about exactly how the popular culture of the two regions diverged. At two centuries' remove, the most striking contrast is the violent and brutal nature of the recreations enjoyed in the west Midlands. It was very generous of a late-nineteenth-century historian of the Black Country to remark that the district's 'outdoor amusements have been marked by a boisterousness';[80] most commentators, both then and since, have condemned them more simply as 'barbarous and brutal'.[81] Yet we need to be wary of placing too much emphasis upon the violent and brutal nature of pastimes in the west Midlands for, as the evidence from the football matches played in the West Riding makes clear, violence was by no means absent from this district either.

Nor indeed was it simply in these two industrialising parts of the country that sports and pastimes involving a high degree of violence were to be

[80] Walsall AS, 'News cuttings', vi, p. 86.
[81] *Aris's Birmingham Gazette*, 4 Feb. 1811.

found. Inter-personal violence was a central component of the sports and recreations of many regions, rural as well as urban, throughout the long eighteenth century. The West Country and Thames Valley, for example, were overwhelmingly pastoral regions, yet the inhabitants of this corner of the land nonetheless enjoyed their own extremely brutal forms of combat sports. This region was the heartland of a family of sports known as cudgelling, single stick, and backsword—forms of combat in which participants used simple sticks both to attack and defend. Do not be deceived by the homely names. Backsword was condemned by William Morris as a 'skull-cracking game'.[82] The object of cudgelling (as a contributor to Hone's *Year Book* helpfully explained), was to 'fetch blood from the other's head; whether by taking a little skin from his pericranium, or drawing a stream from his nose, or knocking out a few of . . . the teeth'.[83] In order to arbitrate justly between combatants, cudgelling contests specified exactly how much blood needed to be 'drawn', adverts usually stipulated one inch.[84] This, clearly, was not a sport for the fainthearted. Violence was integral to the sports and recreations of many different parts of the country; and possibly the most striking characteristic of eighteenth-century sport is not the level of violence it contained, but rather the many different forms in which it could be found.

The pugilism of the Black Country, the football matches of south Yorkshire, and the cudgelling of the West Country were not exceptional; all belonged to a society in which a high degree of violence was not simply tolerated, but was accepted as a part of daily life. The normality of violence is illustrated by the diary of John Clifton, a master craftsman living in the quiet Northamptonshire town of Oundle. Fist-fights and street brawls punctuate Clifton's diary, and his comments upon these events suggest a society very much less sensitive to bloodshed than our own. Clifton looked out upon a 'bungling battle';[85] a 'Severe Battle';[86] and a number of 'Bloody Battle[s]'—and he clearly enjoyed them all.[87] He witnessed fights between

[82] Morris, *Swindon Fifty Years Ago*, p. 134.

[83] Hone, *Year Book*, col. 1525. See also the detailed account of backsword in Morris, *Swindon Fifty Years Ago*, pp. 128–40.

[84] *Jackson's Oxford Journal*, 29 Sept. 1753. See also ibid., 7 Aug. 1762 (Kennington), 6 May 1780 (Uffingham Hill); *Northampton Mercury*, 20 July 1761 (Chesham).

[85] Northamptonshire RO, Clifton's Day Books, 1763–1784, ZA/8732–463, 6 May 1778; 4 Jan. 1772.

[86] Ibid., 9 July 1778.

[87] Ibid., 30 June 1781; 8 Dec. 1781; 9 Feb 1782.

women as well as men.[88] One night he reported upon 'The most Severe Battle fought to Night Opposite my Door as ever I saw in my Life'. He continued:

> they got Collar hold of their Shirts with their left Hands & knocked with their right Fists as many bitter Bangs at each others Ribs as would have served for Ten good fair Battles & it is my Opinion there were more severe sturdy Knocks in this Battle than in all the Battles that have been fought in this Town the last 20 years put together.[89]

Another year he witnessed a fight in which 'a great many sturdy Bangs were exchanged on both sides & a plentiful flow of Blood issued from their Snouts';[90] and another that continued until the combatants 'could hardly be distinguished for Blood'.[91] It is clear that Clifton relished these fights, and found nothing disturbing about the blood and violence they involved. Of course, we should not presume that Clifton's taste for violent sports was shared by all, but the widespread practice of many different forms of combat sports suggests that Clifton was certainly not unusual. Violent combat between animals and humans existed in some form in all parts of the country, and for this reason it is unhelpful to frame the contrast between these two industrial cultures in terms of the presence of violence in one, and its absence in the other.

Besides the brutality or otherwise of the pastimes of these two industrial regions, there are two further qualities that are worth underlining— less colourful, yet no less significant. In the first instance, there is a clear contrast between the two regions in terms of team cooperation. In the West Riding, a degree of organisation and team solidarity is evident in popular recreations, qualities that were largely absent in the west Midlands. The annual matches of football enjoyed in many parts of south Yorkshire called for the inhabitants of one settlement to cooperate as a team against those of another. Around Birmingham and the Black Country, recreations were considerably more individualistic, and team cooperation was essentially unknown. All the sports and pastimes of this region involved pitting individuals (or their animals) against each other: team games barely existed; where they did, they were for boys and young lads, not for adults.

---

[88] Ibid., 30 June 1781; 9 Feb 1782. See also de Saussure, *Letters of de Saussure*, pp. 277–9.
[89] Northamptonshire RO, Clifton's Day Books, 1763–1784, ZA/8732–463, 9 July 1778.
[90] Northamptonshire RO, Clifton's Day Books, 1763–1784, ZA/8732–463, 2 Oct. 1778.
[91] Ibid., 30 March 1771. See also the accounts of fist-fighting given by Joseph Wooley. Nottinghamshire Archives, Joseph Wooley, his book of Memorandums, DD311/1–6, 30 July 1804, 4 Oct. 1804.

And no less important than this distinction is the degree of hostility towards authority that it is possible to detect in Black Country sports. We noted in the last chapter that polite opinion was turning away from blood sports in the late eighteenth century, and the continued support for a wide range of animal combat sports throughout Birmingham and the Black Country was clearly at odds with these new cultural mores. Nor can it be claimed that the workers who participated in cockfighting, bull-baiting, and badger-baiting were unaware of the shifts in opinion that had occurred. By the early nineteenth century, local leaders, no doubt sensitive to the criticisms against blood sports that were being voiced evermore widely, began to take steps to curtail bull-baiting at the wakes, initiatives that were initially disrespected by the working population, and which later ignited serious conflict between the wake-goers and authorities. This hostile response to attempts to reform popular culture is considered in greater detail in Chapter 9, but for the present it is important to emphasise that the followers of these sports were undoubtedly aware that their pastimes were controversial; and, furthermore, that this did nothing but increase the tenacity with which they were held. Sports and recreations were an ongoing source of conflict between the workforce and the authorities in the early nineteenth century, and the industrial workforce of this region revelled in a festive culture that was rebellious and proudly unsubmissive.

These then are the distinctions between the popular culture of the two regions that merit further investigation. It is not the 'violence' of pastimes in the Black Country that was exceptional, but the individualism of the sports and the rebelliousness of the popular culture. Popular culture in the West Riding of Yorkshire differed in both these respects. The sports most highly valued here called for team cooperation and skill, and the local population showed no inclination to battle with social elites over sports such as bull- and bear-baiting, as they rapidly fell from favour.

There are no simple explanations for the distinctive profiles that popular culture had developed in these two regions by the early nineteenth century, though it may be possible to relate the differences to the unique work structures of each. Both regions had undergone rapid industrialisation in the second half of the eighteenth century, but there were significant differences here, as elsewhere, in the outcome of these economic developments. In the West Riding, the growth of the textile industry had been accompanied by new scales of production, and the construction of mills and factories. Not all sectors of the economy were affected equally by these developments, and even in the production of worsteds, where the development of the factory system was most pronounced, many of the new factories were small.

Nonetheless, the early nineteenth century was clearly a period of economic transition, and the introduction of new factory-based forms of production in the region was unmistakeable. The contrast with the west Midlands is clear. In Birmingham and the Black Country, the most notable character-istic of industrialisation was its reliance upon existing skills, tools, and work structures. In this region, economic expansion was achieved almost entirely by the expansion and intensification of existing forms of production, rather than in the introduction of new factories, creating a workforce that continued to exercise considerable control over the hours and pace of work.[92]

The supervision of workers in mills and factories in the cotton and tex-tiles districts was favourably compared by contemporaries with the 'inde-pendence' of labourers in the cottage industries and workshops of the west Midlands. In Disraeli's *Sybil*, for example, the fictional village of Wodgate was 'without a factory or large establishment of any kind', and the workforce was depicted as irreligious, uneducated, and lawless on this account.[93] The few early-nineteenth-century industrial workers in the region who have left any record of their working lives agreed they had enjoyed considerable auton-omy at the time. For example, a Birmingham buckle-maker looking back at the early nineteenth century recalled: 'A workman was a workman in those days . . . and the men were very independent in their whole behaviour. They would not work unless they pleased.'[94] Likewise a Staffordshire worker recalling life in the Potteries in the early nineteenth century believed that the absence of the 'disciplinary grip of machinery' had enabled the workmen to enjoy a lively recreational life, and contributed to the disorderly conduct of the local workforce.[95] Many contemporaries noted that unsupervised work-ing conditions went hand in hand with a vibrant recreational calendar, and this observation may help to explain the regionally specific popular cultures that have been described here.

There is clear evidence that those who participated in blood sports and pugilism in the west Midlands were invariably employed in classic small-scale manufacture. In Wolverhampton in 1815, for example, a miner, screw-filer, snuffer-maker, carpenter, latch-forger, and tin-plate-worker were prosecuted for bull-baiting.[96] On other occasions carters, iron-workers,

---

[92] For the West Riding, see Berg, *Age of Manufactures*, pp. 208–79. For the west Midlands, see Hopkins, *Rise of Manufacturing Town*, pp. 40–61.
[93] Disraeli, *Sybil*. See, in particular, bk 3, ch. 4.
[94] *Morning Chronicle*, 27 Jan. 1855.
[95] [Shaw], *When I was a Child*, pp. 191–2.
[96] *Wolverhampton Chronicle*, 29 Nov. 1815.

gun-barrel-makers, butchers, and colliers were involved.[97] In Oldbury, it was recalled that dog-fighting had been the sport of miners and forge-men;[98] and in Birmingham, a workman in the 'chandelier and gas fitting trade' found himself in trouble for attending a cockfight after the sport had been outlawed in the 1840s.[99] Workers in all these trades worked by the piece rather than the hour, and in small workshops rather than in facto-ries.[100] Low wages and the necessities of survival ensured that here, as else-where, workers usually worked extremely long hours, and it is important that the 'freedom' and 'independence' of these workers should not be exag-gerated. Nonetheless, there is a clear contrast between these occupations and the factory-based employment to be found in south Yorkshire, and there are discernable connections between the working patterns that pre-vailed in each and the recreations they pursued. In the west Midlands, both work and recreation were organised on an individual basis, whilst in the more organised workforce of the West Riding team sports and team cooperation had a far greater hold.

Yet, at the same time it is important not to press this explanation too far; if there were striking differences between the working and employment cultures of the two regions, so were there important similarities, and the complexity of social and economic organisation is likely to undermine simple accounts of the divergences in popular culture described here. Any generalisation about the economy of the West Riding is difficult since the economies of the large towns and industrial hamlets that lay within the region were extremely varied, but it is clear that south Yorkshire was not transformed by mills and factories to the same extent as south Lancashire. Traditional forms of putting-out and artisan manufacture continued well into the nineteenth century, and in some towns the continuation of older methods of production was particularly pronounced—Sheffield, for exam-ple, continued to be dominated by skilled workshop manufacture well into the second half of the nineteenth century.[101] The variety of the many local economies that existed in the West Riding ensured that there were pock-ets with employments patterns similar to those that prevailed in the west

[97] *Aris's Birmingham Gazette*, 7 Nov. 1823; *Pottery Gazette*, 12 Oct. 1822; *Staffordshire Advertiser*, 2 Nov. 1822, 18 Oct. 1828; *Wolverhampton Chronicle*, 8 Oct. 1824.
[98] Walsall AS, 'News cuttings', vi, p. 86.
[99] *Morning Chronicle*, 3 March 1851.
[100] For Birmingham working conditions, see Hopkins, *Rise of Manufacturing Town*, pp. 102–17.
[101] See, in particular, Hudson, *Genesis of Industrial Capital*, pp. 25–48. For Sheffield, see Tweedale, *Steel City*, pp. 27–60.

Midlands, and we must take care, therefore, not to over-exaggerate the economic difference that existed between these two regions. Likewise, the economy of Birmingham and the Black Country, though distinctive in many ways, nonetheless bore continuities with those of other towns. The economy of Birmingham was undoubtedly dominated by small-scale domestic manufacture throughout the period, yet domestic service remained the town's largest employer, a characteristic which it shared with many towns of all kinds, and in every region.[102] In fine, both regions had distinctive yet very complex employment structures and patterns of work. It is certainly possible to delineate a number of real differences between the economies of the west Midlands and south Yorkshire, yet at the same time there were marked continuities, not only across these two regions, but with other parts of the kingdom as well, and there are clearly no simple equations between industrialisation and popular culture to be drawn.

It may well be that history had played its part in creating the distinctive forms of popular culture that have been illustrated here. Although it is tempting to look to the rapid economic changes that were occurring in the late eighteenth century for explanations of these cultural peculiarities, it is possible that the economic changes occurring at this date were played out in districts that already possessed distinct cultural profiles. The popularity of blood sports extended beyond the industrial heart of the west Midlands, throughout rural Staffordshire and into Cheshire, and it is likely that the distribution of these sports and pastimes in the early nineteenth century reflected cultural patterns that had been established in centuries before. Taking this point further is not possible, since we do not have sufficiently detailed information about cultural practice in either region for the early eighteenth century and before, but the spatial distribution of these sports through Staffordshire points strongly to the existence of distinctive patterns prior to the onset of the industrial revolution. Industrialisation in the second half of the eighteenth century and the distinctive work cultures that it produced worked upon popular cultures that were already specific in form, cultures that had in turn been shaped in earlier times by the social and economic context within which they were situated.

As we have seen, industrialisation in the west Midlands was accompanied by greater control over working hours than was usual elsewhere, and this allowed for the creation and development of unique recreational patterns, regardless of whether these patterns were of long-standing or of more

[102] Hopkins, *Rise of Manufacturing Town*, p. 53. See also Rowlands, 'Continuity and change', pp. 103–31.

recent creation. In Birmingham and the Black Country, the practice of St Monday, the custom of remaining away from work on Mondays, and sometimes during part of Tuesday as well, was recalled as frequently as bull-baiting, dog-fighting, and cockfighting, and it is difficult to envisage how the vibrant and rebellious popular culture that has been described here could have become so deeply rooted in the region without this day, devoted each week to the practice of these favoured recreations.[103] St Monday enabled the consolidation and entrenchment of the distinctive popular culture that was flourishing here in the early part of the nineteenth century, and if not the individualism, certainly the rebelliousness and the hostility towards authority could only occur in the context of a workforce not tied to the discipline of the factory.

Popular culture emerges, therefore, as something that is continuously in a state of creation; and there can be no question of reaching backwards in search of an earlier popular culture, of searching for the 'traditional' culture, those sports and pastimes that existed before everything began to change. Popular culture was always changing, being reworked and recreated by successive generations in turn. This research has revealed highly distinctive patterns of popular recreation in two industrial districts separated by a distance of little more than 100 miles. There is no definitive explanation of the causes of this diversity that we can offer, but we can confidently point to the existence of contrasting patterns of employment in each region, and delineate key similarities between these and the recreation patterns with which they coexisted. In each region, popular culture was the product of local social and economic forces. The complex links between local society and local culture created two dynamic and unique popular cultures, and, if the exact nature of these links calls for further investigation, this research has nonetheless succeeded in drawing attention to the power with which small-scale local forces could shape distinctive cultural profiles, and underscores the importance of incorporating a concept of locality into our studies of popular culture.

---

[103] See, for example, *Morning Chronicle*, 3 March 1851; *BWP* Notes and Queries, no. 3368; Shaw, *When I was a Child*, p. 31. See also Reid, 'Decline of Saint Monday', pp. 76–101.

7

Space for recreation in industrial England

737. Is there any accommodation in the nature of public walks in the vicinity of Bury, sufficient to satisfy the growing population of the town?—No, we are greatly wanting in that . . .

756. Does the change of employment that has taken place in your district form in your opinion, a sufficient ground why there should be some accommodation of this kind?—Yes for the factory children, after they have done their work; they might take some exercise by way of straightening their limbs.[1]

This chapter continues the investigation into recreation in industrial areas begun in the last, but brings the focus back to the theme that runs throughout this book: that of space. Here we investigate the spaces that existed for the sports and pastimes described in the previous chapter, and assess how far pressure on space in early-nineteenth-century industrial towns served to constrict the practice of these. The quotes above are taken from a select committee appointed in 1833 to investigate this very issue. The speaker was Richard Walker, member of parliament for Bury, Lancashire, and his bleak assessment of recreation grounds in this industrial town was not unusual. Few by the early nineteenth century could fail to be aware of the urbanisation and industrialisation occurring in Yorkshire, Lancashire, the west Midlands, and the north-east; and the conclusion that many reached from this rapid and unmistakable urban expansion was that an increasingly large number of town dwellers were living without access to open space in which they might take exercise. The Select Committee on Public Walks appointed in 1833 was the government's response to this concern. It noted that owing to urban development and rising property values during the previous fifty years 'many inclosures of open space in the vicinity of Towns have taken place, and little or no provision has been made for Public Walks or Open Spaces, fitted to afford means of exercise or amusement to the

[1] *1833 Select Committee on Public Walks*, p. 394.

middle or humbler classes'.[2] It gathered information from witnesses in London and a further dozen large towns, and sought to establish what remedies for this problem might be found.

The pessimism pervading parliamentary debates concerning the impact of urban growth upon land for sports and pastimes continues to echo through the twentieth-century historiography of popular recreation. Scholarly interest turned towards popular culture in the 1970s, armed with the concepts and assumptions about the industrial revolution then dominant in social history. To a generation of researchers, the contrast between the traditional recreations of pre-industrial England and the recognisably modern patterns of leisure in the nineteenth century and beyond was unmistakable, and it seemed evident that the industrial revolution had been central in powering the lurch from one state to the other.[3] It was presumed to have done so in two distinct ways. In the first instance, the industrial revolution created the factory, whose demands for steady labour reduced the opportunities of the labouring poor for recreation by diminishing their spare hours.[4] Coupled with these demands that the industrial revolution made upon workers' time, were the pressures it placed upon the spaces that had traditionally been used for recreation. Industrialisation and its concomitant, population growth, were swallowing up recreation grounds, leaving communities bereft of the open land upon which earlier generations had played. Together these forces pushed out older patterns of popular recreation; and with these swept away, the stage was left bare for commercial leisure pursuits to be ushered in later in the nineteenth century. In this account, the nineteenth century was considered to be a bleak period in the history of popular recreation, a time when the poor had been stripped of the rich recreational life they had enjoyed in the eighteenth century, and were still awaiting the advent of the capitalist leisure of mature industrial society.

This account is of course premised upon a concept of the industrial revolution that few would accept today, and it is therefore not my intention to

---

[2] *1833 Select Committee on Public Walks*, p. 339.

[3] See, in particular, Malcolmson, *Popular Recreations*, pp. 158–71; Walvin, *Leisure and Society*, pp. 2–17; Hargreaves, *Sport, Power*, pp. 16–56; Marrus (ed.), *Emergence of Leisure*, pp. 1–10; Clarke and Critcher, *Devil Makes Work*, esp. pp. 48–59. See also Thompson, 'Time, work, discipline', reprinted in his *Customs*, pp. 352–403; Storch (ed.), *Popular Culture*, pp. 1–19; Bushaway, 'Rite, legitimation', pp. 110–34. See, however, Cunningham, *Leisure*, pp. 9–56, esp. 9–14; Bailey, *Leisure and Class*, esp. pp. 1–18; Reid, 'Decline of St Monday', pp. 76–101; and Poole, 'Oldham wakes', pp. 71–98.

[4] See, however, Voth, *Time and Work*, esp. pp. 100–6, 118–33, 268–76.

engage systematically with the different parts of this argument. But the assumptions about the relationship between industrialisation and space upon which it is based clearly have relevance to the argument of this book. The contention that demographic expansion diminished the extent of open land in industrial areas is certainly plausible, but the conclusion that this inevitably left industrial communities with nowhere to play needs to be challenged. Of course, open space to which the poor have access is fundamental for plebeian sports and celebrations, but it does not in isolation explain why some pastimes withered and others flourished. The earlier chapters on provincial towns have illustrated this. We noted there a number of significant changes in recreational practice over the course of the long eighteenth century, but these changes can hardly be pinned to changes in the size and number of markets squares and streets, as these spaces remained largely constant. New ideas about the appropriate uses of urban space underpinned the developments outlined in Chapters 3 and 4, and effective police forces forced them through. Thus, it was ideas and power that drove the changes we observed, not alterations in the size or quality of physical space. For this reason, in turning to industrial regions it is not sufficient simply to document the existence or otherwise of streets, fields, and other spaces that might be used for recreation. We need to ask as well: who controlled these places? and how effectively? It is necessary, that is, to explore the territory between local law and local practice.

Parliamentary reports provide the main body of evidence for this chapter. In the 1840s, the 1833 enquiry into public walks was extended with a series of broader enquiries into the health and sanitation of towns in industrial areas. Half a dozen reports produced in the 1830s and early in the 1840s analysed mortality figures, and surveyed the housing stock, water supply, sewerage systems, waste disposal, and scavenging services of large industrial towns. In contrast to the 1833 Select Committee on Public Walks, none of these later enquiries was directly concerned with space for exercise and recreation; nonetheless public walks remained an ongoing concern of sanitary reformers, and all reports furnish some further evidence about the playgrounds that existed in industrial areas.

Inevitably, these blue-book investigations into health and sanitation provide no more than partial answers to the questions that concern us. They are only as well informed as the witnesses they called, and it is clear that some witnesses in fact knew little about the spaces that were used for plebeian sports in their locality. Continuous confusion between committees and witnesses about the land that was suitable for recreation, and the land which, though it might be used for recreation, was not considered suitable

adds to the difficulty of interpreting the information they contain. Moreover, these committees had a political agenda. Chaired by publicly spirited
individuals, concerned about the invidious consequences of enclosure and
convinced that the construction of public walks and gardens was the solu-
tion, they pressed witnesses to expand upon the inadequacy of the playgrounds in their locality, and dwelled upon the most pessimistic parts of
their statements. In spite of these limitations, however, the reports contain
many valuable observations about the availability and use of space for recreation in industrial towns, and provide a unique snapshot into popular recreations in the industrial context in the early nineteenth century. They are
used here together with the local histories and the reminiscences contained
in the Notes and Queries columns of the provincial newspapers that were
used in the last chapter.

In all areas—rural, urban, and industrial—there were many different kinds
of open spaces that might serve as recreation grounds, and many different
uses to which they might be put, but the primary concern of early-
nineteenth-century reformers lay with the availability of land for walking.
In their view, public walks that might be used by all for exercise promised
both physical and social benefits, tending not simply to promote health, but
also to enhance more nebulous qualities such as the morals and integrity of
urban inhabitants. The Select Committee on Public Walks thought that
'having a place to which they [the humbler classes] might resort with their
wives and children decently dressed on a Sunday evening, would tend to
promote that self-respect which is found so advantageous to all classes',[5]
and select committees repeatedly questioned witnesses in all areas whether
walks of this kind existed in their locality, and enquired after the moral
benefits they brought to the neighbourhood.

   The grounds for their concern emerge clearly in the successive select
committees of the 1830s and 1840s for, whereas provincial towns invariably
possessed planted gardens and public walks of some kind, the manufacturing towns in which social reformers were primarily interested were almost
entirely without constructed walks of any description.[6] Newcastle-under-
Lyme, for example, boasted walks 'in good order, and well regulated and
tastefully planted';[7] while Shrewsbury possessed 'a delightful walk on the

---

[5] *1833 Select Committee on Public Walks*, p. 368.
[6] For public walks in provincial towns, see Borsay, 'Rise of the promenade', pp. 125–40.
[7] *1845 Report into State of Large Towns*, p. 181.

banks of the Severn, called "The Quarry"'.[8] The citizens of York enjoyed the use of 'several' walks;[9] and in Chester, the public walks were both 'numerous and spacious'.[10] None of the witnesses from industrial towns was able to furnish such a favourable account of public walks in their locality. When asked, 'Are there any public parks, gardens, or walks, and in what state are they kept, and under what regulations?', witnesses frequently responded that there were none; and there can be no doubt that the various administrative bodies—the corporations, vestries, and town commissioners—that were struggling to govern these rapidly expanding populations were not in the position to provide public walks of the kind that were to be found in an increasing number in provincial market towns. Yet a certain degree of interpretation of these responses is required for, although public parks, gardens, and walks were rarely to be found in manufacturing towns, the facilities for walking were not usually lacking. As one witness from Birmingham said of the town's public gardens and walks: there were 'none, in the sense in which the question is put'.[11] It is clear, however, that there were other spaces that might be used for walking, or, at least, spaces in 'other senses'.

Public walks were largely the preserve of wealthy and well governed market towns, but all towns, both provincial and industrial, were surrounded by ancient public footpaths crossing the fields on their outskirts. Unlike the specially constructed walks beloved of eighteenth-century civic improvers, these were ancient rights of way, functional footpaths, linking one village or homestead to the next; and, despite the expansion of many northern towns, large numbers had managed to survive. A witness from Blackburn informed the committee that the walks in the town consisted in 'footpaths across fields, which lead from farm to farm . . . or from village to village'.[12] In Leeds, there were 'several [public footpaths] on all sides of the town through fields'; whilst in Bradford there were 'footpaths in the fields where they resort'.[13] In Birmingham, there were no places reserved for walking, yet 'there are many places where the working classes have an opportunity of walking at present'.[14] Henry Clarkson, an inhabitant and local historian of Wakefield, remembered a number of walks out of the

[8] *1845 Report into State of Large Towns*, p. 186.

[9] *1844 Report into State of Large Towns*, p. 612.

[10] *1845 Report into State of Large Towns*, p. 183.

[11] Ibid., p. 161.

[12] *1833 Select Committee on Public Walks*, p. 390.

[13] Ibid., p. 387.

[14] *1840 Select Committee on the Health of Towns*, p. 437.

town in the first quarter of the nineteenth century. There was, for instance, 'a very pleasant country walk along the river side'; and another that passed over 'pleasant open fields'. The footpath leading out of the town to the neighbouring hamlet of Thornes 'led over the fields, crossing the stream by a small bridge . . . and continuing over Briggs' garden ground through fields'. It constituted, in Clarkson's opinion, 'a very pleasant walk into the village'.[15] It is necessary to question, therefore, the pessimism to be found in parliamentary papers concerning the facilities for walking. Industrial towns were certainly without the picturesque walks that were maintained at public expense in many market towns, but the evidence from witnesses nonetheless suggests that ancient footpaths were both numerous, and well used for the purpose of walking. Such rights of way are evidently unlike the public walks constructed in order to enhance the appearance and facilities of provincial towns, but they were no less valuable for the purpose of walking for this.

Ancient footpaths and newer turnpike roads ensured that all towns contained some space for walking, no matter how imperfect, but the distribution of larger open spaces for athletic sports was considerably more varied. There were many different kinds of spaces that might be used for recreation, and there was little consistency between committee members and witnesses concerning the suitability of these various spaces as recreation grounds. It is clear, however, that the scale, nature, and pace of urban development in the early nineteenth century varied considerably, and that the outcomes of these developments were far from predictable. The irregular and unplanned nature of urban growth had left some areas well endowed with recreational playgrounds, others much less well so, and this variety makes generalisations about recreation grounds in industrial areas difficult.

Possibly most widespread were the heaths and moors to be found on the outskirts of many large towns in industrialising regions. Urban expansion notwithstanding, a number of industrial towns continued to be surrounded by large tracts of uncultivated common land that might be used by all for walking and exercise. The value of such spaces to the local population was often limited, however, by their distance from the centre of town. The extensive, unstinted commons at Nottingham, for example, could be used by all throughout the year yet they were considered to be 'too distant to be available to the working classes . . . not generally useful'.[16]

---

[15] Clarkson, *Merry Wakefield*, pp. 61–3.
[16] *1844 Select Committee on Commons' Inclosure*, p. 232.

Owing to their distance from the centre of the town, they were used for cricket matches on no more than 'a few days in the year'.[17] Newcastle possessed two fine commons—the Town Moor and Castle Leazes—both 'freely accessible to the inhabitants' and together totalling considerably in excess of 1,000 acres. As in Nottingham, however, witnesses were doubtful about their value to the urban population, being situated at some distance from the town's edge, and being consequently 'far from . . . within the ordinary reach of the great portion of the inhabitants'.[18]

The problem, of course, was one of time. There was wide variation in working patterns throughout industrial districts. In the cottage industries and domestic manufactures in the Midlands, the working week was characterised by an absence from work on Monday and sometimes Tuesday, and very long hours towards the end of the week; while operatives in mills and factories in Yorkshire and Lancashire generally worked regular hours throughout the week. In all areas, however, relentlessly long hours across the seasons precluded the possibility of travelling large distances in search of space for recreation. As one witness explained: 'Work-people have not much spare time, and it is desirable that they should be able to get to an open space of ground to have a game of cricket or football, or whatever it may be, in a short space of time.'[19] Popular recreation called for land that was close to workers' dwellings, and most commentators considered that the commons situated at the edge of many large towns were too distant to answer this purpose.

Heaths and moors were most commonly used, therefore, for the watching, rather than playing, of sports. They provided the location for spectator sports, for the occasional matches between professional sportsmen that could be expected to draw large crowds. When a prize-fight was held on Baildon Moor, for example, a local clergyman recalled that 'large numbers went from Pudsey to see it', travelling a distance of some 6 miles.[20] The Yorkshire moors were frequently used for the regional game of knur and spell: Baildon Moor,[21] Hunslett Moor at Leeds,[22] and Eccleshill Moor at Bradford[23] were all reported as the site of knur and spell matches. Footraces and other spectator sports popular in the north, such as bowling and quoits,

[17] *1844 Report into State of Large Towns*, p. 649.
[18] *1845 Report into State of Large Towns*, p. 562.
[19] *1833 Select Committee on Public Walks*, p. 388.
[20] Lawson, *Progress in Pudsey*, p. 76.
[21] *Wakefield and Halifax Journal*, 16 July 1824; 24 Sept. 1824.
[22] Ibid., 15 Oct. 1824.
[23] Cudworth, *Round about Bradford*, p. 346.

were similarly located on heaths, moors, and commons. The Heath at
Wakefield was the venue one summer for a great footrace, which a 'vast
concourse of spectators, several thousands in number' assembled to watch.[24]
At Newcastle, the Town Moor was put to much the same use. An inhabitant of the town in the 1860s recalled quoits, fives, bowling, and matches of
knur and spell being held on the moor earlier in the century.[25] Finally, prior
to the creation of enclosed race grounds in the second half of the nineteenth century, heaths and commons in all parts of the country formed the
location of the ever popular sport of horse-racing.[26] Large expanses of
common land clearly enhanced the recreational facilities of many industrial
towns, but their value lay in providing space for the watching rather than
playing of sports; and for most inhabitants, trips to distant commons to
watch horse-racing and other spectator sports were made on no more than
an occasional basis.

Commentators were agreed that in addition to common land smaller
spaces closer to the centre of large towns were necessary to provide working people with more regular opportunities for exercise. There was much
variety, however, in the extent of such open land in different industrial
towns. Those of the north-east appear to have been most fortunate. The
inhabitants of Gateshead, for example, enjoyed the use of a 10-acre recreation ground adjoining the town called Windmill Hills. The enclosure acts
of 1809 and 1814 had preserved this recreation ground; and, although there
was some doubt about its future in the 1820s when the freemen who had
been awarded the Windmill Hills began erecting buildings there, the site
remained in continuous use as a recreation ground until being converted
to a public park in the 1860s.[27] North Shields and Sunderland both possessed 'open and convenient' spaces for exercise;[28] and in South Shields it
was thought that the sea beaches and banks provided inhabitants with sufficient suitable grounds for recreation.[29] But the largely positive assessments
of recreation grounds in the coalmining towns of the north-east were
unusual, and witnesses from towns in Yorkshire and Lancashire were more

---

[24] *Wakefield and Halifax Journal*, 19 June 1813.

[25] Adams, *Memoirs*, ii, p. 470. See also Metcalfe, 'Organised sport', pp. 469–95; 'Potshare bowling', pp. 29–44.

[26] For some examples from Yorkshire, see *Leeds Mercury*, 13 June 1727, 4 May 1736, 23 June
1730, 27 March 1745; *Leeds Intelligencer*, 6 May 1760, 25 May 1762. For horse-racing more
generally, see Huggins, *Flat Racing*, esp. pp. 120–6, 143–73.

[27] Manders, *Histroy of Gateshead*, pp. 57, 241.

[28] *1845 Report into State of Large Towns*, pp. 562, 558.

[29] Ibid., p. 541.

doubtful about the quality and quantity of playgrounds in their areas. With
the exception of Bradford, which possessed a space somewhere between 20
and 30 acres in size called Fairweather Green, 'exactly suited' for the purpose of recreation, witnesses consistently replied that local inhabitants were
without adequate spaces for the enjoyment of sports and pastimes.[30] It was
a view from which few dissented.

Yet, although an unmistakable tone of pessimism pervades the parliamentary reports on large towns, their conclusions pose something of a puzzle. They are, at the very least, in stark contrast to the accounts provided by
local histories and by the recollections to be found in the Notes and Queries
columns of the local papers. These sources contain extensive recollections of
the sports that had been enjoyed in the region in the early nineteenth century; and, in contrast to the views of witnesses in front of select committees,
none recalled a scarcity of land imposing restrictions of any kind.

Indeed, the evidence from witnesses is itself more ambiguous than
appears at first sight. Despite the general consensus that urban growth was
destroying recreation grounds in these towns, it is remarkable that most
witnesses were nevertheless able to name some spaces that were habitually
used for recreation. When questioned about open spaces for recreation, a
common response was that there was nowhere to play but the fields. In
Burslem, for example, there were said to be no open spaces for exercise
'except the fields'.[31] It was likewise said of Coventry that there were no
places for recreation beyond 'the fields'.[32] What were these fields? And why
did witnesses tend to discount them when questioned about the playgrounds that existed in their locality? It was the negative elements of these
responses that interested select committees, which were concerned to preserve green spaces in and around large towns and to encourage the creation
of formal parks and gardens upon which no encroachment was possible, but
their interests should not be allowed to obscure the information about
recreational space that local notables brought to the parliamentary committees. At the least, there is some inconsistency between the witnesses'
statements concerning space for recreation, and the politicians' conclusions
that calls for further investigation.

Early-nineteenth-century urban growth was rapid, but it was nevertheless piecemeal. The alarm shared by witnesses and politicians about the loss

---

[30] *1840 Select Committee on the Health of Towns*, p. 391. This witness declared that 'if it had been
set apart for the very purpose, it could not have been more suitable'.
[31] *1845 Report into State of Large Towns*, p. 176.
[32] Ibid., p. 622.

of open space for recreation was fully justified, and their concerns to halt
further depredations laudable. But in the early nineteenth century the
urban sprawl that they feared was by no means complete, and consequently
even the most rapidly growing towns continued to contain central open
spaces of some kind. William Bolling, member of parliament for Bolton,
thought that, despite extensive building in the town during the first third
of the nineteenth century, development had taken place 'in every direction', so that the town was not more 'condensed'. On further questioning,
Bolling agreed that the centre of the town was now further from the country than it had formerly been, but was reluctant to accept the conclusion
that this left significantly fewer open spaces within the town that might be
used for recreation. Fields had been built over he agreed, but 'not densely
so, not filled up', and he believed it was always possible for inhabitants to
find some place in which they could play.[33] And this seems to be a fairly
accurate assessment of the impact of early-nineteenth-century population
growth on popular recreation. The physical appearance of industrial towns
and patterns of landholding within them were changing rapidly, but sports
and pastimes nonetheless continued to thrive. Older customs and practices
were fitted into changing environments; they were certainly under pressure, but it still remained possible to fit them around the interstices of
working life.

Nowhere does the contrast between the witnesses' assessments of the
land to which workers had formal access and inhabitants' accounts of the
land that was in fact available for recreation appear more clearly than in
the case of Birmingham. The witnesses of successive select committees all
concurred on the absence of parks and playgrounds in or near the town. In
the opinion of one there were 'no places where the working-people can
resort for recreation', and it was this 'want of some places of recreation . . .
to which many of their bad habits may be traced'.[34] Another, when questioned whether any open spaces were reserved for the 'youth of the humbler classes' to enjoy athletic games, replied simply: 'there are not any'.[35] But
local inhabitants, reminiscing about sports and pastimes later in the century,
named numerous different sites within the town which had been used for
recreation during these years. Their descriptions of these places were often
vague, yet they suggest the existence of waste and vacant plots within the
town that were simply appropriated for popular recreation when the need

---

[33] *1833 Select Committee on Public Walks*, pp. 392–3.
[34] *1842 Report into the Sanitary Condition of the Labouring Population*, p. 275.
[35] *1833 Select Committee on Public Walks*, p. 370.

arose. One elderly inhabitant, for instance, recalled: 'A sort of arena was fitted up for . . . sports, which consisted of an inclosure containing about
2,000 square yards of land'. He added that it had been much used by men
and boys for this purpose.[36] Others referred to badger-baiting 'in an open
space of ground in Smallbrook-street';[37] and a bull-baiting that took place
on 'a piece of ground' adjoining Easington-street at the back of the
Islington Glass-house.[38] The annual wakes were fitted into vacant sites in
the centre of the town in just the same way. The Bell wake, held in August,
was situated on a 'wide open yard', at the bottom end of Pinfold Street in
the 1820s; when Navigation Street was redeveloped in the 1830s, it relo-
cated to the greater space provided there.[39] These 'spaces', 'pieces of
ground', and 'yards' were all situated in the very heart of the town. Urban
growth in these years was sufficiently halting to ensure that even in the
centre of a large industrial town there were vacant sites that might be used
for recreation. It is not possible to pin down the use and extent of such
spaces, as they came in and out of use as different parts of the town
were developed, yet they indicate that the possibilities for popular recreation in industrial towns were greater than might be inferred from the
select committees' reports.

Nor was it simply undeveloped waste in the centre of the town that
provided the working inhabitants of Birmingham with land for recreation.
Birmingham, despite being the nation's fourth largest town, still covered a
comparatively small surface area. The densely populated town was hemmed
in by fields, and there was consequently space for recreation within easy
access on all sides of the town.[40] To the north, there were fields that one
inhabitant recalled being used for prize-fighting: 'At that time [1834] the
ground from Lancaster Street bridge to Tower Street, and back to the Hos-
pital in Summer Lane, was all fields, and if any houses at all, only one here
and there. It was called the Pignut field, and was the arena where night after
night the fiery spirits of the town fought their fistic duels.'[41] Towards the
east, amateur boxers eager for a fight positioned themselves on 'the waste
ground near Heath Mill Lane and the Floodgates'.[42] Slightly further out in

[36] *Morning Chronicle*, 3 March 1851.
[37] Ibid.
[38] *Aris's Birmingham Gazette*, 15 Sept. 1828.
[39] *BWP* Notes and Queries, no. 1639.
[40] Birmingham was fourth in size to London, Liverpool, and Manchester in 1801. For population estimates, see Sweet, *English Town*, p. 3.
[41] *BWP* Notes and Queries, no. 384.
[42] Ibid., no. 1921.

an eastwards direction, yet still under a mile from the centre of the town was a site known as 'the Knob'. This was used for the Shrovetide sport of cock throwing: it 'was a walk across the fields at the far end of Coventry-road, sometimes called Chain Templefields'.[43] At the south of the town was a plot used for pony-racing: between Main Street and Krywick's-lane, 'lay a stretch of open country well adapted to the purpose'.[44] Again, the area described was comfortably within a mile of the centre of the town. None of these spaces, either within the town or on its outskirts, was formally designated as a recreation ground, and it is purely by historical accident that we know anything about their use. Their existence as recreation grounds was often short-lived; these were ephemeral playgrounds, and there can be no question of attempting to gather comprehensive information about the history of spaces of this kind. Nevertheless, the evidence from Birmingham testifies to the importance of vacant plots and unused wastes in providing the industrial inhabitants of the town with a place to play, and suggests that the recreational facilities of the town cannot be comprehended simply by reference to the legitimate playgrounds and formal walks and gardens they possessed.

The level of detail concerning unofficial recreation grounds in early-nineteenth-century Birmingham is unusual, but it is unlikely that there was anything exceptional about the use of space in this town. In the 1870s, elderly inhabitants of Sheffield recalled a very similar environment, comprising vacant plots within the town, and fields within easy access on its edge. In the early decades of the nineteenth century, the inhabitants of Sheffield had possessed 'a vacant space much used as a play and cricket ground, named Jericho'.[45] This was situated adjacent to the Brocco, in the north-west corner of the town, and was within half a mile of the town's historic centre. And Sheffield, like Birmingham, was still small, comprising a densely populated hub situated in fields and pasture. Another elderly inhabitant of the town recalled: 'From Radford street downwards was, sixty years ago, quite in the country.'[46] Descriptions of Liverpool and Bury suggest very similar pastoral settings.[47] It was not difficult for inhabitants to find somewhere to play in towns of this kind.

---

[43] *Birmingham Gazette and Express*, 9 Oct. 1908.
[44] Ibid.
[45] Leader, *Old Sheffield*, p. 209.
[46] Ibid., p. 206.
[47] *Recollections of Liverpool*, p. 201 (loc. hist.); Barton, *History of Bury*, pp. 41, 68–9.

Furthermore, many of the inhabitants of industrial districts lived out-side large towns such as Birmingham, Sheffield, Liverpool, and Bury. Demographic growth in the century following 1750 took many forms. New employment prospects caused the unprecedented expansion of a dozen or so towns in Lancashire and Yorkshire, and it was this rapid emer-gence of large towns that tended to attract the attention of contemporaries. But in many industrial regions, rural growth was no less significant. Indus-tries such as mining, iron-working, and weaving had historically been located in villages rather than towns; and, as these trades expanded during the classic period of the industrial revolution, so did the numbers living in industrial villages and hamlets. These settlements possessed a wide range of different spaces for recreation, but the pressure upon all of these was con-siderably less acute than that upon land in large and growing towns. Lack of space was not thought to pose problems for the inhabitants of Hyde, Ashton, Staleybridge, and Duckinfield, all suburbs of Manchester, for exam-ple. A witness to the 1840 Select Committee on the Health of Towns agreed there was no place 'reserved where people can take exercise', but continued, 'the towns being small the people can get out into the sur-rounding districts'.[48] Likewise in the townships of the Black Country, space for recreation was not hard to find. The detailed accounts of popular recre-ation in the early nineteenth century provided by local inhabitants rarely gave specific information about the places where sports and pastimes had been held, but they equally never made any suggestion that land for recre-ation was lacking. The site of bull-baitings, for example, was usually given simply as the 'open space'.[49] At Wednesbury, an inhabitant recalled prize-fighting was carried on in a ring 'being an open stretch of pasture land' in the early 1830s;[50] and another remembered there being no fewer than three different places in the town where bull-baitings used to be held.[51] West Bromwich was unique amongst the Black Country townships in possess-ing an especially reserved playground. This was a field of 4 acres that had been provided by the Earl of Dartmouth in order 'to wean the people from bull-baiting and other cruel pastimes, by substituting something better in their place'.[52] The authors of the 1845 Report into the State of Large Towns

---

[48] *1840 Select Committee on the Health of Towns*, p. 457.

[49] *BWP* Notes and Queries, nos 34, 317.

[50] Birmingham RL, 'Newspaper cuttings', 302127, p. 183.

[51] *BWP* Notes and Queries, no. 1510.

[52] *1844 Report into State of Large Towns*, p. 139.

gave their whole-hearted approval of this benevolent gesture, but it is doubtful that the inhabitants of West Bromwich were considerably better provided for than those of other small towns in the west Midlands, particularly given that the park was walled, and that access was permitted only on certain occasions each year.

Elsewhere, large numbers of industrial workers were living in settlements that were still recognisable as villages; these small industrial villages and hamlets had more in common with the agricultural villages of rural areas than they did with the large towns of Lancashire and Yorkshire. Many even possessed the greens and commons that had historically been used for recreation and, in such places, sports and pastimes were unfailingly enjoyed on these traditional spaces.[53] In the West Riding, for example, cricket was played at Pudsey on the village green;[54] and Skelmanthorpe, Conisbrough, and Bentley all had village greens that were noted as the site of recreation.[55] Greens in the iron-working and mining villages of Shropshire were put to just the same use. At the mining village of Oakengates, the green was the location of the annual wake;[56] and at Madeley and Broseley, village greens were the scene of bull-baiting in the early nineteenth century.[57]

No less important than village greens were the common lands that enclosed many industrial villages. In contrast to the heaths and moors surrounding large towns, these were within easy reach of the inhabitants and their value as recreation grounds therefore all the greater. Commons were used for informal sports and games wherever they survived. In south Yorkshire, for example, football matches were played between the villages of Farnley and Thurstonland upon their commons: according to a local schoolmaster, these had provided 'a course of extremely rough country of about three miles long'.[58] At Morley, cricket had been 'played on the highways and commons' in the early decades of the nineteenth century.[59] The rural sector was expanding significantly in the early nineteenth century. This rural growth was an integral part of industrialisation, and industrial villages and hamlets, and their greens and commons, must not be left out of our survey of popular recreation in industrial districts. The social,

---

[53] For a more detailed discussion of the use of greens and commons for recreations, see Chapter 8 below.
[54] [Rayner], *History of Pudsey*, p. 197.
[55] [Marsden], *Reminiscences*, p. 7; Hatfield, *Notices of Doncaster*, i, p. 83.
[56] Burne, *Shropshire Folklore*, ii, p. 446.
[57] Randall, *History of Madeley*, p. 128; Randall, *Broseley*, p. 180.
[58] [Easther], *Glossary of Almondbury*, p. xix.
[59] Smith, *Morley, Ancient and Modern*, p. 129.

economic, and demographic structure of industrial villages was undergoing marked changes, but the topography of these settlements changed far less, and it was not unusual for the land that rural communities had traditionally used for recreation to remain in continuous use.

Even where commons and greens were succumbing to the pressures of demographic expansion, the consequences of this loss of public land for popular recreation were less severe than might be expected. Greens and commons in all parts of the country, both industrial and rural, were under pressure from a wide variety of different sources in the late eighteenth century, and they had been for many centuries. Population growth, agricultural improvements, enclosures, and encroachments had caused the erosion of these recreational spaces throughout their history, and rural communities had long exploited a wide range of other spaces for recreation. Any fallow field might be used for recreation, and all industrial villages, with or without greens and commons, possessed fallow fields of some description. Thus, there were 'open spaces' for bear-baiting at Ecclesfield,[60] Balby, and Doncaster.[61] In Alverthorpe 'a field',[62] in Almondbury a 'triangular piece of ground',[63] and in Pudsey 'the croft'[64] and a 'field called "Greatrails"' were named as recreation grounds.[65] Feasts in Morley were laid out in 'the Bottoms' and spread down to the Pinfold.[66] Pinfolds (fields reserved for the impounding of cattle or other animals) were also the location of cockfighting in a number of districts in and around Doncaster.[67] Every community enjoyed recreation on all and any fallow fields in the village that were suitable. As Joseph Lawson, a clergyman living and working in Pudsey in the early nineteenth century, remarked: 'certain places and lane ends' were used by the young inhabitants of the village for playing at pitch and toss, jumping, boxing, wrestling, knur and spell and other games.[68] Or, as a resident of Honley remembered, a football could be kicked around 'in any old pasture-field'.[69] In sum, rural settlements possessed a variety of different fields and grounds that might be used for recreation. In some instances, the greens

[60] Eastwood, *History of Ecclesfield*, p. 345.

[61] Hatfield, *Notices of Doncaster*, i, pp. 80, 82.

[62] Clarkson, *Merry Wakefield*, p. 60.

[63] [Easther], *Glossary of Almondbury*, p. xv.

[64] [Rayner], *History of Pudsey*, p. 195.

[65] Ibid., p. 179.

[66] Smith, *Morley, Ancient and Modern*, p. 123.

[67] Hatfield, *Notices of Doncaster*, i, p.76.

[68] Lawson, *Progress in Pudsey*, p. 77.

[69] Jagger, *History of Honley*, p. 145.

and commons that had traditionally served as recreation grounds continued in use, but the loss of these spaces did not inevitably imply the end of the games that had been enjoyed on them since privately owned fallow fields, used by inhabitants by custom or agreement rather than by right, were usually sufficiently numerous to make good these losses.

There is a clear contrast between the pessimistic reflections on the absence of fitting recreation grounds to be found in the parliamentary reports, and these recollections written by local inhabitant. Whereas parliamentary reports presented a bleak picture of industrial communities bereft of open spaces for games and recreation, local inhabitants described a wide variety of different locations in which earlier generations had played. But neither account is incorrect: both were describing the same situation from different perspectives. The witnesses speaking to parliament did not set out to deceive, nor were they unaware of the vacant plots, wastes, commons, fields, and greens that were used for recreation in industrial communities of different kinds. They did doubt, however, whether the use the poor made of these spaces was legitimate. Much of the land that was being used for sports and pastimes in industrial towns was privately owned, and its use by the labouring population was therefore trespass. Witnesses from industrial towns repeatedly referred to the ongoing practice of trespass, and both witnesses and the politicians who listened to them took a very dim view of the lawbreaking that it implied. In Birmingham, for example, it was regretted that trespass in the fields was 'very frequently done'.[70] Likewise in Leeds: 'there is a great deal of trespassing on persons' property in the neighbourhood of Leeds'.[71] A witness from Bradford, when questioned whether there was 'not considerable trespass done' in the fields replied: 'Very much so.'[72] In Nottingham, only those freemen with common rights of pasture were permitted to enter the lammas fields surrounding the town but, as one witness observed: 'The public, especially the juvenile portion, does however trespass to a great extent upon these lands while thrown open.'[73] Habitual trespass was common in all industrial towns. The absence of reserved playgrounds in these towns resulted not in a contraction of popular recreation, but in the creation of a tradition of trespass, and it was this that caused parliamentary reformers their greatest worries.

---

[70] *1833 Select Committee on Public Walks*, p. 368.
[71] Ibid., p. 388.
[72] Ibid., p. 389.
[73] *1844 Report into State of Large Towns*, p. 649.

The response of the rightful owners of these fields was varied. At Basford in Staffordshire, an industrial village a few miles north of Stoke-on-Trent, trespass on the part of the young men for the purposes of cricket-playing and other games was 'very common', and the want of open ground for recreation in or around the village was said to be 'a fruitful source of bickering and recrimination between the young men of the parish and the owners and occupiers of lands'.[74] But it is clear that in many instances, the use of private land for recreation was not a source of conflict as landowners simply turned a blind eye to trespass on their fields. In Blackburn, for example, games of football were 'not regarded, about winter-time they do not do much injury';[75] and in Manchester, children played in the fields—'they are very frequently permitted to do so by the tenants, or at least not prevented from doing it'.[76] Likewise in Bolton, football continued on the moor despite its enclosure in the 1790s: 'no person in the neighbourhood prevents them' noted the local member of parliament.[77] In many instances, landowners were absent and, where they were not, they were frequently able to reach an accommodation with workers over the use of land for recreation.

In the smaller townships and suburbs that surrounded large industrial towns, trespass was no less common. In the west Midlands town of Walsall, '*much* trespass [was] committed' in the fields on the edge of the town that the footpaths crossed.[78] In Chorlton, a suburb of Manchester, a space known as Greenheys-field was used as a place for public exercise and, despite being private property, it was, according to one witness, 'habitually trespassed upon'.[79] And it was the lack of designated spaces for recreation that was held responsible for the trespass that was so pervasive in these places. As Mr Ackroyd, a witness from Stourbridge, noted: 'the want of [play-grounds for the children] forces them into thoroughfares, and to trespass on private property'.[80] The problem in industrial areas, both in cities and their suburbs, was not therefore one of a simple lack of space. It was the absence of space that could be legitimately used by all for the purpose of recreation that concerned local elites and sanitary reformers, and it was

---

[74] *1845 Report into State of Large Towns*, p. 618.
[75] *1833 Select Committee on Public Walks*, p. 391.
[76] Ibid., p. 397.
[77] Ibid., p. 393.
[78] *1845 Report into State of Large Towns*, p. 165.
[79] *1844 Report into State of Large Towns*, p. 572.
[80] *1845 Report into State of Large Towns*, p. 140.

the trespass and disrespect for the rights of property that it encouraged that they were most concerned to address.

Trespass was also very much confined to industrial areas. There was no alarm voiced about the problem of trespass in historic market centres growing at a steadier pace. Market towns and county capitals were usually well endowed with public gardens and recreation grounds and there was therefore little call for the labouring poor to turn to undeveloped waste for space to play. The inhabitants of Bristol, for example, enjoyed the use of Clifton and Durdham Downs, both 'much frequented on Sundays and on holidays';[81] and in Chester 'a field of nearly 100 acres of pasture by the riverside, accessible at all times, and in good order' provided inhabitants with abundant land for exercise.[82] In the small Wiltshire town of Frome, the Vallis Vale, property of the Marquis of Bath, filled a similar role.[83] There was clearly no cause for trespass when such fine recreation grounds existed. Elsewhere, old playgrounds, fields that had at one time been set apart or bequeathed to inhabitants for the purpose of sports and games, remained intact. Salisbury had 'abundant space for exercise', made up of a large field that had been left in trust to the corporation for the purpose of recreation, as well as a number of other green spaces.[84] In Norwich, games were permitted in Castle Meadow and Chapel Field.[85] These provincial towns were all expanding, but they were not undergoing the rapid expansion that was transforming towns in the industrialising regions of the north. Urban growth in market towns was both more limited and more controlled, and the commons, parks, and downs that had traditionally provided recreation grounds therefore remained in use.

Here, then, was something that diverse industrial communities had in common. In the previous chapter, we noted many contrasts between patterns of popular culture in the west Midlands and south Yorkshire, but there was also much that both these regions, and others, shared. All industrial towns faced similar problems when searching for somewhere to play. In most market towns, inhabitants enjoyed the use of constructed walks and reserved playgrounds. In industrial towns, such places did not exist, but the consequences of this were not those that politicians and well intentioned reformers feared. The lack of playgrounds did not constrict popular

---

[81] *1845 Report into State of Large Towns*, p. 205
[82] Ibid., p. 183.
[83] Ibid., p. 162.
[84] Ibid., p. 605.
[85] Ibid., p. 645.

recreations, but forced them into spaces on which they had no legitimate claim; it made trespass a way of life, so widespread it was not always even controversial. It is important not to place too great an emphasis on trespass as a universal characteristic of industrial areas since many industrial workers were living outside large towns in villages that still possessed the spaces that had historically been used for recreation. Nevertheless, there is a clear contrast between industrial towns and the market towns surveyed earlier in this book. In all rapidly growing industrial towns a lack of legitimate playgrounds encouraged widespread trespass; it was a custom which had no real parallel in market towns.

These observations are strongly reinforced by witnesses' comments on the practice of bathing in rivers and canals. Like walking, bathing was considered a healthy form of exercise, and successive select committees enquired about the facilities that existed for swimming in different towns. Bathing was the preserve of men and boys; and, since they bathed naked, the committee took the view that a spot specifically reserved for bathing set away from the river banks or towing paths that the public frequented was desirable. In Birmingham, for example, bathing in the canal was considered to be 'very offensive to women walking along the towing path', and it was precisely in order to prevent such scenes of indecency that reformers were keen to promote secluded reservations for the purpose of bathing.[86]

In fact no town of any description had a place on its river or canal banks reserved specifically for bathing, though many had somewhere that was regularly put to this use. Occasionally, a publicly spirited landowner allowed access to a suitable spot for bathing on his lands but, in most places, canals or river banks provided an appropriate place to swim.[87] The residents of Bradford, for example, enjoyed the use of a 'very good place' on the river, not objectionable in point of decency, since it was 'out of the way'.[88] Indeed, the facilities for bathing were often best in industrial areas, since their canals provided better opportunities for bathing than rivers, which were often either too fast flowing, too shallow, or too polluted for safe and convenient bathing. In all areas, however, the place in which communities bathed was determined by local circumstances, and not by the policy or wishes of local leaders. As one witness said of Sheffield, though nowhere

---

[86] *1833 Select Committee on Public Walks*, p. 371.
[87] Ibid., p. 392. William Bolling, the MP for Bolton, allowed the people into his grounds to bathe on Sunday.
[88] Ibid., p. 389.

was reserved specifically for swimming, 'there is just that sort of chance medley bathing that there is in other places'.[89] In most towns, just as in Sheffield, there were one or more convenient places for bathing, and different sites were exploited as circumstances permitted.

But the canals that were so frequently named as the location for bathing were also private property, and their use by local inhabitants for the purpose of bathing was therefore trespass. As might be expected, however, there was a considerable breach between local law and local custom, and the illegality of the practice did little to deter local inhabitants with nowhere else to bathe. In Birmingham, for example, bathing in the canal continued, according to one witness, despite being 'forbid by the proprietors of the canal'.[90] In the pottery towns Hanley and Shelton, children resorted to the canal for bathing, although the practice was illegal.[91] Likewise in Bury, the reservoir was the private property of the canal company, and it was apparently 'rather jealous of trespass'; nonetheless it was the only place in the town resorted to by 'the poorer inhabitants' for the purpose of bathing.[92] Just as the rights of property did not deter the use of land for sports and pastimes, so the industrial workforce had little respect for the restrictions that property owners attempted to impose upon their use for bathing; and, without an adequate police force, canal owners had little real prospect of preventing these incursions on their property. In all industrial areas, it was the force of numbers rather than the forces of law and order that determined the outcome of these disagreements between property owners and local inhabitants.

For the same reason, plebeian street recreations lingered longest in the industrialising towns and townships in northern and central England. As we have seen, plebeian street games were gradually eliminated from market towns over the long eighteenth century, and effective forms of local government were integral to this process. Many industrial towns were struggling to cope with the manifold problems posed by unprecedented population growth with governments that were fitted for much smaller and more stable communities, and they were consequently not in the position to define the legitimate uses of their streets and squares in the same way. The police systems in place in industrial towns could not match the criers,

---

[89] *1833 Select Committee on Public Walks*, p. 404.
[90] Ibid., p. 371.
[91] *1845 Report into State of Large Towns*, p. 178.
[92] *1833 Select Committee on Public Walks*, p. 394.

constables, and watchmen that incorporated towns employed to police their streets; for this reason, industrial streets continued to provide the location for a wide range of plebeian sports and games.[93]

Again our evidence from Birmingham is finest. At the Chapel wake held on the north-east edge of Birmingham, mountebanks and stalls were set up on Gosta Green, whilst Lawrence Street was used for the horse-races.[94] As one contemporary sarcastically commented: 'What singular genius introduced the horse race into a crowded street, I am yet to learn.'[95] During another of Birmingham's wakes, the Bell wake held in August, naked men and boys took the place of horses in the races run through the streets. A local historian remembered 'Boys in a nude state, and females almost in a similar condition' running 'unseemly races in the public thoroughfares';[96] and men 'nude, bedaubed with treacle, and sometimes feathered . . . competing for prizes in the principal streets of the town'.[97] Another inhabitant recalled the sack races held in the streets during the Bell wake. He described the event as follows: 'What should I see but four animated sacks, coming round the corner from Singer's Hill . . . these noble savages in sacks . . . essayed to jump down this incline, and so on round Little Ellis Street, Singer's Hill, Severn Street, and down Fordrough Street, the route of racing. Followed by a shouting rabble, they struggled on . . .'[98] Nor indeed were these exhibitions in the streets confined to the annual wakes. Pony-races, for example were run through the streets at other times of the year as well. There was a local event known as the Sparkbrook Races, held on the Stratford-road, and also more informal pony races 'held frequently on the Coventry-road hill'.[99]

And once again, although there are few towns which possess such a fine level of detail concerning street recreation as Birmingham, it is unlikely that there was anything exceptional about that town. A scattering of references to recreation in both large industrial towns, and in smaller townships and villages in the suburbs, indicates that streets formed the location of a wide range of games and races. Donkey-races, for example, were run through the streets of Sheffield during the Broad Lane wake: an 'open space' at the edge

---

[93] For the policing of street recreation in the later nineteenth century, see Storch, 'Policeman as domestic missionary', pp. 481–509.
[94] *BWP* Notes and Queries, no. 1542. See also ibid., no. 1639.
[95] Hutton, *History of Birmingham*, p. 134.
[96] Birmingham RL, [Jaffray], 'History of Birmingham', ch. 16.
[97] Ibid., ch. 34. See also Hutton, *History of Birmingham*, p. 135.
[98] *BWP* Notes and Queries, no. 1639.
[99] *Birmingham Gazette and Express*, 9 Oct. 1908

of the town was filled with the stalls and booths, but the 'grand expectation and sight were the races'. These were run by donkeys and ponies, and the city's streets formed the race course. An elderly inhabitant of the town marvelled: 'How the riders managed to rush up and down the steepness of Bailey-field, and the narrowness of Bailey-lane without some breaking of the necks or limbs, either of themselves or the spectators, is to me up to this day a mystery.'[100] In Wolverhampton, the bull-baitings enjoyed at the annual wakes were held in Canal Street;[101] and at Bilston, bull-baiting took place on the turnpike road.[102] Dog-fights commonly took place in the streets of industrial suburbs. At Oldbury, for example, it was 'no uncommon occurrence' for dog-fights 'to take place on the public streets by actual arrangement of the owners and backers';[103] and at Pudsey, a clergyman recalled dogs 'fighting on the highways in the village till both animals were nearly dead'.[104] Similarly, games of football and cricket were played in the streets of industrial hamlets. In Lancashire, football was played through the streets of Rochdale between the various hamlets in the parish,[105] and in the centre of Kirkham on Christmas day.[106]

There appears to have been little effort on the part of local authorities to clear play out of central urban districts in industrial areas, which suggests that a very different attitude towards the use of urban space prevailed from that which we found in market towns. The improving civic spirit, we saw, was no friend to popular recreation, but it does not appear to have extended to industrialising towns and townships. It may be that in industrial areas the local authorities' will to prevent street entertainments was greater than their ability to do so; however, if local leaders were growing impatient of these annual street festivities, no evidence for this has survived—the columns of the local newspapers, for example, are empty of complaints about wakes, feasts, and other street games during this period. Certainly large industrial towns and the smaller settlements in their suburbs were without the effective local government that might have translated any wishes that local leaders had for more decorous streets into a reality.

---

[100] Leader, *Old Sheffield*, p. 200.
[101] *Wolverhampton Chronicle*, 4 Nov. 1835, 29 Nov. 1815.
[102] *Aris's Birmingham Gazette*, 7 Nov. 1828.
[103] Hackwood, *Oldbury Round and About*, p. 310. Dog-fights in the street in Leek, *Staffordshire Advertiser*, 27 Aug. 1836.
[104] Lawson, *Progress in Pudsey*, p. 76.
[105] Fishwick, *History of Rochdale*, p. 536.
[106] Idem., *History of Kirkham*, p. 206. For cricket in Pudsey, see [Rayner], *History of Pudsey*, p. 197.

As one resident and historian of the Black Country ruefully observed, dog-fighting in the highway 'discloses the inadequacy with which the town was policed'.[107] Of course, this contrast with market towns should not be pressed too far, as the policing of many of these towns was rudimentary in the extreme.[108] Nonetheless, industrial areas do emerge as a relatively favourable environment for the development of popular recreation; and the availability of poorly policed streets on which entertainments might be organised was an important factor underpinning the resilience of popular entertainments in manufacturing districts well into the second quarter of the nineteenth century.

Once again, simple generalisations about the fate of popular recreations in industrial areas prove elusory. Nonetheless, a number of points that merit emphasis stand out. Most importantly, the gloomy assessments about the impact of industrialisation on popular pastimes uttered by contemporaries and echoed by historians are clearly misplaced. Space for recreation was rarely hard to find in industrial areas. In part this is because many wrokers lived in villages and hamlets where traditional recreation grounds contin-ued in use. Even in the large towns and cities which we more commonly associate with the industrial revolution, however, playgrounds of some description could usually be found. Undeveloped land was often abundant and, together with commons, wasteland and streets, provided sufficient land for plebian recreations of all kinds.

Furthermore, the evidence about the use of space in industrial areas that has been presented here reinforces the conclusions of the previous chapter: these, clearly, were places of cultural vibrancy. Industrial regions were areas of innovation, creation, and change so far as land for popular recreations was concerned. They lacked the historic and fixed recreational spaces of prosperous market towns; but they did not lack space, as com-mons, urban wastes, and streets together provided sufficient land for popu-lar sports. And industrial communities were made up of large populations, and their inhabitants empowered through strength of numbers. Weak local government and the absence of adequate policing structures helped to pro-vide the local population with two fundamental requirements for popular sports and recreations: time and space. Yet they also served to create an atmosphere of permissiveness and freedom for popular recreation, facilitat-ing the creation of new customs, and forging a strong tradition of plebeian cultural autonomy.

---

[107] Hackwood, *Oldbury Round and About*, p. 310. See also [Shaw], *When I was a Child*, pp. 31–3.
[108] Swift, 'Urban policing', pp. 211–57.

8

Village greens

This is to Advertise the Publick, that on TUESDAY the 8th day of *September* next, will be given *gratis*, by Mr Samuel Notley and Mr Christopher Hunt, in a Field near *Lantern Green* in *Eye*, TEN HATS, to be Camp't for by Ten Men of a Side, and the same to be deliver'd to the Winners of the Match, if it appears that there is no Contrivance for carrying them off without fairly playing for the same . . .[1] (1741)

In some parts [of Suffolk] this active game of our ancestors is still much in fashion.[2] (1784)

CAMP. A game formerly much in use among schoolboys, and occasionally played by men in those parts of Suffolk on the sea coast . . . sometimes school against school, or parish against parish.[3] (1823)

Three scarce references to the ancient English sport of camping: the first, an advertisement from an eighteenth-century provincial newspaper, inviting locals to participate in a forthcoming match; the second, published a few decades later, suggesting that camping continued strong; the third, penned half a century on by an obscure scholar of local dialect, the preface to a detailed description of an ancient sport, which has now, it is made clear, been consigned to posterity.

This chapter is not uniquely concerned with the East Anglian game of camping. Nor is the example taken in order to frame a story of the decline of traditional pastimes, the ebbing of time-worn customs during a period of modernisation, though the quotes might be taken to indicate something of the unstable and endlessly changing pattern of sports in rural England. The example is presented rather because it poses the problems with which this chapter is centrally concerned: spaces and the recreations for which they are used. In this chapter we turn finally to the practice of recreation in rural areas, and the focus remains as ever upon the spaces in which games

---

[1] *Ipswich Journal*, 29 Aug. 1741.
[2] Callum, *History of Hawsted*, p. 113.
[3] Moor, *Suffolk Words*, p. 63.

were played. The long-forgotten sport of camping illustrates both the possibilities, and the problems, of using space to explore the history of popular recreations in the rural context.

Camping was an athletic team game, concentrated in the eastern counties of Norfolk, Suffolk, Essex, and Cambridgeshire.[4] It was essentially a form of football, involving two teams of equal size competing to score the highest number of goals within the space of an agreed period of time, often half an hour. One nineteenth-century writer asserted that goals were usually pitched at a distance of between 150 and 200 yards apart, though this, in common with most aspects of pre-industrial sports, could vary considerably.[5] Nevertheless, it is certain that the game required an open space of some size. The traditional open-field farming system, leaving as it did large tracts of land for communal grazing, ensured that such space was not lacking in early modern England; yet, for reasons that are not entirely clear, many East Anglian parishes possessed specially designated fields for the playing of camping. These fields had been bequeathed or given to the parish in perpetuity by individuals, and they are recognisable at several centuries remove through their names—Camping Close, Camping Field, Camping Meadow, Camping Land, and so forth. Field names of this kind provide some of our most valuable evidence for the history of popular recreation in rural areas.

Yet the example of camping also illustrates some of the problems confronting a history of popular sports in rural areas: the incomplete nature of the evidence with which we have to work. Field names tell us how fields had once been used, but names tend to last longer than uses, and they are not reliable as a guide to how spaces were being used at a particular point in history. Consequently, the study of field names, though well adapted to illustrate the spatial extent of a particular cultural practice, is less well equipped to reveal how these uses changed over the course of time.[6] They need, then, to be studied in conjunction with more qualitative evidence, and our three quotes illustrate the unsystematic nature of such qualitative evidence. Newspaper advertisements such as that at the head of this chapter were common in mid-eighteenth-century local newspapers, though they disappeared from the press in the second half of the eighteenth century. A late-eighteenth-century historian thought the game was 'still much in fashion' but, when scholars showed renewed interest in camping in the

---

[4] For a history of camping, see Dymond, 'Camping close', pp. 165–92.
[5] Moor, *Suffolk Words*, p. 64.
[6] For the use of field names as a historical source, see Field, *English Field-names*; and idem, *History of Field-names*.

nineteenth century, the game was always referred to in the past tense. Yet the reasons for the game's demise are unclear from this handful of references. No one explained why the locals were no longer playing the game, and together these sources do no more than record its passage from local practice to local history. And we encounter these difficulties repeatedly when attempting to recover the history of popular recreation in rural areas. Diaries, local histories, and newspapers provide no more than occasional glimpses into sports and pastimes, and there are many areas of the past that they leave undescribed. In the rural context, references to recreation are occasional, incidental, and wholly unsystematic; and, however carefully we piece the evidence together, the picture of the past they produce is regrettably incomplete.

Notwithstanding the difficulties posed by the scarcity of evidence for rural recreations, I return here to two principal themes running throughout this book: the ways in which communities made available land for the purpose of recreation; and the impact of contemporaneous economic change on space for recreation. The motivation for such enquiries may seem less compelling in the rural context, for, intuitively, we should expect problems of land to be less acute in agricultural counties than in the towns and industrialising districts that have previously been considered. Likewise, it is tempting to dismiss the impact of the economic changes traditionally designated the 'industrial revolution' in agrarian counties, because these, by their nature, were largely unaffected by industrialisation. Yet this chapter constitutes an important complement to the work on recreation in urban and industrial England, since local politics and economic change in rural areas did in fact leave their print on space for recreations in ways which were both significant and unpredictable. Open space of the kind required by popular sports, while certainly relatively abundant in rural areas, was not necessarily available for the rural sports of the poor: public access to land was often restricted, and fallow fields provide no unconditional evidence of a place for the people to play. Further, although rural England has no doubt correctly been thought to have been protected from the pressures associated with the industrial revolution, agricultural land was certainly not beyond the reach of market forces—in particular the commercialisation of agriculture associated with the enclosure movement. The fate of popular recreations in rural areas during the eighteenth century is consequently less straightforward than might appear, and a study of the impact of economic and political forces upon the spaces traditionally reserved for recreation in villages and hamlets, whilst made difficult by the limited evidence, will not be without interest.

Although some attempt to address these questions has already been made, there is at present little historical consensus concerning the history of popular sports and pastimes in rural England. In Robert Malcolmson's seminal work it was argued that commercialisation and the rise of the market economy in the late eighteenth century undermined traditional recreations, and rural areas were not believed to be beyond the scope of these forces. In the rural environment, commercialisation took the form of the enclosure movement; parliamentary enclosure diminished the playing spaces available to the rural poor and, in this way, argued Malcolmson, undermined age-old patterns of recreations.[7] However, the evidence that he provided was somewhat inconclusive. Certainly, as Malcolmson demonstrated, nineteenth-century historians did occasionally note that recreational spaces had been lost owing to parliamentary enclosures, but such comments were made surprisingly rarely, and it is difficult to share Malcolmson's confidence that these expressions represent an actual historical trend rather than scholarly nostalgia, that familiar lament for the old way of life. Even assuming the former, Malcolmson's examples suggest a more complex and less uniform trend than his argument admits. He gathered evidence concerning playing grounds spanning nearly two centuries, demonstrating that some were preserved and others lost, with the parliamentary enclosures of the late eighteenth and early nineteenth centuries only rarely implicated in their disappearance. His various examples suggested that communal playing spaces had long been vulnerable to enclosure and encroachment, to appropriation, legal or otherwise, undermining the argument that the loss of rural playgrounds was related to a quickening of the pace of economic change in the late eighteenth century.

Subsequent historians are in disagreement over the fate of rural playgrounds. In the view of Hugh Cunningham the loss of playgrounds consequent upon industrialisation was 'not simply an urban problem'; the enclosure of open fields in rural areas, he argued, had 'quite as great an impact' as sprawling new towns on the availability of playing space.[8] Yet Golby and Purdue have asserted that, notwithstanding the loss of common land, 'space for recreation was only rarely a problem in the countryside'.[9] Given that research into the availability of space for recreation in rural areas has gone no further than the examples collected by Malcolmson, there are at present no good grounds for deciding between these views.

[7] Malcolmson, *Popular Recreations*, pp. 107–10.
[8] Cunningham, *Leisure*, p. 80. See also pp. 76–83.
[9] Golby and Purdue, *Civilisation and Crowd*, p. 102.

The central assumption of all these historians, that enclosure diminished the quantity of common land in rural districts, is beyond dispute. Yet widely differing conclusions concerning the impact of this trend on rural recreations are possible for two reasons. In the first instance, enclosure did not have a uniform impact upon all English counties. Parliamentary enclosure affected regions to very different extents, with some touched only lightly by the process and others dramatically transformed; and this regional diversity makes any generalisations about the impact of enclosure on traditional pastimes easy to undermine. More fundamentally, disagreement about the impact of enclosure on popular recreations is owing to our uncertainty about the role that common land had played in providing space for recreation. It is not clear how widespread the use of common land for recreation ever was, and it is consequently not possible to draw firm conclusions concerning the impact of enclosure on popular recreation. The commons were not the only space available for recreation in rural areas. Many villages possessed specially designated playing fields, such as the camping closes in Suffolk described at the beginning of this chapter. Others possessed large village greens. Both provided suitable land for popular sports, and the impact of enclosure on these spaces is far less clear. Furthermore, the hold of paternalism in rural areas had long ensured that private land had played a role in providing space for recreation, and, again, the impact of enclosure upon this tradition is uncertain.[10]

This chapter sets out to consider what really happened to recreational space in rural England in the early nineteenth century, and is based upon an investigation into the history of the village green during this period. It opens by exploring the cultural uses of these spaces, and then turns to assess the impact of parliamentary enclosures on these spaces and uses in the county of Cambridgeshire. It closes by attempting to draw more general conclusions, concerning the extent to which patterns of recreation had changed in the rural environment by the second quarter of the nineteenth century.

Ancient spaces

In Chapters 3 and 4 we explored an example of urban space in detail: the public streets and squares of provincial market towns. As we saw, these pro-

---

[10] See also the discussion of industrial villages in Chapter 7 above.

vided a valuable space for local celebrations, providing not simply a suitable physical space for games and festivity, but also a location with particular symbolic significance. Furthermore, as we noted there, the use of central commercial spaces for recreation, and consequent eclipse of trade and traffic by pleasure-seekers, served to invest recreations in this environment with a cultural value that went beyond any qualities inherent in the activities themselves. In villages and hamlets, such spaces simply did not exist. Of course, villages did contain streets, and these were oftentimes used as a location for feasts, fairs, football, and other recreations, but the quiet streets of small villages could never provide an equivalent location for recreation. Filling a little used country road with games and crowds did not have the same cultural resonance as filling a busy civic centre; when the streets of villages were used for recreation, it was in a strictly functional, rather than symbolic, way. Yet at the heart of many villages lay a space that had similar, though in no way identical, associations with recreation and celebration. The village green—a large, open, communal space, situated at the heart of the settlement—had long been used for a wide range of rural sports and celebrations. It was in no way a rural market square, but we can nevertheless discern certain parallels with respect to its use as a location for recreation and games.

We know remarkably little about the uses and functions of these ancient rural spaces. They were an established feature of rural settlements by the early Middle Ages and, although in time most became reserved exclusively for the purpose of recreation, it is unlikely that they had originally been created with this purpose in mind. Yet there is little certainty concerning what their original purpose may have been. Some were subject to some form of common grazing, usually the keeping of geese, but others appear never to have been subject to common rights, and it is thought they may originally have been set apart for stock control, or as reservoirs of pasture, possibly to provide protection for the community's livestock during a temporary emergency.[11] It is clear, however, that during the Middle Ages they were also being used by inhabitants for recreations and games. The butts for the archery practice that successive monarchs repeatedly ordered throughout the Middle Ages were invariably set up on the green, and both archery and other sports were enjoyed here. It is this use that proved to be

[11] The literature on village greens is extremely limited. See Thorpe, 'Green villages', pp. 155–80, esp. 160–1; Hoskins, *Making of the Landscape*, pp. 56–7; Hoskins and Stamp, *Common Lands*, pp. 28–34; Wade-Martins, 'Origins of rural settlement', pp. 138–57; Roberts, *Making of the Village*; Williamson, *Shaping Medieval Landscapes*.

Figure 12. Francis Barraud, *The Travelling Show* (Bridgeman Art Library, London).

most enduring. The original function of the village green had been forgotten long before the advent of the eighteenth century. By that date, most
served no economic or agricultural function of any significance, and
existed simply as a place of recreation for local inhabitants.[12]

Situated generally at the centre of the village, the green formed both the
literal and cultural heart of the settlement. It was here, for example, that
communal celebrations were held. Just as central streets and squares were the
customary location for civic celebrations, so was the village green used for
the occasional national celebrations organised by local elites. Thus, for
example, celebrations in the Essex village of Fingrinhoe on account of the
peace between Britain and France were situated on the village green. A local
farmer reported: 'Two large booths were erected on the Green, and, to add
to the general festivity, a bullock was roasted whole and filled with potatoes,
and a great deal of beer with other liquors was given to the populace, all at
the expense of John W Cooper . . . It was supposed that the number of
people of all descriptions assembled was not less than fifteen hundred.'[13] At
East Bergholt, Suffolk, similar celebrations on the village green were held
thirteen years later. The vestry minute books contained a detailed account of
the entertainments provided for the villagers on account of the general peace
with France, and added the following note: 'N.B. The Dinner was Cooked,

---

[12] Hoskins and Stamp, *Common Lands*, p. 28. The legal status is discussed in Eversley,
Commons, pp. 281–89; Hunter, *Preservation of Open Spaces*, pp. 205–20.
[13] Page, 'Diary', 14 Oct 1801, pp. 101–2.

at the Houses of the Principal Families, & served on Tables erected on the Green where the Fair is usually held.'[14] In the Northamptonshire village of Walgrave, celebrations to mark the royal Jubilee in October 1809 were held on the village green;[15] and at Hinxton in Cambridgeshire, the village green was the location of a fete to celebrate the royal coronation in 1831.[16] In contrast to many large towns, celebrations to commemorate events of national significance were held only infrequently in rural areas; and, whereas the use of central civic space was an indispensable requirement of national celebrations in towns, it was not unusual for their rural counterparts to be held on private land, often the estate of the local magnate. On occasion, however, rural communities did celebrate together in public and, although village greens were by no means ubiquitous, where they existed they invariably formed the location of such events.

In addition to occasional celebrations to mark events of national significance, a range of other annual calendar festivals was celebrated on the green. The village green typically formed the central focus of celebrations to commemorate Guy Fawkes. Just as the market square formed the location of every town's bonfires on the Fifth of November, so in villages it was upon the green that the bonfires built by the parish youth were burned.[17] May celebrations took place here,[18] as did morris dancing and music at Whitsun.[19] On such occasions, the village green provided a space that was in some ways similar to the market square of provincial towns. It was a central public space, the natural location for all celebrations that drew in the community at large.

Indeed, these parallels with the market square went deeper than a mere similarity in use. The greens of some villages may have been constructed during the Middle Ages in order to serve as a rural market place and fairground, and their associations with recreation were therefore both deeply rooted and long standing. Certainly the creation of many greens between the twelfth century and fourteenth century is coeval with the proliferation of licences for markets and charters for fairs during these years; and through the following centuries, the green never lost its popularity as a location for feasts and fairs. In the eighteenth century, rural fairs and feasts were invariably situated on the green. A fictional account of a country wake in the

[14] Paterson, *East Bergholt in Suffolk*, p. 151.
[15] *Northampton Mercury*, 4 Nov. 1809.
[16] *Cambridge Independent Press*, 1 Oct. 1831.
[17] Cole, *Blecheley Diary*, 5 Nov 1766, p. 146; Howitt, *Boy's Country-book*, p. 80.
[18] Hutchinson, *Northumberland*, ii, appendix, p. 14. Randall, *Broseley*, p. 182.
[19] Blount, *Fragmenta Antiquitatis*, p. 149.

Spectator described 'their *Green* covered with a promiscuous multitude of all Ages and both Sexes', and the cudgelling and football matches that took place.[20] In most places, the holding of feasts and fairs on the green was simply too obvious to merit comment.

The village green was more than a rural equivalent to the market square, however. In addition to providing space for occasional national celebrations and other annual feasts, fairs, and festivals, the green was also the customary site of athletic sports played at more irregular intervals. Cricket matches, for example, were sometimes recorded on village greens. Diarists from Essex recorded matches of cricket and trap ball on Abberton Green[21] and Passick Green;[22] and Thomas Turner, our cricket-loving shopkeeper from Sussex, twice recorded matches of cricket at Easton's Green.[23] Moreover, the village green was by no means the preserve of gentlemen's cricket, a wide range of more informal and more plebeian recreations was also enjoyed on the green. Occasional spectator events were located on the green. The bull that Lancashire farmer John Blundell sold to his workmen, for instance, was 'Baited upon the Green', before being taken away and slaughtered,[24] and at Madeley and Broseley, village greens were the scene of bull-baiting in the early nineteenth century.[25] Our evidence for informal, plebeian uses of this kind is scarce, but occasional comments describing the activities of local villagers on the green give some indication of the wide range of activities to which village greens were put.

For example, John Denson described how the green had been used by the agricultural labourers of Waterbeach in Cambridgeshire prior to the village's enclosure in 1813. He wrote: 'as the days lengthened, in the evening after our work was done, we assembled on our village-green to spend our time in some rustic amusements, such as wrestling, football, etc'.[26] The Northamptonshire poet John Clare recalled that the green in his village had been put to similar use, though such activities held little appeal for him: 'instead of going out on the green at the town end on Winter Sundays to play football I stuck to my corner stool poreing over a book'.[27] A Banbury shoemaker thought that the 'queer games' that the men and apprentices had

---

[20] *Spectator*, 4 Sept. 1711. See also Clay, *History of Waterbeach*, p. 23.

[21] Page, 'Diary', 29 July 1804, p. 94.

[22] Crosier, 'Diary', June 1785, p. 33.

[23] Turner, *Diary*, 27 Sept. 1756, p. 65; 28 June 1759, p. 186.

[24] Blundell, *Diurnal*, iii, 28 Nov. 1723, p. 121.

[25] Randall, *History of Madeley*, p. 128; Randall, *Broseley*, p. 180.

[26] Denson, *Peasant's Voice*, p. 17.

[27] Clare, *Clare: Selected Poems*, p. 65.

played on the town's green 'would have been worth relating if I could have remembered them', but it is surely not insignificant that he could not.[28] The green was not simply the location of celebrations, feasts, and fairs—all managed and controlled to some degree by village notables. It was also the home of labourers' and children's games, to pastimes and activities that largely lay beyond the gaze or interest of literate commentators, and which, for the same reason, have now almost entirely disappeared from view.

The Buckinghamshire parson William Cole was unusual in the detail with which he recorded the sports and entertainments of his servants and neighbours, and his diary provides further evidence for the value of the green to the rural poor. He one year noted 'Football playing' on the green on Shrove Tuesday;[29] and another recorded 'Bonfires on the Green'[30] on Guy Fawkes night. A remark about a certain Mrs Willis's servants—they 'were sometimes . . . on the Green, at 3 & 4 o'Clock in the Morning in her Absence'[31]—suggests that the green was not simply a location for the young men's athletic sports, but that it was also a place for both sexes to meet and socialise. A description of music on the green by Nicholas Blundell similarly suggests that the green was a place for informal relaxation and socialisation: at Little Crosby, the green one day formed the stage for an informal concert by the local miller; he 'played his Fiddle to the Young People on the Green'.[32] The village green was undoubtedly the location of countless informal and uninstitutionalised rural pastimes. Most of the activities carried on here involved none but village labourers, and were so ephemeral they are only rarely found in historical records. Yet diaries, memoirs, and local histories provide occasional glimpses of rural communities at play, and provide unequivocal evidence that the village green was a significant recreational resource for the rural poor.

At the same time, village greens were by no means ubiquitous, and for this reason it is important not to over-estimate their importance. Not all rural settlements had been originally constructed around a green; some had never possessed a green of any form. Elsewhere, encroachments and piece-meal enclosures through the centuries had left ancient greens much reduced in both size and number long before the eighteenth century. These villages without greens were not without alternative places for games, since

---

[28] Herbert, *Recollections*, p. 66.
[29] Cole, *Blecheley Diary*, 3 March 1767, p. 191.
[30] Cole, *Blecheley Diary*, 5 Nov. 1766, p. 146.
[31] Ibid., 8 June 1766, pp. 56–7.
[32] Blundell, *Diurnal*, i, 22 May 1711, p. 290.

the village green was not the only location for rural recreations. Most villages possessed commons, and all contained quiet streets, which together provided sufficient space for feasts, fairs, and the playing of athletic sports. In addition, there was a long tradition of local landowners lending privately owned fields to the poor for the purpose of recreation. A Sussex farmer once noted a 'smock race in our field', for example;[33] and in Hertfordshire, a diarist recorded that 'the Women met in the orchard to play for a goose' one September evening in the early nineteenth century.[34] A late-eighteenth-century children's writer was presumably referring to this tradition when she described children playing in the local 'Mr Right's field'.[35] In villages without greens, popular recreations were held on commons, streets, and private fields, and it is likely that finding somewhere to play posed few problems in eighteenth-century rural settlements.

Nevertheless, the village green still stands out as an exceptional location for recreation. Its significance lay less in its provision of space, for there were other spaces available for recreation in rural settlements, than in the quality of the space that it offered. Greens were ancient places, usually lying at the heart of the village. Throughout the centuries, they had been the site of communal structures—the pinfold, the stocks, the village pond—and they had been used for recreation for time out of mind. They provided a uniquely valuable space for the festivals and sports of the rural poor, an element in the matrix of space available for recreation in rural areas that cannot be comprehended simply by counting the number of acres they covered. Their value was as much symbolic as practical; and, for this reason, these small spaces merit considerably more scholarly attention than they have hitherto received.

Environmental change

The records for the discussion which follows are drawn from Cambridgeshire in the period 1790–1837. 1790 was chosen as a starting point since this decade marked the beginning of a phase of rapid parliamentary enclosure in Cambridgeshire. This was not the first experience of enclosure in the county, for there had been extensive piecemeal enclosure, by general agreement rather than by parliamentary act, in earlier centuries; however,

---

[33] Marchant, 'Diary', 16 May 1721, p. 189.
[34] Hertfordshire ALS, Carrington's Diary, D/EX3.31, 15 Sept. 1802.
[35] Kilner, *Village School*, ii, p. 41.

the pace of enclosure in the decades after 1790 was quite unlike anything known previously. In the following sixty years, about 70 per cent of Cambridgeshire villages were enclosed to some extent by act of parliament. An estimated 50 per cent of the county's surface area was enclosed, and the enclosures of this period consequently mark a clear break from the past in terms of both the speed and magnitude by which they occurred.[36] In addition, the method of these enclosures, that is by parliamentary act rather than by general agreement, is not unimportant, since enclosure by this means produced the documents that enable a study of village greens to take place. The records that were created during the process of parliamentary enclosure were finer than those created during enclosure by any other means, and their survival rate is also far higher. Although imperfect in some respects, it is only where parliamentary records exist that an analysis of the fortunes of rural playgrounds may be undertaken, and for this reason the discussion cannot be pushed further back than 1790. New legislation passed in 1837 determined the point of closure. This introduced restrictions upon the enclosure of rural playgrounds, and its intentions, implementation, and consequences are all considered below.

In all, eighty-seven of Cambridgeshire's 160 villages and hamlets were enclosed by parliamentary act between 1790 and 1837. This represents over half of the county's rural settlements, and introduced a radical reorganisation of agricultural land in the county. The consequences of these enclosures on different recreation grounds, however, were complex and uneven. The fortunes of common land may be most swiftly summarised, for the loss of commons at enclosure was incontrovertible. In the clear majority of instances, the award left no commons or wastes of any kind in the parish, and enclosure thereby left villages deprived of large tracts of land that had once been used as a location for popular recreation. Since enclosure after 1790 was so extensive in Cambridgeshire, the loss of commons was particularly significant here, and we can be confident that, in this county at least, the process was causing a rapid and very real reduction in the quantity of land available for recreation.

Assessing the impact of these enclosures on village greens is considerably less straightforward, and can be established only through a detailed examination of the enclosure records on a parish basis. Of the ninety-odd villages enclosed by parliamentary act prior to 1837, a small number (sixteen) had to be excluded from the analysis, since either no enclosure

---

[36] All statistics derived from Turner, *English Enclosure*, pp. 32–62. See also the appendices, pp. 176–208.

records have survived, or the records do not contain the kind of detail required. In five villages, no award was enrolled,[37] and the awards of the remaining eleven were insufficiently detailed to establish the existence or otherwise of a village green either before or after enclosure.[38] This study requires the use of field names in awards, since it is only where each plot is named that village greens can be identified. A few of the early awards described allotments with reference either to a numbered map or to the neighbouring plots, rather than describing each allotment by name. In such instances it is not possible to establish the existence of a village green, and these parishes have therefore been excluded.

With these sixteen villages excluded, we are left with a slightly smaller sample of seventy-one villages, representing just under one half of Cambridgeshire's rural settlements. The records for most of these are sufficiently detailed to establish the existence or otherwise of a village green prior to enclosure. It should be emphasised, however, that the style of recording enclosures was not systematic, and the documents for some parishes are more difficult to interpret than others. In consequence, the figures that follow should be approached as estimates: they are certain to capture the fate of the county's village greens during nineteenth-century enclosures in outline, but exact answers concerning the history of some of these greens will always elude us.

Of the seventy-one villages with adequate records, just over two-thirds (forty-eight) appear to have possessed a village green on the eve of enclosure; in the remaining one-third there was either no evidence of a green, or evidence that the green was already in private hands. We shall consider this not insignificant minority of settlements without greens in due course; let us look first, however, at the forty-eight villages in which it is clear that a village green existed prior to enclosure and at the fate of these greens subsequently.

In these villages with greens, the impact of enclosure was unmistakable: in the large majority of parishes the ancient village green was lost. At the time of enclosure, those holding common rights to land in the parish

---

[37] These are Borough Green, Chippenham, Madingley, Soham, and Westerly Waterless.
[38] Cambridgeshire CRO, Great Abington Enclosure Award, 7 July 1804, QRDz5; Conington Enclosure Award, 17 Feb. 1804, QRDz2; Fulbourn Enclosure Award, 20 Aug. 1814, QRDz7; Girton Enclosure Award, 5 March 1814, QRDz7; Pampisford Enclosure Award, 31 Dec. 1801, QRDz6; Snailwell Enclosure Award, 12 July 1806, QRDz4; Swaffham Bulbeck Enclosure Award, 1 Aug. 1801, QRDz6; Trumpington Enclosure Award, 15 May 1809, QRDz6; Wentworth Enclosure Award, 20 May 1830, 'March'; Great Wilbraham Enclosure Award, 2 Feb. 1801, QRDz3; Little Wilbraham Enclosure Award, 2 Feb. 1801, QRDz4.

exchanged their rights for one or more plots of private, hedged land; as the commissioners surveyed the parish in order to assess the land available for enclosure in the parish, it is clear that they usually included the village green as land to which the commoners were entitled. Their final awards created new, enclosed fields and gardens on land that had previously been the village green, and in consequence the county was left with significantly fewer greens by the 1840s than had existed prior to the wave of enclosures that took place after 1790. Only a handful of villages managed to retain their green during these years. In Barrington, an exceptionally large expanse of green was preserved at enclosure, a magnificent and extensive green that still survives today.[39] The fact that the enclosure of Barrington was early and involved only a small number of individuals may have helped to protect it. At the enclosure of the fenland village of Manea in 1810, a 19-acre plot on the expanse of land described as 'green or common' was allotted to the 'Trustees of the Town Estate', and presumably thereby maintained for the inhabitants' use.[40] Enclosure entailed the loss of much of the fine 20-acre green that flanked the road running through the village of Brinkley; nevertheless a not insignificant plot of 5 acres was left unallotted.[41] At Duxford, Histon, Kingston, Teversham, and Waterbeach smaller central greens were left intact at enclosure.[42] In all, a mere six of the fifty village greens that had existed prior to enclosure were left untouched; in a further two, enclosure, though it reduced the green in size, nevertheless left a considerable expanse of green intact. There can be no escaping, therefore, the overwhelmingly destructive impact of parliamentary enclosure on village greens. In nearly forty villages, enclosure left inhabitants with no trace of the former green or greens; and, although a wide range of experiences is encompassed by this statistic, the underlying trend cannot be disputed.

At one end of the spectrum lay a small number of villages in which the change wrought by enclosure was particularly significant. At Wimblington, for example, the inhabitants lost their 'Great Green' of some 25 acres to nine individuals in 1805.[43] An equally fine, ancient green, comprising nearly 20 acres and a large pond, was situated in the southern corner of the village of

[39] Cambridgeshire CRO, Barrington Enclosure Award, 20 Oct. 1800, QRDz2.
[40] Cambridgeshire CRO, Manea Enclosure Award, 15 Dec. 1810, 'March'.
[41] Cambridgeshire CRO, Brinkley Enclosure Award, 24 Jan. 1816, QRDz6.
[42] Cambridgeshire CRO, Duxford Enclosure Award, 12 July 1830, QRDz 10; Histon Enclosure Award, 31 May 1806, QRDz6; Kingston Enclosure Award, 21 Dec. 1815, QRDz8; Teversham Enclosure Award, 20 Dec. 1815, QRDz8; Waterbeach Enclosure Award, 28 Sept. 1818, QRDz8.
[43] Cambridgeshire CRO, Wimblington Enclosure Award, 3 Aug. 1805, 'March'.

Stapleford prior to enclosure, and this too was carved up into numerous private plots at the time of the enclosure of the parish in 1814.[44] A large expanse
of green lay at the centre of Bottisham. It had survived in spite of extensive
ancient enclosure, but it was unable to withstand the parliamentary enclosure of the parish in 1808, at which time all 34 acres of the Goose Green were
allotted to the rector.[45] At Guilden Morden in the south-west corner of the
county, a 'Great Green' of several acres and a much smaller 'Little Green' were
both enclosed in the early nineteenth century.[46] A much larger green at
Harston was allotted to twenty-eight individuals at the same time;[47] and in
Great Shelford, the High Green of some 40 acres was enclosed thirty years
later.[48] The losses in Carlton-cum-Willingham were equally great, though in
this instance owing to the number of greens lost. Here five greens scattered
through the parish ranging in size from 1 to 8 acres were lost during the
enclosure of the parish in 1800—in all 14 acres of former greens were
destroyed.[49] These enclosures resulted in the loss of some of Cambridgeshire's finest village greens. The greens lost were similar in size to the
great green at Barrington which is regarded as one of the finest village
greens, not simply in the county, but in the country. Within the space of fifteen years, six magnificent village greens had been transformed into private
fields and gardens, and two decades later, a seventh went the same way.[50]

Losses of this magnitude were unusual, since few villages possessed such
magnificent greens on the eve of enclosure; nevertheless a further seven
villages lost substantial greens that were over 5 acres in size. Elsworth,
Fordham, Hardwick, and Lode all lost village greens of about 5 acres—in
Elsworth and Fordham two smaller greens of under 2 acres were also lost.[51]
At Horningsea, the green of nearly 7 acres was divided into three allot-

---

[44] Cambridgeshire CRO, Stapleford Enclosure Award, 3 Feb. 1814, QRDz7.

[45] Cambridgeshire CRO, Bottisham Enclosure Award, 3 Oct. 1808, QRDz5.

[46] Cambridgeshire CRO, Guilden Morden Enclosure Award, 1 May 1804, QRDz4.

[47] Cambridgeshire CRO, Harston Enclosure Award, 25 Jan. 1802, QRDc3.

[48] Cambridgeshire CRO, Great Shelford Enclosure Award, 7 Dec. 1825, QRDc50. In this
instance a 1-acre plot in the centre was awarded to the overseers and churchwardens and
reserved for recreation.

[49] Cambridgeshire CRO, Carlton-cum-Willingham Enclosure Award, 6 May 1800, QRDz1.

[50] An eighth village should possibly be included in this category. In Waddon, there were
losses of a similar magnitude when two greens were carved up at enclosure in 1820. An
allotment of over 7 acres was reserved for the private use of the proprietors with common
rights, and was thereby lost to the public without common rights. Cambridgeshire CRO,
Meldreth Enclosure Award, 25 Jan. 1820, QRDz9.

[51] Cambridgeshire CRO, Elsworth Enclosure Award, 11 April 1803, QRDz5; Fordham
Enclosure Award, 9 Aug. 1820, QRDz9; Hardwick Enclosure Award, 30 March 1837,
QRDc15; Bottisham Enclosure Award, 3 Oct. 1808, QRDz5.

ments for the local squire, Thomas Panton.[52] The inhabitants of Dullingham lost a 'place known by the name of Widgeham's Green' at enclosure in 1810.[53] In West Wratting, a 7-acre piece of 'waste called the green' was allotted to one individual at the enclosure of the parish three years later.[54] In these seven villages, enclosure resulted in the loss of greens that were 5 acres or larger. Together with the seven villages that lost much larger greens, this group includes nearly one-third of all the villages that had possessed a green prior to enclosure. Such enclosures represent a very real loss of recreational space in Cambridgeshire.

The county's other greens were rather smaller in size—typically somewhere between 1 and 5 acres—yet this did little to preserve them from the grasp of the enclosers. Experiences such as those of Ashley, Bassingbourne, Croxton, Kirtling, Long Stanton, and Meldreth, where 2-acre greens were allotted to numerous individuals, were therefore common.[55] In Oakington, two greens, the Ale House Green and 'Sheeps Green', both measuring about 2 acres were allotted.[56] At Fen Ditton and Landbeach, greens of just over 3 acres were allotted.[57] Elsewhere in the county, yet smaller greens of around 1 acre were all that were left to enclose. A Rose Green of 1 acre was lost during the enclosure of Balsham; and at Caxton, a Rosemary Green of the same size was lost.[58] Cherry Hinton, Wood Ditton, Harlton, Longstowe, Orwell, Shepreth, and Toft all lost greens of around 1 acre.[59] Weston Colville and Chiswick End also lost village greens, though the enclosure awards do not allow the measurement of these greens.[60] This group of

[52] Cambridgeshire CRO, Horningsea Enclosure Award, 27 April 1810, QRDz6.

[53] Cambridgeshire CRO, Dullingham Enclosure Award, 7 April 1810, QRDz6. The green was 9 acres.

[54] Cambridgeshire CRO, West Wratting Enclosure Award, 27 Oct. 1813, QRDz8.

[55] Cambridgeshire CRO, Ashley Enclosure Award, 26 March 1814, R62/16; Bassingbourn Enclosure Award, 12 Aug. 1806, QRDz3; Croxton Enclosure Award, 23 Sept. 1818, QRDz5; Kirtling Enclosure Award, 26 March 1814, P101/26/1; Long Stanton, All Saints, Enclosure Award, 10 April 1816, QRDz8; Meldreth Enclosure Award, 25 Jan. 1820, QRDz9.

[56] Cambridgeshire CRO, Oakington Enclosure Award, 6 Nov. 1834, QRDc48.

[57] Cambridgeshire CRO, Fen Ditton Enclosure Award, 20 Oct. 1807, QRDz5; Landbeach Enclosure Award, 15 Dec. 1813, QRDz7.

[58] Cambridgeshire CRO, Balsham Enclosure Award, 19 Sept. 1806, QRDz8; Caxton Enclosure Award, 12 May 1835, QRDz10.

[59] Cambridgeshire CRO, Cherry Hinton Enclosure Award, 18 Dec. 1810, QRDz6; Ditton Wood Enclosure Award, 20 May 1823, QRDz/10; Harlton Enclosure Award, 4 Aug. 1810, P84/26; Longstowe Enclosure Award, 22 July 1800, QRDz1; Orwell Enclosure Award, 1 Nov. 1837, QRDc52; Shepreth Enclosure Award, 21 April 1823, QRDz10; Toft Enclosure Award, 25 April 1815, QRDz8.

[60] Cambridgeshire CRO, Weston Colville Enclosure Award, 11 Aug. 1778, QRDz1; Meldreth Enclosure Award, 25 Jan. 1820, QRDz9.

twenty greens constitutes rather over one-third of the villages in the original sample; all these villages contained a green that was somewhere
between 1 and 5 acres in size on the eve of enclosure, and lost it subsequently. In over two-thirds of the county's villages that had possessed a
green prior to enclosure, therefore, enclosure resulted in the permanent
loss of the green. In these villages, historic sites of recreation that had
lain at the heart of the settlement for many centuries were lost forever. It
all amounted to a very rapid reduction in the number of village greens, and
a clear transformation of the Cambridgeshire countryside.

In the small number of remaining villages, the greens that existed prior
to enclosure were less than 1 acre in size. Village greens had long been vulnerable to appropriation, and the enclosure documents reveal that some of
the land going by the name of 'green' was in reality no more than a tiny
patch of grass, often lying at the road's edge, the last remnant of a village
green that had long previously been enclosed. In Hinxton, for example, two
small plots of 18 and 12 perches were all that remained of the village's
Church Green.[61] At Ickleton, the green was a tiny plot of 14 perches in
front of one resident's house.[62] In Whittlesford, the Green and Pound Green
together totalled no more than 2 roods.[63] Most of the green at Bourne had
also been anciently enclosed, and only the last tiny patch of 24 perches was
lost at enclosure in 1820.[64] Greens such as these were so small that their
removal at enclosure was arguably of little consequence for local residents.
If we consider them together with the eight villages in which the greens
survived largely or wholly intact at enclosure, then in one-third of the
villages which had possessed greens on the eve of enclosure, the changes
ushered in by enclosure were of little or no significance.

These last examples, involving the enclosure of small remnants of once
larger greens, demonstrate as well that enclosure was a continuous process.
Piecemeal enclosure since the sixteenth century and earlier had already
reduced the number and size of village greens, and the enclosure records
contain evidence of the traces of many of these. Little Abington,
Longstowe, and West Wickham, for example, had all possessed a village
green at some point in their history; by enclosure in the early nineteenth
century, all had already found their way into the hands of private individ-

---

[61] Cambridgeshire CRO, Hinxton Enclosure Award, 15 Oct. 1833, QRDz10.
[62] Cambridgeshire CRO, Ickleton Enclosure Award, 2 Aug. 1814, QRDz7.
[63] Cambridgeshire CRO, Whittlesford Enclosure Award, 17 Aug. 1815, QRDz9.
[64] Cambridgeshire CRO, Bourne Enclosure Award, 16 June 1820, QRDz9. See also Foxton
Enclosure Award, 10 June 1830, QRDz10; Little Gransden Enclosure Award, 6 April 1826,
QRDz10.

uals.[65] In some villages it is clear that parliamentary enclosures were building on the achievements of earlier centuries. In these, substantial sections of the green had been left open at earlier enclosures, and late-eighteenth- and early-nineteenth-century enclosures were simply completing a process of attrition begun many years earlier. In Croxton, for example, Sir George William Leeds already held two plots on the village green totalling 7 acres prior to enclosure; by an act of enclosure in 1818, the remaining 3 acres were divided into further allotments for Sir George and a road.[66] In Ditton Wood, three of the four greens had been anciently enclosed, and the remaining green, Damp Pond Green, was enclosed by parliamentary act in 1823;[67] whilst at Shepreth three of five greens had been enclosed before enclosure in 1823, at which time the remaining two, Home Lands Green and Huckles Green, were allotted.[68] Many enclosure maps show small central greens hemmed in by ancient enclosures, whilst the layout of the streets suggests the outline of a green that had originally extended much further. It would clearly be mistaken, therefore, to suggest that a golden age of village greens had existed just prior to the parliamentary enclosure movement, as these ancient central spaces had long been vulnerable to encroachment and appropriation, legal or otherwise. Yet the speed with which the parliamentary process of enclosure destroyed ancient village greens is nevertheless quite remarkable. Enclosure was invariably accompanied by the transfer of the green from communal to private property: over two-thirds of the forty-eight villages with greens that were enclosed between 1790 and 1837 lost their green as a consequence of the enclosure. When it is recalled that these enclosures all took place within the space of forty years, the magnitude of the changes that occurred is yet more notable.

It is even doubtful whether these allotments were legal. In most instances it is not possible to establish the exact nature of the rights over the village green that were held by commoners. Where villages had very large greens spreading away from the centre, commoners may have possessed some grazing rights over the land. It is unlikely, for example, that the Great Greens of 20 acres and over in Wimblington and Guilden Morden were entirely free of grazing rights. It is, however, highly unlikely that any

---

[65] Cambridgeshire CRO, Little Abington Enclosure Award, 28 April 1807, QRDz5; Longstowe Enclosure Award, 22 July 1800, QRDz/1; West Wickham Enclosure Award, 16 May 1822, QRDz9.

[66] Cambridgeshire CRO, Croxton Enclosure Award, 23 Sept. 1818, QRDz5 see also the illustration on page 216.

[67] Cambridgeshire CRO, Ditton Wood Enclosure Award, 20 May 1823, QRDz10.

[68] Cambridgeshire CRO, Shepreth Enclosure Award, 21 April 1823, QRDz10.

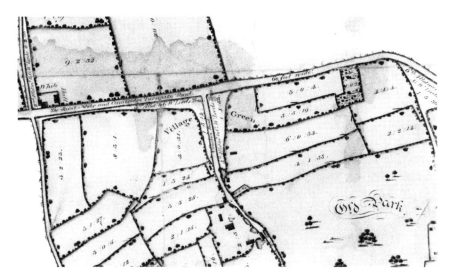

Figure 13.   Croxton Enclosure Map, 1818 (Cambridge County Record Office,
Cambridge, QRDc32.

rights of common existed over the much more numerous smaller, central
greens; and, where this was the case, such land should not have been shared
out amongst the holders of common rights at enclosure. At enclosure, those
who held common rights exchanged those rights for land. Since they did
not in fact possess any rights over the green or greens within the village,
this land should not have been included when evaluating the quantity of
land available for enclosure.[69]

Furthermore, even if rights of common had existed over village greens,
their enclosure would have been legally dubious, since customary rights of
recreation also existed on these spaces, and these rights by law took prece-
dence. The right to play games on the village green (or any other designated close or field) had been upheld in law in 1665, following an
unsuccessful action against the villagers for trespass in a parish in Oxfordshire. The court had upheld the villagers' right to enter the plaintiff's field
for sports and recreation, adding 'it is necessary for inhabitants to have their
recreations'; and this ruling might have been used to prevent the enclosure
of village greens.[70] It is clear, however, that few of those involved in the later
parliamentary enclosure movement were aware of this ruling. In case after
case, the enclosure commissioners did not respect customary playing rights

[69] For more detail concerning those who held common rights, see Shaw-Taylor,
'Parliamentary enclosure', pp. 640–62.
[70] The case is described in Eversley, *Commons*, pp. 281–9.

when making allotments; their awards carved up greens ranging in size from less than 1 acre to 20 acres and more. In the majority of cases no land for recreation was reserved for the poor, and this appropriation of a traditional playing space was rarely contested.

The quiet destruction of village greens went entirely unnoticed for several decades, and it was not until commentators became exercised about the lack of space for recreation in large towns in the 1830s that steps were taken to halt these depredations. As we noted in the previous chapter, a handful of individuals in the House of Commons began to protest about the enclosure of the wastes and commons on the edges of expanding industrial towns during the 1830s, and to argue that recreational space of some kind was necessary to the health of urban dwellers.[71] In order to protect such space the 1836 General Enclosure Act exempted common fields within a certain radius of large towns from enclosure, and this measure was extended in 1837 when the House passed a resolution proposed by Joseph Hume that 'in all Inclosure Bills provision be made for leaving an open space sufficient for the purposes of exercise and recreation of the neighbouring population'.[72] Although parliament's attention was clearly focused on large towns, this new measure had implications for rural playgrounds as well, for Hume's resolution was not in fact confined to urban areas, and enclosure commissioners diligently enforced it in subsequent enclosure awards in all areas.

So far as rural districts were concerned, however, the outcome of Hume's resolution was decidedly mixed. Certainly new recreation grounds were laid out, and the situation which had prevailed prior to 1837, where enclosed villages were usually left bereft of any open space, was brought to a close. Yet the new regulation did little to preserve ancient rural greens, and these continued to be destroyed as enclosure continued unabated in the following years. At Sutton and Haddenham, for example, small greens of less than 1 acre were exchanged for small recreation grounds 1 acre in size at enclosure.[73] At Comberton, a green of over 2 acres was exchanged for a rather more generously sized 'Allotment for the recreation of the Inhabitants' of 4 acres at enclosure.[74] The village of Swavesey lost six greens—the

---

[71] See Hammond and Hammond, *Age of Chartists*, pp. 121–43.

[72] Ibid., pp. 124–5. For the changing legal status of greens, see Scrutton, *Commons and Common Fields*, pp. 157–8; and Hunter, *Preservation of Open Spaces*, pp. 223–30.

[73] Cambridgeshire CRO, Sutton Enclosure Award, 4 June 1840, 'March'; Haddenham Enclosure Award, 4 Aug. 1847, 'March'.

[74] Cambridgeshire CRO, Comberton Enclosure Award, 18 Dec. 1840, QRDc57. At Fowlmere, a 3–acre ground, the Butts, was awarded for recreation (Fowlmere Enclosure Award, 19 April 1850, QRDc70).

Green, Cow Fen Green, Thistle Green, Gibralter Green, Church Green, and the Great Green—at the enclosure in 1840. The Green was no more than a very long, thin roadside verge, but Cow Fen Green, Thistle Green, Gibralter Green, and Church Green were all fine central greens of between 2.5 and 10 acres, and the Great Green was yet larger still. The 4-acre recreation ground that was awarded to the churchwardens in return was arguably rather poor compensation for these losses.[75] Even where the new recreation grounds were greater in size than the greens that had been enclosed, it is far from evident that they constituted adequate compensation for the space that had been lost. The new, symmetrical recreation grounds that were created, often on village outskirts, bore little resemblance to the centuries-old spaces that had once lain at the heart of the village. Some were placed on the outskirts of the village; that at Comberton, for example, was tucked away in fields a little under a mile away from the centre of the village. There must be some doubt whether this new, remote recreation ground was commensurate with the ancient central green that it replaced.

It was not until a further eight years had passed that parliament finally called a decisive halt to the destruction of village greens. The General Enclosure Act of 1845 excluded all town and village greens from the land that might be enclosed under the act, and gave the commissioners new powers to set out recreation grounds. But, by this date, there were precious few greens in Cambridgeshire left to preserve, and the legislation was therefore little used. Half a century of extensive enclosure came to an almost complete close just before this legislation was passed, and there were no more than a dozen further enclosure acts in the county after 1845.[76] Extensive enclosure prior to 1837 had demolished many of the greens that had existed in the late eighteenth century: two-thirds of those villages with a green, or one-half of all the villages enclosed during this period, lost their greens as a consequence of enclosure. Furthermore, the next decade, although it saw the creation of a number of recreation grounds, witnessed the further destruction of many greens. The impact of enclosure on the county's village greens is therefore quite clear: it caused a rapid and significant despoliation of these ancient rural spaces.

[75] Cambridgeshire CRO, Swavesey Enclosure Award, 18 Dec. 1840, QRDc56.
[76] The county's enclosures are listed in Tate, *Domesday of Enclosures*, pp. 72–7.

Cultural continuity

There can be no doubt that the impact of enclosure in Cambridgeshire was significant: a half century of enclosure left the extent of both commons and greens in the county much diminished. but how did the experience of Cambridgeshire compare with that of other regions? And what were the ramifications of these developments, both within the county and beyond, for the history of recreation more broadly?

Neither of these questions is straightforward to answer, though the first, concerning the typicality of the experience of Cambridgeshire, perhaps poses rather fewer problems than the second. There is of course no 'typical' county, as the experience of enclosure varied so widely from one county to the next. However, if generalisations of some kind could be made, it is unlikely that Cambridgeshire would conform to any general patterns. This is because enclosure in this county occurred notably later than elsewhere, and was also very much more rapid once it began.[77] From 1790 to the middle of the nineteenth century, 136 acts of enclosure were passed, involving something well in excess of 50 per cent of the county's surface area. Nearly 80 per cent of villages were affected to some extent by parliamentary enclosure during this period, making this one of the most rapidly enclosed counties in England.[78] These enclosures introduced a swift and far-reaching reorganisation of the county's agricultural land, and one social consequence of this was the loss of the common land that had once formed a valuable source of land for popular sports and recreations. It is doubtful, however, that many other counties witnessed such comprehensive and rapid destruction of rural playgrounds in this period. There were no more than a handful of counties—Bedfordshire, Huntingdon, Leicestershire, Northamptonshire, Oxfordshire, and the East Riding of Yorkshire—that were so rapidly and extensively enclosed. In all of these counties, enclosure began earlier, usually in the first half of the eighteenth century, and the pace of enclosure was considerably slower; none saw such extensive enclosure concentrated in so few years. In most other parts of the country, the pace of enclosure was yet slower still, spanning centuries rather than decades.

---

[77] For overviews of the geography of enclosure, see Tate, *Domesday of Enclosure*, pp. 32–62; Turner, *English Enclosure*. For mechanisms of enclosure, see Gonner, *Common Land*, pp. 43–94; Yelling, *Common Field and Enclosure*, pp. 11–45; Allen, *Enclosure and Yeoman*, pp. 25–55; Mingay, *Parliamentary Enclosure*, pp. 55–82.

[78] Turner, *English Enclosure*, pp. 32–62.

Even acknowledging the marked regional diversity of the enclosure movement, the experience of enclosure in Cambridgeshire stands out as unusual. Yet it was not entirely exceptional either. It was the timing of the enclosure in this county that set it apart from other counties, rather than its extent; and, as the process wound down in the 1840s, Cambridgeshire came increasingly to resemble most other English counties, which had either been enclosed in the eighteenth century or earlier, or in some instances may never have been fully open. In other words, the heavy enclosure of Cambridgeshire after 1790 was largely owing to the fact that so much of the county had remained open for so long, and the rapid enclosure subsequently may perhaps be best understood as a process of catching up. Although in most places occurring earlier and at a much gentler pace, enclosure in the eighteenth century was extensive, and the underlying trend is undeniable. The enclosure of commons was consistent and relentless, and certainly left most rural areas with very much less space to play by the century's end.

The extent to which the loss of village greens in Cambridgeshire was typical is more uncertain. It is likely, however, that losses here were unusually high, even when contrasted with other heavily enclosed counties. Our evidence for the existence of village greens in the present day is frail; nevertheless, the information that we have indicates that modern Cambridgeshire has amongst the fewest greens of any county. The list of commons and greens in each county assembled by Stamp and Hoskins in the 1970s places Cambridgeshire in a small group of counties with fewer than a dozen reported greens.[79] Yet other counties that were heavily enclosed after 1700 are not found in this group, which suggests that something other than enclosure might have been responsible for the poor survival rate of village greens in Cambridgeshire.

Once again, it is the timing of enclosure that underpins the county's distinctive experience. Enclosure here was not only extensive; it also occurred considerably later than elsewhere, and this factor is significant since the timing of enclosure appears to have affected its nature. As the movement gathered pace in the late eighteenth century, commissioners became increasingly rigorous in their approach, allotting even the smallest plots of waste and verges—scraps of land that had usually been left

---

[79] For lists of village greens by county, see map and table (pp. 30–1) and the appendix (pp. 245–350) in Hoskins and Stamp, *Common Lands*. It is known that many greens are missing from this list, but there are no grounds for assuming the omissions are greater in the case of Cambridgeshire than elsewhere, and the distribution of greens between counties is likely to be broadly correct.

untouched by an earlier generation of enclosers. In consequence, counties that were enclosed late were transformed by the process to a greater extent than those where enclosure had occurred earlier. The experience of enclosure in neighbouring Hertfordshire was very different. The county's suitability for the cultivation of corn and its close proximity to London had encouraged enclosure at a much earlier date, mostly prior to 1700, but at this date enclosers had rarely included village greens when drawing up their surveys of the land over which common rights were held; and this early enclosure no doubt helps to explain why the number of registered commons and greens in Hertfordshire is considerably greater than that in Cambridgeshire.[80] Enclosure had been a feature of rural life in most counties for many centuries, yet it had not traditionally been associated with the appropriation of the village green; and, through much of history, these spaces had been preserved, at least in part, during the process of enclosure. It was the misfortune of Cambridgeshire that enclosure was delayed until after 1790, since by this time the customary respect that had long protected village greens seems to have been largely eroded.

The second of our questions, concerning the impact of these changes in landholding upon the practice of popular recreation is rather more problematic. It is clear that the eighteenth century saw the steady erosion of traditional playing spaces in many parts of rural England, but what happened to the recreations that had once been played on them? Enclosure records tell us nothing about the uses of space, and, in order to answer this question, we need to turn to the writings of folklorists, antiquaries, historians, and others who took an interest in popular customs and recreations. Unfortunately, however, their ideas about the practice of athletic sports in the early nineteenth century were confused, and often contradictory, and no clear account of the fortunes of popular recreations in enclosed rural areas is contained within them.

It is difficult, for example, to know how to interpret the claims of nineteenth-century commentators that traditional forms of football no longer held the place in rural communities that they once had. The historian of popular sports, Joseph Strutt, writing at the turn of the century, believed that football 'was formerly much in vogue among the common people of England, though of late years . . . seems to have fallen into disrepute, and is but little practised'.[81] Another commentator agreed that football had 'dwindled down to nothing, compared to the estimation in which it was

---

[80] Hoskins and Stamp list 116 village greens in Hertfordshire. Ibid., pp. 254–5, 287–90.
[81] Strutt, *Sports and Pastimes*, p. 92.

formerly held'.[82] A few writers even suggested that enclosure was responsible for the game's recent demise. William Howitt, for example, noted that football required a 'wide space for its exercise', and concluded that it had 'gone out of use' owing to the enclosure of waste and commons.[83] And there is some evidence to support these views, a few documented examples of enclosure removing the land on which football matches had traditionally been played. In Holme, in Cumbria, for example, a historian noted that football had formerly been played upon the extensive commons of the district, but continued to observe that 'from this [the people] have been excluded ever since the time of the enclosure'.[84] In Hornsea in Yorkshire, a historian noted that football had 'necessarily been disused' following the enclosure of common land in 1809.[85] Likewise at Seascale in Cumbria, the great annual match was brought to an end when the Furness railway company bought up the land on which it had been played.[86]

But these writers appear to have been referring to the great set matches that the young men from neighbouring parishes had traditionally played over large expanses of common land. Such games had never been universal. In the eighteenth century they were confined to outlying regions in the north and south-west of England, and in most of southern and central England they were unknown. They may well have gone into decline in the course of the eighteenth century as a consequence of enclosure but, since they had never been particularly widespread, it is doubtful that this development entailed a significant contraction of popular recreation in rural England.

There had always been a tradition of football that did not range over large tracts of commons, but which was played in a form much closer to the modern game with which we are familiar—on small pitches of regular size, and between teams of equal numbers. In contrast to the annual set matches, these games received very little attention from commentators, but it should not be presumed from this that the game was not widespread. A sporting manual written in 1837 described football played on pitches where 'the goals are placed at the distance of eighty or one hundred yards from each other'.[87] Clearly, large commons were not necessary for games of this kind, and there is evidence to suggest that football in this form continued

[82] Litt, *Wrestliana*, p. 51. See also Aspin, *Picture of Manners*, p. 215.
[83] Howitt, *Rural Life*, ii, p. 244.
[84] Whellan, *History of Cumberland*, p. 235. He made similar observations of Isell. Ibid., p. 364.
[85] Bedell, *Account of Hornsea*, p. 88.
[86] Parker, *Gosforth District*, p. 36.
[87] Walker, *Games and Sports*, p. 253.

to be played throughout the nineteenth century. At the same time as folk-lorists and historians were recording the recent demise of football, the sporting newspapers were regularly reporting football matches in all parts of the country, apparently unaware that the game was now 'disused'. Downs, meadows, race grounds, fields, commons, parks, and private land were named as some of the places at which the game was played, and though our evidence for nineteenth-century football is limited there is little to indicate that lack of space hindered the game.[88] It is certain that the enclosure of common fields deprived the inhabitants of at least some rural districts of their traditional playing grounds yet, rather than undermine football, it is likely that this development simply prompted it to migrate to other spaces.

This point seems to be confirmed by the history of nineteenth-century cricket. In contrast to football, there were no expressions of concern about the recent decline of popular cricket: in fact its popularity was far more frequently noted. In the view of one writer: 'far and wide is spread the love of cricketing, and it may now be safely ranked as the prince of English athletic games'.[89] Nor was this popularity founded upon the middle and upper classes alone, for it was widely agreed that all social groups participated in the sport. The popular writer Mary Russell Mitford described a village match in which teams consisted in 'a little farmer's second son', a day labourer, and blacksmith;[90] and her account suggested to one contemporary that she 'well [understood] the subject'.[91] In the middle of the nineteenth century, commentators continued to insist that cricket was 'in every sense a game of the people generally, from the highest to the lowest; it excites no envy by its exclusiveness, as it equally enjoys the attention of the prince and the peasant'.[92] Elsewhere it was claimed that the game was 'participated in by all ranks of society', and that this maintained a 'healthy and kindly feeling' between the peer and the peasant.[93] Such commentary runs right through the nineteenth century; and, though it no doubt contains a certain degree of polemic, the ongoing popularity of cricket with the rural poor cannot be denied. Given that enclosure, in at least some parts of the

[88] For references, see Goulstone, 'Origins of football', pp. 135–43; Harvey, 'Football's missing link', pp. 92–116.
[89] Howitt, *Rural Life*, ii, p. 274.
[90] Mitford, *Our Village*, p. 147.
[91] Egan, *Book of Sports*, p. 311.
[92] Blaine, *Encyclopaedia of Sports*, p. 134.
[93] Eardley-Wilmot, *Reminiscences of Assheton Smith*, p. 54. See also Swanton and Woods, *Bygone Haslemere*, p. 297.

country, was depriving rural labourers of their traditional recreation grounds, one is led to question why plebeian cricket was not disappearing along with commons and greens; where was the village cricket now being played?

Since nineteenth-century commentators rarely gave the location of village cricket, there is very little direct evidence with which such questions may be answered. However, the history of Cambridgeshire's ancient 'camping closes' provides some clues to why cricket was not disappearing in enclosed counties. Camping closes were the specially designated playing fields found in villages across Cambridgeshire, as well as in Suffolk and Norfolk discussed at the start of this chapter. They had usually been bequeathed to the parish for its inhabitants' use in perpetuity, though by the eighteenth century many of these communal playing spaces had already been transferred to private hands.[94] Certainly in Cambridgeshire the transfer from communal to private ownership had been largely completed by the nineteenth century. In Landbeach and Milton, the rectors had appropriated the camping closes by the early eighteenth century;[95] and enclosure awards from the early nineteenth century indicate that by that date many more were in the hands of private individuals. A 'camping close' was mentioned in the enclosure awards of thirteen villages—Little Abingdon, Bottisham, Bourne, Dullingham, Fulbourn, Girton, Histon, Kirtling, Long Stanton, Milton, Oakington, Trumpington, and West Wickham[96]—and every single one of these closes was described as an 'ancient enclosure'. Additional records for Landbeach, Littleport, Little Shelford, Waterbeach, and Whittlesford reveal that the camping closes belonging to these villages were also privately, rather than communally, owned.[97] In all eighteen villages in which there is evidence of a camping close in the early nineteenth

---

[94] See Dymond, 'Camping close', pp. 165–79.

[95] Clay, *History of Landbeach*, p. 60; Clay, *History of Milton*, p. 21.

[96] Cambridgeshire CRO, Little Abington Enclosure Award, 28 April 1807, QRDz5; Bottisham Enclosure Award, 3 Oct. 1808, QRDz5; Bourne Enclosure Award, 16 June 1820, QRDz9; Dullingham Enclosure Award, 7 April 1810, QRDz6; Fulbourn Enclosure Award, 20 Aug. 1814, QRDz7; Girton Enclosure Award, 5 March 1814, QRDz7; Histon Enclosure Award, 31 May 1806, QRDz6; Kirtling Enclosure Award, 26 March 1814, P101/26/1; Longstanton Enclosure Award, 10 April, 1816, QRDz8, Milton Enclosure Award, 1 Aug. 1802, QRDz5; Oakington Enclosure Award, 6 Nov. 1834, QRDc48; Trumpington Enclosure Award, 15 May 1809, QRDz6; West Wickham Enclosure Award, 16 May 1822, QRDz9.

[97] Clay, *History of Landbeach*, p. 60; Cambridge UL, Littleport Tithe Apportionment, 1839, EDK T; Wale, *Grandfather's Pocket Book*, 24 Feb. 1786, p. 257 (diar.); Clay, *History of Waterbeach*, p. 23. Cambridgeshire CRO, Maynard Manuscripts, R58, Whittlesford, v, p. 269.

century, the records indicate that the close had been transferred to private hands at some point in the preceding centuries.

In some instances, the new owner of the land had terminated rights of recreation in the camping close. This appears to have happened at Little Shelford, for example, where a farmer 'sent for Field keeper to forbid boys playing in Camping Close' in the 1780s.[98] A nineteenth-century researcher likewise found that at Haverhill in Suffolk the camping close was 'long since closed to the public', and that the camping close at Boxted in Essex was no longer in use as a recreation field.[99] But it is remarkable how many camping closes did continue to be used by inhabitants, despite being privately rather than communally owned. In Dullingham, a field invested in the village as a camping close in 1558 was clearly described as an 'old inclosure' in the award of 1810,[100] yet a late-twentieth-century historian found that the camping close nevertheless continued to be used nearly two centuries later.[101] Nor is this an isolated example. In Littleport, a tithe map of 1839 indicates that a large camping close of over 6 acres was in private hands; however twentieth-century researcher Enid Porter recorded that children played games here every Shrove Tuesday until the late nineteenth century, when a factory was built on the site.[102] Cambridgeshire folklorist and historian Henry Maynard established that the camping closes at Duxford and Whittlesford, both enclosed villages, were being used by children in the middle of the nineteenth century; and similarly at Burgh Castle, Suffolk, the village camping close was still being used in the nineteenth century.[103] Camping closes at Needham Market, Bures, Pakenham, and Swaffham have all survived as open playing spaces until the present day.[104]

These examples are not presented in order to suggest that cricket migrated from greens and commons to ancient playgrounds following enclosure. Nor are they intended to suggest that the assumption of property rights did nothing to reduce recreation grounds in rural areas. Many private owners did attempt to prevent popular recreation on their land, and the long-term trend, the eventual termination of rights of recreation, is

---

[98] Wale, *Grandfather's Pocket Book*, 24 Feb. 1786, p. 257 (diar.).

[99] Cambridgeshire CRO, Maynard Manuscripts, R58, vii, pp. 9, 12.

[100] Cambridgeshire CRO, Dullingham Enclosure Award, 7 April 1810, QRDz6.

[101] Personal communication with David Dymond.

[102] Cambridge UL, Littleport Tithe Apportionment, 1839, EDR T; Porter, *Folklore of East Anglia*, pp. 58–93.

[103] Cambridgeshire CRO, Maynard Manuscripts, R58, v, Whittlesford, p. 269; x, Duxford, p. 278. Dutt, *Highways of East Anglia*, pp. 151–2.

[104] Dymond, 'Camping close', pp. 176, 179.

Figure 14. Charles Shayer, *Village Cricket, c. 1870* (Marylebone Cricket Club, London).

Figure 15. John Ritchie, *Village Cricket*, 1855 (Marylebone Cricket Club, London).

undeniable. The point rather is to highlight the breach that existed between the legal and customary status of these closes over long periods of time. Although most camping closes had become private property in the eighteenth century or earlier, landowners were decidedly slower to assert their rights than might be imagined, and rights of recreation continued to be exercised in many camping closes well into the nineteenth century and beyond. It is impossible to measure how often and how long such customary rights endured, but nevertheless it is clearly important to recognise that custom and tradition were powerful forces in the rural environment throughout the period of this study, and served to mitigate the damage wrought by enclosure suggested by official records.

Notwithstanding the disappearance of traditional playgrounds consequent upon enclosure, fallow fields remained abundant in most rural areas, and alternative sites for recreation appear to have been found without great difficulty. There was a long tradition of landowners lending fields to local villagers for recreations, and much evidence for the continuation of this custom throughout the nineteenth century. The Cambridgeshire newspapers contain regular accounts of local landowners lending their fields for a variety of different recreational and social activities. In Fulbourn, for example, Mr Payne 'who loves to see cricket, and is always ready to do what he can to promote the game' lent meadows and closes during the 1850s and 1860s.[105] In Swavesey, cricket was played in the field of Mr Carter.[106] School treats were held in private fields in Teversham, Stretham, and Fulbourn. In Over, there were sports in Mr Gifford's close.[107] At Soham, the feast was held on land owned by the Crown Inn in the 1870s.[108] And so on. Although private estates did occasionally provide the location of public celebrations in urban areas, the routine use of private land and gardens for plebeian recreation in towns was rare. In rural areas a very different culture existed. Privately owned land had formed a central component of provision of space for rural sports and pastimes throughout the eighteenth century and, although social and economic change in some rural areas was both rapid and pervasive, this culture persisted well into the following century.

It is also clear that, in many instances, landowners simply turned a blind eye to popular recreation in their fallow fields. A nineteenth-century Cambridgeshire landowner, Wedd Nash, speaking to the Select Committee

---

[105] See, for example, *Cambridge Chronicle*, 5 Sept. 1846. Quote from ibid., 20 June 1863.
[106] Ibid., 5 Sept. 1846.
[107] Ibid., 18 July 1874.
[108] Ibid., 23 June 1877.

on Commons' Inclosure in 1844 summarised the situation in the following way. When questioned whether he believed it was necessary during enclosure to set apart a parcel of ground 'where the people might go to play at cricket, or amuse themselves', he replied:

> I have never known an instance where parties have been deprived of an opportunity of resorting to those games, whether commons have been inclosed or not; there is always some ground which the proprietors will not object to being used in this way; in all those parishes with which I am acquainted, those games are as prevalent as they were before the Inclosures.[109]

Of course, as a supporter and beneficiary of enclosure Nash might be suspected of downplaying any negative consequences of the process, yet this seems doubtful since Nash in fact supported the introduction of a parliamentary act stipulating the setting aside of a recreation ground in all instances of enclosure 'because in hundreds of cases it may be very important'; repeating once again, however, that 'in those cases which come within my knowledge, I have seen no mischief arising from the want of it'.[110] An elderly villager's recollections of her childhood in Wilburton in the nineteenth century support this account. Dorothy Porter remembered 'a great playing area' in fields around the parish church; the children appear to have preferred these to the 2-acre recreation ground laid out at enclosure in 1845, and their preference met no challenge.[111] The rural poor were certainly losing the common land and village greens on which they had traditionally held rights of recreation, and the loss of these rights should not be underestimated. However, changes in landholding patterns were not matched by marked changes in the attitude of landowners towards rural sports and recreations. Farmers and landowners continued to regard popular recreations sympathetically; and, as common land and village greens diminished, patronage played an increased role in providing land for popular recreations.

   When contrasted with the findings of earlier chapters, considering the history of popular sports in provincial towns and in the industrial Midlands and north, it is possible both to delineate a number of continuities between

---

[109] *1844 Select Committee on Commons' Inclosure*, p. 294.
[110] Ibid., p. 294.
[111] Cambridgeshire LSL, Porter, 'These are my times', Cambridgeshire Collection, p. 7. See also Garrett, 'Village memories', Cambridgeshire Collection, i; and the comments of Charlotte Burne, the Shropshire folklorist: villagers from Baschurch on their way home from Shrewsbury market would 'turn aside into some friendly farmer's field to rest, and there have a picnic meal and a dance on the grass before going home'. Burne, *Shropshire Folklore*, ii, p. 473.

different areas, and to bring into relief a characteristically rural culture. The similarities between rural and industrial areas, for instance, are striking. In both, there was a considerable breach between local law and local custom, and it is clear that the practice of popular recreation cannot be fully comprehended simply by measuring and counting the designated spaces in which the poor were permitted to play. It is likely, however, that the factors underpinning this similarity were different in each case. In industrial areas it seems that a combination of indifference and ineffective governance enabled popular recreations to flourish on wasteland, undeveloped sites, and city streets; whilst in rural areas it was the enduring hold of paternalism and a well entrenched tolerance for popular recreation that ensured the continuation of existing forms of recreation well into the second half of the nineteenth century.

In respect of provincial towns, the contrasts are yet greater. Compared to the close supervision and control of the small village, the town has generally been seen as a place of freedom, and it is certainly true that in some respects towns did provide a propitious environment for popular recreation.[112] As we have noted, the size and wealth of large towns enabled them to develop complex and large-scale entertainments capable of attracting large numbers of visitors from surrounding districts. The recreational calendar of towns was undeniably both richer and more varied than that of smaller rural settlements but, if the resources of villages and hamlets were more limited, these places nonetheless formed an environment that was in its own way favourable to popular recreations. Villages lacked the mechanisms of control—the criers, watchmen, and magistrates—who were policing urban recreations increasingly effectively throughout the nineteenth century, and serving to define their timing and location. Perhaps more significantly, however, the hostility towards recreation that was developing in many market towns was largely absent in smaller settlements. And this indeed is the most striking characteristic of popular recreation in rural areas throughout this period. Although the rural environment was changing rapidly and profoundly in some parts of the country, patterns of recreation were not being transformed at a similar rate. Economic and social change was possibly as profound and pervasive in parts of rural England as it was anywhere, yet deeply rooted traditions of custom and paternalism served to ensure the survival of older patterns of sports and pastimes.

---

[112] According to Golby and Purdue, for example: 'In the cities and larger towns especially, the individual [was] free from the suffocating embrace and the unofficial pressures of small communities'. Golby and Purdue, *Civilisation and Crowd*, p. 63.

9
The demise of bull-baiting

This book has returned repeatedly to the ancient sport of bull-baiting. It is clear that the pastime was endlessly adaptable, fitting into the recreational calendar of different communities in a number of distinct ways. Although originally a butchers regulation intended to improve the quality of meat, bull-baiting had migrated into other contexts. In the eighteenth century, it continued as an occasional plebeian sport practised in the centre of provincial market towns, divest of the slaughtering customs that had long been associated with it; and it also featured at the wakes, feasts, and fairs of many communities both rural and urban. At the same time, bull-baiting was more than a plebeian pastime, it was also a concept, a cultural reference point. As Chapter 5 made clear, the sport had an existence beyond country feasts and the market squares of provincial towns; it was also an idea intimately tied up with contemporary hopes and fears about social progress.

At some point, these things have all ceased to be. For reasons that are not yet clear, bull-baiting in all these contexts has disappeared, and it is arguably only as an idea—as historical evidence of the barbarity of an earlier age—that the sport lives on. It is fitting therefore that at the close of this book we should turn to consider this. It is time to tie the threads of these different histories together, and to offer some explanation of the process by which a widespread social custom passed into history.

In fact establishing the manner in which bull-baiting disappeared is difficult, and uncovering the reasons for this yet more so; for, just as bull-baiting had occupied a distinct position in different communities, so was the demise of the sport played out in a number of different ways. Bull-baiting had always existed in diverse contexts and forms, and as a consequence of this diversity it is not possible to provide a single unified account of the sport's eventual decline. Instead two distinct patterns stand out. In most respects, the demise of bull-baiting was not dramatic. In almost all parts of the land—urban, rural, and industrial—the sport that formed the focus of so much disgust by the early nineteenth century simply disappeared. Bull-baiting did not divide local communities: there were no battles waged over bull-baiting, no action taken to maintain the custom, and no attempt to suppress it. Popular interest simply ebbed away, and this loss of plebeian interest sapped the forces that had kept the sport alive for so many centuries. No less striking, however, than the quiet and uncontested departure of bull-baiting from markets squares, feasts, and fairs, was the one exception to this pattern. In Birmingham and the Black Country, the sport refused to disappear. In complete contrast to elsewhere, in this region bull-baiting increased rather than decreased in popularity, and in the late eighteenth century became the source of repeated social conflict. It was only when the forces of law and order were effectively mobilised in the 1820s and 1830s that the sport was eventually eliminated from this region. We are faced, therefore, with two very different problems to explain. In the first instance, why did the popular support that had sustained bull-baiting through the centuries fall away at this time? And in the second, why did the west Midlands diverge so strikingly from this pattern?

Invented reformers

The disappearance of bull-baiting from England is not a problem that has courted historical controversy. Throughout the nineteenth century, commentators on popular sports proudly appropriated responsibility for the suppression of blood sports for the middle classes; and, although the honour of this claim is viewed more doubtfully in some recent discussions, it is nevertheless still widely accepted by historians of all political persuasions that bull-baiting was eliminated only though the efforts of middle-class reformers. The case was put in particularly flamboyant terms by the cultural commentator, William Howitt. With typical aplomb, he wrote: 'The brutal and vulgarised condition of the people flashed on the perception of the middle classes, which amid all the noise of [the French Wars] had been progressing in intelligence and refinement . . . A better spirit, a better sense of our duties and responsibilities towards the people awoke.'[1] Howitt's language was no doubt a little more florid than that of most nineteenth-century commentators, but the sentiments he expressed were typical, for few doubted that the benign influence of the middle classes was responsible for the recent disappearance of bull-baiting and other popular blood sports.

Yet this account contains something of a puzzle, for these claims are not backed up by the official records in the way that we should expect. We

---

[1] Howitt, *Rural Life*, ii, p. 268.

noted in Chapter 3 of this book that recreation in the market square was common through most of the century following the Restoration, and that bull-baiting was firmly established as one of the plebeian pastimes traditionally practised here. Chapter 4 documented a steady process of attrition upon plebeian recreation in the market square and public streets in the second half of the eighteenth century, yet in this chapter bull-baiting slipped from view. Nor was this the consequence of an authorial decision to reserve discussion of bull-baiting until a later chapter. Bull-baiting was absent from that chapter because it largely slips from official records following the end of payments for the civic bull-ring. And this disappearance of bull-baiting from official records is far from what we should expect, if bull-baiting had indeed been suppressed in the way that commentators claimed.

Once civic authorities had made their final contribution to their municipal bull-ring, it becomes difficult to trace accurately the fortunes of bull-baiting, though it is clear that the pastime continued as an urban sport in many towns for a number of decades, the end of payments notwithstanding. Certainly the bull-rings remained in place: town authorities had been making only small payments and those who provided the sport could easily absorb the cost of bull rope and bull collars. Thus in Great Yarmouth, for example, the corporation ceased its payments for bull rope and bull collars in 1755, but enterprising local men continued to organise sport at the bull-ring for at least another two decades. In 1775 a local gentleman noted in his diary (with some displeasure) that 'About 4 o'clock this afternoon there was a BULL BAITED in the Market by Bull Dogs till 6 o'clock. Jos Bamaby and one Whitehead were there, Proprietors.'[2] In Cambridge, where the city chamberlains made no contributions to the bull-ring after 1660, a manuscript history of the town written in the early nineteenth century by a local resident, John Bowtell, remarked that 'so late as about the year 1766 this diversion continued'.[3] Bowtell recalled that two bull-rings remained in place, 'at the great hill, near to the conduit, and the beast market hill', until the 1790s when they were removed during the paving of the town following a recently procured act of parliament.[4] This was over a century after the city chamberlains' final payments for the bull-ring.

Local newspapers confirm that bull-baiting continued at civic bull-rings for some years following the end of official payments, though their

[2] Norfolk RO, Youell's Diary, 1771–75, D87/10, 25 Aug. 1775.
[3] Downing College Library, John Bowtell, Unpublished History of Cambridge, vii, Bowtell Bequest/63, 2756.
[4] Ibid., pp. 2756–7.

reports were infrequent and usually occasioned only by some mishap. We know, for example, that there was a bull-baiting at Stockton in 1793, but only because on this occasion the bull slipped its chain and injured a man.[5] Similarly, there is a record of bull-baiting at Derby in 1772—in this instance because a man the crowd had observed picking pockets was thrown over a bridge into the stream.[6] It is not possible to provide an accurate reconstruction of the mechanisms that lay behind the disappearance of bull-baiting from English towns on the basis of occasional references such as these. For all the extensive debates considered in Chapter 5, simple questions about the frequency and form of bull-baiting in towns during this period remain impossible to answer, as do more fundamental ones about the manner of its eventual demise.

It does seem unlikely, however, that the disappearance of bull-baiting from English towns owed much to the reforming endeavours of the middle classes. It is certain that reforming activity of this kind would have left its mark on the historical record—as it did, for example, in Essex, when a bull-baiting got out of hand, and the ringleaders were rounded up and prosecuted at the town's quarter sessions. Court records reveal that in 1758 two men were indicted for 'a Riot and baiting a Bull in the town of Chelmsford in an Improper place and afterwards letting him loose in the said town'.[7] This was an attempt to regulate bull-baiting rather than abolish it, though as the record indicates if the authorities of Chelmsford had wanted to abolish bull-baiting in the town they would have been able to do so at quarter sessions. Yet no more bull-baiting cases appear in the indictment books.[8] So far as we can know, bull-baiting continued in Chelmsford in its proper place, but ceased before it became controversial; and in this it mirrored the pattern in many other towns from all parts of England. Across the country, bull-baiting was disappearing from towns that had in the recent past promoted the sport, but evidence that civic authorities were driving this trend is not forthcoming.

Town records and local newspapers are not scarce for this period and, where civic authorities took steps to prevent plebeian recreations, these actions were invariably recorded in local records. Yet borough records (both town order books and accounts) and local newspapers very rarely recorded

---

[5] Richmond, *Stockton and Neighbourhood*, p. 92.
[6] Davison, *Derby: Its Rise and Progress*, p. 109. For an account of bull-baiting in Newark market place, see *Nottingham Journal*, 6 Jan. 1781.
[7] Essex RO, Process Book of Indictments, 1742–1762, Q/SPb/14, p.86.
[8] Essex RO, Process Books of Indictment, 1747–1840, Q/SPb/14–22.

official attempts to prevent bull-baiting in towns—a silence which forms a marked contrast to the abundant evidence of civic attempts to eliminate throwing at cocks at Shrovetide, and bonfires and fireworks at Guy Fawkes, and which must correspond to an absence of attempts to suppress the sport in urban areas. For example, in Cambridge and Great Yarmouth, where we have just noted diarists describing the custom in the second half of the eighteenth century, official records provide no evidence that the local authorities ever attempted to bring an end to these occurrences.[9] Similarly in Oundle, there is no record of official attempts to prohibit the Christmas bull-running recorded in John Clifton's diary between 1768 and 1784.[10] In Wokingham, the annual bull-baiting on St Thomas's day continued for some thirty years following the members of the corporation's resolution to absent themselves from the annual event.[11] A local historian claimed there were occasional breaches of the peace in following years, and gaol sentences for the organisers of a bull-bait in 1825, though this account is not corroborated by either the official record or the local papers.[12] Similar claims about the suppression of bull-running in Wisbech[13] and of bull-baiting in Windsor[14] are also not backed up by official records. It may be that the failure of official endeavours to prohibit bull-baiting to show up in the records of these towns is anomalous, but the near total absence of evidence for any such official action across the country is not so easily explained away.

[9] Cambridgeshire CRO, Cambridge Common Day Books, 1770–1792, Shelf c.13–13; Minute Book of Town Sessions, 1769–1771, Box 2.6; *Cambridge Chronicle*. Norfolk RO, Great Yarmouth Assembly Books, 1771–1801, Y/C19/14–15; *Norfolk Chronicle*; *Norwich Mercury*.

[10] The bull-running is described in Chapter 3 above. Northamptonshire RO, Quarter Sessions Presentment Book, 1754–90, Misc Q53; Recognizance Books 1787–1830, Misc Q54–8; *Northampton Mercury*.

[11] Adverts in the local paper indicate that a bull for baiting was provided by subscription until at least 1819. See *Reading Mercury*, 14 Dec. 1807, 20 Dec. 1813, 18 Dec. 1817, 20 Dec. 1819.

[12] Readwin, *Account of Wokingham*, pp. 73–6. Berkshire RO, Quarter Sessions Files, January 1836, SR244.

[13] A local historian claimed a new mayor put a stop to the custom in the 1790s. See Gardiner, *History of Wisbech*, p. 25. There is no account of his actions in either the town order book or local newspapers. Wisbech Museum, Wisbech Town Book, not catalogued; *Ipswich Journal* and *Cambridge Chronicle*.

[14] Capel Lofft claimed his father had suppressed bull-baiting. See *Monthly Magazine*, xii, 1 Jan. 1802, p. 480. There is nothing recorded in the town order books for the period of Lofft's mayoralty. See Berkshire RO, Windsor Sessions Book, 1750–1787, W1/JQ1/3; Windsor Chamberlains' Accounts, 1637–1806, W/FA1/2–3.

Throughout the county of Yorkshire, for example, there is no record of reforming activity, although there is extensive evidence that baiting bulls had been a popular custom during the eighteenth century and earlier. As we noted in Chapter 6, bull- and bear-baiting were both widely practised at annual feasts throughout the industrial hamlets and villages of the West Riding of Yorkshire, yet there is scant evidence that these events were brought to an end by the interference of civic elites. Local histories written in the second half of the nineteenth century often included recollections of bear-baiting at the local feasts: the man with the wandering bear was recalled by historians and their neighbours, so too was the site of the bear-baitings. What no one seems to have remembered, however, was any attempt to prevent bear-baiting, and almost none of the local historians in this region proved able to provide any detail about when or why the itinerant bearwards had stopped their periodic visits to the feast.[15] At Ecclesfield, for example, an open space by the churchyard was remembered in the 1860s as the site of bear-baitings by one historian; and the bull and two bears maintained by an inhabitant of the village for the purpose of baiting were recalled by another; neither, however, appears to have known when or why bear-baiting disappeared from the annual feast.[16] Even the most well informed historians gave no information about the eventual demise of the sport. Thus Charles Hatfield, in an exceptionally detailed account of recreations in Doncaster, stated that the mayor of that town, Dr Chorley, had attempted to prevent bear-baiting at Balby and Hexthorpe, two suburbs, in July 1824; but though he thought that bear-baiting had subsequently returned, he gave no indication of how it was finally suppressed beyond gesturing to a 'change in public opinion'. He was equally vague about the end of bear-baiting in the nearby villages of Conisbrough, Mexbrough, and Bentley, though he had amassed a considerable amount of evidence of the popularity of it in each of these places.[17] Only in Pudsey had a researcher uncovered information about the disappearance of bull-baiting: a historian in the 1860s had spoken to persons 'recently living' who had informed him that the last bull-baiting had ended in fines for the

[15] See Clarkson, *Merry Wakefield*, pp. 59–60; [Easther], *Glossary of Almondbury*, p. xv; Jagger, *History of Honley*, pp. 147–9; Roberts, *History of Lofthouse*, p. 46; Leader, *Old Sheffield*, pp. 209–11; Holmes, *Keighley Past and Present*, pp. 149–50; Speight, *Chronicles of Bingley*, p. 274; [Marsden], *Reminiscences*, p. 7.
[16] Eastwood, *History of Ecclesfield*, p. 354; Gatty, *Life at One Living*, p.25 (diar.).
[17] Hatfield, *Notices of Doncaster*, i, p. 80.

owner of the bull—a man named Jack Sheldon—and several others who had taken an active part in the sport.[18]

Examples of official attempts to prevent bear-baiting are equally scarce in the local newspapers; only two instances appear to have been reported over the first quarter of the nineteenth century. The first of these was in the parish of Darton, near Barnsley, in August 1820, where the minister and churchwardens had unspecified 'success' in preventing the 'inhuman and disgraceful practice of bear-baiting'.[19] The second was in Beeston, a village 2 miles south of Leeds where the magistrates imposed fines on the ringleaders of bull-baiting at the parish feast in two consecutive years, 1825–6.[20] Yet prosecutions for bull-baiting were newsworthy: the *Leeds Mercury* reported such cases from as far afield as Shropshire and the Black Country. It may be that a handful of other local prosecutions for bull- and bear-baiting escaped the notice of the local papers, yet it is safe to conclude that the small number of local cases reported also indicates a relatively low level of prosecutions in the area.

Beyond the industrial hamlets of the West Riding, in the market towns of north Yorkshire, the same pattern is evident. The ancient butchers regulation requiring the baiting of bulls before slaughter was enforced in several Yorkshire towns—Hedon, Bridlington, and Easingwold, for example, all collected fines from butchers who had failed to bait bulls before slaughter in the late seventeenth century.[21] Hull, Thirsk, and Skipton continued to enforce the custom until the middle of the eighteenth century.[22] In addition, many bull-rings were scattered across the county, usually in towns though sometimes on rural manorial estates as well. It is not always clear who had paid for these rings, as they were not generally recorded in town accounts. Their existence, however, is undoubted: they were noted by local historians and folklorists in the nineteenth century in Carlton, Hornsea, Leyburn and Middleham, Masham, Harewood, Easingwold, Bradford,

---

[18] [Rayner], *History of Pudsey*, pp. 195–6.

[19] *Sheffield Mercury*, 12 Aug. 1820.

[20] *Leeds Mercury*, 10 Sept. 1825, 2 Sept. 1826.

[21] East Riding of Yorkshire AO, Hedon Quarter Sessions Minute Book and Court Leet, 1657–1745, DDHE/5/1. Presentments 15 July 1659, 21 Jan. 1660, 3 Oct. 1662, 3 Jan. 1665, 4 Oct. 1667, 5 Oct. 1669. Purvis, *Bridlington*, pp. 247, 252, 254, 259. Cowling, *History of Easingwold*, p. 58.

[22] Hull CA, Chamberlains' Accounts, 1661–1800, BRF/2/517–698. Fines for the slaughter of unbaited bulls collected most years down to 1750. North Yorkshire CRO, Thirsk Manor Court Book, 1739–94, MIC 163. Presentments and orders at courts on 5 Oct. 1739, 10 Oct. 1740, 2 Oct. 1741, 5 Oct. 1744, 9 Oct. 1747, 11 Oct. 1754. Yorkshire Arch. Soc., Skipton Manor Jurors' Verdicts, 1700–1766, DD121/12. Fines in several years down to 1764.

Ingleton, and Kilham.[23] The bull-ring at Askrigg remained visible until at least the 1950s.[24]

However, none of these commentators could remember the baiting of any bulls at these rings. The closest any got to recalling bull-baiting was John Fisher, of Masham, who thought he had 'some slight glimmering of the recollection of Suzy Fleetham's bull being baited [in the market place]'.[25] William Grainge's experiences in Thirsk appear to have been more typical. He wrote that 'the bull-baitings have been so long discontinued as to be only a matter of tradition, the oldest inhabitant having no recollection of such an event'.[26] In the centre of Bradford, the bull-ring remained in place many decades into the nineteenth century but 'the most aged inhabitants of Bradford, speaking of the last eighty years [i.e. since the 1780s] all aver the bull-baiting was, by no means, a common occurrence here'.[27] Similarly at Halifax, bull-baiting was described in the past tense as early as 1775.[28] Henry Clarkson, 'never [recollected] Bull Baiting, nor [did he] remember to have heard [his] father speak of having witnessed it in Wakefield'.[29] A resident of Bedale, writing in the first decade of the nineteenth century, could only remember having seen one bull baited, and that was not in town, but at Masham fair in 1789.[30] It is not clear from these sources exactly why bull-baiting had ceased in these towns, but they do suggest that it had done so before the end of the eighteenth century. Furthermore, they lend small support to the claim that the pastime was eliminated only owing to the reforming efforts of local notables.

Finally, the evidence from the Yorkshire newspapers once again points in the same direction. These contain no record of plans either to organise or prevent bull-baiting in local towns. Yet, when the MPs of Beverley began to revive the custom of providing a bull for baiting on the mayor's swearing-in day in the early nineteenth century, the newspapers complained

---

[23] Carlton (Fairfax-Blakeborough, *Yorkshire Village*, p. 15); Hornsea (Bedell, *Account of Hornsea*, ii, p. 88); Leyburn and Middleham (Barker, *History of Wensleydale*, p. 163); Masham (Fisher, *History of Masham*, p. 58); Harewood (Jones, *History of Harewood*, p. 168); Easingwold (Cowling, *History of Easingwold*, p. 73); Bradford (James, *Continuations of Bradford*, p. 249); Ingleton (Balderston and Balderston, *Ingleton*, p. 20); Kilham (Le Blanc Smith, 'Snitterton bull ring', p. 143).

[24] Hartley and Ingilby, *Yorkshire Village*, p. 100.

[25] Fisher, *History of Masham*, p. 58.

[26] Grainge, *Vale of Mowbray*, p. 113.

[27] James, *Continuations of Bradford*, p. 249.

[28] Watson, *History of Halifax*, p. 202.

[29] Clarkson, *Merry Wakefield*, p. 56.

[30] Hird, *Annals of Bedale*, p. 240.

loudly, so such events were clearly thought to be newsworthy.[31] When a man turned up in Hull with a baiting bull in April 1810, the local newspaper seemed to be genuinely bemused by the reappearance of the sport.[32] These responses suggest that the lack of commentary on bull-baiting in local newspapers through the late eighteenth and early nineteenth centuries stemmed from its absence in the area. The many bull-rings in Yorkshire had fallen into disuse before the nineteenth century, and the disappearance of bull-baiting from these towns during the eighteenth century had almost certainly not been accompanied by any serious conflict.

Few counties contained so many towns in which bull-rings remained in place into the nineteenth century, but there were certainly numerous towns scattered throughout the country in which bull-rings survived. Local historians frequently recorded the place where the bull-ring had been, or sometimes still was, situated. As in Yorkshire, however, they were almost always unable to recall any occasion on which it had been used, and they were noted simply as objects of antiquarian curiosity. It was the unexpected return of bull-baiting in 1813 that an inhabitant of Horsham in Sussex found remarkable: 'many people appear to think that this "sport" was frequently and regularly indulged till that year, but it was not so,' wrote a local resident, Henry Burstow. 'Mr Gilburd, my old master . . . told me he well remembered that in 1813 the bull ring was quite covered over with dirt and grass, and had to be "found" for this last occasion, and that he could remember no previous indulgence of the pastime'.[33] In most places, of course, bull-baiting made no such unexpected return, and the final bull-baiting had been held at a time when the sport had been neither newsworthy, nor controversial.

There are no more than a handful of exceptions to the generally peaceful disappearance of bull-baiting from the many market towns that had promoted the sport at some time during the century following the Restoration. At Lincoln, the annual bull-baitings held at Guy Fawkes were suppressed only following repeated threats, fines, and gaol sentences from the city magistrates in the first quarter of the nineteenth century.[34] A similar

---

[31] *Hull Advertiser*, 11 Oct. 1817, 2 Oct. 1819, 13 Oct. 1820.

[32] *Rockingham and Hull Weekly Advertiser*, 28 April 1810.

[33] Burstow, *Reminiscences*, pp. 62–3. Bull-baiting returned to Swindon 'somewhere about the years 1810 or 1812' in a similar way. See Morris, *Swindon Fifty Years Ago*, pp. 119–21.

[34] *Stamford Mercury*, 11 Nov. 1808, 10 Nov. 1809, 10 Nov. 1815, 10 Nov. 1818, 12 Nov. 1819, 10 Nov. 1820, 9 Nov. 1821, 8 Nov. 1822, 11 Nov. 1825, 10 Nov. 1826, 9 Nov. 1827.

tradition of bull-baiting at Guy Fawkes in Bury St Edmunds had been suppressed with considerably greater ease at the turn of the century.[35] In Aylesbury, the regular bull-baitings that continued until 1820s were brought to an end when a local magistrate, Colonel Browne, instructed the constables to prevent bull-baiting in the town in 1821.[36] There may be evidence from other towns that took steps to prevent bull-baiting that has yet to come to light, but it will not undermine the broad trends outlined here. In most towns, bull-baiting became ever more infrequent in the second half of the eighteenth century, and popular support for the sport had ebbed away years before reforming zeal crystallised.

One way in which bull-baiters might avoid open conflict with civic authorities was to move their sport out of the urban centre into more permissive and less closely policed rural areas, and there is some evidence that this did indeed occur. But, although bull-baiting lingered longer in rural areas, the same pattern is evident: the authorities rarely took action to prevent bull-baiting since the popular following that had once sustained the sport dissipated without official interference. At Ipswich, for example, a local historian remembered bull-baiting continuing in fields and inns around the town in the first decade of the nineteenth-century, but concluded: 'it is evident, from the frequency of their occurrence, that the authorities took no steps to stop such brutal amusements'.[37] The authorities in Norwich, given their thirty-year campaign against throwing at cocks, would certainly have stepped in to prevent bull-baiting in the city, but they appear never to have been prompted to do so. Instead the entertainment moved just outside the town. The *Norfolk Chronicle* carried reports of bull-baits in districts just outside the city's jurisdiction, at Thorpe, Bishop's Gate, and Carrow Hill.[38] Two reports of bull-baiting at Carrow Hill in 1815 and 1818 reveal that a game-bull was making his reputation there as an animal that no dog could pin, and suggest that the bull-baitings at Carrow Hill were more frequent than the occasional newspaper reports indicate. Had the authorities wished, they might have indicted the organisers of these events at quarter sessions, yet the court records indicate that

[35] *Bury and Norwich Post*, 14 Nov. 1792, 21 Nov. 1799, 10 Nov. 1802. Oakes, *Diary*, i, 13 Nov. 1792, p. 286.

[36] Buckinghamshire RO, Case Book Easter 1821–Epiphany 1812, QS/JC/6, 123–6; Gibbs, *History of Aylesbury*, pp. 558–9.

[37] Glyde, *Ipswich*, pp. 51–2.

[38] *Norfolk Chronicle*, (Thorpe) 3 March 1781; (Bishop's Gate) 14 March 1807; (Carrow Hill) 21 Jan. 1815, 23 June 1818.

they did not choose to do so.[39] Likewise in Nottinghamshire, bull-baitings were apparently carried on at Kimberley, just outside Nottingham, for four days in 1818;[40] here again, there is no evidence that the justices attempted to prevent them.[41] In the counties of Wiltshire, Hertfordshire, and Northamptonshire, there is only one instance of official interference in bull-baiting during the period.[42] Although the disappearance of bull-baiting from rural areas may sometimes have occurred at a later date than in towns, the process was essentially the same. The forces of law and order were rarely mobilised against bull-baiting, and the disappearance of this plebeian pastime owed more to waning popular demand than to the enlightenment and humanity of the well-to-do.

The legislation that was finally introduced by parliament to prohibit the baiting of bulls and bears needs to be seen in this context. Legislation against bull-baiting was first initiated in 1800, and a second unsuccessful attempt followed in 1802;[43] a broader animal protection bill also failed in 1809.[44] There was limited success in 1822, when Richard Martin's Bill to Prevent Cruelty to Horses and Cattle received royal assent. Bull-baiting was not explicitly mentioned in this act and, although provincial magistrates widely assumed that the act prohibited bull-baiting through its provisions to prevent cruelty to cattle, politicians were aware that it did not, and continued to agitate for further reform throughout the 1820s.[45] In 1835, the original act was consolidated: the prohibition of bull-baiting was made explicit, and extended to badger-baiting and dog-fighting; cockfighting was abolished seven years later.[46]

This animal protection legislation has long been regarded as evidence of increasing humanitarian concern amongst social elites, but it is important not to overestimate the practical significance of these laws. Bull-baiting

---

[39] Norfolk RO, Quarter Sessions Minute Book, 1815–21, Case 20a/27.

[40] *Nottingham Journal*, 31 Oct. 1818.

[41] Nottinghamshire Archives, Quarter Sessions Minute Book, 1817–1820, QSM/1/38.

[42] Wiltshire RO, Quarter Sessions Instructions for Indictments Books, 1790–1839, A1/170/1–4. In Hertfordshire, the constables claimed expenses for preventing a bull-baiting at Hertingfordbury in 1776. *Hertfordshire County Records*, viii, p. 250.

[43] *Parliamentary History*, xxxv (1800), pp. 202–14; xxxvi (1803), pp. 829–54.

[44] *Parliamentary Debates*, xiv (1809), pp. 851–3, 989–90, 1029–41, 1071; xvi (1810), pp. 726, 845–6.

[45] *Parliamentary Debates*, n.s. ix (1824), pp. 433–5; x (1825), pp. 130–4, 368–9, 486–96; xii (1825), pp. 657–61, 1002–13; xiv (1826), pp. 647–52; xxi (1829), pp. 1319–20.

[46] Nineteenth-century animal protection legislation is summarised in Harrison, 'Animals and the state', pp. 788–9; the law concerning bull-baiting is addressed in Turner, *Heaven in a Rage*, pp. 104–40.

had largely disappeared from England prior to even the earliest of these measures, and there was therefore little scope for the operation of the laws that were finally passed. Moreover, civic authorities had long possessed the powers necessary to prohibit bull-baiting, and the need for new legislation must therefore be questioned. Bull-baiting was a plebeian sport requiring a large open space; and, since the poor rarely possessed land of this type, it was almost always played on publicly owned land. The authorities who controlled these spaces already possessed the power to indict anyone conducting any activities they regarded as illegitimate or a public nuisance. It was in this way that the civic authorities in Lincoln, Bury St Edmunds, and Aylesbury had all managed to draw the bull-baitings that continued within their jurisdiction to an end. Indeed, during the course of the eighteenth century, these powers were extended in many towns by means of new improvement acts, since these invariably contained clauses explicitly prohibiting bull-baiting and bull-running in the streets of the town. Local authorities were thus fully armed with the powers they needed to prohibit bull-baiting, and had been for many years. It is remarkable that they had so seldom used these powers, and their enthusiastic response to the introduction of further sanctions yet more so. But the 1835 Cruelty to Animals Act was arguably important as an ideological statement, rather than as a political act. Its significance lay not in the new powers it introduced, but in the cultural message, concerning a civilised and enlightened ruling class, that it embodied.

We need therefore to reconsider the mechanisms that underpinned the disappearance of bull-baiting from England. At a few centuries' remove, the decline of bull-baiting looks very much like an example of nineteenth-century social progress, and we are used to looking to social elites to explain progressive cultural shifts of this kind. The evidence presented here, however, suggests that it is necessary to turn away from social elites, to the more nebulous and unquantifiable domain of plebeian cultural tastes, if we are to understand the disappearance of bull-baiting. This is clearly something very much harder to capture, since plebeian perceptions of bull-baiting were essentially unarticulated and are recoverable only in the crudest outline. It is possible to delineate a declining interest in the sport in the second half of the eighteenth century but, in the absence of any discussion from those involved, the exact forces underpinning this development are beyond direct investigation. Yet, if there is little direct evidence which addresses this problem, it may nevertheless be possible to pursue it indirectly, for there was one region which diverged strikingly from this general pattern. By turning to consider the place where the disappearance of bull-baiting was far from quiet and uncontroversial, it may be possible to get a better grasp of the forces that underlay the unexpected general trend that has been outlined here.

Social conflict

In Birmingham and the west Midlands, the demise of bull-baiting occurred in a very different way. Here, popular enthusiasm for bull-baiting did not simply evaporate as the eighteenth century drew to a close. In this region, there was no peaceful disappearance of bull-baiting; the elimination of the sport was both protracted and difficult. The bull-baiting that opened the wakes throughout the region emerged as a predictable point of conflict between local officials and the labouring population; and, by the 1820s, popular resistance to the authorities became established as an integral part of the wakes entertainments. Nor can this distinctiveness be explained simply with reference to the industrialisation witnessed in this region through the eighteenth century. In the no less industrial region of the West Riding of Yorkshire, conflict over bull-baiting was almost as uncommon as it was in rural or provincial England; and, although the sport proved a source of conflict in a handful of industrial hamlets in Lancashire and Shropshire, these battles were both occasional and localised when contrasted with the long-running conflicts across the west Midlands. The extent of support for bull-baiting throughout Birmingham and Staffordshire far exceeded that witnessed elsewhere, making the cultural history of this district clearly distinct not only from provincial towns and rural areas, but also from that of other industrialising parts of the country.

The earliest challenge to traditional sports in the west Midlands was made in the regional capital, Birmingham. In 1780 the town commissioners began a campaign to eliminate popular games and celebrations from the administrative centre of the city, issuing orders against fireworks and bonfires at Guy Fawkes.[47] This resolution 'not appearing to have had the desired effect', it was decided that year that a handbill should also be prepared, and the following year another resolution to prevent bonfires and fireworks at Guy Fawkes was passed.[48] This was the first of several attempts to regulate

---

[47] Birmingham CA, Commissioners of the Birmingham Street Acts Minutes, 1776–1785 (not catalogued), 7 Oct. 1780.
[48] Ibid., 7 Nov. 1780, 6 Nov. 1781. See also Constables' Accounts, 1778–1842, 661859 ZZ334, years 1781–3, pp. 88, 116, 138.

unofficial recreations in the streets over the next two decades. In 1781 the authorities attempted to prevent a wake at Walmer Lane taking place;[49] and in 1788 a small payment was made to 'Tart for sending ye Bull away'.[50] Further expenses were incurred in 1797 'for assistance at ye bull-baiting'.[51] In the 1790s there were orders against cockfighting and throwing at cocks on Shrove Tuesday.[52]

This was a fairly wide-ranging attack on popular recreation, though the orders appear to have been an attempt to deal with the crowds and disorder consequent on the influx of high-spirited labourers, rather than an attempt to prevent recreation altogether. This is made evident in the only clear statement of the authorities' motivation that appears to have been made. In 1777 officials announced their intention to suppress bull-baiting:

> There having been great Disturbances in the Hamlets of Deritend, Erdington, Saltley, and other Places, in or near this town [Birmingham], occasioned by Bull-baiting, and other Methods made use of to collect disorderly People together, to the great Annoyance of the Publick Peace . . .[53]

This campaign was therefore very similar to those occurring in market towns that we explored in Chapter 4, and the authorities' actions would appear to belong to a broader eighteenth-century commitment to clearing games out of town centres. It reinforces the view that hostility towards the unsanctioned use of the streets by the populace was emerging across the country, and it also confirms that this hostility was focused on the location of sports, rather than the propriety of sports or games themselves.

At the very end of the eighteenth century, however, the region witnessed the emergence of new concerns about popular recreation, a change which became apparent when a group of local residents determined to suppress the bull-baiting at the Chapel wake in Birmingham. The Chapel wake was held annually in late August and lasted nearly a week. During this time, stalls and entertainments spread over streets and wasteland in the north-west of the city; and, like all good Birmingham wakes, it opened with a bull-bait. In 1798 it was planned that the baiting should take place in a field behind Snow Hill, in the north-west of the city, thereby removed from both the trading and living quarters of the north-west outskirts of the city. The decision of local residents to suppress a recreation located on waste

---

[49] Birmingham CA, Constables' Accounts, 1778–1842, 661859 zz334, 1781, p. 116.

[50] Ibid., 1788, p. 210.

[51] Ibid., 1797, p. 280.

[52] Ibid., 1795, p. 261. *Aris's Birmingham Gazette*, 28 Jan. 1799.

[53] Ibid., 10 July 1777.

ground consequently marks a departure from eighteenth-century concerns about the nuisance of sports and games in crowded urban streets.

To achieve their ends, the residents enlisted the support of the members of the Birmingham Loyal Association, a volunteer militia formed by local tradesmen. At the appointed hour they marched 'with colours flying and drums beating' to the bull-baiting, which had by now transferred to Birmingham Heath, where they captured the bull before the baiting took place, and triumphantly walked him back through the town.[54] In the event, these actions were ineffectual so far as preventing bull-baiting was concerned, which was eliminated neither from the district nor the wake. The 'highly-respected' inhabitant who provided this account conceded that the bull-baiting moved just beyond the jurisdiction of the militia into neighbouring Handsworth, and it appears to have maintained its links with the Chapel wake because the local paper reported a 'dreadful catastrophe' at a bull-baiting at the wake a decade later, in 1811.[55] But the militia's interference did indicate a new trend in the policing of popular sports. Although the residents only succeeded in moving the bull-baiting from one field to another, this clearly had not been their intention. Their attention was focused very clearly on one, in their view particularly objectionable, element of the wakes holiday. They opposed the bull-baiting not simply because it was a nuisance—the stalls in the streets would have been a far greater intrusion than the bull-baiting tucked away in a field—but because they found the recreation distasteful. The aim was to interfere in the way that people spent their free time: morality had been introduced into the policing of sports.

After this initial attempt to prevent bull-baiting at the wakes, popular entertainments were largely left alone for nearly two decades. As parliament debated John Dent's Bill to Prevent Bull-Baiting in April 1802, several petitions in favour were sent from Black Country towns, but there is no evidence in the local newspapers that the petitions were being matched with actions.[56] The *Staffordshire Advertiser* routinely noted the wakes in rural Staffordshire, but rarely objected to bull-baiting, which it rather indulgently

---

[54] Account based on memory of a local man published in *Birmingham Journal*, 10 March 1856. The event was not recorded in contemporary local papers.

[55] *Aris's Birmingham Gazette*, 2 Sept. 1811. An elderly inhabitant thought that this had been the final bull-baiting at Chapel wake. *Morning Chronicle*, 3 March 1851.

[56] *Journal of Commons,* lvii (1802). Petitions from Walsall and Wolverhampton (13 April); Wednesbury (14 April); Darlaston (15 April); Dudley 'and neighbours' (26 April); Tipton and Sedgeley (28 April).

considered to be one of those 'rustic sports' that local people enjoyed on
such occasions. The more censorious Birmingham newspapers roundly
condemned bull-baiting when accidents occurred, but otherwise generally
remained silent about all aspects of the wakes. Beyond these occasional outbursts of moral outrage, no action appears to have been taken until over a
decade later, when the magistrates of Wolverhampton announced their
determination to prevent bull-baiting at the town's wakes.

These wakes were held annually in November on waste land in
Tettenhall, a suburb to the north-west of the town. In 1815 the authorities
paid for adverts in the *Wolverhampton Chronicle* announcing that 'a STRICT
WATCH will be kept, and that the FULL PENALTY will be levied'
against any one involved in bull-baiting at the forthcoming Tettenhall
wake;[57] and prosecuted several workmen for organising bull-baiting in both
the town centre and at Tettenhall wakes in defiance of these orders.[58] The
same order was repeated the following year, and further convictions were
made.[59] And so it continued. The people of Wolverhampton organised bull-
baits over and over again in defiance of the authorities' wishes.[60] In 1835
the paper reported that the constables were still attempting to prevent bull-
baiting at the wake, and on this occasion one of the constables was 'much
abused and kicked' for his endeavours.[61] The final attempt to provide a
bull-baiting was made the following year.[62] The sport had remained a
continuous source of conflict in the town for over two decades.

During the 1820s authorities from every part of the west Midlands
began taking similar steps to prevent bull-baiting. So long as the bull-
baiting took place on public streets, the authorities usually had no difficulty
prosecuting those involved for nuisance. At Brewood, for example, during
a case of bull-baiting at quarter sessions in 1820, the prosecution claimed
that it had no quarrel with the principle of bull-baiting, and that the case
was 'confined to the nuisance of baiting in the *public street or highway*'.[63] In
fact, reformers certainly were concerned about the principle of bull-
baiting, but it was widely appreciated that the magistrates' power to suppress bull-baiting extended only to events organised on public streets. In

---

[57] *Wolverhampton Chronicle*, 4 Oct. 1815.
[58] Ibid., 29 Nov. 1815.
[59] Ibid., 9 Oct. 1816.
[60] Convictions and orders against bull-baiting at the wakes in, for example, ibid., 8 Nov.
1818, 13 Oct. 181; *Rockingham and Hull Weekly Advertiser*, 28 Nov. 1818; *Times*, 8 Oct. 1824.
[61] *Wolverhampton Chronicle*, 4 Nov. 1835.
[62] *Staffordshire Advertiser*, 24 Sept. 1836.
[63] Ibid., 22 April 1820.

such circumstances, prosecutions were generally unproblematic, but when bull-baitings took place on private land the situation was less clear. Possibly in order to protect the ancient sport, the 1822 Act to Prevent the Cruel and Improper Treatment of Cattle did not extend to bulls, but it is clear that the majority of magistrates in the west Midlands believed it did. The act received the royal assent in July 1822, and was used by JPs across Staffordshire against bull-baiting during the following wake season. The newspapers did not systematically report such cases, though it remains possible to sketch in outline the authorities' responses to the new legislation. The constables at Hanley announced their intention to use the new act to prevent bull-baiting during the wakes,[64] and there were convictions made for bull-baiting in the market place at Uttoxeter and Leek.[65] In 1823 there were further convictions at Eccleshall.[66] The newspapers reported that the convictions had been made under the recent act but, since most of the bull-baits had taken place on public streets, the offences were already indictable at common law.

Similarly in the Black Country, numerous attempts to prevent bull-baiting were made through the 1820s, many based on the belief that the 1822 act made the sport illegal. At West Bromwich, for example, the parish vestry instantly resolved to appoint a special constable to prevent bull-baiting at the wakes.[67] The Birmingham papers reported that bull-baiting had been discontinued at the Tipton and Bilston wakes in 1823, which was probably accomplished through the interference of the authorities, for it returned the following year; convictions were also made that year at West Bromwich.[68] Magistrates fined bull-baiters at the wakes at Tipton, Wednesbury, and Beech Lanes (Birmingham) and Ninevah in 1824.[69] The papers frequently noted that the convictions were made under the 1822 act. All the prosecutions were made summarily or at petty sessions; and, owing to the patchy way the papers covered such cases, it is probable that others were made but not reported.

The 1822 act authorised magistrates to impose fines of up to 5 pounds but, in almost all of these instances, the full penalty was not levied. Instead,

---

[64] Turner, *Reckoning*, pp. 39–40.
[65] *Staffordshire Advertiser*, 3 Aug. 1822, 28 Sept. 1822, 2 Nov. 1822.
[66] Ibid., 5 Oct. 1823.
[67] Sandwell Community History and AS, West Bromwich Vestry Minutes, 1820–1896, pp. 120–2.
[68] *Aris's Birmingham Gazette*, 17 Nov. 1823.
[69] Ibid., 9 Aug. 1824, 4 Oct. 1824, 1 Nov. 1824, 10 Jan. 1825.

magistrates preferred to impose small fines, in return for promises from the offenders not to repeat the offence. At Tipton, for example, when the first conviction in the parish was made, a labourer, John Edmunds, was fined 20 shillings, 'the object being the prevention rather than the punishment of the offence'; and two men who 'acknowledged the impropriety of their action, and promised never to be guilty of the same again' were not convicted at all.[70] In contrast, William Bates, a journeyman butcher from West Bromwich, was fined 5 pounds and spent a month in gaol in default of payment, when he was convicted for bull-baiting under the 1822 act for a second time.[71]

In 1827 it was realised that some of the recent convictions for bull-baiting might have been made illegally, following the conviction of six men by Richard Spooner of Birmingham for bull-baiting at West Bromwich on 7 November 1827. The six men refused to pay their 5 pound fines, arguing they had not broken the law, and were put in gaol on a warrant issued by Spooner. A writ of habeas corpus was applied for in the case of one of the offenders, John Hill, and a rule was granted. When the rule was argued the following month at the King's Bench it was made absolute, on the grounds that bulls had been intentionally omitted from the act.[72]

This ruling did not stop the tide of prosecutions for bull-baiting in public streets: there were further convictions at the Edgbaston and Handsworth wakes in Birmingham; the Greenhill, Great Haywood, and Burslem wakes in Staffordshire; and at Willenhall, Bilston, and Oldbury in the Black Country.[73] However, the protection it assured the sport when organised on private land ensured its continuation in many of the townships of the Black Country (including some of those where the authorities were actively suppressing the sport on the streets), as well as in a dwindling number of towns and villages in Staffordshire.[74] In Cheadle, for instance, bull-baiting continued at the wakes until 1830, when the owners of the bull, unable to find anyone willing to lend private land for the annual sport, baited the bull on the turnpike road—and were promptly prosecuted

[70] *Aris's Birmingham Gazette*, 9 Aug. 1824.

[71] Ibid., 17 Nov. 1823.

[72] *Short Authentic Account*, p. 4.

[73] *Aris's Birmingham Gazette*, 15 Sept. 1828, 3 Oct. 1828; *Staffordshire Advertiser*, 25 Oct. 1828, 9 Oct. 1830, 27 Sept. 1834; *Aris's Birmingham Gazette*, 17 Nov. 1828; *Birmingham Journal*, 12 Sept. 1829; William Salt Library, Broughton's Scrap Book, p. 241.

[74] It continued, for example, in Smethwick (*Times*, 15 Nov. 1828); West Bromwich (*Staffordshire Advertiser*, 1 March 1828); Wolverhampton (ibid., 18 Oct. 1828); Bilston (ibid., 21 Aug. 1830).

[75] *Staffordshire Mercury*, 11 Dec. 1830.

for it.[75] It returned the subsequent year, however, when the owner of a beershop was persuaded to lend the bull-baiters his yard.[76]

The difficulties faced by the authorities were described in a letter sent by an inhabitant from Rowley Regis to *Aris's Birmingham Gazette* in 1833, outlining the steps that had been taken by the parish officers to prevent bull-baiting at the wake that year. The writer explained that the officers had prepared a handbill which all the victuallers and beersellers of the town were requested to sign, agreeing not to 'countenance or encourage bull-baiting or bear-baiting, or any of those cruel wanton sports'. All but two of the town's victuallers signed, one of whom subsequently organised a bull-baiting in one of his own fields for several days: twenty-six dogs entered, 'brought by the lowest rabble from Birmingham, Walsall and Wednesbury'. A second victualler who had signed the paper also procured a bull, and 'caused it to be tied to a stake in his own premises for the amusement of the rabble tippling at his house'.[77] There was nothing the constables could do to prevent these occurrences, though the writer suggested that at the next brewster sessions licenses could be refused those publicans guilty of organising bull-baits.

The struggles over bull-baiting in the west Midlands, which had lasted for nearly two decades, were brought to a relatively swift conclusion in the years after 1835, with the passage of the Cruelty to Animals Act which extended the provisions of the 1822 act to bulls, and included clauses explicitly prohibiting the baiting of animals.[78] This legislation is best regarded as a national response to what had become an almost entirely local problem. Throughout the Black Country and the pockets of Staffordshire where bull-baiting continued, the authorities effectively used the new law to suppress the sport. In Cheadle, West Bromwich, and Sedgley it was put down in 1835;[79] and in Rowley Regis, Tean, and Walsall the final prosecutions for bull-baiting were made in 1836.[80] That year also saw the eventual elimination of the sport from the Wolverhampton wakes held at Tettenhall.[81] In Smethwick, the new legislation galvanised the parish vestry into action. It resolved that the constable for the town should inform the magistrates of any bull-baiting planned so that it might be prevented, and

---

[76] *Staffordshire Advertiser*, 9 Oct. 1835.

[77] *Aris's Birmingham Gazette*, 26 Sept. 1833.

[78] Malcolmson, *Popular Recreations*, p. 124.

[79] *Staffordshire Advertiser*, 3 Oct. 1835, 21 Nov. 1825.

[80] Ibid., 1 Oct. 1836, 15 Oct. 1836, 22 Oct. 1836.

[81] Ibid., 24 Sept. 1836.

that the constable for Harborne should be appointed 'Special Deputy Constable' for the occasion of Smethwick wake, to help him towards this end; these actions appear to have been effective.[82] The vestry at West Bromwich made similar resolutions, and the sport was suppressed there in 1835;[83] as did the vestry at Stone, where the sport was finally suppressed in 1837.[84] The final reference to bull-baiting in the local papers occurred in 1839, when *Aris's Birmingham Gazette* smugly noted that there had been no bull-baiting at the Brierley Hill wake that year.[85] Since the newspapers did not systematically report bull-baiting cases the fine detail of the disappearance of bull-baiting from west Midlands wakes is unknown; the broad trends, however, are clear. The new legislation rapidly accomplished what several decades of uncoordinated local efforts had been unable to achieve. By the early 1840s, bull-baiting had been entirely eliminated from the region.

The history of bull-baiting in Birmingham and the Black Country differs profoundly from the history of the sport in other regions. Whether in urban, industrial, or rural England, conflict over bull-baiting rarely materialised, since support for the sport from its traditional participants, the labouring poor, was ebbing away decades before civic leaders took steps to suppress it. It was in this respect that the Black Country differed from elsewhere. Here popular enthusiasm for the sport did not wane. Bull-baiting continued to occupy a central position in the annual wakes festivities, in spite of the opprobrium the sport was increasingly attracting by the early nineteenth century. Nor did periodic harassment of bull-baiting after 1800 hasten any decline in its popularity. Official interference served only to increase the sport's popularity with the local community; and, by the 1820s, conflict with the authorities had arguably become as integral a part of the wakes holidays as the sport itself. With no real parallel elsewhere in the land, the battles waged over bull-baiting in the west Midlands form a distinctive historical episode, and it is therefore worth pausing to consider this conflict in further detail.

[82] Birmingham CA, Harborne Parish Church Minute Book, 1829–1857, DRO61/3/(1), 29 Sept. 1835, p. 138.

[83] Sandwell Community History and AS, West Bromwich Vestry Minutes, 1820–1896, pp. 137–8; *Staffordshire Advertiser*, 21 Nov. 1825.

[84] Resolutions for Stone printed in full in *Staffordshire Advertiser*, 10 Oct. 1835. The final prosecutions were made in 1837; see ibid., 4 Nov. 1837.

[85] *Aris's Birmingham Gazette*, 30 Sept. 1839.

Interpretations

As the local authorities of Birmingham and the Black Country struggled to put an end to the bull-baits that punctuated the annual wakes season, they could hardly fail to be aware of the condemnation of the sport in newspapers and periodicals in all corners of the land. Although bull-baiting scarcely continued in most places, there was no shortage of criticism, and opposition was invariably framed in the language of morality. Writers and commentators claimed to be unable to comprehend the continued allegiance of the working classes to popular sports which involved combats between animals, and urged those more enlightened to take a decisive lead. They argued that the populace was simply too degraded to know better, and concluded that they were under a moral imperative to lead the way—though, as one writer assured his readers, it was noble and useful employment 'cleansing the vulgar mind from those barbarous prejudices'.[86]

This account of the ongoing popularity of bull-baiting amongst the lower orders in the first half of the nineteenth century was repeated endlessly throughout the second half of the century by all those with any interest in the manners of the poor. And, where reformers had predicted the abolition of bull-baiting would encourage an improvement in popular manners and morals, the next generation agreed that this had indeed occurred. The many local historians whose researches have been used in this study were united in dismissing bull-baiting as a 'barbarous custom',[87] a 'brutal amusement'.[88] All agreed that the disappearance of bull-baiting, dog-fighting, cockfighting, and to a lesser degree prize-fighting, provided a satisfactory testimony to the great improvement in the manners of the working population that had occurred over the nineteenth century. Thus concluded one: 'In the gradual decline of cockfighting, bear-baiting, bull-baiting, and badger-baiting may be traced the slow but sure progress of civilisation and refinement.'[89] The sporting recollections of two gentlemen from Birmingham were thought to interest readers of the *Morning Chronicle* who 'delight to trace the progress of civilisation in the refinement of manners'.[90]

---

[86] Lawrence, *Treatise on Horses*, i, p. 143. See also ibid., i, pp. 120–43. More detail on national debates may be found in Chapter 5 above.
[87] For example, [Easther], *Glossary of Almondbury*, p. xv.
[88] For example, Bedell, *Account of Hornsea*, ii, p. 88.
[89] Hatfield, *Notices of Doncaster*, i, p. 72.
[90] *Morning Chronicle*, 3 March 1851.

Furthermore, similar connections between bull-baiting and savagery continue to haunt more recent historiography addressing the enduring popularity of blood sports in industrial districts. Sympathetic late-twentieth-century commentators, whilst dropping the confident narrative of progress, have nonetheless hardly moved beyond this interpretation of the place of blood sports in working-class culture in early industrial England. People with such harsh living conditions could not be expected to share our sensitivities: 'the common people lived rough lives, and enjoyed rough, unrefined pleasures,' it is argued.[91] This formula makes it possible for us to understand the culture of violence that persisted for decades in the west Midlands, without condemning the people we are studying. But blood sports remain, as ever, no more than an indicator of brutality.

There is no doubt some validity in this common-sense view of how people could tolerate what disgusts us today; yet stressing the brutality and degradation common to both the sport and the people arguably obscures as much as it reveals. In particular, this approach has not encouraged a serious analysis of the suppression of the sport: given its association with the basest elements of human nature, the elimination of bull-baiting is seen quite simply as an inevitability. Consequently, historians who have been struck by the violent excesses of wakes in certain industrial districts have nevertheless had very little to say about why bull-baiting was suppressed, beyond gesturing vaguely to a rise in humanitarian sentiment emanating from the higher social orders.[92] Nor has the enduring popularity of the sport in the Black Country been questioned. If bull-baiting was nothing more than an occasion to indulge in brutalities, then it goes without saying that brutalised miners and metal-workers would be its chief votaries.

We need to recognise that this is exactly the story that reformers themselves liked to tell. This narrative has been derived from individuals who, if not campaigning for a specific programme of reform, were at least in sympathy with it; and consolidated through the endless repetitions of a second generation who approved of their actions. Understanding popular behaviour through stereotypes formulated by elites with a political agenda seems to be a sterile approach. It is time to explore the different meanings that might have lain behind the actions critics were quick to label atavistic. We should be aware that there can be as much rebellion and dissent in a bull-baiting as there is cruelty and degradation. We need to abandon the tired

[91] Reid, 'Beasts and brutes', p. 14. See also Raven, *Urban Songs*, p. 131; Ede, *History of Wednesbury*, p. 156.
[92] Hutton, *Stations of the Sun*, pp. 357–8; Poole, 'Wakes, holidays', pp. 128–9 (diss.).

cliché of a degraded, brutalised populace, and think more carefully about the politics of recreation.

Just as the extensive discussion about bull-baiting that emerged in the late eighteenth century identified the backwardness and ignorance of those who enjoyed the sport as the main target for reform, so in the west Midlands, where bull-baiting was a practical, not simply ideological problem, the same language of morality was employed. Local residents voiced a familiar complex of concerns about the sport's demoralising tendencies and of the pernicious consequences of permitting the practice to continue unchecked. For example, when inhabitants from Wednesbury petitioned parliament for the suppression of bull-baiting, they argued that 'a continuance of that savage sport must demoralise all who partake in it'; and a letter on the same subject sent to *Aris's Birmingham Gazette* pontificated on the continuance of these 'debasing and demoralizing' exhibitions in Staffordshire.[93]

In practice, however, local leaders in this region were troubled not simply by the demoralising effects of bull-baiting upon the local population. Civic elites in the west Midlands were also faced with the problem of insubordination. As conflict over bull-baiting intensified in the early nineteenth century, so their power and authority appeared increasingly insecure, adding a new dimension to the campaign. Sir Oswald Mosley, a Staffordshire magistrate, recalled with disgust that during the annual Tutbury bull-running 'all authority was set at defiance', and this loss of authority was at least as distressing to local leaders as any animal suffering that might have occurred.[94] The exasperation of local elites is apparent in the letter of one resident from:

> [one of] those places where the worst disposed people can, as respects bull-baiting, have everything their own way; and where, as in the dense populations of our manufactories in this neighbourhood, they can always collect a numerous mob in support of them. But, in the meantime, is the better, and it is to be hoped, the larger portion of the inhabitants of West Bromwich, Dudley, Wednesbury, Darlaston &c, to have their feelings outraged, and be doomed from year to year to witness such brutalities as I dare not repeat, because a few debased individuals choose publicly to perpetrate or encourage cruelties?[95]

---

[93] *Journal of Commons*, xxcii (1826), p. 407; *Aris's Birmingham Gazette*, 24 March 1828.
[94] Moseley, *History of Tutbury*, p. 89.
[95] *Times*, 31 Oct. 1828.

The critique of bull-baiting might have originated in discussions about popular manners but, as attempts to suppress the sport in the west Midlands gathered pace, the refusal of the populace to obey their orders raised the stakes considerably. The continuation of bull-baiting was interpreted by local leaders as a challenge to their authority, and they responded by redoubling their attempts to eliminate the sport.

There is of course little written testimony by working people to indicate what the defence of bull-baiting meant to them. There are no clear statements from those involved about their struggles to preserve bull-baiting at wakes. Yet the records do contain accounts of their actions, and in the absence of written evidence we may endeavour to return a voice to the defenders of bull-baiting by reading these. Certainly, their actions imply that more than a love of blood sports was involved, that this was more than an uncontrolled eruption of brutality stemming from an inability to recognise their cruelty. We have observed numerous bull-baitings organised in defiance of the authorities' orders, and the patchy reporting of such events implies that many more occurred; and this act of organising prohibited events over and over again suggests a political context for the battles waged over bull-baiting. These events consistently held in opposition of the authorities' orders suggest a working population at odds with its leaders, and not fearful of confrontation with them. Though the enthusiasm of the labouring population for the sport may indicate a certain lack of sensibility and refinement, their actions also reveal their commitment to their cultural traditions. And the vigour with which they defended their customs undermined the authorities' endeavours to suppress them for nearly three decades, a not insignificant period of time in the lives of the local population.

Occasional accounts of the fierce resistance that constables might encounter on arrival at bull-baitings underscore the tenacity with which the local community held on to this custom. The organiser of a bull-baiting at the wakes in Leek had no time for the constables who came to prevent the bull-baiting; he persisted 'in defiance of all authority';[96] in a Shropshire mining town, Madeley, the population 'offered the most determined resistance', when a Methodist clergyman attempted to 'put a check' upon their customary amusements.[97] This behaviour was motivated by more than sheer love of the sport: the right to self-expression was at stake here. The political overtones of interference in popular recreation were understood in the following way by William Dyott, a Staffordshire gentleman visiting the

[96] *Times*, 2 Nov. 1822.
[97] Randall, *History of Madeley*, p. 128.

Ashbourne wakes in 1824. He believed that 'if interfering resistance had not
. . . given particular importance to the Bull beat, it would have met the fate
of all the diversions of its date and would have sunk to rise no more'.[98]
Dyott considered that it was the act of interference that caused the vigorous defence of bull-baiting, rather than any deeper attachment to the custom, and his contention was no doubt correct. Official interference in this
popular pastime unfailingly served to unify the local population, no matter
what conflicts divided them at other times. As was noted by a researcher in
Shropshire, 'colliers and bargemen, who, though they fought each other
every market day, were ready to make common cause against the disturbers
of their cruel sport'.[99]

Resistance to local law-keepers sometimes involved physical violence.
At Eccleshall, for example, the vicar, having freed the bull, found himself
'surrounded by a crowd of roughs, who tore his gown off his back, and otherwise maltreated him, until he was rescued by more sensible parishioners';[100]
and at Rowley Regis it was claimed for the parish curate, George Barrs,
that he had had his teeth knocked out attempting to prevent a bull-
baiting.[101] Acts of physical violence were swiftly condemned, and used by
critics as further evidence of the need to reform a brutalised populace. Yet
violence is also the tactic of the powerless: the defenders of bull-baiting had
little other recourse to protect their cultural traditions. By equating the violence encountered with ignorance and barbarity, reformers adroitly glossed
over the motivation that underpinned these actions and the political context
in which they occurred.

A number of less aggressive ways to undermine the authorities' actions
were also found. Following a set of successful prosecutions for bull-baiting
at Handsworth, the *Birmingham Journal* lamented that the neighbourhood
was nonetheless determined to protect the practice of bull-baiting, raising

---

[98] Staffordshire CRO, Dyott's Diary, 1814–1830, D661/11/2/3/1/11, 26 Aug. 1824.

[99] Burne, *Shropshire Folklore*, ii, p. 448.

[100] Yonge, *Bye-paths of Staffordshire*, p. 105.

[101] *BWP* Notes and Queries, no. 2076. There has no doubt been some exaggeration in the
heroic role played by the local clergy. This account of Barrs' role in suppressing bull-baiting
in Rowley Regis is not supported by his diaries. Barrs' personal journal contains a reference
to bull-baiting in the neighbourhood one wakes Monday. He apparently felt 'very much
grieved, and in some degree angry' when he saw his neighbours engaged in bull-baiting.
However, though 'they made [his] heart bleed, and drew tears from [his] eyes', the journal
gives no hint that he stepped outside and attempted direct interference. He remained safely
indoors, where 'God kept my mind, and suffered not their noise to disturb my thoughts'.
See Barrs, *Private Journals*, pp. 82–3.

a considerable subscription for the purpose of paying the fines imposed.[102] The solidarity amongst bull-baiters that was created by an attack on the sport was neatly summarised by an inhabitant of Blythemarsh, a village in northern Staffordshire. After a bull-baiting which continued, the reader is asked to believe, unabated for three days, one resident eventually went to the magistrate at Lane End with the names of nine of the participants. The magistrate dismissed the case. Once freed, the nine men returned home 'collected their abettors, got drunk, hoisted their colours, pressed a rustic piper into their services, rolled, and roared, and shouted, and piped up and down the village in true style. But their rage fell chiefly upon their worthy neighbours.'[103] The writer concluded that this must be stopped—though whether he was referring to the bull-baiting or to the rabble's insubordination was not made clear.

It is evident that a number of meanings adhered to the annual bull-bait in the west Midlands in the early nineteenth century. In this district, the sport was perceived as an integral part of a traditional festivity, all aspects of which had long been organised and determined by working people themselves, and official attempts to interfere with this culture during the first half of the nineteenth century were deeply resented. The numerous acts of defiance indicate not simply degradation, brutality, and backwardness; they also reveal a community with a clear sense of its own autonomy. The working community in this industrial region had established its own sporting and festive traditions, independent of elite guidance and control, and was prepared to go to considerable lengths in defence of these local customs.

Above all, this episode dovetails with the picture of a regionally specific popular culture in the west Midlands described Chapter 6. The spirited defence of bull-baiting that we have seen here is clearly of a piece with the west Midlands' popular culture detailed above. We noted there not only that blood sports were deeply rooted in the region, but also that sports there tended to be individualistic in nature. The decades of defiance surrounding the wakes holidays' bull-baitings amply confirm this, reinforcing the picture of an insubordinate workforce, with a suitably rebellious popular culture.

Moreover, these peculiarities in the west Midlands help us in some way to understand the quiet and uncontroversial way in which bull-baiting disappeared from most other parts of the land. As we saw in the first part of this chapter, bull-baiting rarely emerged as a source of conflict outside the west Midlands, but it should not be concluded from this that the labouring

---

[102] *Birmingham Journal*, 11 Oct. 1828.
[103] *Staffordshire Advertiser*, 6 Dec. 1828.

poor were more passive or quiescent elsewhere. The well documented battles over Guy Fawkes celebrations that ran in many towns throughout the nineteenth century should warn against this. Those conflicts suggest that the inhabitants of small provincial towns could be equally difficult to govern as those in industrial districts, and that an annual day of misrule was a characteristic common to many towns. The point rather is that there was considerable variety between urban communities concerning the dates and activities that local inhabitants prized the most. Guy Fawkes night and bull-baiting were both part of a shared popular culture, but different settlements and communities accorded each a separate worth; and, in most places, bull-baiting was simply not a pastime over which the labouring poor were prepared to wage battle.

We can see now exactly how far the extensive discussion about blood sports that raged in the press and periodicals in the early nineteenth century was divorced from reality. Since the late eighteenth century, discussions of bull-baiting have invariably positioned it as a pastime to which the poor and uneducated were peculiarly attached, but inhabitants of all areas shared a complex cultural heritage, subject to many regional and topographical peculiarities, and bull-baiting was just one part of the mosaic that made up each region's popular culture. There is no need to search for great cultural shifts to explain changes in the composition of different regions' popular culture, and there should be no prior expectation that the working classes would hold tenaciously to every pastime they had ever known. Popular culture was constantly changing over time, and this is all we need to appreciate in order to explain the disappearance of bull-baiting from provincial towns.

Finally, it is important to stress once again the exceptional nature of these battles over blood sports. By conflating a unique episode confined to the west Midlands with the nation at large, a number of generalisations about the poor, both unflattering and inaccurate, have been created and sustained. At the same time, the true extent of regional peculiarities has been obscured. As this book has repeatedly demonstrated, there was no single popular culture in existence during the period, and overarching generalisations about plebeian culture are therefore not helpful. Throughout the country and across different types of settlement, a recognisable set of shared practices was enjoyed, but the precise form of these practices and their local significance varied endlessly, and an appreciation of the role of the region and locality is fundamental to understanding this diversity.

10

Conclusion

How may the different threads of this book be tied together? The first generation of research into the history of popular culture offered us grand narratives, but no general conclusion concerning the history of popular sports and recreations during the long eighteenth century emerges from this book. There is no overarching point that deserves especial emphasis; and no new turning point or historical moment, around which divergent trends, contradictions, and differences may all be resolved, has been identified. Instead, this book celebrates the diversity of popular culture and plebeian experience. The three case studies describe a complex picture of both decline and expansion, with different recreations (blood sports, athletic sports, political celebrations, and wakes and fairs) and different locations (urban, industrial, rural) all experiencing change in unique ways. It is clear that sports did not respond to political and economic changes in a predictable and straightforward fashion, and it is therefore necessary to reconceive the historical development of popular sports and pastimes during the period of modernisation.

In place of a grand narrative, this book offers a number of conclusions worthy of emphasis. As was noted at the outset of this study, there exists a long tradition of historical research into popular sports and recreations. Antiquarian interest in plebeian pastimes may be dated from the end of the eighteenth century, and it should by now be clear that this early work has cast a long shadow over our understanding of popular sports and recreations during the period. Nineteenth-century research not only provided formulas for explaining the decline and emergence of certain sports and pastimes that have continued to be repeated until the present, but has also influenced the questions that subsequent generations have sought to answer. Yet it is doubtful that early antiquarians produced a reliable account either of the recreations of their social inferiors, or of the ways in which these patterns of recreation changed over time. They did not, for example, describe the dismantling of medieval customs of street entertainment in the century following the Restoration, or the elimination of plebeian street recreations towards the end of the eighteenth century. Their account of the decline of blood sports, counterpoising as it did a humane and enlightened middle class with the unreconstructed plebeian masses, was not only laden with class stereotypes that served to justify existing social inequalities, it was also frankly inaccurate. And, in contrast to the fanfare surrounding the reformers' rather insignificant contribution to the decline of bull-baiting, nineteenth-century scholars kept very quiet about the destruction of ancient village greens, a process the responsibility for which unquestionably lay with educated social elites. It has been in records that were not produced for public consumption that the evidence for these social and cultural changes was found, and this suggests that any attempt to reconstruct patterns of popular recreation solely from descriptive accounts produced by social elites is likely to be incomplete. Each of the case studies here points to the existence of a significant discontinuity between popular culture and middle-class perceptions of that culture, and demonstrates the necessity of developing ways of traversing this breach if popular habits and mores are to be properly understood. I hope to have demonstrated that by delving behind the polished account left by social elites, a far richer and truer account of the past may be uncovered.

More critically, the value of the theoretical basis of this work should now appear clear. The three case studies, exploring patterns of recreation from the perspective of the spaces in which they were played, deepen our understanding of eighteenth-century society on many levels. The chapters on provincial towns (Chapters 3 and 4) have made inroads into an entirely unexplored facet of historical experience—the market square as a cultural and recreational space. They demonstrate that streets and squares in early modern England served a cultural function that went beyond the traffic and trading with which they are now so closely associated, and provide a rudimentary chronology of change. The survey of town accounts indicates that civic authorities routinely funded sports and entertainments in town streets for much of the century following the Restoration; that by the middle of the eighteenth century such financial support for recreation had ebbed; and that by the early nineteenth century most authorities had taken some measures to prevent the continuation of street recreations. This suggests a very gradual redefinition of the legitimate uses of this central urban space involving the progressive closing down of its recreational functions. The chronology proposed here might well be questioned. Does the Restoration really represent the beginning of this process? Have the uses of town centres ever ceased changing in the nineteenth or twentieth centuries? It is possible that each generation reconsiders and redefines the appropriate uses of the civic space, and, although the start and end dates employed here suggest a process of terminal decline over a discrete period, it is arguably more accurate to envisage a process of ongoing change. Yet for all that this research into the history of recreation in market towns raises almost as many questions as it answers, it has nevertheless succeeded in bringing back into focus a feature of urban life that had entirely receded from the historical record.

The two chapters on industrial England (Chapters 6 and 7) address a problem that has attracted greater historiographical attention: the impact of the industrial revolution on popular culture. Counter to expectations, this research reveals that industrial areas provided a propitious environment for popular sports, enabling traditional recreations to flourish and expand, and encouraging the development of new traditions. Yet this work also reveals that significant cultural and sporting differences existed between different industrial areas, demonstrating in particular that blood sports were more deeply rooted in the popular culture of the Black Country than that of the West Riding, and confirming once again that sports and traditions differed between geographical communities as well as between social groups. Sports and recreations have long been viewed through the prism of class, and a generation of historians has sought to understand cultural peculiarities with reference to a hierarchal scheme of social difference. But, as we have seen here, it is also possible to conceptualise social difference geographically. This study of popular recreation in early industrial England indicates that local economic characteristics were key factors determining the nature of popular culture, and has demonstrated the necessity of introducing the concept of locality into our analyses of social change.

The third case study, addressing popular sports in rural England, is, like the first, largely unrelated to existing historiographical concerns. Just as the market square has not previously been identified as a topic for historical investigation, so the subject of this case study — the cultural use of the village green — has never formed the focus of sustained scholarly attention. Chapter 8 illustrates the range of recreational uses to which these ancient spaces were customarily put, and demonstrates a steady reduction in the size and number of village greens in the county of Cambridgeshire consequent upon the wave of enclosures that crossed the county in the final decade of the eighteenth century and the first half of the nineteenth. It attempts to determine how far these changes altered traditional patterns of recreation, and concludes that paternalism helped to ensure the continuation of most traditional sports despite the disappearance of the communal land on which they had long been played. This research is suggestive rather than definitive — in particular it is necessary to question how far the destruction of village greens that occurred in Cambridgeshire was mirrored in other parts of the country. But, once again, its aim is to open new avenues of enquiry rather than to settle existing historical debates; and, if it succeeds in establishing the village green as a subject worthy of further analysis, its purpose will have been accomplished.

This book might be criticised for containing many omissions. There is nothing, for instance, about horse-racing, one of the most popular and rapidly expanding eighteenth-century sports; and a whole family of fighting sports—pugilism, boxing, cudgels, wrestling—has likewise been largely ignored. There is much here for the critic who seeks a history of popular sports. Yet these omissions are less problematic than might be imagined, for this is not, and has never claimed to be, an historical encyclopaedia of popular sports. Nor does this work stake its worth on a general conclusion about the history of popular sport during the period of modernisation. Should any such verdict be attempted, the neglect of many sports might well be considered suspect, their exclusion serving to ensure that grand conclusions hold out. Rather, this study has set out to explore the relationship between sports and space. It has looked at the ways in which different types of community made space available for popular recreations, at changes in their agreements concerning the use of land, and at the causes and consequences of these changes. The need to provide a comprehensive account of all popular sports is less compelling in a project of this kind.

Each study has picked up themes that could be explored in far greater depth. Each has uncovered historical trends concerning, for example, reform movements, working patterns, the efficiency of local government and policing, and the enclosure movement, that deserve fuller treatment than they have received here. There inevitably remain many unanswered questions about the local peculiarities described here, but by retaining a narrow focus on the interplay of sports and space it has been possible to identify contrasts between the three plebeian cultures, and to throw into relief a set of characteristics unique to each.

It was in market towns that interference in popular culture was most persistent and most effective. Moreover, historic county and market towns were the home not only of reform movements, but also of the policing that realised reformers' visions. In consequence, although the urban workforce was by no means quiescent, it was possible for social elites to shape their sporting traditions in ways that were both significant and enduring. In industrialising areas there is less evidence of the reforming spirit, and the mechanisms of control were certainly far weaker than in established urban communities. At the same time, industrialisation created a workforce that was comparatively independent, combative, and aggressive, and these factors came together and served to forge a popular culture that was innovative, expanding, and changing. Finally, in rural areas hostility towards popular sports from local elites was rarely encountered, and enduring paternalism ensured that popular recreations did not emerge as a source of conflict. The rural environment was the home of strong cultural continuities—continuities which are even more striking when the profound economic and agrarian changes that rural communities were undergoing are taken into consideration.

In all three studies, popular culture emerges as the outcome of negotiations between different sections of society, negotiations which were sometimes acrimonious, sometimes harmonious, always complex. There can be no returning to the idea that popular culture was the property of the poor, for their culture was neither so socially restricted nor so autonomous. Although the participants of the sports this book considers were overwhelmingly plebeian, this section of society did not have the power to determine all elements of the form, location, and timing of their recreations. Eighteenth-century England was a profoundly uneven society, and the ways in which this shaped the culture of the poor should not be forgotten.

Bibliography

Primary literature

Manuscript records

Bath and North East Somerset Record Office

Bath Chamberlains' Accounts, 1657–1724, 650/1/2.

Berkshire Record Office, Reading

Borough records
Abingdon Chamberlains' Accounts, 1702–1787, A/FAc/5–10.
Hungerford Constables' Accounts, 1658–1789, H/Fac/1–2.
Maidenhead Bridgewarden Accounts, 1662–1738, M/FBa/2.
Newbury Borough Sessions Minute Book, 1739–1785, N/JQ/1/2.
  Court Leet Book, 1640–1723, N/AM1/1.
Reading Chamberlains' Accounts, 1690–1771, R/FA3/52–94.
Windsor Chamberlains' Accounts, 1637–1806, W/FA1/2–3.
  Sessions Book, 1750–1787, W1/JQ1/3.

Parish records
Wokingham Overseers' Accounts, 1766–1773, D/P154/12/3.
  Minutes of Common Council, 1749–1833, Wo/AC1/1/2.
  Parish Register, 1761–1812, D/P154/1/2.

Quarter Sessions records
Quarter Sessions Files, January 1836, SR244.

Birmingham City Archives

Borough records
Birmingham Constables' Accounts, 1748–1749, 37784 ZZ63B.
  Constables' Accounts, 1778–1842, 661859 ZZ334.
  Commissioners of the Birmingham Street Acts Minutes, 1776–1800, 2 vols (uncatalogued).

Parish records
Harborne Parish Church Minute Book, 1829–1857, DRO61/3/1(1).

Birmingham Reference Library

'Birmingham Notes and Queries', vols A–G, 144951–144957 (bound volumes of
　　cuttings of Notes and Queries columns from *Birmingham Weekly Post*).
'Newspaper cuttings', 302127.
'Newspaper cuttings', 302129.
'Newspaper cuttings', 302135.
[Jaffray], 'Hints for a history of Birmingham', 174534.

Buckinghamshire Record Office

Quarter Sessions Case Book, Easter 1821–Epiphany 1824, QS/JC/6.

Cambridge University Library

Littleport Tithe Apportionment, 1839, EDR T.

Cambridgeshire County Record Office, Cambridge

Borough records
Cambridge Common Day Books, 1770–1792, Shelf c.12–13.
　　Minute Book of Town Sessions, 1769–1771, Box 2.6.

Enclosure records
Abington, Great, Enclosure Award, 7 July 1804, QRDz5.
　　Map P1/26/1–2.
Abington, Little, Enclosure Award, 28 April 1807, QRDz5.
　　Map P2/26/2.
Ashley Enclosure Award, 26 March 1814, R62/16.
　　Map R60/24/2/74.
Balsham Enclosure Award, 19 Sept. 1806, QRDz8.
　　Map R60/24/2/2.
Barrington Enclosure Award, 20 Oct. 1800, QRDz2.
　　Map P8/26/1
Bassingbourn Enclosure Award, 12 Aug. 1806, QRDz3.
　　Map QRDc11.
Bottisham Enclosure Award, 3 Oct. 1808, QRDz5.
　　Map QRDc12.
Bourne Enclosure Award, 16 June 1820, QRDz9.
　　Map QRDc35.
Brinkley Enclosure Award, 24 Jan. 1816, QRDz6.
　　Map R60/24/2/9.
Burwell Enclosure Award, 27 June 1817, QRDz9.
　　Map QRDc29.

Carlton-cum-Willingham Enclosure Award, 6 May 1800, QRDz1.
  Map R60/24/2/12.
Caxton Enclosure Award, 12 May 1835, QRDz10.
  Map QRDc49.
Cherry Hinton Enclosure Award, 18 Dec. 1810, QRDz6.
  Map QRDc13.
Comberton Enclosure Award, 18 Dec. 1840, QRDc57.
  Map QRDc57.
Conington Enclosure Award, 17 Feb. 1804, QRDz2.
  Map R60/24/2/16a.
Croxton Enclosure Award, 23 Sept. 1818, QRDz5.
  Map QRDc32.
Ditton Wood Enclosure Award, 20 May 1823, QRDz10.
  Map P55/26/2.
Doddington and Manea Enclosure Award, 6 March 1834, 'March'.
  Map 'March'.
Dry Drayton Enclosure Award, 30 July 1811, QRDz4.
  Map QRDc15.
Dullingham Enclosure Award, 7 April 1810, QRDz6.
  Map QRDc14
Duxford Enclosure Award, 12 July 1830, QRDz10.
  Map QRDc4.
Elsworth Enclosure Award, 11 April 1803, QRDz5.
  Map R60/24/2/22.
Fen Ditton Enclosure Award, 20 Oct. 1807, QRDz5.
  Map R60/L4/2/24.
Fordham Enclosure Award, 9 Aug. 1820, QRDz9.
  Map QRDc33.
Fowlmere Enclosure Award, 19 April 1850, QRDc70.
  Map QRDc70.
Foxton Enclosure Award, 10 June 1830, QRDz10.
  Map QRDc45.
Fulbourn Enclosure Award, 20 Aug. 1814, QRDz7.
  Map ARDc21.
Girton Enclosure Award, 5 March 1814, QRDz7.
  Map QRDc17.
Grantchester and Coton Enclosure Award, 12 Feb. 1803, QRDz4.
  Map P79/26/2.
Graveley Enclosure Award, 7 Aug. 1805, QDz5.
  Map QRDc7.
Great and Little Eversden Enclosure Award, 14 May 1814, QRDz7.
  Map QRDc19.
Haddenham Enclosure Award, 4 Aug. 1847, 'March'.
  Map 'March'.

Hardwick Enclosure Award, 30 March 1837, QRDc15.
    Map QRDc51.
Harlton Enclosure Award, 4 Aug. 1810, P84/26.
    Pre-enclosure map 124/P52.
    Map P84/26.
Harston Enclosure Award, 25 Jan. 1802, QRDc3.
    Map QRDc3.
Haslingfield Enclosure Award, 23 June 1820, QRDz9.
    Map QRDc36.
Hinxton Enclosure Award, 15 Oct. 1833, QRDz10.
    Map QRDc47.
Histon Enclosure Award, 31 May 1806, QRDz6.
    Map QRDc8.
Horningsea Enclosure Award, 27 April 1810, QRDz6.
    Map P94/26/2.
Ickleton Enclosure Award, 2 Aug. 1814, QRDz7.
    Map QRDc20.
Kennet Enclosure Award, 14 July 1830, QRDz10.
    Map QRDc43.
Kingston Enclosure Award, 21 Dec. 1815, QRDz8.
    Map QRDc25.
Kirtling Enclosure Award, 26 March 1814, P101/26/1.
    Map P101/26/1.
Knapwell Enclosure Award, 18 Many 1776, QRDz10.
    Map QRDc1.
Landbeach Enclosure Award, 15 Dec. 1813, QRDz7.
    Map QRDc18.
Litlington Enclosure Award, 21 Jan 1830, QRDz10.
    Map QRDc46.
Little Gransden Enclosure Award, 6 April 1826, QRDz10.
    Map QRDc41.
Long Stanton, All Saints, Enclosure Award, 10 April 1816, QRDz8.
    Map QRDc27.
Longstowe Enclosure Award, 22 July 1800, QRDz/1.
    Map 71/P7.
Manea Enclosure Award, 15 Dec. 1810, 'March'.
    Map 'March'.
Meldreth Enclosure Award, 25 Jan. 1820, QRDz9.
    Map QRDc34.
Milton Enclosure Award, 1 Aug. 1802, QRDz5.
    Map QRDc4.
Morden, Guilden, Enclosure Award, 1 May 1804, QRDz4.
    Map P121.
Morden, Steeple, Enclosure Award, 31 Jan. 1816, QRDz8..
    Map QRDc28.

Oakington Enclosure Award, 6 Nov. 1834, QRDc48.
  Map QRDc48.
Orwell Enclosure Award, 1 Nov. 1837, QRDc52.
  Map QRDc52
Pampisford Enclosure Award, 31 Dec. 1801, QRDz6.
  Map QRDc2.
Papworth Everard Enclosure Award, 31 Aug. 1826, QRDz10.
  Map QRDc42.
Sawston Enclosure Award, 25 June 1811, QRDz3.
  Map P136/26/1B.
Shelford, Great, Enclosure Award, 7 Dec. 1825, QRDc50.
  Map QRDc50.
Shelford, Little, Enclosure Award, 23 Nov. 1815, QRDz7.
  Map QRDc24.
Shepreth Enclosure Award, 21 April 1823, QRDz10.
  Map QRDc40.
Snailwell Enclosure Award, 12 July 1806, QRDz4.
  Map R55/7/48/4
Stapleford Enclosure Award, 3 Feb. 1814, QRDz7.
  Map R60/24/2/64
Stetchworth Enclosure Award, 30 Nov. 1820, QRDz9.
  Map QRDc37
Strethem Enclosure Award, 6 Sept. 1837, 'March'.
  Map 'March'.
Sutton Enclosure Award, 4 June 1840, 'March'.
  Map 'March'.
Swaffham Bulbeck Enclosure Award, 1 Aug. 1801, QRDz6.
  Map L87/3.
Swaffham Prior Enclosure Award, 1 Dec. 1814, QRDz7.
  Map R60/24/2/67.
Swavesey Enclosure Award, 18 Dec. 1840, QRDc56.
  Map QRDc56.
Teversham Enclosure Award, 20 Dec. 1815, QRDz8.
  Map QRDc22.
Toft Enclosure Award, 25 April 1815, QRDz8.
  Map QRDc23.
Trumpington Enclosure Award, 15 May 1809, QRDz6.
  Map.
Waterbeach Enclosure Award, 28 Sept. 1818, QRDz8.
  Map QRDc31
Wentworth Enclosure Award, 20 May 1830, 'March'.
  Map 'March'.
West Wickham Enclosure Award, 16 May 1822, QRDz9.
  Map QRDc39.

West Wratting Enclosure Award, 27 Oct. 1813, QRDz8.
    Map P184/26/2.
Weston Colville Enclosure Award, 11 Aug. 1778, QRDz1.
    Map lost.
Whittlesford Enclosure Award, 17 Aug. 1815, QRDz9.
    Map P171/26/2.
Wilbraham, Great, Enclosure Award, 2 Feb. 1801, QRDz3.
    Map QRDc9.
Wilbraham, Little, Enclosure Award, 2 Feb. 1801, QRDz4.
    Map P175/26/16.
Wimblington Enclosure Award, 3 Aug. 1805, 'March'.
    Map 'March'.
Witchford Enclosure Award, 1 March 1813, 'March'.
    Map 'March'.

Personal papers
Maynard Manuscripts, R58, v, vii, x.

Cambridgeshire Local Studies Library, Cambridge

Dorothy Porter, 'These are my times', Cambridgeshire Collection.
F. J. Garrett, 'Village memories', i, Cambridgeshire Collection.

Centre for Kentish Studies, Maidstone

Faversham Accounts Rolls, 1661–1707, Fa/Ac/80–111.
    Wardmote Book, 1741–1820, Fa/ACS.
    Draft Orders, Fa/AZ/79.
Gravesend Chamberlains' Accounts, 1653–1784, Gr/FAc/2–4.
Dover Chamberlains' Accounts, 1660–1829, Do/FCa/6–8.
Maidstone Chamberlains' Accounts, 1693–1750, Md/FCa/1693–1750.
    Chamberlain's Vouchers, 1711–1720, Md/FCv2/4.
Queenborough Chamberlains' Account, 1611–1785, Qb/FAg/1–3.
Sandwich Treasurers' Accounts, 1664–1779, Sa/FAt/40–1.
    Notices and Orders, Sa/Z6.

Coventry City Archives

Wardens' and Chamberlains' Accounts, 1637–1709, BA/A/A/26/3.

Doncaster Archives Department

Doncaster Chamberlains' Accounts, 1661–1717, AB/6/1/2/22–47.

Downing College, Cambridge

Borough records
Cambridge Treasurers' Accounts, 1661–1787, Bowtell Bequest/E3–6.

Family papers
John Bowtell, Unpublished History of Cambridge, Bowtell Bequest/63, vii.

East Riding of Yorkshire Archive Office, Beverley

Beverley Account Rolls, 1660–1728, BC/II/6/70–126.
   Account Book, 1735–1791, BC/IV/1/2.
Hedon Quarter Sessions Minute Book and Court Leet, 1657–1745, DDHE/5/1.

Essex Record Office, Chelmsford

Borough records
Maldon Court Leet Presentments, D/B3/3/161.
Chamberlains' Accounts, 1660–1690, D/B3/3/89–107.
Chamberlains' Accounts, 1737–1760, D/B3/3/P524–39.

Parish records
Chelmsford Poor and Rate Book, 1713–1739, D/P94/12/5.

Quarter Sessions records
Process Books of Indictments, 1742–1762, Q/SPb/14.
Process Books of Indictments, 1747–1840, Q/SPb/14–22.

Guildhall Library, London

Playbills Collection (fairs).
Osborne, 'Bartholomew Fair', Gr. 3.3.1.
'Bartholomew Fair', MS. 01514.
Noble Collection, C. 26.5.
Main Print Collection, Pr. L.26.5.

Hampshire Record Office, Winchester

Andover Chamber Accounts, 1663–1794, 37M85/4/AC/8–29.
Lymington Town Book, 1613–1729, 27M74/DBC2.
Winchester Index to Ordinance Books, W/B1/18.
   City Accounts, 1726–1822, W/E1/148–202.
   Mayor's Accounts, 1741–1743, W/E7/2.

Hertfordshire Archives and Local Studies, Hertford

Family papers
John Carrington's Diary, 1797–1810, D/EX3.31.

Parish records
Minute Book of Special Sessions for the Half Hundred of Hitchen, 1808–1825,
   PS12/2/3.

Hull City Archives

Hull Chamberlains' Accounts, 1661–1800, BRF/2/517–698.

Kings Lynn Borough Archives

Kings Lynn Hall Book, 1684–1731, KL/C7/12.
  Chamberlains' Accounts, 1669–1708, KL/C39/105–8.

Lancashire Record Office, Preston

Preston White Book, 1662–1741, PMC/1/2.

Lincolnshire Archives, Lincoln

Boston Chamberlain and Treasurer Accounts, 1695–1787, 4/B/4–80.
Lincoln Chamberlain Rolls, 1685–1720, 150/1685–134/1720.
  Accounts of Corporation, 1764–1812, L1/4/1 /1–2.
Louth Wardens' Account Book, 1551–1686, Louth Grammar School/B/3/1.
  Wardens' Account Book, 1735–1834, Louth Grammar School/B/3/2–3.
  Corporation Minute Book, 1774–1824, Louth Grammar School/D/1.

Liverpool Record Office and Local History Service

Liverpool Cash Books, 1730–1784, 352/Tre/1/4/1–7.
  Town Book, 1671–1803, Bk. 4, 352/Min/Coul.
  Town Book, 1702–1731, Bk. 6, 352/Min/Coul.

Norfolk Record Office, Norwich

Borough records
Norwich Chamberlains' Accounts, 1700–1721, Case 18b/1–21.
  Court of Mayoralty Books, 1719–1776, Case 16a/28–33.
Great Yarmouth Audit Books, 1707–1757, Y/C27/4–8.
  Assembly Books, 1771–1801, Y/C19/14–15.
  Liber Ordinum, Y/C18/3.

Family papers
John Youell's Diary, 1771–1775, D87/10.

Quarter Sessions records
Norwich City Quarter Sessions Minute Book, 1815–1821, Case 20a/27.

North Yorkshire County Record Office, Northallerton

Borough records
Richmond Chamberlain Accounts, 1663–1692, 1776–1832, MIC 3386.
Ripon Mayors' Accounts, 1656–1819, MIC 2140.
Scarborough Chamberlains' Accounts, 1660–1683, MIC 1345.
  Chamberlains' Accounts, 1729–1826, MIC 2415, 2423.

Family papers
Henry Thirlway's Journal, 1835–1859, MIC 2563.

Manorial records
Thirsk Manor Court Book, 1739–1794, MIC 163.

Northamptonshire Record Office, Northampton

Borough records
Northampton Chamberlains' Accounts, 1690–1750, 8/1.

Family papers
John Clifton's Day Books, 1763–1784, ZA/8732–46.

Quarter Sessions records
Presentment Book, 1754–90, Misc Q53.
Recognizance Books, 1787–1830, Misc Q54–8.

Nottinghamshire Archives, Nottingham

Borough records
Nottingham Chamberlains' Accounts and Vouchers, 1716–1724, CA/1800E–G, 1801A–E, 1803E.

Family papers
Will and 4 Codicils of Sir Thos. Parkyns, Bart., PR3 13.
Joseph Wooley, his Book of Memorandums, DD311/1–6.

Parish records
Worksop Constables' Accounts, 1720–1811, PR 22,770.

Quarter Sessions records
Quarter Sessions Minute Books, 1767–1782, QSM/1/29–31.
Quarter Sessions Minute Bbook, 1817–1820, QSM/1/38.

Saffron Walden Town Council

Saffron Walden Accounts of the Guild of Holy Trinity, 1652–1835, ref. 314.

Sandwell Community History and Archive Service

West Bromwich Vestry Minutes, 1820–1896.
'Wednesbury Notes and Queries' (3 bound volumes of cuttings of Notes and Queries columns from *Midlands Advertiser*, compiled by F. W. Hackwood).

Sheffield Archives

Sheffield Burgery Accounts, 1566–1811, TT13–14.

Southampton Archives Service

Southampton Chamberlains' Accounts, 1660–1723, SC/3/23–41.

Staffordshire Record Office, Stafford

Borough records
Stafford Chamberlains' Accounts, 1699–1704 and 1729–44, D(W)O/8/2.
   Chamberlains' Accounts, 1765–1796, D1031/1.

Family papers
William Dyott's Diary, 1814–1830, D661/11/2/3/1/11.

Suffolk Record Office, Bury St Edmunds

Bury St Edmunds Book of Accounts, 1695–1778, D6/5/2.
   Court Minutes, 1760–1805, D4/1/4.
   Sessions Files, January 1803, D8/1/3.
Sudbury Book of Orders and Decrees, 1658–1681, EE501/2/8.
   Town Clerk's Book EE501/6/170.

Suffolk Record Office, Ipswich

Ipswich Chamberlains' Accounts, 1672–1785, C9/11/89–207.
Orford Chamberlains' Accounts, 1714–1767, EE5/5/1.

Surrey Record Office, Guildford Muniments Room

Guildford Hallwardens' Accounts, 1666–1787, BR/OC/6/2–3.
Mayors' Proclamations, BR/OC/2/7.

Walsall Archives Service

Walsall Mayors' Accounts, 1633–1714, 277/13/56–102.
'News cuttings', vi (uncatalogued).

Warwickshire County Record Office, Warwick

Borough records
Warwick Corporation Accounts, 1693–1729, CR1618 W/13/5.
   Corporation Accounts, 1728–1732, CR1618 W/13/8.

Manorial records
Atherstone Miscellaneous Papers: The Manor and Manorial Court, 1595–1804,
   MIR/9.

William Salt Library, Stafford

Broadsides and Ballads, 132/2/91.
Broughton's Scrap Book.

Wiltshire and Swindon Record Office, Trowbridge

Borough records
Calne General Book and Accounts, 1561–1814, G18/1/1.
Marlborough General Account Books, 1572–1771, G22/1/205/2–3.
Salisbury Chamberlain and Treasurer Account Rolls, 1683–1712, G23/1/47.
   Chamberlain and Treasurer Account Book, 1714–43, G23/1/48.
Wilton Burgess and Chamber Accounts, 1640–1811, G25/1/92–3.

Quarter Sessions records
Instructions for Indictments Books, 1790–1839, A1/170/1–4.

Wisbech Museum

Wisbech Town Book (uncatalogued).

Wolverhampton Archives and Local Studies

Wolverhampton Town Constables' Accounts, 1688–1737 and 1746–50, DX/79/1.
   Town Constables' Accounts, 1790–1813, DX/79/2.

Yorkshire Archaeological Society, Leeds

Skipton Manor Jurors' Verdicts, 1700–1766, DD121/12.

Parliamentary papers

Journal of the House of Commons, lvii (1802); lxxxiii (1826); xxcii (1826).
Parliamentary Debates, xiv (1809); xvi (1810).
Parliamentary Debates, n.s. ix–x (1824–1825); xii (1825); xiv (1826); xxi (1829).
Parliamentary History, xxxv–xxxvi (1800–1803).
First Report of the Commissioners for Inquiring into the State of Large Towns and Populous Districts, *Parliamentary Papers*, 1844, xvii.
Second Report of the Commissioners for Inquiring into the State of Large Towns and Populous Districts, *Parliamentary Papers*, 1845, xviii.
Report from the Poor Law Commissioners into the Sanitary Condition of the Labouring Population of Great Britain, *House of Lords Sessional Papers*, 1842, xxvi–vvvii.
Report from the Select Committee on Commons' Inclosure, *Parliamentary Papers*, 1844, v.
Report from the Select Committee on the Health of Towns, *Parliamentary Papers*, 1840, xi.
Report from the Select Committee on Public Walks, *Parliamentary Papers*, 1833, xv.

Books and pamphlets

An Address to the Public from the Society for the Suppression of Vice (London, 1803).
Alken, Henry, *The National Sports of Great Britain* (London, 1821).

Annals of Cambridge, iv, ed. Charles Henry Cooper (Cambridge, 1852).

Aspin, Jehosaphat, *A Picture of Manners, Customs, Sports, and Pastimes of the Inhabitants of England* (London, 1829).

Aubrey, John, *Remaines of Gentilisme and Judaisme, 1686–7*, ed. James Britten (London, 1881).

Barry, Edward, *Bull Baiting! A Sermon on Barbarity to God's Dumb Creation, Preached in the Parish Church of Wokingham, Berkshire* (Reading, 1802).

Baxter, Richard, *A Christian Directory: Or, a Summ of Practical Theologie and Cases of Conscience* (London, 1673).

Beverley Corporation Minute Book, 1707–1835, ed. K. A. MacMahon, Yorkshire Archaeological Society, 122 (1958).

Bewick, Thomas, *A General History of Quadrupeds* (Newcastle-upon-Tyne, 1790).

Bigland, John, *Letters on Natural History* (London, 1806).

Bingley, William *Animal Biography*, 3 vols (London, 1805).
 Memoirs of British Quadrupeds (London, 1809).

The Black Book of Warwick, ed. Thomas Kemp (Warwick, 1898).

Blaine, D. P., *An Encyclopaedia of Rural Sports* (London, 1840).

Blome, Richard, *The Gentleman's Recreation* (London, 1686).

Blount, Thomas, *Fragmenta Antiquitatis* (London, 1679).

Brand, John, *Observations on Popular Antiquities: Including the Whole of Mr. Bourne's Antiquitates Vulgares, with Addenda to Every Chapter* (Newcastle upon Tyne, 1777).

Chester, J. Greville, *Statute Fairs: Their Evils and their Remedy* (York and London, 1856).

Clare, John, *Clare: Selected Poems and Prose*, ed. Eric Robinson and Geoffrey Summerfield (London, 1966).

Clemency to Brutes: The Substance of Two Sermons Preached on Shrove Sunday (London, 1761).

The Constables' Accounts of the Manor of Manchester, 1743–1766, iii, ed. J. P. Earwaker (Manchester, 1892).

The Court Leet Records of the Manor of Manchester, 1552–1686 and 1731–1846, 12 vols, ed. J. P. Earwaker (Manchester, 1884–90).

Coventry Constables' Presentments, 1629–1742, ed. Levi Fox (Oxford, 1986).

Defoe, Daniel, *A Tour Through the Whole Island of Great Britain*, ed. D. G. H. Cole and D. C. Browning (London, 1974).

Denson, John, *A Peasant's Voice to Landowners, on the Best Means of Benefiting Agricultural Labourers, and of Reducing Poor Rates* (Cambridge, 1830).

Descriptive Catalogue of the Charters, Minute Books and other Documents of the Borough of Weymouth and Melcombe Regis, 1252–1800, ed. H. S. Moule (Weymouth, 1833).

The Devil at Greenwich Fair: Being a True Account of Old Nick's Visit to Greenwich, on Easter Monday last (London, 1841).

Dillon, R. C., *A Sermon on the Evils of Fairs in General and of Bartholomew in Particular* (London, 1830).

Disraeli, Benjamin, *Sybil, or the Two Nations* (London, 1845).

Drummond, William H., *The Rights of Animals, and Man's Obligation to Treat Them with Humanity* (London, 1838).

Egan, Pierce, *Life in London: Or of the Day and Night Scenes of Jerry Hawthorn, esq. and his Elegant Friend Corinthian Tom* (London, 1822; repr. 1859).

Book of Sports and Mirror of Life (London, 1832).

Ellis, Henry (ed.), *Observations on Popular Antiquities by J. Brand: Arranged, Revised and Greatly Enlarged*, 2 vols (London, 1813).

Extracts from the Records in Portsmouth, ed. Richard J. Murrel and Robert East (Portsmouth, 1884).

Familiar Essays on Interesting Subjects (London, 1789).

Gaskell, Elizabeth, *The Life of Charlotte Bronte* (London, 1901).

Granger, James, *An Apology for the Brute Creation: Or Abuse of Animals Censured* (London, 1772).

Harewood, Harry, *A Dictionary of Sports* (London, 1835).

Hertfordshire County Records, Calendar to the Sessions and other Sessions Records, 1701–1751, viii, ed. W. J. Hardy (Hertford, 1905).

Hone, Wiliam, *The Every-day Book*, 2 vols (London, 1825–7).

The Year Book (London, 1832).

Houghton, John, *A Collection for the Improvement of Husbandry and Trade* (London, 1727).

Howitt, William, *The Rural Life of England*, 2 vols (London, 1838).

The Boy's Country-book: Being the Real Life of a Country Boy, Written by Himself (London, 1839).

Kilner, Dorothy, *The Village School: A Collection of Entertaining Histories for . . . Children* (London, 1828).

Lawrence, John, *A Philosophical and Practical Treatise on Horses, and on the Moral Duties of Man Towards the Brute Creation*, 2 vols (London, 1796–8).

Litt, W., *Wrestliana: Or, an Historical Account of Ancient and Modern Wrestling* (Whitehaven, 1823).

Macaulay, James, *Essay on Cruelty to Animals* (Edinburgh, 1839).

Markham, Gervase, *Country Contentments, or, the Husbandmans Recreations*, 5th edn (London, 1633–7).

[Maxwell, W. H.], *The Field Book, or Sports and Pastimes of the British Isles* (London, [1833]).

Mitford, Mary Russell, *Our Village: Sketches of Rural Character and Scenery*, 5 vols (London, 1824–32).

Moffett, Thomas, *Health's Improvement: Or Rules Comprising and Discovering the Nature . . . and Manner of Preparing all Sorts of Food used in the Nation* (London, 1655).

Morley, H., *Memoirs of Bartholomew Fair* (London, 1859; facs. repr. 1973).

Ogilby, John and William Morgan, *The Traveller's Pocket Book* (London, 1759).

Osbaldiston, William A., *The British Sportsman* (London, 1795).

Owen, William, *An Authentic Account . . . of all the Fairs in England and Wales*, 2nd edn (London, 1759).

Pegge, Samuel, 'The bull-running at Tutbury, in Staffordshire, considered', *Archaeologia*, 2 (1773), pp. 86–91.

'A memoir on cockfighting', *Archaeologia*, 3 (1775), pp. 132–50.

Pennant, Thomas, *British Zoology*, 4 vols, 4th edn (London, 1776–7).

Popular Pastimes, Being a Selection of Picturesque Representations of the Customs and Amusements of Great Britain (London, 1816).

Records of the Borough of Leicester, iii, ed. Mary Bateson (Cambridge, 1905).

Records of the Borough of Northampton, 1550–1835, ii, ed. Christopher Markham and Charles Cox (Northampton, 1898).

Records of the Borough of Nottingham, 1485–1800, iv–vii (Nottingham, 1900–47).

R. H., *The Royal Pastime of Cockfighting* (London, 1709; facs. repr. Alton, 1988).

Richmond, Legh, *A Sermon on the Sin of Cruelty toward the Brute Creation* (Bath, 1802).

Selections from the Records of the City of Oxford, ed. William H. Turner (Oxford, 1880).

Seymour, Richard, *The Compleat Gamester*, revised by Charles Johnson, 8th edn (London, 1754).

Sheldrake, William, *A Picturesque Description of Turton Fair, and its Pernicious Consequences: A Poem* (London, 1789).

A Short Authentic Account of the late Decision on the Bull-baiting Question (Dudley, 1827).

[Southey, Robert], *Letters from England*, ed. Jack Simmons (Oxford, 1951).

The Sportsman's Dictionary: Or the Country Gentleman's Companion to all Rural Recreations, 2 vols (London, 1735).

Strutt, Joseph, *Glig-Gamena Angel-Deod: Or the Sports and Pastimes of the People of England*, 2nd edn (London, 1833).

Stubbes, Philip, *Anatomie of Abuses* (London, 1583; facs. repr. Amsterdam, 1972).

Styles, John, *Animal Creation* (London, 1839).

Taplin, William, *The Sporting Dictionary and Rural Repository* (London, 1803).

Transcripts from the Municipal Archives of Winchester, ed. Charles Bailey (Winchester, 1856).

Walker, Donald, *Games and Sports: Being an Appendix to 'Manly Exercises' and 'Exercises for Ladies'* (London, 1837).

Woodward, G. M., *Eccentric Excursions, or Literary and Pictorial Sketches of . . . Different Parts of England* (London, 1796).

The Writings and Speeches of Oliver Cromwell: The Protectorate, 1653–55, iii, ed Wilbur Cortez Abbott (Oxford, 1988).

Youatt, William, *The Obligation and Extent of Humanity to Brutes, Principally Considered with Reference to the Domesticated Animals* (London, 1839).

Young, Thomas, *An Essay on Humanity to Animals* (London, 1809).

Local histories

Balderston, Robert and Margaret Balderston, *Ingleton, Bygone and Present* (London, [1888]).

Banks, W. S., *Walks in Yorkshire: Wakefield and its Neighbourhood*, 2nd edn (Wakefield, 1871).

Barker, W. G. M. Jones, *History and Topographical Account of Wensleydale* (London, 1856).

Barton, B. T., *History of the Borough of Bury and Neighbourhood* (Bury, 1874).

Batty, John, *The History of Rothwell* (Rothwell, 1877).

Bedell, E. W., *An Account of Hornsea, in Holderness, in the East-Riding of Yorkshire* (Hull, 1848).

Bell-Irving, E. M., *Mayfield: The Story of an Old Wealden Village* (London, 1903).

Biden, W. D., *The History and Antiquity of Kingston upon Thames* (Kingston, 1852).

Bracket, C. W., *A History of Plymouth and her Neighbours* (Plymouth, 1931).

Brewster, John, *The Parochial History and Antiquities of Stockton-upon-Tees* (Stockton-upon-Tees, 1829).

Burne, Charlotte S., *Shropshire Folklore: A Sheaf of Gleanings from the Collections of Georgina Jackson*, 2 vols (London, 1883; facs. repr. East Ardsley, 1973).

Callum, Sir John, *The History and Antiquities of Hawsted, in the County of Suffolk* (London, 1784).

Chapple, William, *A Review of Part of Risdon's Survey of Devon* (Exeter, 1785; facs. repr. Barnstaple, 1970).

Chope, R. Pearse, 'Football on Good Friday', *Devon and Cornwall N&Q*, 10 (1918–19), pp. 113–14.

Clarkson, Christopher, *The History and Antiquities of Richmond in the County of York* (Richmond, 1821).

Clarkson, Henry, *Memories of Merry Wakefield* (Wakefield, 1889; facs. repr. East Ardsley, 1969).

Clay, William Keatinge, *A History of the Parish of Waterbeach in the County of Cambridge* (Cambridge, 1859).
   A History of the Parish of Landbeach in the County of Cambridge (Cambridge, 1861).
   A History of the Parish of Milton in the County of Cambridge (Cambridge, 1869).

Cole, John, *The History and Antiquities of Higham Ferrars* (Wellingborough, 1838).

Collections towards a Parochial History of Berkshire (London, 1783). Included in vol. 4 of *Nichols's Bibliotheca Topographica Britannica*, 10 vols.

Cooper, Isaac, *Helmsley, or Reminiscences of One Hundred Years Ago* (York, [1890?]).

Cowling, Geoffrey O., *The History of Easingwold* (Huddersfield, n.d.).

Cradock, H. C., *History of the Ancient Parish of Birstal, Yorkshire* (London, 1933).

Cudworth, William, *Round about Bradford: A Series of Sketches* (Bradford, 1876).

Curwen, John F., *Kirkbie Kendall* (Kendal, 1900).

Davison, A. W., *Derby: Its Rise and Progress* (London, 1908).

Dawson, William Harbutt, *History of Skipton* (Skipton, 1882).

Deering, Charles, *The History of Nottingham* (Nottingham, 1751; facs. repr. East Ardsley, 1970).

Dent, Robert, K., *Old and New Birmingham*, 3 vols (Birmingham, 1878–80).

A Description of the Town of Ludlow with an Historical Account of the Castle (Ludlow, 1811).

Dixon, D. D, 'Old Coquetdale customs', *Archaeolgia Aelinea*, n.s. 15 (1892), p. 144.

Drakard, John, *The History of Stamford* (Stamford, 1822).

Drake, James, *The Picture of Birmingham* (Birmingham, 1825).

Dunkin, John, *The History and Antiquities of Bicester* (London, 1816).

   The History and Antiquities of Dartford (London, 1844).

Dutt, William A., *Highways and Byways of East Anglia* (London, 1901).

[Easther, Alfred], *A Glossary of the Dialect of Almondbury and Huddersfield*, ed. Thomas Lees (London, 1883).

Eastwood, J., *The History of the Parish of Ecclesfield* (London, 1862).

Ede, J. F., *History of Wednesbury* (Birmingham, 1962)

Fairfax-Blakeborough, J., *Life in a Yorkshire Village* (Stockton, 1912).

Farey, John, *General View of the Agriculture of Derbyshire*, 3 vols (London, 1811–17).

Fisher, John, *The History and Antiquities of Masham and Mashamshire* (London, 1865).

Fishwick, Henry, *The History of the Parish of Kirkham, in the County of Lancaster*, Publications of the Chetham Society, 92 (1874).

   The History of the Parish of Rochdale in the County of Lancaster (Rochdale, 1889).

Fletcher, J. S., *A Book about Yorkshire* (London, 1908).

'Football in the North', *North-country Lore and Legend*, February 1889, pp. 54–6.

Forby, Robert, *The Vocabulary of East Anglia*, 2 vols (London, 1830; facs. repr. Newton Abbot, 1970).

Fumess, William, *History of Penrith from the Earliest Record to the Present Time* (Penrith, 1894).

Gardiner, Frederick, *History of Wisbech and Neighbourhood, 1848–1898* (Wisbech, 1898).

Gibbs, Robert, *A History of Aylesbury* (Aylesbury, 1885).

Giles, John Allen, *History of the Parish and Town of Bampton, with the Districts and Hamlets Belonging to It* (Bampton, 1848).

Glover, Stephen, *The History and Gazateer of the County of Derby*, 2 vols (Derby, 1831).

Glyde, John, *The Moral, Social and Religious Condition of Ipswich* (Ipswich, 1850; facs. repr. East Ardsley, 1971).

   Folklore and Customs of Suffolk (Wakefield, 1976; facs. repr. of idem, 'The New Suffolk Garland', 1866).

Grainge, William, *The Vale of Mowbray* (London, 1859).

   The History and Topography of the Townships of Little Timble, Great Timble, and the Hamlet of Snowdon (Otley, 1895).

Hartley, M. and J. Ingilby, *Yorkshire Village* (London, 1953).

Hasted, Edward, *The History and Topographical Survey of the County of Kent*, xii, 2nd edn (Canterbury, 1801).

Hatfield, Charles William, *Historical Notices of Doncaster*, 3 vols (Doncaster, n.d.).

Heaviside, Henry, *The Annals of Stockton-on-Tees* (Stockton-on-Tees, 1865).

Hemmingway, Joseph, *The History of Chester* ([Chester], 1831).

Hemstone, Lucy and J. W. Clay Hemstone, *Olde Eland: Being Reminiscences of Elland* (Elland, 1901).

Henslow, J. S., *Suggestions towards an Enquiry into the Present Condition of the Labouring Population of Suffolk* (Hadleigh, 1844).

Hewitson, Anthony, *The History of Preston* (Preston, 1883).

Hodgson, George, *The Borough of South Shields* (Newcastle-upon-Tyne, 1903).

Holmes, Richard, *Keighley Past and Present* (London, 1858).

Humphries, Arthur, *The Materials for a History of Wellington* (London, 1889).

Hutchinson, William, *A View of Northumberland*, 2 vols (Newcastle, 1778).

   The History of the County of Cumberland, 2 vols (Carlisle, 1794–7; facs. repr. East
      Ardsley, 1974).

Hutton, William, *An History of Birmingham*, 2nd edn (Birmingham, 1781).

Jagger, Mary A., *The History of Honley* (Honley, 1914).

James, John, *Continuations and Additions to the History of Bradford* (Bradford, 1866;
      facs. repr. Manchester, 1973).

Jones, John, *The History and Antiquities of Harewood, in the County of York* (London,
      1859).

Keys, J., *Reminiscences of Old Derby* (Derby, 1850).

Latimer, John, *The Annals of Bristol in the Seventeenth Century*, iii (Bristol, 1900).

Lawson, Joseph, *Progress in Pudsey* (Stanningley, 1887; facs. repr. Firle, 1978).

Le Blanc Smith, G., 'Snitterton bull ring', *Derbyshire Archaeological Society Journal*, 30
      (1908), pp. 143–54.

Leader, Robert Eadon, *Reminiscences of Old Sheffield* (Sheffield, 1875).

Longstaffe, W. H. D., *The History and Antiquities of the Parish of Darlington* (Darlington,
      1854).

Manders, F. W. D., *A History of Gateshead* (Gateshead, 1973).

Moor, Edward, *Suffolk Words and Phrases* (London, 1823).

Morris, Rupert H., *Chester in the Plantagenet and Tudor Reigns* (Chester, 1894).

Morris, William, *Swindon Fifty Years Ago: Reminiscences, Notes and Relics of ye Old
      Wiltshire Town* (Swindon, [1885]).

Mosley, Sir Oswald, *History of the Castle, Priory and Town of Tutbury* (London,
      1832).

Noake, John, *Worcester in Olden Times* (London, 1849).

Oliver, George, *The History and Antiquity of the Town and Minster of Beverley, in the
      County of York* (Beverley, 1829).

Ormerod, George, *The History of the County Palatine and City of Chester*, i (London,
      1819).

Parker, C. A., *The Gosforth District: Its Antiquities and Places of Interest* (Kendal, 1904;
      facs. repr. Whitehaven, 1986).

Paterson, T. F., *East Bergholt in Suffolk* (Cambridge, 1923).

Pilkington, James, *A View of the Present State of Derbyshire*, 2 vols (London, 1789).

Plot, Robert, *Natural History of Staffordshire* (Oxford, 1686).

Pobjoy, Harold N., *A History of Mirfield* (Driffield, 1969).

Porter, Enid, *The Folklore of East Anglia* (London, 1974).

Pratt, Charles Tiplady, *A History of Cawthorne* (Barnsley, 1882).

Purvis, J. S., *Bridlington: Charters, Court Rolls and Papers from the Fifteenth to the
      Nineteenth Centuries* (London, 1926).

Randall, John, *Broseley and its Surroundings* (Madeley, 1879).

   The History of Madeley (Madeley, 1880).

[Rayner, Simon], *The History and Antiquities of Pudsey*, ed. William Smith (London, 1887).

Readwin, T. A., *An Account of the Charities in the Town and Parish of Wokingham* (Wokingham, 1845).

Recollections of Old Liverpool by a Nonagenarian (Liverpool, 1863).

Richmond, Thomas, *The Local Records of Stockton and the Neighbourhood* (London, 1868; facs. repr. Stockton, 1972).

Ripley, Henry, *The History and Topography of Hampton-on-Thames* (London, 1884).

Roberts, George, *The Topography and Natural History of Lofthouse*, 2 vols (Leeds, 1885).

Robinson, C. Clough, *Dialect of Leeds and Its Neighbourhood* (London, 1862).

Scarratt, William, *Old Times in the Potteries* (Stoke-on-Trent, 1906).

Sedgwick, Adam, *Adam Sedgwick's Dent, 1868–70*, ed. David Boulton (Dent, 1984).

Shaw, Stebbing, *The History and Antiquities of Staffordshire*, 2 vols (London, 1798–1801).

Smith, William (ed.), *The History and Antiquities of Morley* (London, 1876).
　Old Yorkshire (London, 1882).
　Morley, Ancient and Modern (London, 1886).

Speight, H., *Chronicles and Stories of Old Bingley* (Elliot Stock, 1898).

Stainthorpe, T. W., 'Ye ancient bull ring at Totnes', *Reports and Transactions of the Devonshire Association*, 32 (1900), pp. 106–10.

Sugden, John, *Slaithwaite: Notes of the Past and Present* (Manchester, 1905).

Swanton, E. A. and P. Woods, *Bygone Haslemere: A Short History of the Ancient Borough* (London, 1914).

Tate, George, *The History of the Borough, Castle and Barony of Alnwick*, 2 vols (Alnwick, 1866–9).

Throsby, John, *The History and Antiquities of the Ancient Town of Leicester* (London, 1791).

Troughton, Thomas *The History of Liverpool* (London, 1810).

Turner, Roger, 'The Great George Inn, Petworth', *Sussex Archaeological Collection*, 19 (1868), pp. 134–44.

Watson, John, *The History and Antiquities of the Parish of Halifax in Yorkshire* (London, 1775).

Weeks, William Self, *Clitheroe in the Seventeenth Century* (Clitheroe, [1927]).

Whellan, William, *The History and Topography of Cumberland and Westmorland* (Pontefract, 1860).

Whitaker, Cuthbert W., *An Illustrated Historical, Statistical and Topographical Account of the Urban District of Enfield* (London, 1911).

Willis, Cloudesley S., *A Short History of Ewell and Nonsuch* (Epsom, 1931).

Yonge, Weston E. Vernon, *Bye-paths of Staffordshire*, 4th edn (Stafford, 1991).

Printed diaries, journals, autobiographies, reminiscences, and letters

Adams. W. E., *Memoirs of a Social Atom*, 2 vols (London, 1903).

Asplin, Jonas, 'Jonas Asplin, Doctor of Prittlewell, 1826–28', in *Essex People 1750–1900, from their Diaries, Memoirs and Letters*, ed. A. F. J. Brown, Essex Record Office Publications, 59 (1972).

Barrs, George, *Four Sermons by the Late Reverend George Barrs . . . together with Copious Extracts from his Private Manuscript Journals*, 2nd edn (Birmingham, 1897).

Bee, Jacob, 'Diary of Jacob Bee', in *Six North Country Diaries*, Publications of the Surtees Society, 118 (1910).

Blundell, Nicholas, *The Great Diurnal of Nicholas Blundell of Little Crosby, Lancashire, 1702–1728*, ed. Frank Tyrer, 3 vols, Record Society of Lancashire and Cheshire, 110–14 (1968–72).

Buckley, John, *A Village Politician: The Life-story of John Buckley*, ed. J. C. Buckmaster (London, 1897).

Burgess, John, *No Continuing City: The Diary and Letters of John Burgess, a Sussex Craftsman, 1785–1810*, ed. Donald F. Burgess (Redhill, Surrey, 1989).

Burstow, Henry, *Reminiscences of Horsham: Being Recollections of Henry Burstow, the Celebrated Bellringer and Songsinger* (Horsham, 1911).

Carter, Thomas, *Memoirs of a Working Man*, ed. Charles Knight (London, 1845).

Cole, William, *The Blecheley Diary of the Rev. William Cole, 1765–1767*, ed. Francis Griffin Stokes, with an introduction by Helen Waddell (London, 1931).

Collings, Jesse, *Life of the Right Honourable Jesse Collings* (London, 1920).

Cossins, James, *Reminiscences of Exeter Fifty Years Since* (Exeter, 1877).

Crosfield, Thomas, *The Diary of Thomas Crosfield*, ed. Frederick S. Boas (London, 1935).

Crosier, John, 'John Crosier, Maldon miller, 1753–78', in *Essex People 1750–1900, from their Diaries, Memoirs and Letters*, ed. A. F. J. Brown, Essex Record Office Publications, 59 (1972).

[Darter, William Silver], *Reminiscences of Reading: An Octogenarian* (1889), ed. Daphne Philips (Newbury, 1985).

Eardley-Wilmot, John E., *Reminiscences of the late Thomas Assheton Smith, esq.*, 6th edn (London, 1902).

Evelyn, John, *The Diary of John Evelyn, 1647–1676*, ii, ed. Austin Dobson (London, 1906).

Gatty, Alfred, *A Life at One Living* (London, 1884).

Gyll, Thomas, 'Diary of Thomas Gyll', in *Six North Country Diaries*, Publications of the Surtees Society, 118 (1910).

Hardy, Mary, *Mary Hardy's Diary, 1773–1809*, ed. B. Cozens-Hardy, Norfolk Record Society, 37 (1968).

Hentzner, Paul, *A Journey into England, in the year 1598*, trans. Richard Bentley (Strawberry-Hill, 1757).

Herbert, George, *Shoemaker's Window: Recollections of Banbury in Oxfordshire before the Railway Age*, 3rd edn, ed. C. S. Cheney and B. S. Trinder (Banbury, 1979).

Heywood, Oliver, *The Rev. Oliver Heywood, B.A., 1630–1702: His Autobiography, Diaries, Anecdote and Event Books*, ed. J. H. Turner, 4 vols (Brighouse and Bingley, 1881–5).

Hird, Robert, *Hird's Annals of Bedale, 1808–1812*, ed. Lesley Lewis, North Yorkshire CRO Publications, 2 (1975).

Hobley, Frederick, 'From the autobiography of Frederick Hobley, a nineteenth-century schoolteacher', *Alta: The University of Birmingham Review*, 6 (1968), pp. 331–7.

Hobson, John, 'The Journal of Mr John Hobson', in *Yorkshire Diaries*, Publications of the Surtees Society, 65 (1877).

Holland, William, *Paupers and Pig Killers: The Diary of William Holland, a Somerset Parson*, ed. Jack Ayres (Gloucester, 1984).

Kay, Richard, *The Diary of Richard Kay, 1716–1751, of Baldingstone, near Bury: A Lancashire Doctor*, ed. W. Brockbank and F. Kenworthy, Publications of the Chetham Society, 3rd ser., 16 (1968).

Keys, J., *Reminiscences of Old Derby* (Derby, 1850).

Lowe, Roger, *The Diary of Roger Lowe of Ashton-in-Makerfield, Lancashire, 1663–74*, ed. William L. Sachse (London, 1938).

Marchant, Thomas, *The Marchant Diary*, ed. Rev. Edward Turner, Sussex Archaeological Collection, 25 (1873), pp. 163–203.

[Marsden, Isaac], *Reminiscences of Isaac Marsden*, ed. John Taylor (London, 1883).

Mayett, Joseph, *The Autobiography of Joseph Mayett of Quainton, 1783–1839*, ed. Ann Kussmaul, Buckinghamshire Record Society, 23 (1986).

Mildmay, Humphrey, *Humphey Mildmay, Royalist Gentleman: Glimpses of the English Scene*, ed. Philip Lee Ralph (New Brunswick, 1945).

Misson, Henri M., *Misson's Memoirs and Observations in his Travels over England, 1627*, ed. John Ozell (London, 1719).

Muralt, Béat Louis de, *Letters Describing the Character and Customs of the English and French Nations*, 2nd edn (London, 1726).

Neville, Sylas, *The Diary of Sylas Neville, 1767–88*, ed. Basil Cozens-Hardy (Oxford, 1850).

Newcome, Henry, *The Diary of Henry Newcome, 1661–3*, ed. Thomas Heywood, Publications of the Chetham Society, 18 (1849).
  Autobiography of Henry Newcome, 2 vols, ed. Richard Parkinson, Publications of the Chetham Society, 26 (1852).

Oakes, James, *The Oakes Diaries: Business, Politics and the Family in Bury St Edmunds, 1778–1827*, ed. Jane Fiske, Suffolk Records Society, 32–3 (1990–1).

Oakey, J. A., *Winchcombe, 1935: Reminiscences* ([Winchcombe?], 1936).

Page, Joseph, 'Joseph Page, farmer of Fingrinhoe, 1799–1803', in *Essex People 1750–1900, from their Diaries, Memoirs and Letters*, ed. A. F. J. Brown, Essex Record Office Publications, 59 (1972).

Paynter, William, *Old Saint Ives: The Reminiscences of William Paynter* (St Ives, [1928]).

Pepys, Samuel, *The Diary of Samuel Pepys, 1660–2*, ed. Robert Latham and William Matthews, 11 vols (London, 1970–83).

Platter, Thomas, *Thomas Platter's Travels in England, 1599*, trans. and ed. Clare Williams (London, 1932).

Prescott, Henry, *The Diary of Henry Prescott, LL. B., Deputy Registrar of Chester Diocese, 1704–1711*, i, ed. John Addy, The Record Society of Lancashire and Cheshire, 127 (1987).

de la Pryme, Abraham, *The Diary of Abraham de la Pryme*, ed. Charles Jackson, Publications of the Surtees Society, 54 (1870).

Rathgeb, Jacob, 'A true and faithful narrative of the bathing excursion, which his serene highness, Frederick, Duke of Wirtemberg . . . made a few years ago in the far-famed Kingdom of England, 1592', in *England as Seen by Foreigners*, ed. William B. Rye (London, 1865).

Richards, John, 'Extracts from the diary of John Richards, 1697–1702', *Retrospective Review*, 1 (1853), pp. 97–101, 201–5, 408–18.

Rogerson, Joseph, 'The diary of Joseph Rogerson, scribbling miller, of Bramley, 1808–1814', in *The Leeds Woollen Industry, 1780–1820*, ed. W. B. Crump, Publications of the Thoresby Society, 32 (1929).

Rose, Charles, *Recollections of Old Dorking* (1878), ed. Margaret K. Kohler (Dorking, 1977).

de Saussure, César, *A Foreign View of England in the Reigns of George I and George II: The Letters of Monsieur César de Saussure to his Family*, ed. Madame van Muyden (London, 1902).

Sharpe, Robert, *The Diary of Robert Sharp of South Cave: Life in a Yorkshire Village, 1812–1837*, ed. Janice E. Crowther and Peter A. Crowther, Records of Social and Economic History, new ser., 26 (1997).

[Shaw, C.], *When I was a Child, by 'an Old Potter'* (London, 1903; facs. repr. Wakefield, 1969).

Shellinks, William, *The Journal of William Shellinks' Travels in England*, trans. and ed. Maurice Exwood and H. L. Lehrmann, Camden Series, 5th ser., 1 (1993).

Skinner, John, *Journal of a Somersetshire Rector*, ed. Howard Coombs and A. N. Bax (London, 1930).

Smith, William, 'The memoir of William Smith', ed. B. S. Trinder, *Transactions of the Shropshire Archaeological Society*, 58 (1966), pp. 178–85.

Spershott, James, *The Memoirs of James Sperchott*, ed. Francis W. Steer, Chichester Papers, 30 (1962).

[Stapley, Richard], 'On the domestic habits and mode of life of a Sussex gent', ed. Edward Turner, *Sussex Archaeological Collections*, 23 (1871).

Thomson, Christopher, *Autobiography of an Artisan* (London, 1847).

[Tompkins Family], 'The Tompkins diary', ed. G. W. Eustace, *Sussex Archaeological Collection*, 71 (1930), pp. 11–56.

Turner, Thomas, *The Diary of Thomas Turner, 1754–1765*, ed. David Vaisey (Oxford, 1984).

von Uffenbach, Zacharias Conrad, *London in 1710: From the Travels of Zacharias Conrad von Uffenbach*, trans. and ed. W. H. Quarrel and Margaret Mare (London, 1934).

Wale, Henry John, *My Grandfather's Pocket Book from A. D. 1701–1796* (London, 1883).

Watkin, Absalom, *The Diaries of Absalom Watkin: A Manchester Man, 1787–1861*, ed. Magdalen Goffin (Stroud, 1993).

[Wharton family], 'Rural life and manners in the neighbourhood of Bidstone and Upton', ed. Reud Canon Hume, *Transactions of the Historical Society of Lancashire and Cheshire*, 3rd ser. 3 (1875).

Whitaker, Jeffrey, *The Diaries of Jeffery Whitaker Schoolmaster of Bratton, 1739–1741*, ed. Marjorie Reeves and Jean Morrison, Wiltshire Record Society, 44 (1988).

Wire, William, 'William Wire, Watchmaker and Postman of Colchester, 1842–57', in *Essex People 1750–1900, from their Diaries, Memoirs and Letters*, ed. A. F. J. Brown, Essex Record Office Publications, 59 (1972).

Wood, Anthony, *The Life and Times of Anthony Wood, Antiquary, of Oxford, 1632–1695, described by Himself*, i, ed. Andrew Clark, Oxford Historical Society, 19 (1891).

Woodforde, James, *The Diary of a Country Parson, 1758–1802*, ed. John Beresford, 5 vols (Oxford, 1924–31).

National newspapers and periodicals

Adventurer
Analytical Review
Blackwood's Magazine
British Critic
British Review
Critical Review
Eclectic Review
Edinburgh Review
European Magazine
European Review
Gentleman's Magazine
Gray's Inn Journal
Guardian
Literary Magazine
London Magazine
Methodist Magazine
Mirror of Literature, Amusement, and Instruction
Monthly Magazine
Monthly Review
Morning Chronicle
Primitive Methodist Magazine
Public Advertiser

Quarterly Review
Rambler
Spectator
Sporting Magazine
Tatler
The Times
Universal Magazine
Wesleyan Methodist Magazine
World

Local newspapers

Aris's Birmingham Gazette
Bath Journal
Berkshire Chronicle
Birmingham Daily Mail
Birmingham Gazette and Express
Birmingham Journal
Birmingham Weekly Post (BWP)
Brighton Herald
Bristol and Bath Magazine
Bury and Norwich Post
Cambridge Chronicle
Cambridge Independent Press
Chelmsford Chronicle
Derby Mercury
Hampshire Chronicle
Hull Advertiser
Hull Advertiser and Exchange Gazette
Ipswich Journal
Jackson's Oxford Journal
Leeds Intelligencer
Leeds Mercury
Lewes Journal
Lincoln Mercury
Lincoln, Rutland and Stamford Mercury
Liverpool General Advertiser
Manchester Mercury
Newcastle Courant
Norfolk Chronicle
Northampton Mercury
Norwich Mercury
Nottingham Journal
Reading Mercury
Rockingham and Hull Weekly Advertiser

Sheffield Independent
Sheffield Iris
Sheffield Mercury
Staffordshire Advertiser
Stamford Mercury
Sussex Weekly Advertiser
Wakefield and Halifax Journal
Williamson Liverpool Advertiser
Wolverhampton Chronicle
York Courant

Secondary literature

Books and journal articles

Addison, William, *English Fairs and Markets* (London, 1953).

Alexander, Matthew, 'Shrove Tuesday football in Surrey', *Surrey Archaeological Collections*, 77 (1986), pp. 197–205.

Alexander, Sally, *St Giles Fair, 1830–1914: Popular Culture and the Industrial Revolution in Nineteenth-century Oxford* (Oxford, 1970).

Allen, Robert C., *Enclosure and the Yeoman* (Oxford, 1992).

Bailey, Peter, *Leisure and Class in Victorian England: Rational Recreation and the Contest for Control, 1830–1885*, 2nd edn (London, 1987).

Berg, Maxine, *The Age of Manufactures, 1700–1820: Industry, Innovation and Work in Britain*, 2nd edn (London, 1995).

Berlin, Michael, 'Civic ceremony in early modern London', *Urban History Yearbook* (1986), pp. 15–27.

Biersack, Aletta, 'Local knowledge, local history: Geertz and beyond', in Lynn Hunt (ed.), *The New Cultural History* (Berkeley, CA, 1989), pp. 72–96.

Birley, Derek, *A Social History of English Cricket* (London, 1999).

Borsay, Peter, 'The English urban renaissance: the development of provincial urban culture, c.1680–c.1760', *Social History*, 5 (1977), pp. 581–603.

'"All the town's a stage": urban ritual and ceremony, 1660–1800', in Clark (ed.), *Transformation of English Towns*, pp. 228–58.

'The rise of the promenade: the social and cultural use of space in the English provincial town, 1660–1800', *British Journal of Eighteenth-century Studies*, 9 (1986), pp. 125–40.

The English Urban Renaissance: Culture and Society in the Provincial Town, 1660–1770 (Oxford, 1989).

Bowen, Rowland, *Cricket: A History of its Growth and Development throughout the World* (London, 1970).

Brailsford, Dennis, *Bareknuckles: A Social History of Prize-fighting* (Cambridge, 1988).

A Taste for Diversions: Sport in Georgian England (Cambridge, 1999).

Bristow, Edward J., *Vice and Vigilance: Purity Movements in Britain since 1700* (London, 1977).

Brookes, Christopher, *English Cricket: The Game and its Players through the Ages* (London, 1978).

Burke, Peter, *Popular Culture in Early Modern Europe* (London, 1978).

'Popular culture in seventeenth-century London', in Barry Reay (ed.), *Popular Culture in Seventeenth-century England* (Beckenham, 1985), pp. 31–58.

Bushaway, Bob, *By Rite: Custom, Ceremony and Community in England, 1700–1880* (London, 1982).

'Rite, legitimation, and community in southern England, 1700–1850: the ideology of custom', in Barry Stapleton (ed.), *Conflict and Community in Southern England* (Stroud, 1992), pp. 110–34.

Chambers, E. K., *The Elizabethan Stage*, ii (Oxford, 1923).

Chartier, Roger, 'Culture as appropriation: popular culture uses in early modern France', in Kaplan (ed.), *Understanding Popular Culture*, pp. 229–54.

The Cultural Use of Print in Early Modern France (Princeton, NJ, 1987).

Clapson, Mark, *A Bit of a Flutter: Popular Gambling and English Society, 1823–1961* (Manchester, 1992).

Clark, Peter (ed.), *The Early Modern Town: A Reader* (London, 1976).

(ed.), *The Transformation of English Provincial Towns, 1600–1800* (London, 1984).

Clarke, John and Charles Critcher, *The Devil Makes Work: Leisure in Capitalist Britain* (London, 1985).

Corfield, P. J., *Impact of English Towns 1700–1800* (Oxford, 1982).

'Small towns, large implications: social and cultural roles of small towns in eighteenth-century England and Wales', *British Journal for Eighteenth-century Studies*, 10 (1987), pp. 125–38.

'Walking the city streets: the urban odyssey in eighteenth-century England', *Journal of Urban History*, 16 (1990), pp. 132–74.

Cowell, Ben, 'The Commons Preservation Society and the campaign for Berkhamstead Common, 1866–70', *Rural History*, 13 (2002), pp. 145–60.

Cressy, David, *Bonfires and Bells: National Memory and the Protestant Calendar in Elizabethan and Stuart England* (London, 1989).

'The Fifth of November remembered', in Roy Porter (ed.), *Myths of the English* (Cambridge, 1992), pp. 68–90.

Croll, Andy, 'Street disorder, surveillance and shame: regulating behaviour in the public spaces of the late Victorian British town', *Social History*, 24 (1999), pp. 250–68.

Cunningham, Hugh, 'The metropolitan fair: a case study in the social control of leisure', in A. P. Donajgrodzki (ed.), *Social Control in Nineteenth-century Britain* (London, 1977), pp. 163–84.

Leisure in the Industrial Revolution, c.1780–1880 (London, 1980).

Daunton, Martin, *House and Home in the Victorian City: Working-class Housing, 1850–1914* (London, 1983).

Delves, Anthony, 'Popular recreation and social conflict in Derby, 1800–1850', in Yeo and Yeo (eds), *Popular Culture*, pp. 89–127.

Dentith, Simon, *Society and Cultural Forms in Nineteenth-century England* (London, 1998).

Dunning, E. and K. Sheard, *Barbarians: Gentlemen and Players* (Oxford, 1979).

Dymond, David, 'A lost social institution: the camping close', *Rural History*, 1 (1990), pp. 165–92.

Easton, Susan et al., *Disorder and Discipline: Popular Culture from 1550 to the Present* (Aldershot, 1988).

Eastwood, David, *Government and Community in the English Provinces, 1700–1870* (London, 1997).

Estabrook, Carl B., *Urbane and Rustic England: Cultural Ties and the Social Spheres in the Provinces, 1660–1780* (Manchester, 1998).

Everitt, Alan, 'The market towns', in Clark (ed.), *The Early Modern Town*, pp. 168–204.

Eversley, Lord, *Commons, Forests and Footpaths*, revised edn (London, 1910).

Field, John, *English Field-names: A History* (Newton Abbot, 1972).
    A History of English Field-names (London, 1993).

Geertz, Clifford, *The Interpretation of Cultures: Selected Essays* (New York, 1973).

Girouard, Mark, *The English Town* (Yale, 1990).

Golby, J. M. and A. W. Purdue, *The Civilisation of the Crowd: Popular Culture in England, 1750–1900*, revised edn (Stroud, 1999).

Golding, Sally, 'The importance of fairs in Essex, 1750–1850', *Essex Journal*, 10 (1975), pp. 20–67.

Gonner, E. C. K., *Common Land and Inclosure* (London, 1912).

Goodman, Jordan, 'History and anthropology', in M. Bentley (ed.), *Companion to Historiography* (London, 1997), pp. 783–804.

Goulstone, John, 'The working-class origins of modern football', *International Journal of the History of Sport*, 17 (2000), pp. 135–43.

Green, Richard, *Anti-Methodist Publications issued during the Eighteenth Century* (London, 1902).

Griffin, Emma, 'Popular culture in industrialising England', *Historical Journal*, 45 (2002), pp. 619–65.

Hackwood, Frederick W., *Old English Sports* (London, 1907).

Hammond, J. L. and Barbara Hammond, *The Age of the Chartists 1832–1854: A Study of Discontent* (London, 1930).

Hargreaves, John, *Sport, Power and Culture: A Social and Historical Analysis of Popular Sports in Britain* (Cambridge, 1986).

Harris, Tim, *London Crowds in the Reign of Charles II: Propaganda and Politics from the Restoration until the Exclusion Crisis* (Cambridge, 1987).
    'Problematising popular culture', in idem (ed.), *Popular Culture in England*, pp. 1–27.
    (ed.), *Popular Culture in England, 1500–1850* (Hampshire, 1995).

Harrison, Brian, 'Animals and the state in nineteenth-century England', *English Historical Review*, 88 (1973), pp. 786–820.

Harrison, Mark, 'Symbolism, "ritualism" and the location of crowds in early nineteenth-century English towns', in Denis Cosgrove and Stephen Daniels (eds), *The Iconography of Landscape: Essays on the Symbolic Representation, Design and Use of Past Environments* (Cambridge, 1988), pp. 194–213.

Harwood, Dix, *Love for Animals and How it Developed in Great Britain* (New York, 1928).

Harvey, A., 'Football's missing link: the real story of the evolution of modern football', *European Sports History Review*, 1 (1999), pp. 92–116.

Heaton, H., *The Yorkshire Woollen and Worsted Industries* (Oxford, 1965).

Henricks, Thomas S., *Disputed Pleasures: Sport and Society in Pre-industrial England* (New York, 1991).

Hindle, Steve, 'Custom, festival and protest in early modern England: the Little Budworth wakes, St Peter's day, 1596', *Rural History*, 6 (1995), pp. 155–78.

Holt, Richard, *Sport and the British: A Modern History* (Oxford, 1989).

(ed.), *Sport and the Working Class in Modern Britain* (Manchester, 1990).

Hopkins, Eric, *The Rise of the Manufacturing Town: Birmingham and the Industrial Revolution* (Stroud, 1998).

Hoskins, W. G., *The Making of the English Landscape*, 3rd edn with an introduction by Christopher Taylor (London, 1988).

and L. Dudley Stamp, *The Common Lands of England and Wales* (London, 1963).

Hotson, J. Leslie, 'Bear gardens and bear-baiting during the Commonwealth', *Publications of the Modern Language Association*, 40 (1925), pp. 276–88.

Hudson, Pat, *The Genesis of Industrial Capital: A Study of the West Riding Wool Textile Industry, 1750–1850* (Cambridge, 1986).

Huggins, Mike, *Flat Racing and British Society, 1790–1914: A Social and Economic History* (London, 2002).

Hulbert, N. F., 'A survey of the Somerset fairs', *Proceedings of the Somersetshire Archaeological and Natural History Society*, 82 (1936), pp. 83–159.

Hunter, Robert, *The Preservation of Open Spaces and Footpaths and Other Rights of Way* (London, 1896).

Hutton, Ronald, *The Rise and Fall of Merry England: The Ritual Year, 1400–1700* (Oxford, 1994).

The Stations of the Sun: A History of the Ritual Year in Britain (Oxford, 1996).

Innes, Joanna, 'Politics and morals: the reformation of manners movement in later eighteenth-century England', in Eckhart Hellmuth (ed.), *The Transformation of Political Culture: England and Germany in the Late Eighteenth Century* (Oxford, 1990), pp. 57–118.

Isaacs, Tina, 'The Anglican hierarchy and the reformation of manners, 1688–1738', *Journal of Ecclesiastical History*, 33 (1982), pp. 301–411.

Judd, Mark, '"The oddest combination of town and country"; popular culture and the London fairs, 1800–1860', in Walton and Walvin (eds), *Leisure in Britain*, pp. 11–30.

Kaplan, Steven, *Understanding Popular Culture: Europe from the Middle Ages to the Nineteenth Century* (Berlin, 1984).

Kean, Hilda, *Animal Rights: Political and Social Change in Britain since 1800* (London, 1998).

King, Peter, 'Gleaners, farmers and the failure of legal sanction in England, 1750–1750', *Past and Present*, 125 (1989), pp. 116–50.

Klein, Benjamin, '"Between the bums and the bellies of the multitude": civic pageantry and the problem of the audience in late Stuart London', *London Journal*, 17 (1992), pp. 18–26.

Krantz, Frederick (ed.), *History from Below: Studies in Popular Protest and Popular Ideology in Honour of George Rude* (Montreal, 1985).

McCutcheon, K. L., *Yorkshire Fairs and Markets,* Publications of the Thoresby Society, 39 (1940).

McInnes, Angus, 'The emergence of a leisure town: Shrewsbury, 1660–1760', *Past and Present*, 120 (1988), pp. 53–87.

McKibbin, Ross, 'Working-class gambling' and 'Work and hobbies', both reprinted in his *Ideologies of Class: Social Relations in Britain, 1880–1950* (Oxford, 1990), pp. 101–66.

MacMaster, Neil, 'The Battle for Mousehold Heath, 1857–1884: "popular politics" and the Victorian public park', *Past and Present*, 127 (1990), pp. 117–54.

Malcolmson, Robert W., *Popular Recreations in English Society, 1700–1850* (Cambridge, 1973).

Manley, L., *Literature and Culture in Early Modern London* (Cambridge, 1995).

Marples, Morris, *A History of Football* (London, 1954).

Marrus, Michael (ed.), *The Emergence of Leisure* (New York, 1974).

Metcalfe, Alan, 'Organized sport in the mining communities of south Northumberland, 1800–1889', *Victorian Studies*, 25 (1982), pp. 469–95.

'Football in the mining communities of East Northumberland, 1882–1914', *International Journal of the History of Sport*, 5 (1988), pp. 269–91.

'"Potshare bowling" in the mining communities of east Northumberland, 1800–1914', in Holt (ed.), *Sport and the Working Class*, pp. 29–44.

Miller, John, *Popery and Politics in England, 1660–1688* (Cambridge, 1973).

Mingay, G. E., *Parliamentary Enclosure in England: An Introduction to its Causes, Incidence and Impact, 1750–1850* (London, 1997).

Mitchell, Ian, 'The development of urban retailing 1700–1815', in Clark (ed.), *Transformation of English Towns*, pp. 259–83.

Montano, J. P., 'The quest for consensus: the lord mayor's day shows in the 1670s', in G. MacLean (ed.), *Culture and Society in the Stuart Restoration: Literature, Drama, History* (Cambridge, 1995), pp. 31–51.

Mullan, John and Christopher Reid (eds), *Eighteenth-century Popular Culture: A Selection* (Oxford, 2000).

Muncey, R. W., *Our Old English Fairs* (London, [1935?]).

Nead, Lynda, *Victorian Babylon: People, Streets and Images in Nineteenth-century London* (New Haven, CT, 2000).

O'Gorman, Frank, 'Campaign rituals and ceremonies: the social meaning of elections in England, 1780–1860', *Past and Present*, 135 (1992), pp. 79–115

Owens, Gary, 'Nationalism without words: symbolism and ritual behaviour in the repeal "Monster Meetings" of 1843–5', in James Donnelly and Kerby Miller (eds), *Irish Popular Culture, 1650–1850* (Dublin, 1998), pp. 242–69.

Page, John, *The Story of the Manchester Fairs* (Manchester, 1887).

Paz, D. G., 'Bonfire night in mid-Victorian Northants: the politics of a popular revel', *Historical Research*, 63 (1990), pp. 316–28.

Phythian-Adams, Charles, 'Ceremony and the citizen: the communal year at Coventry 1450–1550', in Clark (ed.), *Early Modern Town*, pp. 106–28.

Poole, Robert, *Popular Leisure and the Music Hall in Nineteenth-century Bolton* (Lancaster, 1982).

    'Oldham wakes', in Walton and Walvin (eds), *Leisure in Britain*, pp. 71–98.

Poole, Steve, '"Till our liberties be secure": popular sovereignty and public space in Bristol, 1780–1850', *Urban History*, 26 (1999), pp. 40–54.

Porter, J. H., 'Cockfighting in the eighteenth and nineteenth centuries: from popularity to suppression', *Report and Transactions of the Devonshire Association for the Advancement of Science, Literature and Art*, 118 (1986), pp. 63–71.

Radzinowicz, L., *History of English Law: The Reform of the Police*, iii (London, 1936).

Raven, Jon, *The Urban and Industrial Songs of the Black Country and Birmingham* (Wolverhampton, 1977).

Reay, Barry, *Popular Cultures in England, 1550–1750* (Harlow, 1998).

Reed, Michael, 'The transformation of urban space, 1700–1840', in Peter Clark (ed.), *The Cambridge Urban History of Britain, 1540–1840*, ii (Cambridge, 2000), pp. 615–40.

Reid, Douglas, 'The Decline of St Monday, 1766–1876', *Past and Present*, 71 (1976), pp. 76–101

    'Interpreting the festival calendar: wakes and fairs as carnivals', in Storch (ed.), *Popular Culture*, pp. 125–53.

    'Beasts and brutes: popular blood sports c.1780–1860', in Holt (ed.), *Sport and the Working Class*, pp. 12–28.

Ritvo, Harriet, *The Animal Estate: The English and Other Creatures in the Victorian Age* (Cambridge, MA, 1987).

Roberts, Brian K., *The Making of the English Village* (Harlow, 1987).

Rogers, Nicholas, *Crowds, Culture, and Politics in Georgian Britain* (Oxford, 1998).

Rosenfeld, Sybil, *The Theatre of the London Fairs in the Eighteenth Century* (London, 1960).

Rowlands, Marie B., *The West Midlands from AD 1000* (Harlow, 1987).

    'Continuity and change in an industrialising society: the case of the west Midlands industries', in Pat Hudson (ed.), *Regions and Industries: A Perspective on the Industrial Revolution in Britain* (Cambridge, 1989), pp. 103–31.

Rowley, Trevor, *Villages in the Landscape* (London, 1987; repr. London, 1994).

Ryder, Richard D., *Animal Revolution: Changing Attitudes towards Speciesism* (Oxford, 1989).

Samuel, Raphael, 'Reading the signs', *History Workshop Journal*, 32 (1991), pp. 88–109.

    'Reading the signs II', *History Workshop Journal*, 33 (1992), pp. 220–51.

Sandiford, Keith A. P., 'The Victorians at play: problems in historiographical methodology', *Journal of Social History*, 15 (1981), pp. 271–88.

    Cricket and the Victorians (Aldershot, 1994).

Scribner, Bob, 'Is a history of popular culture possible?', *History of European Ideas*, 19 (1989), pp. 175–91.

Scrutton, Thomas Edward, *Commons and Common Fields: Or the History and Policy of the Laws Relating to Commons and Enclosures in England* (Cambridge, 1887).

Shaw-Taylor, L., 'Parliamentary enclosure and the emergence of an English agricultural proletariat', *Journal of Economic History*, 61 (2001), pp. 640–62.

Short, Brian, 'Conservation, class and custom: lifespace and conflict in a nineteenth-century forest environment', *Rural History*, 10 (1999), pp. 127–54.

Stearns, Peter N., 'The effort at continuity in working-class culture', *Journal of Modern History*, 52 (1980), pp. 626–55

Stobart, Jon, 'Shopping streets as social space: leisure, consumerism and improvement in an eighteenth-century county town', *Urban History*, 25 (1998), pp. 3–21.

Storch, R. D., 'The policeman as domestic missionary: urban discipline and popular culture in northern England, 1850–1880', *Journal of Social History*, 9 (1976), pp. 481–509.

(ed.), *Popular Culture and Custom in Nineteenth-century England* (London, 1982).

'"Please to remember the fifth of November": conflict, solidarity and public order in southern England, 1815–1900', in idem (ed.), *Popular Culture*, pp. 71–99.

Suggett, Richard, 'Festivals and social structure in early modern Wales', *Past and Present*, 152 (1996), pp. 79–112.

Summerfield, P., 'The Effingham Arms and the Empire: deliberate selection in the evolution of music hall in London', in Yeo and Yeo (eds), *Popular Culture*, pp. 209–40.

Sweet, Rosemary, *The Writing of Urban Histories in Eighteenth-century England* (Oxford, 1997).

The English Town, 1680–1840: Government, Society and Culture (Harlow, 1999).

Swift, Roger, 'Urban policing in early Victorian England, 1835–1886: a reappraisal', *History*, 73 (1988), pp. 211–37.

Tate, William Edward (ed.), *The English Village Community and the Enclosure Movement* (London, 1967).

A Domesday of English Enclosure Acts and Awards (Reading, 1978).

Thomas, Keith, 'History and anthropology', *Past and Present*, 24 (1963), pp. 3–24.

'Work and leisure in pre-industrial society', *Past and Present*, 29 (1964), pp. 50–62.

Man and the Natural World: Changing Attitudes in England 1500–1800 (London, 1983).

Thompson, E. P., 'Folklore, anthropology and social history', *Indian Historical Review*, 3 (1978), pp. 247–66.

Customs in Common (London, 1991).

Thompson, F. L. M., 'Nineteenth-century horse sense', *Economic History Review*, 29 (1976), pp. 60–81.

Thorpe, 'The green villages of county Durham', *Transactions, Institute of British Geographers*, 15 (1951 for 1949), pp. 155–80.

Trinder, Barrie, 'Industrialising towns 1700–1840', in Peter Clark (ed.), *Cambridge Urban History of Britain, 1540–1840*, ii (Cambridge, 2000), pp. 805–29.

Turner, E. S., *All Heaven in a Rage* (London, 1964).

Turner, James, *Reckoning with the Beast: Animals, Pain and Humanity in the Victorian Mind* (Baltimore, MD, 1980).

Turner, Michael, *English Parliamentary Enclosure: Its Historical Geography and Economic History* (Folkestone, 1980).

Tweedale, Geoffrey, *Steel City: Entrepreneurship, Strategy and Technology in Sheffield, 1743–1993* (Oxford, 1995).

Underdown, David, *Revel, Riot and Rebellion: Popular Politics and Culture in England, 1603–1660* (Oxford, 1985).

Start of Play: Cricket and Culture in Eighteenth-century England (London, 2000).

'Regional cultures? Local variations in popular culture during the early modern period', in Harris (ed.), *Popular Culture*, pp. 28–47.

Vamplew, Wray, *Pay Up and Play the Game: Professional Sport in Britain, 1875–1914* (Cambridge, 1988).

Vicinus, M., *The Industrial Muse* (London, 1974).

Vincent, David, 'The decline of the oral tradition in popular culture', in Storch (ed.), *Popular Culture*, pp. 20–47.

Voth, Hans-Joachim, *Time and Work in England, 1750–1830* (Oxford, 2000).

Wade-Martins, Peter, 'The origins of rural settlement in East Anglia', in P. J. Fowler (ed.), *Recent Work in Rural Archaeology* (Bradford-on-Avon, 1975), pp. 137–57.

Walford, Cornelius, *Fairs, Past and Present: A Chapter in the History of Commerce* (London, 1883).

Walker, Wendy, *Essex Markets and Fairs*, Essex Record Office Publications, 83 (1981).

Walsh, Martin, 'November bull-running in Stamford Lincolnshire', *Journal of Popular Culture*, 30 (1996), pp. 233–47.

Walton, John K. and Robert Poole, 'The Lancashire wakes in the nineteenth century', in Storch (ed.), *Popular Culture*, pp. 100–24.

and James Walvin, *Leisure in Britain 1780–1939* (Manchester, 1983).

Walvin, James, *Leisure and Society, 1830–1950* (London, 1978).

The People's Game (Edinburgh, 1984).

Warren, Leland, 'Turning reality round together: guides to conversation in eighteenth-century England', *Eighteenth-century Life*, n.s. 8 (1983), pp. 65–85.

Waters, Ronald K.G., 'Signs of the times: Clifford Geertz and historians', *Social Research*, 47 (1980), pp. 537–56.

Williams, Raymond, *The Country and the City* (London, 1973).

Williamson, Tom, *Shaping Medieval Landscapes: Settlement, Society, Environment* (Macclesfield, 2003).

Wilson, Adrian (ed.), *Rethinking Social History: English Society 1570–1920 and its Interpretation* (Manchester, 1993).

Wilson, Kathleen, *Sense of the People, Culture and Imperialism in England, 1715–1785* (Cambridge, 1995).

Winter, *London's Teeming Streets, 1830–1914* (London, 1993).

Wrightson, Keith and David Levine, *Poverty and Piety in an English Village: Terling, 1525–1700* (Oxford, 1995).

Yelling, J. A., *Common Field and Enclosure in England 1450–1850* (London, 1977).

Yeo, Eileen and Stephen Yeo (eds), *Popular Culture and Class Conflict, 1590–1914: Explorations in the History of Labour and Leisure* (Brigton, 1981).

Unpublished dissertation

Poole, R. J. R., 'Wakes, holidays and fairs in the Lancashire cotton district, c.1790–1890', PhD dissertation, Lancaster, 1895.

Index